P9-DUV-753

Twelve PLAYS

OTHER PLAYS BY JOYCE CAROL OATES

Three Plays: Ontological Proof of My Existence
Miracle Play
The Triumph of the Spider Monkey

Joyce Carol Oates

Twelve
PLAYS

A WILLIAM ABRAHAMS BOOK

DUTTON

DUTTON
Published by the Penguin Group
Penguin Books USA Inc., 375 Hudson Street, New York, New York 10014, U.S.A.
Penguin Books Ltd, 27 Wrights Lane, London W8 5TZ, England
Penguin Books Australia Ltd, Ringwood, Victoria, Australia
Penguin Books Canada Ltd, 10 Alcorn Avenue, Toronto, Ontario, Canada M4V 3B2
Penguin Books (N.Z.) Ltd, 182–190 Wairau Road, Auckland 10, New Zealand

Penguin Books Ltd, Registered Offices: Harmondsworth, Middlesex, England

First published by Dutton, an imprint of New American Library,
a division of Penguin Books USA Inc.
Distributed in Canada by McClelland & Stewart Inc.

First Printing, November, 1991
10 9 8 7 6 5 4 3 2 1

Copyright © The Ontario Review, Inc., 1991
All rights reserved

 REGISTERED TRADEMARK—MARCA REGISTRADA

Library of Congress Cataloging-in-Publication Data
Oates, Joyce Carol, 1938–
Twelve plays / by Joyce Carol Oates.
p.   cm.
"A William Abrahams book."
Contents: Tone clusters — The eclipse — How do you like your
meat? — The ballad of Love Canal — Under/ground — Greensleeves —
The key — Friday night — Black — I stand before you naked — The
secret mirror — American holiday.
ISBN 0-525-93376-X
I. Title.
PS3565.A8T87   1991
812'.54—dc20   91-14055
                                                                          CIP

Printed in the United States of America
Designed by Eve L. Kirch

for Jon Jory
and
Michael Dixon

CONTENTS

I

Part

Tone Clusters

A Play in Nine Scenes

CHARACTERS

FRANK GULICK: fifty-three years old
EMILY GULICK: fifty-one years old
VOICE: male, indeterminate age

These are white Americans of no unusual distinction, nor are they in any self-evident way "representative."

Tone Clusters is not intended to be a realistic work, thus any inclination toward the establishment of character should be resisted. Its primary effect should be visual (the dominance of the screen at center stage, the play of lights of sharply contrasting degrees of intensity) and audio (the VOICE, *the employment of music—"tone clusters" of Henry Cowell and/or Charles Ives, and electronic music, etc.). The mood is one of fragmentation, confusion, yet, at times, strong emotion. A fractured narrative emerges which the audience will have no difficulty piecing together even as—and this is the tragicomedy of the piece—the characters* MR. *and* MRS. GULICK *deny it.*

In structure, Tone Clusters *suggests an interview, but a stylized interview in which questions and answers are frequently askew. Voices trail off into silence or may be mocked or extended by strands of music. The* VOICE *is sometimes overamplified and booming; sometimes marred by static; sometimes clear, in an ebullient tone, like that of a talk-show host. The* VOICE *has no identity but must be male. It should not be represented by any actual presence on the stage or*

3

within view of the audience. At all times, the VOICE *is in control: the principals on the stage are dominated by their interrogator and by the screen, which is seemingly floating in the air above them, at center stage. Indeed the screen emerges as a character.*

The piece is divided into nine uneven segments. When one ends, the lights dim, then come up again immediately. (After the ninth segment the lights go out completely and darkness is extended for some seconds to indicate that the piece is ended: it ends on an abrupt cutoff of lights and images on the screen and the monitors.)

By degree the GULICKS *become somewhat accustomed to the experience of being interviewed and filmed, but never wholly accustomed: they are always slightly disoriented, awkward, confused, inclined to speak slowly and methodically or too quickly, "unprofessionally," often with inappropriate emotion (fervor, enthusiasm, hope, sudden rage) or no emotion at all (like "computer voices"). The* GULICKS *may at times speak in unison (as if one were an echo of the other); they may mimic the qualities of tone-cluster music or electronic music (I conceive of their voices, and that of the* VOICE, *as music of a kind); should the director wish, there may be some clear-cut relationship between subject and emotion or emphasis—but the piece should do no more than approach "realism," and then withdraw. The actors must conceive of themselves as elements in a dramatic structure, not as "human characters" wishing to establish rapport with an audience.*

Tone Clusters is about the absolute mystery—the not knowing— at the core of our human experience. That the mystery is being exploited by a television documentary underscores its tragicomic nature.

Scene 1.

Lights up. Initially very strong, near-blinding. On a bare stage, middle-aged FRANK *and* EMILY GULICK *sit ill-at-ease in "comfortable" modish cushioned swivel chairs, trying not to squint or grimace in the lights (which may be represented as the lights of a camera crew provided the human figures involved can be kept shadowy, even indistinct). They wear clip-on microphones, to which they are unaccustomed. They are "dressed up" for the occasion, and clearly nervous: they continually touch their faces, or clasp their hands firmly in their laps, or fuss with fingernails, buttons, the microphone cords, their hair. The nervous mannerisms continue throughout the piece but should never be too distracting and never comic.*

Surrounding the GULICKS, *dominating their human presence, are the central screen and the TV monitors and/or slide screens upon which, during the course of the play, disparate images, words, form-less flashes of light are projected. Even when the* GULICKS' *own images appear on the screens they are upstaged by it: they glance at it furtively, with a kind of awe.*

The rest of the time, the monitors always show the stage as we see it: the GULICKS *seated, glancing uneasily up at the large screen. Thus there is a "screen within a screen."*

The employment of music is entirely at the director's discretion. The opening might be accompanied by classical tone cluster piano pieces—Henry Cowell's "Advertisement," for instance. The music should never be intrusive. The ninth scene might well be completely empty of music. There should certainly be no "film-music" effect. (The GULICKS *do not hear the music.)*

The VOICE *too in its modulations is at the discretion of the director. Certainly at the start the* VOICE *is booming and commanding. There should be intermittent audio trouble (whistling, static, etc.); the* VOICE, *wholly in control, can exude any number of effects throughout the play—pomposity, charity, condescension, bemusement, false chattiness, false pedantry, false sympathy, mild incredulity (like that of a television emcee), affectless "computer talk." The* GULICKS *are entirely intimidated by the* VOICE *and try very hard to answer its questions.*

Screen shifts from its initial image to words: IN A CASE OF MURDER—*large black letters on white.*

VOICE

In a case of murder   (taking murder as an abstraction)   there is always a sense of the Inevitable   once the identity of the murderer
     is   established. Beforehand there   is   a sense   of
disharmony.
And humankind fears and loathes disharmony,
Mr. and Mrs. Gulick of Lakepointe, New Jersey, would you comment?

FRANK

. . . Yes I would say,   I think that

EMILY

What is that again, exactly?   I . . .

FRANK

My wife and I, we . . .

EMILY

Disharmony . . .?

FRANK

I don't like disharmony.   I mean, all the family,
we are a law-abiding family.

VOICE

A religious family   I believe?

FRANK

Oh yes.   Yes,
We go to church every

EMILY

We almost never miss a,   a Sunday
For a while,   I helped with Sunday School classes
The children,   the children don't always go but they believe,
our daughter Judith for instance she   and Carl

FRANK

oh yes   yessir

EMILY

and Dennis,   they do believe they were raised to
believe in God and, and Jesus Christ

FRANK

We raised them that way because   we were raised that way,

EMILY

there *is* a God whether you agree with Him   or not.

VOICE

"Religion" may be defined as   a sort of adhesive matter invisibly
holding together   nation-states, nationalities, tribes, families

for　　the　　good　　of　　those　　so
held together,
would you comment?

FRANK

Oh,　　oh yes.

EMILY

For the good of . . .

FRANK

Yes I would say so,　　I think so.

EMILY

My husband and I, we were married in church, in

FRANK

In the Lutheran Church.

EMILY

In Penns Neck.

FRANK

In New Jersey.

EMILY

All our children,

BOTH

they believe.

EMILY

God sees into the human heart.

VOICE

Mr. and Mrs. Gulick　　from your experience would you　　theorize for
our audience:　　is the Universe "predestined"　　in every particular
or　　is　　man　　capable　　of　　acts　　of　　"freedom"?

BOTH

. . .

EMILY

. . . I would say,   that is hard to say.

FRANK

Yes. I believe that man is free.

EMILY

If you mean like, I guess   choosing good and evil?   Yes

FRANK

I would have to say   yes.   You would have to say
mankind is free.
Like moving my hand. (*moves hand*)

EMILY

If nobody is free   it wouldn't be right would it
to punish anybody?

FRANK

There is always   Hell.
I believe in Hell.

EMILY

Anybody at all

FRANK

Though I am not free to, to   fly up in the air am I? (*laughs*)
because   Well I'm not built right for that am I? (*laughs*)

VOICE

Man is free.   Thus man is   responsible for his acts.

EMILY

Except, oh   sometime if,   maybe for instance if
A baby born without

FRANK

Oh one of those "AIDS" babies

EMILY

poor thing

FRANK

"crack" babies
Or if you were captured   by some enemy, y'know   and tortured
Some people never have a chance.

EMILY

But God sees into the human heart,
God knows who to forgive   and who not.

Lights down.

Scene 2.

Lights up. Screen shows a suburban street of lower-income homes; the GULICKS *stare at the screen and their answers are initially distracted.*

VOICE

Here we have Cedar Street   in Lakepointe, New Jersey   neatly kept
homes (as you can see)   American suburb   low crime rate,
single-family homes   suburb of Newark, New Jersey
     population twelve thousand   the neighborhood of
     Mr. and Mrs. Frank Gulick the parents of   Carl Gulick
     Will you introduce yourselves to our audience please?

(*House lights come up.*)

FRANK

. . . Go on, you first

EMILY

I, I don't know what to say

FRANK

My name is   Frank Gulick, I   I am fifty-three years old
that's our house there   2368 Cedar Street

EMILY

My name is Emily Gulick, fifty-one years old,

VOICE

How employed,   would you care to say?   Mr. Gulick?

FRANK

I work for the post office,   I'm a supervisor for

EMILY

He has worked for the post office for twenty-five years

FRANK

. . . The Terhune Avenue branch.

VOICE

And how long have you resided   in your attractive home   on Cedar
    Street?

(*House lights begin to fade down.*)

FRANK

. . . Oh I guess, how long   if this is
this is 1990?

EMILY

(oh just think: 1990!)

FRANK

we moved there in, uh   Judith wasn't born yet so

EMILY

Oh there was our thirtieth anniversary a year ago,

FRANK

wedding
no that was two years ago

EMILY

was it?

FRANK

or three, I   twenty-seven years, this is 1990

EMILY

Yes: Judith is twenty-six,   now I'm a grandmother

FRANK

Carl is twenty-two

EMILY

Denny is seventeen, he's a senior in high school
No none of them are living at home now

FRANK

not now

EMILY

Right now poor Denny is staying with my sister in

VOICE

Frank and Emily Gulick you have been happy here   in Lakepointe
    raising your family like any   American couple   with your
hopes and aspirations
        until recently?

FRANK

. . . Yes, oh yes.

EMILY

Oh for a long time we *were*

FRANK

oh yes.

EMILY

It's so strange to,   to think of
The years go by so

VOICE

You have led a   happy family life   like so many millions
of Americans

EMILY

Until this,   this terrible thing

FRANK

Innocent until proven guilty—that's a laugh!

EMILY

Oh it's a, a terrible thing

FRANK

Never any hint beforehand of   the meanness of people's hearts.
I mean the neighbors.

EMILY

Oh now don't start that,   this isn't the

FRANK

Oh God you just try to   comprehend

EMILY

this isn't the place, I

FRANK

Like last night: this carload of kids
drunk, beer-drinking   foul language in the night

EMILY

oh don't, my hands are

FRANK

Yes but you know it's the parents   set them going
And telephone calls   our number is changed now, but

EMILY

my hands are shaking so
we are both on medication   the doctor says,

FRANK

oh you would not believe, you would not   believe   the hatred
like Nazi Germany

EMILY

Denny had to drop out of school,   he loved school he is
an honor student

FRANK

everybody turned against us

EMILY

My sister in Yonkers, he's staying with

FRANK

Oh he'll never be the same   boy again.
none of us will.

VOICE

In the development of   human identity   there's the element
of chance,   and there is genetic determinism.
    Would you comment please?

FRANK

The thing is,   you try your best.

EMILY

oh dear God yes.

FRANK

Your best.

EMILY

You give all that's in your heart

FRANK

you
can't do more than that can you?

EMILY

Yes but there is certain to be   justice.
There *is* a, a sense of things.

FRANK

Sometimes there is a chance, the way they   turn out
but also   what they *are*.

EMILY

Your own babies

VOICE

Frank Gulick   and Mary   what is your assessment of
        American civilization   today?

EMILY

. . . it's Emily.

FRANK

My wife's name is,

EMILY

it's
Emily.

VOICE

Frank and EMILY   Gulick.

FRANK

. . . The state of the   civilization?

EMILY

It's so big,

FRANK

We are here to   tell our side of,

EMILY

. . . I don't know: it's a,   a Democracy

FRANK

the truth is,   do you want the truth?
the truth is where we live
Lakepointe
it's changing too

EMILY

it has changed

FRANK

Yes but it's all over, it's
terrible, just terrible

EMILY

Now we are grandparents we fear for

FRANK

Yes what you read and see on TV

EMILY

You don't know what to think,

FRANK

Look: in this country   half the crimes
are committed by the,   by half the population against
the other half.   (*laughs*)
You have your law-abiding citizens,

EMILY

taxpayers

FRANK

and you have the   rest of them
Say you went downtown into a city like   Newark, some night

EMILY

you'd be crazy if you got out of your car

FRANK

you'd be dead.   That's what.

VOICE

Is it possible,   probable   or in your assessment *im*probable
that the slaying of   fourteen-year-old   Edith Kaminsky
      on February 12, 1990   is related to

the social malaise
of which you speak?

FRANK

. . . "ma-lezz"?

EMILY

. . . oh it's hard to,   I would say yes

FRANK

. . . whoever did it, he

EMILY

Oh it's terrible the things that
keep happening

FRANK

If only the police would arrest the right person,

VOICE

Frank and Emily Gulick   you remain adamant in your belief
in your faith in your twenty-two-year-old son   Carl
that he is innocent   in the death of
fourteen-year-old Edith Kaminsky
on February 12, 1990?

EMILY

Oh yes,

FRANK

oh yes that is
the single thing we are convinced of.

EMILY

On this earth.

BOTH

With God as our witness,

FRANK

yes

EMILY

Yes.

FRANK

The single thing.

Lights down.

Scene 3.

Lights up. Screen shows violent movement: urban scenes, police pa-
trol cars, a fire burning out of control, men being arrested and herded
into vans; a body lying in the street. The GULICKS *stare at the screen.*

VOICE

Of today's pressing political issues   the rise in violent crime
most concerns American citizens   Number-one political issue of
      Mr. and Mrs. Gulick   tell our viewers your opinion?

FRANK

In this state,
the state of New Jersey

EMILY

Oh it's everywhere

FRANK

there's capital punishment supposedly

EMILY

But the lawyers   the lawyers get them off,

FRANK

you bet
There's public defenders the taxpayer pays

EMILY

Oh, it's   it's out of control
(like that, what is it   "acid rain"

FRANK

it can fall on you anywhere,

EMILY

the sun is too hot too:

BOTH

the "greenhouse effect")

FRANK

It's a welfare state by any other name

EMILY

Y'know who pays:

BOTH

the taxpayer

FRANK

The same God damn criminal, you pay for him   then he
That's the joke of it (*laughs*)
the same criminal who slits your throat (*laughs*)
He's the one you pay bail for, to get out.
But it sure isn't funny.   (*laughs*)

EMILY

Oh God.

FRANK

It sure isn't funny.

VOICE

Many Americans have come to believe   this past decade   that
capital punishment is one of the   answers: would you
comment please?

FRANK

Oh in cases of actual, proven   murder

EMILY

Those drug dealers

FRANK

Yes *I* would have to say, definitely   yes

EMILY

I would say so yes

FRANK

You always hear them say   opponents of the death penalty
"The death penalty doesn't stop crime"

EMILY

Oh that's what they say!

FRANK

Yes but *I* say, once a man is dead   he sure ain't gonna commit
any more crimes, is he.   (*laughs*)

VOICE

The death penalty *is* a deterrent to crime   in those cases
when the criminal has been   executed

FRANK

But you have to find the right,
the actual murderer.

EMILY

Not some poor innocent*   some poor innocent*

Lights down.

Scene 4.

*Lights up. Screen shows a grainy magnified snapshot of a boy about
ten. Quick jump to a snapshot of the same boy a few years older.
Throughout this scene images of "Carl Gulick" appear and disappear
on the screen though not in strict relationship to what is being said,
nor in chronological order. "Carl Gulick" in his late teens and early
twenties is muscular but need not have any other outstanding char-
acteristics: he may look like any American boy at all.*

* "innocent" is an adjective here, not a noun

VOICE

Carl Gulick, twenty-two years old   the second-born child of Frank
and Emily Gulick   of Lakepointe, New Jersey   How would you
describe your son, Frank and Emily

FRANK

D'you mean how he looks or . . .?

EMILY

He's a shy boy, he's   shy   Not backward just

FRANK

He's about my height I guess   brown hair, eyes

EMILY

Oh! no I think   no he's much taller Frank
he's been taller than you   for years

FRANK

Well that depends on how we're both standing.
How we're both   standing
Well in one newspaper it said six feet one inch, in the other
six feet three inches, that's the kind of

EMILY

accuracy

FRANK

reliability of the news media
you can expect!

EMILY

And oh that terrible picture of,
in the paper
that face he was making   the police carrying him
against his will   laying their hands on him

FRANK

handcuffs

EMILY

Oh that isn't *him*

BOTH

that isn't our son

(GULICKS *respond dazedly to snapshots flashed on screen.*)

EMILY

Oh! that's Carl   age I guess about

FRANK

four?

EMILY

that's at the beach one summer

FRANK

only nine or ten, he was big for

EMILY

With his sister Judith

FRANK

that's my brother George

EMILY

That's

FRANK

he loved Boy Scouts,

EMILY

but
Oh when you are the actual parents it's
a different

FRANK

Oh it is so different!
from something just on TV.

VOICE

In times of disruption   of fracture   it is believed that
human behavior moves   in unchartable leaps   History is a formal
record of such   leaps   but in large-scale demographical   terms
      in which the   individual   is   lost
            Frank and Emily Gulick it's said your son   Carl   charged
in the savage slaying of   fourteen-year-old   shows no sign of
      remorse   that is to say, *awareness* of the act:
thus the question we pose to you   Can guilt reside in those
      without conscience,
or is memory   conscience, and conscience memory?
      can "the human" reside in those
            devoid of "memory"

EMILY

. . . Oh the main thing is,
he is innocent.

FRANK

. . . Stake my life on it.

EMILY

He has always been   cheerful, optimistic

FRANK

a good boy, of course he has not
forgotten

BOTH

He is innocent.

EMILY

How could our son "forget" when he has nothing to

BOTH

"forget"

FRANK

He took that lie detector test voluntarily didn't he

EMILY

Oh there he is   weight-lifting, I don't remember
who took that picture?

FRANK

When you are the actual parents you see them every day,
you don't form judgments.

VOICE

And how is your son employed, Mr. and Mrs. Kaminsky?
Excuse me: GULICK.

FRANK

Up until Christmas he was working in
This butcher shop in East Orange

EMILY

. . . it isn't easy, at that age

FRANK

Before that, loading and unloading

EMILY

at Sears at the mall

FRANK

No: that was before, that was before the other

EMILY

No: the job at Sears was

FRANK

. . . Carl was working for that Italian, y'know that

EMILY

the lawn service

FRANK

Was that before?   or after
Oh in this butcher shop   his employer

EMILY

yes there were hard feelings, on both sides

FRANK

Look: you can't believe a single thing   in the newspaper or TV

EMILY

it's not that they lie

FRANK

Oh yes they lie

EMILY

not that they lie, they just   get everything wrong

FRANK

Oh they do lie!   And it's printed and you can't stop them.

EMILY

In this meat shop, I never wanted him to work there

FRANK

In this shop there was pressure on him
to join the union.

EMILY

Then the other side, his employer
did not want him to join.
He's a sensitive boy,   his stomach and nerves
He lost his appetite for weeks, he'd say "oh if you could see
some of the things I see"   "the insides of things"
and so much blood

VOICE

There was always a loving   relationship   in the household?

EMILY

. . . When they took him away he said,   he was so brave
he said Momma I'll be back soon
I'll be right back,   I am innocent he said
I don't know how she came to be in   our house

I don't know,   I don't know he said
I looked into my son's eyes and saw   truth shining
His eyes have always been   dark green,
like mine.

VOICE

On the afternoon of   February 12 you have told police that
no one was home   in your house?

EMILY

I, I was . . . I had a doctor's appointment,
My husband was working, he doesn't get home until

FRANK

Whoever did it,   and brought her body in

EMILY

No: they say she was   they say it,   it happened there

FRANK

No I don't buy that,   He brought her in   carried her
whoever that was,
I believe he tried   other houses
seeing who was home and who   wasn't
and then he

EMILY

Oh it was like lightning striking

VOICE

Your son Dennis   was at Lakepointe High School attending a meeting
of the yearbook staff,   your son Carl has told police he
      was   riding   his   motor scooter
            in the park,

FRANK

They dragged him like   an animal
put their hands on him like
Like Nazi Germany,

EMILY

it couldn't be any worse

FRANK

And that judge
it's a misuse of power, it's

EMILY

I just don't understand

VOICE

Your son Carl on and after   February 12   did not exhibit
(in your presence) any unusual sign of   emotion?
       agitation? guilt?

EMILY

Every day in a house,   a household
is like the other days.   Oh you never step back,   never *see*.
Like I told them, the   police,   everybody. *He did not.*

Lights down.

Scene 5.

*Lights up. Screen shows snapshots, photographs, of the murdered
girl Kaminsky. Like Carl Gulick, she is anyone at all of that age:
white, neither strikingly beautiful nor unattractive.*

VOICE

Sometime in the evening of February 12 of this year forensic reports
say   fourteen-year-old Edith Kaminsky daughter of   neighbors
2361 Cedar Street, Lakepointe, New Jersey   multiple stab wounds,
sexual assault   strangulation
An arrest has been made but   legally or otherwise,   the absolute
identity of the murderer has yet to be

EMILY

Oh it's so unjust,

FRANK

the power of a single man
That judge

EMILY

Carl's birthday is   next week
Oh God he'll be in that terrible   cold place

FRANK

"segregated" they call it
How can a judge refuse to set bail

EMILY

oh I would borrow a million dollars
if I could

FRANK

Is this America or   Russia?

EMILY

I can't stop crying

FRANK

. . . we are both under medication you see but

EMILY

Oh it's true he wasn't himself   sometimes.

FRANK

But that day when it happened, that wasn't one of the times.

VOICE

You hold out for the possibility that   the true murderer
      carried Edith Kaminsky into your house,   into your basement
thus meaning to throw suspicion on your son?

FRANK

Our boy is guiltless that's the main thing, I will never doubt that.

EMILY

Our body is innocent . . .   What did I say?

FRANK

Why the hell do they make so much of
Carl lifting weights, his   muscles
He is not a freak.

EMILY

There's lots of them   and women too, today   like that,

FRANK

He has other interests he used to collect stamps   play baseball

EMILY

Oh there's so much misunderstanding

FRANK

actual lies
Because the police do not know who the murderer *is*
of course they will blame   anyone they can.

Lights down.

Scene 6.

Lights up. Screen shows the exterior of the Gulick house seen from
various angles; then the interior (the basement, evidently, and the
"storage area" where the young girl's body was found).

VOICE

If, as is believed, "premeditated" acts arise   out of a
mysterious sequence of neuron discharges   (in the brain)
out of what source   do
       "unpremeditated"   acts   arise?

EMILY

Nobody was down in,   in the basement
until the police came.   The storage space is behind the
water heater,   but

FRANK

My God if my son is   so shiftless   like people are saying
just look: he helped me paint the house last summer

EMILY

Yes Carl and Denny both,

FRANK

Why are they telling such   lies, our neighbors?   We have never
wished them harm,

EMILY

I believed a certain neighbor was my friend,   her and I, we
we'd go shopping together   took my car
Oh my heart is broken

FRANK

It's robin's-egg blue,   the paint turned out brighter than
when it dried, a little brighter than we'd   expected

EMILY

I think it's pretty

FRANK

Well.   We'll have to sell the house,   there's no choice
the legal costs   Mr. Filco our attorney has said

EMILY

He told us

FRANK

he's going to fight all the way, he believes Carl is   innocent

EMILY

My heart is broken.

FRANK

My heart isn't,
I'm going to fight this all the way

EMILY

A tragedy like this,   you learn fast who is your friend and who
is your enemy

FRANK

Nobody's your friend.

VOICE

The Gulicks and Kaminskys were   well acquainted?

EMILY

We lived on Cedar first,   when they moved in I don't remember:
my mind isn't right these days

FRANK

Oh yes   we knew them

EMILY

I'd have said Mrs. Kaminsky   was my friend, but
that's how people are

FRANK

Yes

EMILY

Carl knew her,   Edith
I mean, we all did

FRANK

but not well,

EMILY

just neighbors
Now they're our declared enemies, the Kaminskys

FRANK

well,   so be it.

EMILY

Oh! that poor girl   if only she hadn't,
I mean, there's no telling who   she was with,   walking home
walking home from school I guess

FRANK

Well she'd been missing overnight,

EMILY

yes overnight

FRANK

of course we were aware

FRANK

The Kaminskys came around ringing doorbells,

EMILY

then the police,

FRANK

then
they got a search party going,   Carl helped them out

EMILY

Everybody said how much he helped

FRANK

he kept at it for hours
They walked miles and miles,
he's been out of work for a while,

EMILY

he'd been looking
in the *help wanted* ads but

FRANK

. . . He doesn't like to use the telephone.

EMILY

People laugh at him he says,

FRANK

I told him no he was imagining it.

EMILY

This neighborhood:

FRANK

you would not believe it.

EMILY

Call themselves Christians

FRANK

Well　　some are Jews.

EMILY

Well it's still white isn't it　　a white neighborhood,　　you expect
better.

VOICE

The murder weapon　　has yet to be found?

FRANK

One of the neighbors had to offer an opinion,　　something sarcastic
I guess

EMILY

Oh don't go into *that*

FRANK

the color of the paint　　on our house
So Carl said, You don't like it, wear sunglasses.

EMILY

But,
he was smiling.

VOICE

A young man with a sense of　　humor.

FRANK

Whoever hid that poor girl's
body
in the storage space of our
basement well clearly it
obviously it was　　to deceive
to cast blame on our son.

EMILY

Yes   if there were fingerprints down there,

BOTH

that handprint they found on the wall

FRANK

well for God's sake it was from when Carl
was down there

BOTH

helping them

FRANK

He cooperated with them,

EMILY

Frank wasn't home,

FRANK

Carl led them downstairs

EMILY

Why they came to our house, I don't know.
Who was saying things   I don't know,
it was like everybody had gone   crazy
casting blame on all sides.

VOICE

Mr. and Mrs. Gulick   it's said that from your son's room
Lakepointe police officers confiscated   comic books, military
magazines, pornographic magazines   a cache of more than one dozen
        knives including   switchblades   plus
a U.S. Army bayonet (World War II)   Nazi memorabilia
    including a "souvenir" SS helmet   (manufactured in Taiwan)
a pink plastic skull   with lightbulbs in eyes
        a naked Barbie doll, badly scratched   bitten
            numerous pictures of naked women
        and women in fashion magazines,   their eyes
breasts   crotches   cut out with a scissors

(pause)
Do you have any comment   Mr. and Mrs. Gulick?

                            FRANK

. . . .
Mainly they were hobbies,

                            EMILY

I guess I don't,

                            FRANK

we didn't know about

                            EMILY

Well   he wouldn't allow me in his room,   to vacuum, or

                            FRANK

You know how boys are

                            EMILY

Didn't want his mother

                            FRANK

poking her nose in

                            EMILY

So . . .

(EMILY *upsets a glass of water on the floor.*)

                            VOICE
Police forensic findings   bloodstains, hairs, semen
      and DNA "fingerprinting"   constitute a tissue of
            circumstance   linking your son to

                       EMILY *(interrupting)*
Mr. Filco says   it's all pieced together
"Circumstantial evidence," he says   not proof

                            FRANK

I call it bullshit   *(laughs)*

EMILY

Oh Frank

FRANK

I call it bullshit   (laughs)

VOICE

Eyewitness accounts disagree,   two parties report
having seen Carl Gulick and Edith Kaminsky   walking together
   in the afternoon, in the alley   behind Cedar Street
      a third party   a neighbor   claims to have seen
the girl   in the company of a   stranger   at approximately
         4:15 p.m.   And Carl Gulick insists
he was "riding his motor scooter"   all afternoon

FRANK

He is a boy

EMILY

not capable of lying

FRANK

Look: I would have to discipline him sometimes,

EMILY

You have to, with boys

FRANK

Oh yes you have to, otherwise

EMILY

He was always a good eater   didn't fuss

FRANK

He's a quiet boy

EMILY

You can't guess his thoughts

FRANK

But he loved his mother and father   respected

EMILY

Always well behaved at home
That ugly picture in the paper, oh

FRANK

THAT WASN'T HIM

EMILY

You can't believe   the cruelty in the human heart

FRANK

Giving interviews! his own teachers from the school

EMILY

Telling lies   cruel   nasty

FRANK

His own teachers from the   school

VOICE

Mr. and Mrs. Gulick   you had no suspicion
                no   awareness
    you   had   no   sense   of   the   fact
        that the battered   raped   mutilated body of
            fourteen-year-old Edith Kaminsky
                was hidden in your basement   in a storage space
                    wrapped in plastic garbage bags
for approximately   forty   hours

GULICKS

. . . .

VOICE

No consciousness of   disharmony
    in your household?

FRANK

It was a day like

EMILY

    It *was*,   I mean, it wasn't

FRANK

I keep the cellar clean, I   There's leakage

EMILY

Oh
Last week at my sister's   where we were staying,
we had to leave   this terrible place
in Yonkers I was crying,   I could not stop   crying
downstairs in the kitchen   three in the morning
I was standing by a window and there was suddenly   it looked
like snow!
it was moonlight moving in the window and there came a   shadow I
guess
like an eclipse?   was there an eclipse?
Oh I felt so, I felt   my heart stopped   Oh but I, I wasn't scared
I was thinking   I was seeing how the world is
how the universe *is*
it's so hard to say, I feel like a   a fool
I was gifted by this, by   seeing   how the world *is* not
how you see it   with your eyes, or talk   talk about it
I mean names you give to,   parts of it   No I mean how it *is*
when there is nobody there.

VOICE

A subliminal conviction of disharmony   may be nullified by   a
    transcendental leap of   consciousness;   to a "higher plane"
        of celestial harmony,
        would you comment   Mr. and Mrs. Gulick?

EMILY

Then Sunday night it was,

FRANK

this last week

EMILY

they came again

FRANK

threw trash on our lawn

EMILY

screamed
Murderers! they were drunk, yelling   in the night *Murderers!*

FRANK

There was the false report that Carl was released on   bail
that he was home with us,

EMILY

Oh dear God if only that was true

FRANK

I've lost fifteen pounds since February

EMILY

Oh Frank has worked so hard   on that lawn,
it's his pride and joy and in the neighborhood   everybody knows,
they compliment him,   and now
Yes he squats right out there, he pulls out crabgrass   by hand
Dumping such such ugly nasty disgusting things
Then in the A&P a woman followed me   up and down the aisles
I could hear people   *That's her, that's the mother of*
the murderer   I could hear them   everywhere in the store
Is that her,   is that the mother of the murderer? they were saying
Lived in this neighborhood, in this town   for so many years
we thought we were welcome here and now
Aren't you ashamed to show your face!   a voice screamed
What can I do with my face,   can I hide it forever?

FRANK

And all this when our boy is   innocent.

VOICE

Perceiving the inviolate nature of   the Universe   apart from human
suffering   rendered you happy, Mrs. Gulick   is this so?
            for some precious moments?

EMILY

Oh yes, I was crying but
not because of

no   I was crying because
I was happy I think.

Lights down.

Scene 7.

Lights up. Screen shows neurological X-rays, medical diagrams, charts as of EEG and CAT-scan tests.

VOICE

Is it possible that in times of   fracture, of evolutionary
unease   or, perhaps, at any time   human behavior mimics that
of minute   particles   of light?   The atom is primarily emptiness
          the neutron dense-packed
The circuitry of the human brain   circadian rhythms   can be tracked
but never,   it's said comprehended.   And then   in descent
from "identity"—(memory?)   to tissue to cells to cell-particles
          electrical impulses   axon-synapse-dendrite
                    and beyond, be-
                         neath
                    to subatomic bits
               Where is "Carl Gulick"?

(GULICKS *turn to each other in bewilderment. Screen flashes images: kitchen interior; weightlifting paraphernalia; a shelf of trophies; photographs; domestic scenes, etc.*)

VOICE

Mr. and Mrs. Gulick you did not notice anything   unusual   in
your son's behavior on the night of February 12   or the following
day,   to the best   of your recollection?

EMILY

. . . Oh we've told the police this so many   many times

FRANK

Oh you forget what you remember,

EMILY

That night, before we knew there was anyone missing   I mean, in
the neighborhood   anyone we knew

FRANK

I can't remember.

EMILY

Yes but Carl had supper with us like always

FRANK

No I think,   he was napping up in his room

EMILY

he was at the table with us:

FRANK

I remember   he came down around nine o'clock,   but he did eat.

EMILY

Him and Denny, they were at the table with us

FRANK

We've told the police this so many times, it's
I don't know any longer

EMILY

I'm sure it was Denny too.   Both our sons.
We had meatloaf   ketchup baked on top, it's the boys'
favorite dish just about   isn't it?

FRANK

Oh anything with hamburger and ketchup!

EMILY

Of course he was at the table with us,   he had his usual appetite.

FRANK

. . . he was upstairs, said he had a touch of   flu

EMILY

Oh no he was there.

FRANK

It's hard to speak of your own flesh and blood,   as if
they are other people
it's hard   without giving false testimony against your will.

VOICE

Is the intrusion of the "extra-ordinary"   into the dimension of the
"ordinary"   an indication that such Aristotelian categories are
invalid?   If one day fails to resemble the preceding
          what does it resemble?

FRANK

. . . He has sworn to us, we are his parents
He did not touch a hair of that poor child's head   let alone the rest.
Anybody who knew him, they'd know

EMILY

Oh those trophies!   he was so proud
one of them is from the, I guess the Lakepointe YMCA
there's some from the New Jersey competition   at Atlantic City
two years ago?

FRANK

no, he was in high school
the first was, Carl was only fifteen years old

EMILY

Our little muscleman!

VOICE

Considering the evidence of thousands of years   of human culture
of language   art   religion   the judicial system   "The family
unit"   athletics   hobbies   fraternal organizations
charitable impulses   gods of all species
is   it   possible   that   humankind   desires
          not   to   know
               its   place   in
                    the
                    food cycle?

EMILY

One day he said
he wasn't going back to school,
my heart was broken.

FRANK

Only half his senior year ahead
but you can't argue,   not with

EMILY

oh his temper!   he takes after,
oh I don't know who

FRANK

we always have gotten along together
in this household   haven't we

EMILY

yes but the teachers would laugh at him he said
girls laughed at him he said   stared and pointed at him he said
and there was this pack of   oh we're not prejudiced
against Negros,   it's just that
the edge of the Lakepointe school district
well

FRANK

Carl got in fights sometimes
in the school cafeteria and   I guess the park?

EMILY

the park isn't safe for law-abiding people these days
they see the color of your skin,   they'll attack
some of them are just like animals   yes they *are*

FRANK

Actually our son was attacked first   it isn't like he got
into fights by himself

EMILY

Who his friends are now, I don't   remember

FRANK

He is a quiet boy, keeps to himself

EMILY

he wanted to work
he was looking for work

FRANK

Well: our daughter Judith was misquoted about that

EMILY

also about Carl having a bad temper   she never said that
the reporter for the paper twisted her words
Mr. Filco says   we might sue

FRANK

Look: our son never raised a hand against anybody let alone against

EMILY

He loves his mother and father,   he respects us

FRANK

He is a religious boy at heart

EMILY

He looked me in the eyes he said   Momma you believe me don't
you?   and I said Oh yes   Oh yes   he's just my baby

FRANK

nobody knows him

EMILY

nobody knows him the way we do

FRANK

who would it be, if they did?
I ask you.

Scene 8.

House lights come up, TV screen shows video rewind. Sounds of audio rewind. Screen shows GULICKS *onstage.*

VOICE

Frank and Mary Gulick we're very sorry   something happened to
the tape we're going to have to re-shoot   Let's go back just to,
we're showing an interior   Carl's room   the trophies
I will say,   I'll be repeating
Are you ready?

(House lights out, all tech returns to normal.)
Well Mr. and Mrs. Gulick your son has
quite a collection of trophies!

FRANK

. . . I,   I don't remember what I

EMILY

. . . yes he,

FRANK

Carl was proud of   he had other hobbies though

EMILY

Oh he was so funny, didn't want his mother   poking in his room
he said

FRANK

Yes but that's   how boys are

EMILY

That judge refuses to set bail, which I don't   understand

FRANK

Is this the United States or   is this the Soviet Union?

EMILY

we are willing to sell our house to stand up for what is

VOICE

You were speaking of your son Carl   having quit school,
    his senior year?   and then?

EMILY

. . . He had a hard time, the teachers   were down on him.

FRANK

I don't know why,

EMILY

we were never told
And now in the newspapers

FRANK

the kinds of lies they are saying

EMILY

that he got into fights, that he was

FRANK

that kind of thing is all a distortion

EMILY

He was always a quiet boy

FRANK

but he had his own friends

EMILY

they came over to the house sometime, I don't remember   who

FRANK

there was that one boy what was his name

EMILY

Oh Frank   Carl hasn't seen him in years
he had friends in grade school

FRANK

Look: in the newspaper there were false statements

EMILY

Mr. Filco says   we might sue

FRANK

Oh no: he says we can't,   we have to prove "malice"

EMILY

Newspapers and TV are filled with lies

FRANK

Look: our son Carl never raised a hand against anybody let alone against

EMILY

He loves his mother and father,

FRANK

he respects us

VOICE

Frank and,   it's Emily isn't it   Frank and Emily Gulick
         that is very moving.

Lights down.

Scene 9.

Lights up. Screen shows GULICKS *in theater.*

VOICE

The discovery of radioactive elements   in the late nineteenth
century enabled scientists to set back the estimated age of the Earth
      to several billion years,   and the discovery in more
recent decades   that the Universe is expanding,   thus that
there is a point in Time when the Universe   was tightly
compressed   smaller than your tiniest fingernail!
      thus that the age of the Universe is many billions
         of   years
         uncountable.
Yet   humankind resides in Time,   God bless us.
      Frank and Emily Gulick as we wind down *our* time together
         What are your plans for the future?

FRANK

. . . Oh that is, that's hard to   that's hard to answer.

EMILY

It depends I guess on

FRANK

Mr. Filco has advised

EMILY

I guess it's,
next is the grand jury

FRANK

Yes: the grand jury.
Mr. Filco cannot be present for the session   to protect our boy
I don't understand the law, just the prosecutor is there
swaying the jurors' minds
Oh I try to understand but I can't,

EMILY

he says we should be prepared
we should be prepared for a trial

VOICE

You are ready for the trial   to clear your son's name?

FRANK

Oh yes . . .

EMILY

yes that is a way of,   of putting it
Yes.   To clear Carl's name.

FRANK

. . . Oh yes you have to be realistic.

EMILY

Yes but before that   the true murderer of Edith Kaminsky
might come forward.
If the true murderer is watching this   *Please come forward.*

FRANK

. . . Well we both believe Carl is protecting someone, some
friend   another boy

EMILY

the one who really   committed that terrible crime

FRANK

So all we can do is pray.   Pray Carl will come
to his senses   give police the other boy's name, or
I believe this: if it's a friend of Carl's
he must have some decency   in his heart

VOICE

Your faith   in your son remains unshaken?

EMILY

You would have had to see his   toes,
his tiny baby toes in his bath.
His curly hair,   splashing in the bath.
His yellow rompers or no: I guess that was Denny

FRANK

If your own flesh and blood looks you in the eye,
you believe

EMILY

Oh yes.

VOICE

Human personality, it might be theorized, is a phenomenon of memory
yet memory   built up from cells, and   atoms does not "exist":
      thus memory   like mind   like personality
            is but a fiction?

EMILY

Oh   remembering backward is so hard!
oh it's,

FRANK

it pulls your brain in two.

EMILY

This medication the doctor gave me, my mouth   my mouth is so
dry
In the middle of the night I wake up drenched in

FRANK

You don't know who you are   until a thing like this happens,
then you don't know.

EMILY

It tears your brain in two, trying to   remember,
like even looking at the pictures
Oh you are lost

FRANK

in Time you are lost

EMILY

You fall and fall,
. . . ever since the,   the butcher shop
he wasn't always himself   but
who he was then, I don't know.   But
it's so hard, remembering why.

FRANK

Yes my wife means thinking backward the way   the way the police
make you, so many questions   you start forgetting right away
it comes out crazy.
Like now,   right here   I don't remember anything up to now
I mean, I can't swear to it: the first time, you see, we just
lived. We lived in our house. I am a, I am a post office employee
I guess I said that?   well, we live in our,   our house.
I mean, it was the first time through.   Just living.
Like the TV, the picture's always on if nobody's watching it
you know?   So,   the people we were then,
I guess I'm trying to say
those actual people, me and her   the ones you see *here*
aren't them. (*laughs*)
I guess that sounds crazy,

VOICE

We have here the heartbeat   of parental love and faith, it's
a beautiful thing   Frank and Molly Gulick. please comment?

FRANK

We are that boy's father and mother.
We know that our son is not a murderer and a,   a rapist

EMILY

We know, if that girl came to harm,   there is some reason
for it to be revealed, but
they never found the knife, for one thing

FRANK

or whatever it was

EMILY

They never found the knife, the murderer could tell them where
it's buried, or   whatever it was.
Oh he could help us so   if he just would.

VOICE

And your plans for the future,   Mr. and Mrs. Gulick of Lakepointe,
    New Jersey?

FRANK

. . . Well.
I guess,   I guess we don't have any.

(*Long silence, to the point of awkwardness.*)

VOICE

. . . Plans for the future, Mr. and Mrs. Gulick of Lakepointe, New Jersey?

FRANK

The thing is, you discover   you need to be protected
from your own thoughts sometimes,   but
who is there to do it?

EMILY

God didn't make any of us strong enough I guess.

FRANK

Look: one day in a family like this, it's   like the next day
and the day before.

EMILY

You could say it *is* the next day, I mean the same   the same day.

FRANK

Until one day it isn't

Lights slowly down, then out.

(THE END)

The Eclipse

A Play in Eight Scenes

CHARACTERS

MURIEL WASHBURN: seventy-six years old
STEPHANIE WASHBURN: thirty-eight years old
AILEEN STANLEY: mid-thirties
SEÑOR RÍOS: mid-fifties

NOTE: *Though there are occasional surreal or fanciful elements in the play, its dominant tone is serious; it should never be allowed to degenerate into situation comedy. The actress playing* MURIEL *should be particularly wary of succumbing to a stereotypical comic stance vis-à-vis the audience. To the contrary, both* MURIEL *and* STEPHANIE *are intelligent, troubled, complex women who employ humor for the sake of relief or diversion.*

As the play unfolds in quick scenes, the shadow of the eclipse moves slowly but inexorably across the stage. At certain times, as indicated, it is noticed (by MURIEL*); most of the time it appears to have been assimilated into the unexamined routine of their lives.*

Scene 1.

Lights up. The WASHBURNS' *apartment, or a stylized approximation of it. Stage right, toward rear, is* MURIEL's *bedroom (dimly seen); stage left, toward rear, is* STEPHANIE's *bedroom (dimly seen); center stage, a living area. Suggestion of old but good furniture, somewhat heavy in design; a cluster of new, brightly colored pillows on a sofa; a well-worn Oriental carpet on the floor; old-fashioned oak bookcases crammed with books, both hardcover and paperback. On the wall above the sofa there is a framed work of art that appears to be in the style of abstract expressionism but is really a photograph of a planetary nebula. On a portable wheeled table is a television set. Though the apartment is empty, the television set is turned on with its volume high.*

In this first scene the eclipse is a sliver of darkness at extreme stage right, scarcely noticeable as it blends with the shadowy interior of MURIEL's *room.*

Door in rear wall opens: MURIEL WASHBURN *enters, followed closely by her daughter* STEPHANIE, *who, though burdened with packages, is trying to assist her even as* MURIEL, *offended and upset, shrinks away.*

MURIEL *is an older woman of quicksilver moods. She is attractive, though superficially flamboyant, hyperactive, "busy"; her mannerisms, in imitation of nervousness, may in fact be designed to disguise nervousness. Here is a woman approaching old age—disintegration, death—and alternately fascinated by and terrified of the changes occurring in her. In this scene she is wearing a brassy wig which is slightly askew on her head (but only slightly—it must not be comically crooked). She wears a raincoat with iridescent threads, a hood, deep pockets—a coat that is much too large for her, reaching almost to her ankles—and she carries an oversized shopping bag or purse, with a gold or silver sparkle to it. Beneath the coat she is wearing what appear to be pedal pushers and a sweater. In contrast,* STEPHANIE *is wearing a beige tweed blazer and matching pants; a dark brown turtleneck sweater; fashionable shoes or boots; she carries an attractive handbag of dark brown leather as well as an armful of grocery packages and a skirt or a dress from the dry cleaner's.* STEPHANIE *is a handsome woman who looks younger than her age; she is slender but strong-bodied; she moves forthrightly and with confidence, a "public" person, except at such times—and this is one of those times—when she is frightened and angry, having lost control of a situation. Her exasperation with* MURIEL *should not entirely obscure the fact of her intense love for the woman.*

STEPHANIE (*close to tears, her fear expressed as anger*): *Why* did you do that, Mother, when you promised!? Why such a—deranged thing!

MURIEL (*facing audience, back to* STEPHANIE: *agitated but trying to appear calm*): How dare you call me deranged! Who are *you*!

STEPHANIE (*voice raised to be heard over the television*): Behaving like that—in *that* store! Now we'll have to get our groceries over at the A&P on Third Avenue. (*As she sets down her packages, one tips over and spills several oranges, which, distracted, she stoops to pick up.*) God damn it, Mother—

MURIEL: I'm Muriel.

STEPHANIE: —you *promised*.

MURIEL: I—I didn't want them to charge us twice.

STEPHANIE: Nobody was going to charge us twice.

MURIEL (*as if groping*): It's easy to be cheated in those stores. The way the checkout woman slides those things along, everything automatic . . . (*With increasing anger*) They were watching us. As soon as we came in, they started. The—what's the word?—the surveillance people—I can sense it.

STEPHANIE (*switching off television*): Nobody was watching you, Mother. Why would anyone watch *you*!? (*Laughs dispiritedly*) Behaving the way you do, so entirely unpredictable, dressed like you are, why would anyone watch *you*!?

MURIEL (*clapping her hands over her ears, dislodging her wig just perceptibly*): It's too quiet in here suddenly. It isn't natural.

STEPHANIE (*ironically*): I turned off the television, Mother. Now that we're home we can make our own noises, to scare off burglars.

MURIEL: I don't like too much quiet—my head echoes.

STEPHANIE: You promised you wouldn't act . . . that way. You promised.

MURIEL: It wasn't "that way." It was . . . (*pause*) . . . another way.

STEPHANIE: There are people who recognize me in those stores— from my picture in the newspaper, from television. I'm so ashamed. (*As the items from the dry cleaner's begin to slide to the floor,* STEPHANIE *snatches them up and tosses them back down onto the sofa.*) You know better, God damn it. And flirting like that with the butcher—!

MURIEL: *He* was flirting with *me.* One of my students from the old days—now he's almost my age—an old man. Y'know why? Because particles speed up as they approach black holes—cross the "event horizon." (*As if warningly*) I don't get any younger, but the rest of you get older, fast.

STEPHANIE: That butcher? He was a student of yours?

MURIEL: Look, I had a long teaching career. Half the goddamn city—half the goddamn *country*—are former students of Mrs. Washburn, Commodore Stephen Decatur Junior High School. (*Laughs*) There's no escape!

STEPHANIE: And that ridiculous coat of yours—I'm going to throw it away. You've become a clown!

MURIEL (*backing off*): Oh, no you don't. (*Hugs coat tightly about her*)

STEPHANIE: Why did you behave the way you did?

MURIEL: What way?

STEPHANIE: Why did you throw those things on the floor?

MURIEL: I didn't throw them—they fell.

STEPHANIE: Yes? Up over the side of the cart?

MURIEL: Don't you raise your voice to *me*, baby.

STEPHANIE: Then stop talking so fast. Practically punching me when I touched you!

MURIEL (*pained*): I—didn't know who it was—laying hands on me. (*Hesitates*) These icy-cold little hands. Out of nowhere.

STEPHANIE (*incensed*): Behaving like a madwoman.

MURIEL: Who are you calling a madwoman? *You*—theorist!

STEPHANIE: You said you wanted to go shopping—said you were bored at home. And then—you betrayed me.

MURIEL (*defiantly*): Who said I was bored? I'm never bored. Somebody else must've said that.

STEPHANIE: Losing control like that. In public.

MURIEL (*drawing in a deep breath, pausing, then shrieking*): I DID NOT LOSE CONTROL! I DO NOT LOSE CONTROL!

(*There is a long tense moment: the women stand motionless, perfectly poised. We sense how skillfully* MURIEL *holds* STEPHANIE *in check.*)

MURIEL (*calmer, almost conversationally*): I am *never* bored when alone. I am *only* bored in company.

STEPHANIE (*retreating, taking a package out of one of the grocery bags, murmuring to herself*): Oh—it's leaking. All over the inside of—

MURIEL: It's just they were watching me. From the first instant I stepped through the—what do you call it—(*snaps fingers, trying to remember term*)—the seeing-eye door.

STEPHANIE: You cracked the damn thing—the plastic container. (*Peering inside*) "Seafood combo"—eight dollars and twenty-five cents a pound. Half of it isn't even real, it's "sea legs." Manufactured in Japan from parts of fish scraps and dyed pink.

MURIEL (*earnestly*): Not just watching—I could live with that. I was born in this century. But *taping*. On *microfilm*. Hiding up in the ceiling, the surveillance people. Putting us all on file. (*Hugs herself again in the coat: we see that the pockets are bulging.*)

STEPHANIE: If you're so afraid of people watching you, why the hell make a spectacle of yourself?

MURIEL (*shrewdly*): To distract them, Stevie. It's an old, old trick of evolution: distracting predators. (*Flaps her arms, mugs, winks toward audience*) First principle of teaching junior high school.

(MURIEL *does a little tap dance; she is surprisingly agile.*)

STEPHANIE (*close to tears, yet amused; then reverts to her reproachful tone*): Now I can't shop at that Kroger's anymore, and the A&P is a mile away. And you caused such a fuss in the Italian bakery—

MURIEL: It's all in your imagination—we could go back any time.

STEPHANIE: —and the Rexall's. (*Laughs dispiritedly*) If this keeps up, we'll have to move out of the neighborhood.

MURIEL (*as if serious*): The elderly provoke the acceleration of objects in their vicinity: things *fly* into their pockets. Clocks speed up. Calendars. Pulses.

STEPHANIE: It isn't funny. How can I possibly go to Denver next month and leave you alone . . . ?

MURIEL (*continuing, with eerie precision*): If—and when—the earth's density increases, its volume must contract; and when its volume contracts to the size of a pea (*with thumb and forefinger raised overhead, she indicates the size of a pea*), it will implode— and become a black hole. And time will cease. And all our problems will be solved.

(*A moment's silence.* STEPHANIE *makes an impatient gesture.*)

STEPHANIE: No wonder you scared your students! (*Pause*) When is *that* going to happen? In a million million years?

MURIEL (*shrugs*)

STEPHANIE: You've been so—almost—sensible—for weeks, and now this. What am I going to do?

(MURIEL *has drifted off toward stage right, though not in the direction of her bedroom at the rear. She has placed her left hand over her left eye and seems to be testing her vision. As* STEPHANIE, *not noticing, carries one of the grocery bags into another room—presumably into the kitchen, offstage—*MURIEL *behaves oddly, removing her hand from her eye, replacing it quizzically, testing her other eye. It is the "eclipse"—a shadow growing in her brain—which she sees or senses.*)

MURIEL: My eye . . . A blade of—dark.

STEPHANIE (*calling out to her, preoccupied*): At least take off that coat. Help me put the things away.

MURIEL: Or is it in both eyes? No. Yes . . .

STEPHANIE: Mother? What is it?

(MURIEL *mutters to herself, inaudibly.* STEPHANIE *approaches her.*)

STEPHANIE: Your eye? Your vision? What?

MURIEL: Nothing.

STEPHANIE: Is something wrong? (STEPHANIE *is impeccably well groomed, but at this moment she runs a hand through her hair, disheveling it.*) You know your eyes are sensitive to light, but you don't protect them. That bright sun—

MURIEL (*with a sudden harsh laugh*): I'm all right—mind your own business. Your own eyes.

STEPHANIE (*uncertainly*): Mother, please? Is something wrong?

MURIEL (*muttering as if frightened, defensive*): Nothing wrong with me—what's wrong with *you*? Always spying on me—the lot of you.

STEPHANIE: Mother—

MURIEL: Who's "Mother"? I'm Muriel.

STEPHANIE: Look—if something is wrong, you'd better tell me. I'll make an appointment with Dr. Weisbord.

MURIEL: Oh—hell. Go fly off to Denver, fly off to Paris, or Istanbul, or Hoboken—wherever. Who needs you? I have my own friends.

(STEPHANIE *advances upon her, but* MURIEL *wards her off.*)

STEPHANIE (*half pleading*): Mother—should I call Dr. Weisbord? You haven't seen him since July.

MURIEL: Who's "Mother"? You're a feminist, baby. I'm a feminist. Oh boy, am *I* a feminist! I was there when it was invented. So who's "Mother"?

STEPHANIE: Oh, for God's sake, here we go again.

MURIEL (*addressing third party*): Who gets stuck with "Mother" gets stuck scrubbing the toilets, right?

STEPHANIE (*exasperated*): *You* haven't scrubbed a toilet in this apartment in thirty years!

MURIEL: And it looks it, too.

STEPHANIE: *Are* you all right? Just tell me.

MURIEL (*takes a hand mirror out of her pocket, shoves it in* STEPHANIE's *face in a brusque gesture*): Look at yourself, baby, not me. You're the Ph.D. You're the professor. You pay the bills around here, not me.

(STEPHANIE *flinches from the sight of her own reflection, oddly; then renews her tack.*)

STEPHANIE: I'd better call Dr. Weisbord.

MURIEL (*quickly*): The problem is—you're ashamed of me. Of your own dear mother—ashamed. "Prominent Feminist Ashamed of Her Own Dear Mother."

STEPHANIE: I am not—ashamed. I'm worried.

MURIEL: "I'm worried!"

STEPHANIE (*clutching* MURIEL's *wrist, trying to hold her still so she can look into her eyes*): Don't mock me, please. It isn't you. It's —that other person.

(*A pause.* MURIEL *disengages herself, with an air of dignity.*)

STEPHANIE: The way you lost control in the store—it wasn't you, was it?

MURIEL (*defiantly*): I told you: I didn't want those crooks to charge us twice.

STEPHANIE: God damn it, Mother—you know it's just routine— when we pay at the deli counter, they staple the—the (*she becomes nervous, rattled, speaking rapidly*)—receipts to the bags—from the deli counter—you know that. (*She locates one of the bags, with a stapled receipt, to show to* MURIEL, *who airily ignores it.*) Nobody was going to make us pay twice. And even if, if—if they tried to —why throw things onto the *floor*? Like a madwoman?

MURIEL (*contemptuously*): What do you—*you*—know about madness!

(*A pause.* MURIEL *changes tone, reverts to her flamboyant, stagey self. From this point until the end of the scene, the lights should be dim at the periphery of the action, focusing upon* MURIEL *and* STEPHANIE, *with* MURIEL *at the center, as if greedy for attention.*)

MURIEL: She who lasts, laughs. (*She pats one of her deep pockets, pulls out an item—a box of gourmet chocolates; professes surprise.*) Why—what have we here? (*Out of that same pocket she pulls a jar of fancy cocktail shrimp.*) Uh-oh—what's this? (*Out of another pocket, a mango.*) And *this*?

(STEPHANIE *is utterly astonished, watching with wide, childlike eyes. A strand of hair has fallen into her face, and her posture is less assured than it was only a few minutes ago.*)

STEPHANIE: Oh my God, Mother—what have you done?

MURIEL (*winking at audience*): Who's "Mother"? I'm Muriel.

STEPHANIE: But—when did you take those things? How? I was watching you every second.

MURIEL (*chuckling*): Now you see it, *voilà!* (*A small jar of caviar appears in the palm of her hand, then disappears up her sleeve.*) Now you don't!

STEPHANIE: How could you! I trusted you!

MURIEL: Treat time for my little girl! Things you can't afford on your salary!

STEPHANIE (*growing angry*): I'll have to take those things back to the store.

MURIEL: What?

STEPHANIE: Back to the store. Right now. (*Half sobbing*) Oh—I should have known better. God damn it, I should have known.

MURIEL: Oh, no you're not, baby. These're *mine.*

(MURIEL *tosses the mango to* STEPHANIE, *who has no choice but to catch it. She laughs, rather shrilly.*)

STEPHANIE: (*sadly*): It's all a joke to you now, isn't it?

MURIEL: What's a joke? (*Sniffs under an arm*) Where?

STEPHANIE: Life. (*Speaking slowly, not quite accusingly*) The life remaining to you.

MURIEL: Nah—I'm imbued with "the tragic sense of life," you betcha. Teach in any American public school for forty years, it's natural.

STEPHANIE (*quietly furious*): Now I have to take these things back. These—god—damned—*things.* (*It is evident that* STEPHANIE *is deflecting her deep concern for* MURIEL'*s health along lines of a more conventional emotional exasperation and disgust. She picks up the items flamboyantly, wiping tears from her eyes.*) God *damn,* and *damn,* and *damn.*

MURIEL: Aw, Stevie, where's your sense of humor? (*She snatches one of the items from her, drops it in her pocket.*)

STEPHANIE: Give that back! Mother—damn *you!*

MURIEL (*less certainly*): Hey—Stevie?

STEPHANIE: Don't call me that ridiculous name—I hate it!

MURIEL: Don't yell at me, baby. (*As* STEPHANIE *snatches at one of the items*) These things're *mine. Loot.*

(*A brief, ineffectual scuffle.* STEPHANIE, *though furious, sobbing in frustration, is timid about using force against her mother. When a jar falls to the floor, she gives a little scream and kicks it offstage. By this time only the two women are fully illuminated.*)

MURIEL (*hands over ears; repentant; perhaps genuinely frightened*): Baby—why are you crying? I—I won't do it again—I promise. (*Pause*) I won't go shopping with you again.

STEPHANIE (*wiping face, calmer*): That's why I'm crying, Mother— you won't go shopping with me again. Today was the last time.

(*Lights darken. The* WOMEN *stand motionless. As lights go out:*)

MURIEL (*with bravado*): Who's "Mother"? I'm Muriel.

Lights out.

Scene 2.

Lights up. Several days later, evening. MURIEL, *in an attractive quilted bathrobe, a colorful turban wrapped around her head, sits on the sofa composing a letter on numerous sheets of pink stationery. A vase of slightly (not overly) wilted gladioli, flame-colored, is on the coffee table, and* MURIEL *glances up frequently at it as if for inspiration.*

The "blade of dark" is slightly more prominent now, stage right, cutting through MURIEL's *bedroom at the rear.*

In the doorway of her own bedroom, observing her mother closely and out of the range of MURIEL's *vision,* STEPHANIE *stands talking in an apparently surreptitious way on the telephone. In this scene both women speak clearly enough to be heard by the audience and yet not by each other.* STEPHANIE *has recovered from her upset of the previous day and is again impeccably groomed, in tweed trousers, turtleneck sweater, medallion necklace around her throat. As she speaks, her eyes drift about in the characteristic manner of one talking on the telephone, yet always return to* MURIEL. *Unconsciously* STEPHANIE *winds the telephone cord around her fingers, wrist, etc.*

STEPHANIE: Except for last Thursday, she's been fine. Even docile. (*Laughs*) For *her*.

MURIEL (*writing her letter, cheerily*): "Señor Ríos, thank you so much for the *lovely* flowers."

STEPHANIE: The reason I'm calling, Jill, is—well, you know I've been nominated for executive director of the Council, I need to be in Denver and I thought maybe—I'd hoped—(*in a rush*) you could come stay with Mother for a few days?

MURIEL: "How did you know (*peering at gladioli*) flame-colored glads, fluorescent-bright glads, are my favorite flowers?"

STEPHANIE: No, she isn't listening in on the extension, Jill. I can *see* her.

MURIEL: "I wish I could speak Spanish to express my sentiments more lyrically. . . ."

STEPHANIE (*watching* MURIEL): I was never Mother's favorite, really. She loved us equally. I mean, *loves*. She asks after you all the time. And David and Betsey. And Jenny. *Yes.*

MURIEL (*alternately girlish and seductive*): "Of course, there *is* a minor age discrepancy. For forty-two years I taught . . ." (*hesitates; rethinks*) . . . No, dummy, strike that. "For a *number* of years I taught junior-high-school science."

STEPHANIE: Jill, I can't. She refuses to allow any nurse in this apartment since . . . you know. And it *is* her apartment really . . . in spirit . . . though I pay the rent. (*Listens; nods; frowns impatiently*)

MURIEL: "Señor Ríos, you make me shy. The other day in the park . . ."

STEPHANIE: Yes, but *no*. I couldn't! A home is absolutely out of the question. You saw what happened when she was in the hospital: begging everybody to be allowed to die.

MURIEL: "I've been a widow for so long . . ." (*Pauses; rethinks*) Naw! What if he finds out the truth! (*Crumples letter, tosses it down; takes up another sheet of stationery*)

STEPHANIE (*urgent*): Would you like to talk to her? . . . She *does*. Oh, she *does*. . . . Jill, please, we aren't small children anymore, we aren't *rivals*. Women must stop perceiving themselves as *rivals*. We're *sisters*.

MURIEL (*musing*): "Perhaps you don't believe in divorce in your native country, Señor Ríos . . . but my husband and I parted . . . *divorced* . . . in 1957. Oh, he was a cruel, cold-hearted son of a—" (*Pauses*) "Oh, he meant well—he was just ineffectual, sort of *not there*."

STEPHANIE (*intense*): Only for a week, Jill. I simply must attend this conference. . . . No, there isn't "internal disagreement," that's just the media. The issue is—some of us believe it's time for women to form a third political party. And I *have* to be there.

MURIEL (*continuing with a flourish*): "But when genuine love, old-fashioned romance, is involved . . . I am, you'll discover, practically a girl again; a *virgin*."

STEPHANIE: Oh, she's writing a letter. This latest "friend"—"man friend."

MURIEL: "I hope to be swept away."

STEPHANIE: Of course it's a delusion—what else? (*Nervous laugh*) He even sends her flowers. . . .

MURIEL (*who has overheard Stephanie*): Huh?

STEPHANIE: . . . arranged by Mother herself . . .

MURIEL: What's this?

STEPHANIE: Or, I guess retrieved out of the garbage dumpster—which is what these look like.

(MURIEL's *mood suddenly changes; we see that she is susceptible to swift emotional swings as if, indeed, another person had entered her being. She clumsily tries to hide the letter she has been writing, muttering to herself, "Can't let . . . evidence used against me . . . spies . . . surveillance . . . ," but these words need not be clearly articulated.* STEPHANIE *sees that* MURIEL *is upset, but it is too late.*)

MURIEL (*furious, as vase of gladioli capsizes*): LOOK WHAT YOU MADE ME DO! Clumsy, clumsy—idiot! Spying on your own flesh and blood!

(*As* MURIEL *tries awkwardly to gather up the gladioli,* STEPHANIE *hastily concludes her conversation.*)

STEPHANIE (*in an undertone*): Oh, God. I have to hang up. . . . Will you think about it, please? . . . Good-bye.

(STEPHANIE *hurries to help* MURIEL, *who appears to have banged her knee on the coffee table.* MURIEL *slaps at her.*)

MURIEL: I caught you! Red-handed! Spying on me! In my own house!

STEPHANIE: Oh, Mother, I—

MURIEL: Who were you talking to? Reporting to?

STEPHANIE (*placatingly, guiltily*): I was talking to a—

MURIEL: Don't lie! It was the school board, wasn't it?

STEPHANIE: The school board?

MURIEL: Those fools! Is that who it was? Checking up on me? And my own daughter cooperating?

STEPHANIE: Oh, no—no. It wasn't the school board, Mother. It was—a colleague of mine. (STEPHANIE *replaces the gladioli in the vase, dabs up some of the water spilled on the coffee table, carries the vase offstage as if to replenish the water; she continues speaking, trying to calm* MURIEL.) A colleague of *mine.* A—

MURIEL: Spying on me. And I am helpless. (*She presses her left hand against her left eye, a pained expression on her face.*) Paralyzed under the . . . anesthetic.

(STEPHANIE *returns with the flowers in the vase, sets the vase down. But* MURIEL *is too upset to be placated.*)

STEPHANIE (*with forced sincerity*): It was . . . a friend. A woman from the Council.

MURIEL: Whosit?

STEPHANIE: The Council. The Feminist Majority Council. Where I'm running for office.

MURIEL: So why are they spying on *me*? *I'm* not running for office. (*Laughs angrily*)

STEPHANIE: Nobody was spying on you.

MURIEL: *You* were. I saw you.

STEPHANIE: For God's sake, Mother. I was just standing there. I have to stand somewhere.

MURIEL: You're saying the apartment is too small? I should leave? Is that it? You're hinting I should leave?

STEPHANIE: What? Of course not.

MURIEL (*with bravado*): I can leave, just like that (*snaps her fingers*). I've had . . . invitations. To be a house guest. I've had a proposal . . . to elope.

STEPHANIE: Don't be silly—it's your apartment.

MURIEL: It used to be—now it's yours. Too small for two career women. Matter and antimatter. Protons. Trouble. *You* own it now—you can do as you please. (*Breathing hard, incensed*) All I need is enough boxes.

STEPHANIE: Enough what?

MURIEL: Boxes.

STEPHANIE: What about boxes?

MURIEL: To pack my things.

STEPHANIE (*laughing*): Oh, Mother, really!

MURIEL: Who's "Mother"? I'm—

STEPHANIE: Muriel.

MURIEL: *I'm* Muriel.

(STEPHANIE *notices the sheets of stationery* MURIEL *has tried to hide under one of the pillows, but makes it a point to ignore them. Instead, she arranges the pillows in order to conceal them better.* MURIEL *rubs rather dazedly at her eyes.*)

STEPHANIE: It's late—we should both get to bed.

MURIEL: You think I'm deluded, don't you?

STEPHANIE: What?

MURIEL: You *thought* it—I could hear you.

STEPHANIE: I—did not think it.

MURIEL: Baby, Muriel Washburn has worn out more delusions than most other people have worn out Kleenex in their lifetimes. So don't tell me about delusions.

STEPHANIE: Oh, Mother—you make too much of things.

MURIEL: It's possible to read thoughts, if you know how. Microwave radiation. Permeating the universe. It was only discovered in 1964, but I could sense it all my life. . . .

STEPHANIE: I'm sorry I upset you. Why don't you—

MURIEL (*earnestly*): It *was* the school board, wasn't it? The super-intendent's office?

STEPHANIE: No, Mother. All that was—a long time ago.

MURIEL: Those liars. Calling me "hysterical." They wouldn't believe how I was followed, and that . . . that bloody chicken foot in my desk (*a shiver of disgust*). They wouldn't take me seriously until I was murdered. In my own classroom.

STEPHANIE: Yes, but you're all right now. You're fine now. You're retired.

MURIEL: A twelve-year-old with a razor. They wouldn't believe *me*.

STEPHANIE: You're retired now—the hell with them. Why don't I run a bath for you—?

MURIEL: It *was* the school board, wasn't it? Just tell the truth.

STEPHANIE: I—I am telling the truth. It was a friend of mine.

MURIEL (*regarding her closely, searchingly*): And you weren't talking about me behind my back?

STEPHANIE: Of course not, Mother.

(MURIEL *seems about to believe* STEPHANIE, *then changes her tone.*)

MURIEL: Nah—I don't believe you. There's proof.

STEPHANIE: Proof?

MURIEL: The glad—glad— (*She is pointing to the gladioli but having difficulty pronouncing the word.*) Glad-a-lol—

STEPHANIE (*mispronounces the word too, stammering*): Glad—glad-e-o-lee . . .

MURIEL: Glad-e-o-lee . . . Oh, shit—these *things*, these—*flowers*. They're ruined now.

STEPHANIE: Oh, no—they're fine. They're beautiful.

MURIEL: Nah—they're ruined. All withered.

STEPHANIE: Oh, I think they're beautiful.

MURIEL: My friend sent them to me. He's a gentleman, but shy. Dances the tango. But *shy*.

STEPHANIE: Señor—César?

MURIEL: Ríos. Señor Ríos.

(*The light begins to fade, centering upon* MURIEL, *who executes a few dance steps vaguely resembling the tango. Brief rise of tango music, then fade.*)

MURIEL: All I need is a box. (*Pause*) Boxes.

(*Lights out*).

STEPHANIE'S VOICE (*shrilly*): Oh, Mother—you make too much of things!

Scene 3.

Lights up, but only to focus upon MURIEL, *who stands in her quilted bathrobe and turban, center stage.*

MURIEL (*reciting, in a girl's bell-like voice*):

I saw Eternity the other night,
Like a great ring of pure and endless light . . .

(*In silence,* MURIEL *removes her turban: exposes her bare head. She has had neurosurgery, and her gunmetal-gray hair is cropped short. At the left side of her head and across the crown there is a patch of fuzz, beneath which a jagged scar nine or ten inches in length is prominent.*

MURIEL *stands with her head bowed, turban unwound in her fingers, as the lights fade slowly to darkness.*)

Scene 4.

Lights up. A lively, boisterous episode, in contrast with the preceding. Here is MURIEL *in one of her hyperkinetic moods watching a boxing match (Tyson–Biggs) on television. She is wearing crimson stretch pants, a velour shirt, jogging shoes, and the brassy wig of scene 1. Her color is good, her eyes bright. She stands in front of the set mimicking certain of the boxers' movements—feinting, jabbing, throwing punches, footwork, "slipping" punches by turning her head swiftly. The television screen is not seen by the audience, but there are crowd noises, an announcer's voice, the sound of an occasional bell.* MURIEL, *caught up in the action, mutters, "C'mon!" "Yeah—like that!" "Deck 'im!" "Don't let 'im get away!" "C'mon, Mike—ice 'im!" etc.*

STEPHANIE *is visible in her bedroom, pacing about, papers in hand, practicing a speech;* she pauses to contemplate herself in a mirror. Very shortly, however, the noise from the living room distracts her and brings her out. By this time the eclipse covers about two-fifths of the stage, from stage right.* MURIEL's *bedroom is dark.*

STEPHANIE (*approaching the set, staring in revulsion*): What are you watching? Oh, Mother! My God! *Boxing?*

(MURIEL *continues with her feinting, jabbing, etc.*)

STEPHANIE: You're watching a *boxing* match?

MURIEL (*waving her off*): Don't distract me—go away.

STEPHANIE: Mother, are you serious? When have you gotten interested in—

MURIEL: Shhhh! It's Mike Tyson! (*Cringing, excited*) Oh, wow—what a left hook!

STEPHANIE (*fascinated, disgusted*): Which one is Mike Tyson?

MURIEL: If you have to ask, you can't be told.

---

* See Appendix (pp. 94–95) for Stephanie's speech.

(MURIEL *stands stock-still, whistling thinly through her teeth as the bell rings signaling the end of a round.* STEPHANIE *switches the set off primly.*)

STEPHANIE: You can't be serious. You're just—

MURIEL (*offended*): Hey—whadja *do?* What the hell?

STEPHANIE: —just pretending.

MURIEL: I don't interfere with *your* cultural interests.

STEPHANIE: I couldn't hear myself think, with this on so loud. It sounded like the monkey house at the zoo.

(MURIEL *switches the set back on;* STEPHANIE *switches it off again.*)

STEPHANIE: You know you shouldn't get excited. Worked up. (*With a despairing laugh*) I can't *believe* this.

MURIEL (*flippantly*): Seein's believin'! (*She switches the set back on, prevents* STEPHANIE *from switching it off. Her face registers intense empathetic interest.*)

STEPHANIE: Which one did you say is Mike Tyson?

MURIEL: The little one.

STEPHANIE: *That* one?

(*The bell rings again, signaling the start of the next round.* MURIEL *resumes her crouch and her comical movements;* STEPHANIE *watches with disdain.*)

MURIEL: C'mon! Like that! Ummmmm—what a left hook! Didja see that left hook!

STEPHANIE: Is that *real?*

MURIEL: Huh?

STEPHANIE: Is that *real? Real blood?* On that poor man's face?

MURIEL (*wincing*): Oh, wow!

STEPHANIE: Mother—you *are* crazy. I can't *believe* this.

(MURIEL *pushes her vaguely to one side, but* STEPHANIE *manages to switch off the set again.*)

MURIEL: Why can't I watch?

STEPHANIE: It excites you too much, that's why not. (*Passes a hand over her face*) My God—it's horrible. Why anyone in her right mind would want to see it I can't imagine.

MURIEL (*cheerfully, insolently*): Yah, so what—it's only a replay. I saw it already—I know how Mike winds it up. (*Throws a zippy left hook*) Vintage Tyson 1989.

STEPHANIE: You've seen it already? That fight? You were watching it for the second time?

MURIEL (*mopping her face with her shirt*): Muriel does lots of things, sweetie, nights you're out campaigning.

STEPHANIE (*stung*): Mother, I do not "campaign."

MURIEL: "Networking," then.

STEPHANIE: I do not "network." I—

MURIEL: Old-fashioned politicking, then. Whatever.

STEPHANIE: You do this sort of thing to upset me, don't you? It's a pattern.

MURIEL (*laying a heavy hand on* STEPHANIE's *shoulder*): Oh— pfffff! Your father always made that accusation. "You do it to upset me, don't you! Me, me, me!" (*Shakes her head*) Some people imagine the universe revolves around their precious navels.

STEPHANIE (*calmly*): You know this is a crucial period in my career. I've been working for the Council for years and I—I deserve some national recognition. On Sunday, when I leave, I won't know if— if I can trust you here. If—I can trust you.

MURIEL (*airily*): That's for me to know and you to find out. (*She places a hand over one of her eyes, quizzically, though not concerned or upset.*) One of these light bulbs is burned out, I guess. (*She sits on the sofa, leans back to peer up inside the shade of a floor lamp, turns the switch experimentally. It is a lamp with three light bulbs of varying watts.*) Why's it so dark in here . . . ?

(STEPHANIE, *pacing about, takes no notice. She runs her hands through her hair, disturbing its smoothness.*)

STEPHANIE: It's a pattern, isn't it? I begin to see. To see clearly. (*As if presenting a classroom analysis, brisk, grim, satisfied*) You,

Mother, are of that generation of women who "sacrificed" for their daughters; who wanted us to "go beyond" you. And now that we have, now you resent us. You boast about us to your friends—or did—but secretly you resent us.

MURIEL (*fussing with the lamp*): Oh—damn!

STEPHANIE: Just when I need your support, need to trust you, you —start behaving . . . (*a pause*) . . . like that. Like . . . (*another pause*) . . . that other person.

MURIEL (*a strange bodiless cry*): I don't know who it is.

(A *moment's tension: then* STEPHANIE *consciously breaks the spell, moving briskly about, pushing the television off to one side; tidying up.*)

STEPHANIE: My father—Dwight James Washburn—who *was* he? Why is he such a mystery? You've never even shown Jill and me pictures of him.

MURIEL (*resuming her earlier mood*): He didn't photograph.

STEPHANIE: What?

MURIEL: Some people aren't photogenic—your father wasn't photographic. He didn't *develop*.

STEPHANIE: You make a joke of everything. The fact is—you erased half of our heritage. Jill and me. No wonder she married the first man who asked her—

MURIEL: And you ran from the first man who asked *you*.

STEPHANIE: Men don't "ask" women to marry them these days. You're behind the times. It's—different.

MURIEL: Whatever he asked you, you sure ran.

STEPHANIE (*irritably*): There wasn't a "he." I mean—there were several. I mean (*stammering*) th-there were friends, colleagues who were men, but—but it didn't work out.

MURIEL (*stretching*): That was quite a workout—I'm famished! Time for midnight snack!

STEPHANIE: (*a mild gesture of revulsion*): Not me, thank you.

(MURIEL *bounces up from the sofa and trots into the kitchen.* STEPHANIE *is aware of the darkness on one side of the living room, but only casually turns on a small table lamp extreme stage right.*)

STEPHANIE (*in an ordinary voice, as if addressing an invisible audience*): It was unjust to Jill and me, depriving us of a father.

MURIEL (*offstage, cheerily*): So sue me!

(STEPHANIE *presses her fingertips to her eyes in a gesture reminiscent of* MURIEL.)

MURIEL (*returning with two cans of beer, a quart container of ice cream, two spoons*): Working out in the ring, you get *famished.* C'mon, baby. (*She sits luxuriantly on the sofa, but* STEPHANIE *refuses to join her.*)

STEPHANIE: Is he—alive? Our father?

MURIEL (*shrugging*): "Our" father—who he?

STEPHANIE: Dwight James Washburn.

MURIEL (*singing, to her own tune*):

My sweetheart's the man in the moon.
I'm gonna be meeting him soon . . .

STEPHANIE: What did he look like, at least? Do I—resemble him?

MURIEL (*offering a beer to* STEPHANIE, *who politely declines; opens the other for herself*): I was born in 1914. The year the Imperial German Army rose up. Entropy on the march! Through Brussels to France! (*Shudders, excited*) There's been a hot time globally ever since.

STEPHANIE: I was four years old when he—disappeared. But I can't remember him.

(MURIEL *spoons ice cream into her mouth in a slow, sensuous manner; offers some to* STEPHANIE, *who politely declines.*)

MURIEL (*gravely*): I'm approaching a watershed.

STEPHANIE: What?

MURIEL: I like French Vanilla Bean Candy Almond *almost* as much as Dutch Chocolate Mint Raspberry. Yum! Try some!

STEPHANIE (*declining the proffered spoon*): I try to summon back a face—but I can't. But (*angry laugh*) the person I'm addressing, in my lectures, in my books—even my speech to the women's council—it's *him.*

MURIEL (*sharply*): The hell with that, baby. Dwight James Washburn *evaporated.* On a gusty autumn night in 1957. When you were four, and Jill was three—months short of being born. And where he went, the s.o.b. soon forgot to maintain child support.

STEPHANIE: You drove him out, though.

MURIEL (*spooning ice cream*): Who says?

STEPHANIE: You. You used to boast. When Jill and I were children.

MURIEL (*shrugging*): Now, Señor Ríos . . . he's different.

STEPHANIE: Who?

MURIEL (*quietly*): Señor Ríos. My friend.

STEPHANIE (*with an impatient gesture, rolling her eyes*): Oh. Him.

MURIEL: Completely different from your basic American man. He's Spanish . . . from an ancient family.

STEPHANIE: I thought he was Hispanic. From Puerto Rico.

MURIEL (*adamantly*): *Spa*nish. The real thing. From Castellón de la Plana.

STEPHANIE: From where?

MURIEL (*rolling the syllables on her tongue*): Castellón de la Plana. The Ríoses are an old noble family. Medieval. (*She shivers, hugs herself.*) He's so . . . romantic. Not like your Anglo men, all anemic, cold-fish types. He's warm . . . warm-blooded . . . *dark.* His eyes are like gems, shiny and dark . . . but the whites so *white.* And his teeth . . . so white. (*Pause*) I'm undecided about the moustache.

STEPHANIE (*skeptically*): And you met this Señor Ríos in the park? In May? The night of the—eclipse, was it?

MURIEL (*seems confused for a moment*): No . . . I met Señor Ríos— that's to say *he* met *me,* introduced himself to *me*—the night there were shooting stars. *You* weren't there.

STEPHANIE: Where was I, then?

MURIEL: They were streaking across the sky . . . the northeast . . . one or two a minute. Even with the air pollution, they were beautiful. Incandescent.

STEPHANIE: There aren't shooting stars, really. That's just a—fairy tale.

MURIEL (*annoyed*): So? So they're meteors? They're real enough.

STEPHANIE: Meteors?

MURIEL: A shower of 'em, all afire. Thrown off from a comet. (*Dreamily*) A comet's a wild, beautiful thing, but the fact of it is, it's *precise*. It won't let you down.

STEPHANIE (*a little cruelly*): Was that the night, last May, I came home and found you on the sofa here, you woke up and didn't know where you were? Chattering nonstop about shooting stars, like the stars could care about *you*? But no mention then of Señor Ríos.

MURIEL (*hurt, angry*): So—the stars don't care about us—we can care about *them*. They got the beauty, we got the brains.

STEPHANIE: So that's how Señor Ríos entered your life.

MURIEL: No need to be jealous—it's strictly platonic. Thus far.

STEPHANIE: He calls you, when I'm not home? Sends you flowers?

MURIEL: We have a date to go dancing—when you're in Denver.

STEPHANIE: Do you!

MURIEL: No need to be jealous.

STEPHANIE (*stung*): Of course not, Mother. *No* need.

MURIEL (*in her bright, insouciant way*): Who's "Mother"? I'm— whosit. (*Sipping beer and eating ice cream contentedly*) Y'know why I like boxing? Why I'm a fan of Mike Tyson?

STEPHANIE (*after a perceptible pause, yet with an almost innocent cruelty*): Because it's about brain damage—other people's.

(*A long, awkward pause. We see that* MURIEL *has been wounded only by the way her spoon freezes in midair. But* MURIEL *shrugs the remark aside.*)

MURIEL (*brightly*): Yah—why I like Mike Tyson, it's not what you're thinking, probably—'cause I'm lily-white watching black men beat up on their brothers for money. No, and it's not 'cause I'm thirsty for blood, or bored, or sadistic, or—any of that. Nah, I like Mike Tyson for just one thing—when he's good there's nobody better. He knows how to get the job done!

STEPHANIE: Better go to bed now, Mother. It's late, and you over-excited yourself.

MURIEL (*chuckling, almost coarsely*): Yah—*he knows how to get the job done.* The rest of 'em . . . cold fish.

STEPHANIE (*standing over* MURIEL): You'll have to take your medication tonight.

MURIEL: I already did.

STEPHANIE: You did *not.*

MURIEL: I say I *did.*

STEPHANIE: I can't endure another night like the last time you were—overexcited.

MURIEL: You take the pills, then. (*Laughs*) You got the problem, you take the pills.

STEPHANIE: Now, Mother.

(MURIEL *suddenly scrambles to her feet, backs off. She has dropped her beer, the ice cream container, the spoon—a quicksilver change of mood.*)

MURIEL: I'm not "Mother"!—don't blame me!

STEPHANIE: Mother, please—don't.

MURIEL: I don't know where she is. She's—gone. *Don't blame me.*

(STEPHANIE *hides her face in her hands as the lights darken.*
Lights out; then up. Later that night. STEPHANIE *is in a chair.*)

STEPHANIE (*in a pure, bell-like voice, to herself*): "Though I walk through the Valley of the Shadow of Death, I will fear no evil: for thou art with me: thy rod and thy staff they comfort me. Thou preparest a table before me in the presence of mine enemies. . . ."

Lights out.

Scene 5.

Lights up. A few days later. Baroque harpsichord music is playing (a record or CD of STEPHANIE's*); the mood is subdued.*

By now the eclipse is at the halfway point: stage right is dark, or would be if no lamps were on; stage left is illuminated normally. MURIEL's *bedroom would be entirely dark except that she has turned on a bedside crook-necked lamp with a small, intense bulb. In her quilted bathrobe, a towel wrapped loosely around her head,* MURIEL *sits up in bed, feverishly writing a letter. Her door is shut.*

STEPHANIE, *in tailored slacks and a striking cable-knit sweater, stands in the doorway of her bedroom, talking on the telephone. Her room is brightly lit; we see an open suitcase on a chair, clothes laid across her bed.*

As she talks on the telephone, STEPHANIE *repeatedly glances in the direction of* MURIEL's *room.* MURIEL, *intent upon her letter, does not glance around.*

STEPHANIE *(in a good mood)*: . . . No, no, everything is fine, Barbara. I finished the speech. I think it will be effective. And I've conferred with . . . Yes, right. I've been at the university all day, on the phone. Sally Mack—she's head of the women's studies program at Berkeley—she's going to introduce me . . . *(Listens, nodding)* Yes, Mother is fine. She is.

(From out of the relative shadows stage right, AILEEN STANLEY *appears, walking slowly, as if cautiously. She is a solid-bodied woman with glasses, a close-cropped practical haircut, and a habit of squinting frequently and brushing at her nose. She wears nondescript clothes, perhaps a pantsuit, and carries a handbag and a well-worn briefcase. She shifts between uneasiness and professional arrogance, as of a naturally shy person invested with a measure of bureaucratic authority.)*

STEPHANIE *(a bit impatient, but confident)*: Of course I won't let any of you down. I'll be there. If we are ever to establish a viable third party, a true women's party, a *majority* party, this is the time. This is an exciting time! The abortion issue alone—

*(*AILEEN STANLEY *rings the front doorbell of the apartment.)*

STEPHANIE *(murmuring)*: Oh, excuse me—someone's at the door. *(She hangs up the phone and hurries to answer the door.)*

(MURIEL, *still absorbed in her letter writing, takes no notice. The harpsichord music continues in the background.*)

STEPHANIE (*with a polite smile*): Yes? Hello?

AILEEN (*blinking at* STEPHANIE, *whom she apparently recognizes: she is startled, confused, and embarrassed*): Oh—! Hello . . .

STEPHANIE: Yes?

AILEEN (*consults a piece of paper, as if to disguise her awkwardness*): I . . . I've come to see . . . Is this the residence of Muriel Washburn? (*Squints at the paper*) "Retired schoolteacher"? "Thwarted astrophysicist"?

STEPHANIE (*perplexed*): Well—Muriel Washburn is my mother. We share this apartment.

AILEEN (*blinking, smiling nervously, almost at a loss for words*): I guess . . . it *is* you? I thought maybe, the name . . . I mean, I was wondering . . . unless it was a coincidence . . . You don't remember, but we met once, a few years ago, at a women's conference in Boston. (*Laughs nervously*) You *are* . . . Stephanie Washburn, of course?

STEPHANIE (*trying to remain cordial*): Yes, I am, but . . . what do you want?

(AILEEN *thrusts out her hand:* STEPHANIE *has no choice but to shake it.*)

AILEEN (*quickly*): My name is Aileen Stanley and I'm a social worker for the county, but, oh!—you wouldn't remember *me*! I wouldn't expect you to remember *me*.

STEPHANIE: You wanted to see my . . . mother?

AILEEN (*easing inside the door, fluttery, nervous, yet a bit aggressive*): (*Laughs nervously*) I can't claim to have read your book . . . but I've read essays . . . like, I guess, on gender? Role playing in the professions? The misuse of power?

STEPHANIE (*perplexed, a bit annoyed*): But it's . . . Mother you want to see? Muriel Washburn?

AILEEN (*having eased into the living room, glancing quickly about, both abashed and frankly inquisitive*): Oh, isn't this attractive! So many books! Such nice music! One of these good old apartments with high ceilings and good hardwood floors . . . so different from what I usually see. (*A pause*) May I speak with your mother, Stephanie? Is she here?

STEPHANIE: Is she expecting you?

AILEEN: I think so, yes.

STEPHANIE (*mildly incredulous*): Yes?

AILEEN (*quickly*): Oh, it's . . . routine. I mean, there is probably some . . . misunderstanding. . . . (*Speaking rapidly, embarrassed*) I'm from the County Hot-Line Crisis Center for Senior Citizens, and—

STEPHANIE: The county what?

AILEEN: Your mother *is* here?

STEPHANIE: She's asleep. She's under medication.

(MURIEL *now looks up, alert. She lays aside her letter, goes to the door of her room, listens.*)

AILEEN: May I see her . . . anyway?

STEPHANIE: (*stiffly*): What do you mean? If Mother is asleep you can't see her—Miss—Stanley.

(STEPHANIE, *beginning to be agitated, goes to switch off the harpsichord music.* MURIEL *opens the door of her room a crack, peers out.*)

AILEEN: Oh—Aileen! Please call me—

STEPHANIE: If you want to see my mother, Aileen, I suggest you come back another time. Tomorrow? Monday? Mother is at her most coherent in the mornings.

AILEEN: Most coherent?

STEPHANIE: Please—what do you want?

AILEEN: I . . . I've told you. I want to speak with Muriel Washburn. (*Awkwardly, yet aggressively; opening briefcase and removing papers*) I think you had better . . . comply, Stephanie, with our . . . office.

(*At this point, we see that* MURIEL *has opened the door of her room a crack and is peering out.*)

STEPHANIE (*her own authority now evoked*): Are you threatening me?

AILEEN: If I don't see Mrs. Washburn and determine her . . . condition . . . I'm afraid I will have to return with a . . . warrant and a . . . police officer.

(MURIEL *has shut the door and withdrawn. She hurriedly puts on a wig; changes her robe for a good, but not overly dressy, dress; hastily applies makeup before the mirror. Her wig is silvery-white, stylish and dignified, appropriate for a woman of her age. Before the mirror, she mutters to herself, chiding, upset, not fully audible:* "Oh, now!" "Now what!" "Such fuss!" "Why don't they let us alone!" "Spying on us!" *etc.*)

STEPHANIE (*astonished*): A . . . police officer?

AILEEN (*indicating the documents*): Your mother filed a . . . complaint against you. With our office.

STEPHANIE (*groping backward; sitting on arm of sofa*): I can't believe this.

AILEEN: Yes, indeed, she telephoned in, left a message with one of our staff—

STEPHANIE (*with a little cry*): Oh, God! I can't believe this!

AILEEN: She sounded sort of . . . emotionally distressed. Said she'd been—locked in her room? In the dark? Tied in her bed? (*Peers at document*) "Refused a view of the sky"—?

STEPHANIE (*faint wail edged with anger*): Mother! How could you!

AILEEN (*reading*): "Mental cruelty . . . force-feeding of narcotics . . . physical and mental coercion . . . mistrust . . . spiritual deprivation." (*Laughs nervously*) Of course, not all of these charges could stand up in court.

STEPHANIE (*as if dazed*): Mother isn't well. She hasn't been well for . . . a while.

(STEPHANIE *begins to stand, sinks back on sofa as if light-headed. Where at the start of the scene she was in control, now she appears almost childlike, helpless. She runs her fingers unconsciously through her hair.)*

AILEEN (*sympathetic even while still "official"*): Even if it's a false alarm, Stephanie, I have to see her. It's—the law.

(STEPHANIE *hides her face in her hands.*
MURIEL *throws open her door to make a dramatic entrance. Emerging into the light, she appears quite striking in her elegant wig, attractive dress, flattering makeup. Unfortunately, she is bare-legged and has forgotten her shoes.)*

MURIEL (*imperial tone*): What on earth is this? All this commotion?

AILEEN (*a bit intimidated*): You are . . . Muriel Washburn?

MURIEL (*loftily*): And who, may I inquire, are *you?*

AILEEN: I am Aileen Stanley of the Meridian County Hot-Line Crisis Center, Senior Citizen Division. (*Extends her hand as if for a handshake, but the gesture is ignored.*) I believe you called us yesterday, Mrs. Washburn?

MURIEL (*coolly*): Stephanie, who is this person? One of your campaigners?

(STEPHANIE *looks away, hurt, offended.*)

AILEEN: Mrs. Washburn, I—

MURIEL: *Ms.*

AILEEN: *Ms.* Washburn, you did telephone us, didn't you? Our emergency hot-line number? (*Checks document*) Friday—October 6—three-fifty P.M.?

MURIEL (*approaches* STEPHANIE *cautiously; a bit guiltily*): Stephanie—?

(STEPHANIE, *rather like a stubborn child, shrugs, looks away.*)

MURIEL (*to* AILEEN, *quickly*): Look here, Ms.—Stanley? I don't know who you are or what your true business is, but I will not allow false accusations to be made against my daughter, or me. (*Indignant*) We will not be spied on, do you hear?

AILEEN: You telephoned the Crisis Center, didn't you? To report being *abused?*

MURIEL (*cupping hand to ear, haughtily*): Report *who*?

AILEEN (*reading*): "Systematic and repeated abuse."

MURIEL: Hugh? Hugh *who*?

AILEEN: "Abuse."

MURIEL (*to* STEPHANIE): Hear this! It's one of our neighbors complaining about us. Somebody named "Hugh"?

AILEEN (*half shouting*): "*Abuse.*"

MURIEL (*offended*): You needn't shout, young lady. No one here is deaf.

AILEEN: Mrs. Washburn, I'm here to help you if you need help. May I speak with you in private?

MURIEL: Where did you say you're from? (*Suspicious*) The school board? You want to revoke my pension after forty-two years?

AILEEN: No, I'm from the County Crisis Center. The Senior Citizens Program. I'm here to investigate your complaint of—abuse.

MURIEL (*haughtily, indicating her dress*): Do I look like a person with a complaint? I am—(*groping*)—an object of gentrification.

AILEEN: Oh, that is a pretty dress, Mrs. Washburn. You look very nice. But according to our records—

MURIEL: Do I look like a senior citizen? (*Winking toward audience*) I may be senior, but I sure ain't a citizen.

AILEEN (*laughs weakly*): I certainly don't want to intrude, Mrs. Washburn. But we tape all our hot-line calls, and we do have a record of a call from you, Mrs. Washburn—do you remember making it?

MURIEL (*growing excited*): A what? A *tape*? A *tape* of *me*? How dare you!

AILEEN: It's policy.

MURIEL: I—will not be spied upon. Not by the FBI, or TV monitors in the grocery store, or the school board, or—you. I will not be taped, and reduced to microfilm, like—somebody dead. (*Begins waving her hands*) I am alive, I am not—that other. *I am alive, can't you see!?*

AILEEN (*to* STEPHANIE: Is she always like this?

MURIEL (*furious*): "She" is the cat's mother!

AILEEN (*edging away, yet trying to maintain some measure of authority*): I—I'm sorry to upset you, Mrs. Washburn, but you *did* call our office—didn't you? With a complaint against a party you identified as your daughter?

MURIEL (*to* STEPHANIE, *now stony-faced*): Don't believe a word of it, Stevie—it's all a tissue of lies.

AILEEN (*doggedly*): I only want to help, Mrs. Washburn. If . . . there is any substance to your complaint . . .

MURIEL: Yes! The school board has been abusing me for years. Refused to believe me—took the word of pathological liars over mine. *I* ended up being called a racist—*I*!

AILEEN (*confused*): Oh, dear. But this present complaint—

MURIEL: Do I look like a person with a complaint? I'm in exemplary health. There were thirty-seven staples in my head, but they're gone now.

AILEEN (*edging backward, as* MURIEL *advances*): I—I do have a directive to interview you, and to arrange for a medical examination . . .

MURIEL: Nobody touches me! Nobody unclothes me! Ever again!

AILEEN: The—the county assumes all expenses.

MURIEL (*snaps her fingers*): Ah—I got it.

AILEEN: Yes?

MURIEL: *I* understand your confusion, miss—you're in the wrong apartment. There's an old woman down on the third floor—*she* called you. She's the victim you want.

AILEEN: But *you* are Muriel Washburn—aren't you?

MURIEL (*with bravado*): Who's "Muriel"? I'm Mother.

Lights out.

Scene 6.

Lights up. Immediately following the preceding scene. Stage left, in a segment of light cast by a single lamp, STEPHANIE and AILEEN STANLEY sit, having tea. Both MURIEL's and STEPHANIE's bedrooms are dark. In this scene, STEPHANIE oscillates between her dawning awareness of MURIEL's state and her career-worry that her reputation might be injured.

STEPHANIE (*in a strange, impersonal voice*): It wasn't a brain tumor she had to have removed last winter, it was a capillary angioma. She'd been having a headache and wouldn't tell me and finally had to tell me so I took her for tests and it turned out she'd had a minor hemorrhage. . . . They discovered she'd had two or three over the course of her life . . . there was this accumulation of blood in her midbrain that had to be removed. A tight little ball of capillaries. Mother said, "Oh boy, I have my own private black hole."

AILEEN: She is what you'd call . . . delusional.

STEPHANIE: I love Mother—I can't institutionalize her. She won't even allow a nurse in here, or a sitter, or . . . anyone except me.

AILEEN (*cautiously*): Oh, but they're all like that. At first.

STEPHANIE: I love Mother. I am defined as . . . as the person who loves her. (*Loudly*) For each of us on earth is so defined, by who we love, and who loves us.

AILEEN: The things I see in my line of work! Oh, it's . . . just tragic sometimes. I mean, you wouldn't believe how *sad*. Elderly people *do* get abused.

STEPHANIE: You say . . . there is a tape of Mother's conversation with one of your staff members? It's . . . a permanent record?

AILEEN: Oh dear, yes, I'm afraid so. But our records are *private*.

STEPHANIE (*awkwardly*): Even if . . . if her charges turn out to be . . . delusional?

AILEEN: It's the law. (*Cheerfully*) But don't worry, Stephanie, no one will ever know. (*A pause*) Outside our office.

STEPHANIE: I see. (*A pause; then she speaks in her impersonal voice, as if for the record.*) Mother is a woman of enormous energy and intelligence. She should have been something more ambitious than a junior-high science teacher. . . . She did apply to graduate school, to study astrophysics—but it was 1935, women weren't wanted. I think in fact she showed up at Cal Tech demanding an interview and they . . . laughed at her. (*Peculiar smile*) Not that I blamed them, or anyone—Mother *can* be funny.

AILEEN (*as if misunderstanding*): Oh my, yes—so witty! For a woman of her age.

STEPHANIE: Mother was such a popular teacher—for years. Her students loved her—she was so funny. Demanding, and—a disciplinarian—but fair. Then . . . in the sixties . . . things began to shift. The school district, the population . . . the racial mix. Mother tried to maintain the old ways, but her students rebelled, some of them actually . . . threatened her . . . or she claimed they did. And the younger teachers weren't sympathetic. (*With more emotion*) She was followed leaving the school building one day, she was knocked down on the street . . . another time she was slashed with a razor. But the boy denied it, and . . . (*with a resigned gesture*) and there was such controversy . . . the school board advised early retirement.

AILEEN (*too buoyant for the situation*): You'd never know she's had brain surgery! Gee whiz, some of those patients I see . . . they're paralyzed, or aphasiac, or blind, or . . . just plain *not there*. (*Pause; unintentional irony*) Your mother would fit in real well in a good nursing home where there was, y'know, lots of activities. Social life. Muriel Washburn would be a real mover and shaker.

STEPHANIE (*as if not hearing; bitter*): . . . Mother said the boy had a razor—he slashed her forearm, threatened to . . . slash her throat. The boy said she'd cut herself on the edge of his locker! It was his word and his parents' and friends' against Mother's. . . . She never got over it.

(*Pause*)

AILEEN (*a sort of professional cheeriness*): So, Stephanie—you're flying out to Denver tomorrow?

STEPHANIE: I . . . intend to.

AILEEN: Give 'em hell! Wish I could come along.

STEPHANIE (*abstractly*): What is real, what is invented . . . the distinction isn't always clear. (*Pause*) Mother used to tell us, Jill and me, that the way the stars twinkle is just an optical illusion. Delusion? It's the movement of Earth's atmosphere, actually—the way the atmosphere bends light rays that causes it.

AILEEN (*self-absorbed*): I'm thinking of quitting my job. The nasty things I see—the hot-line cases—brrrrr!

STEPHANIE (*slowly, as if just realizing*): The eye invents so much. Especially in the heavens.

AILEEN (*briskly picks up briefcase, prepares to leave*): Well, look—here's my card. Any time you need the name of a good registered nurse, or, y'know, just someone to watch over Muriel when you're away. Male nurses are great: even the gays have some muscle. And when it's time for the nursing home . . . I know all the inside dope.

STEPHANIE (*staring at the card for a long pained moment*): Oh. Thank you.

AILEEN (*shaking hands with* STEPHANIE, *at the door*): Well! Stephanie Washburn! It's an honor to sit and chat with you—even in these circumstances.

STEPHANIE (*barely concealing her distaste; forced cordiality*): Oh . . . it was very nice to meet you. I'm just sorry about the—misunderstanding.

AILEEN (*cheerfully*): No problem. About 20 percent of the calls we get are filed under the code "Cuckoo"—I mean, "delusional"—but we have to investigate them all. It's state law.

STEPHANIE (*trying to disguise how much this point means to her*): And . . . the tape can't be erased?

AILEEN (*nudging* STEPHANIE, *familiarly*): Oh, now, Stevie—don't worry! Nobody's gonna leak classified information to the press!

(AILEEN *leaves. Light fades to illuminate* STEPHANIE, *who stands frozen, insulted, an expression of cold fury on her face.*)

STEPHANIE (*as the mask drops*): I don't love anyone! Any of you! I mean *you*! I hate hate hate (*as she tears* AILEEN's *card to bits and*

scatters the pieces) you all! (*Begins to pack a suitcase furiously*)
But I'm going anyway.

Lights out.

Scene 7.

Lights up. The following night. MURIEL, *in the apartment alone, is
speaking over the telephone. She wears her oversized sweater, pedal
pushers, and jogging shoes; her turban is wrapped loosely around
her head and affixed with a gaudy jeweled brooch.*

*Approximately four-fifths of the stage is now in an umbral darkness,
converging on stage left, front, where* MURIEL *paces about in a circle
of light cast by a floor lamp. She does a good deal of squinting and
blinking, and, during this speech, several times presses her fingertips
against her forehead or eyes, with a suggestion of pain, dizziness, or
fatigue. But her voice is generally upbeat, ebullient.*

A chair has been placed in front of the door as a sort of barricade.

MURIEL (*gaily*): No, no, *no*, I don't need anyone to stay with me.
Stevie knows better than to try that again. . . . (*Voice rising*) *I
don't need any caretaker, thank you. I'm of sound mind and body.*
(*Relents somewhat*) Well—I have my own friends. . . . Yes. I have
a . . . a special friend. . . . Yes: male. Tomorrow night is eclipse
night and we're going out dancing. (*Girlish laughter*) He's from an
old Spanish family . . . from Castellón de la Plana. . . . What d'you
mean, is he my age? . . . Oh, yes—she knows. Sure, she's a wee
bit jealous, but . . . that's her problem. (*Excited*) Tomorrow night
is the lunar eclipse, the first time in seven years we'll be able to
see an eclipse clearly in North America. Oh, I can't wait! It will
begin here about nine-twenty P.M. and by ten-thirty it should be
at its fullest. The moon might be orangish, or dark red, depending
. . . on the earth's atmosphere: how discolored, I mean. Be sure
the children see it, Jill? Promise? (*A bit too urgently*) Jill? *Promise?*

(*From extreme stage right,* STEPHANIE *appears out of the darkness,
in the corridor outside the* WASHBURNS' *apartment. She is carrying
her handbag, suitcase, and a small package under one arm. She is
wearing an attractive belted trenchcoat, but the belt is twisted in
back; her hair is windblown; her eyes are oddly bright. She walks
with studied care, as if mildly,and unaccustomedly, drunk.*)

MURIEL (*querulously*): Jill, I'm having a hard time hearing you. I wonder if it's *you-know-who* with their *you-know-what* devices. (*Disguising her voice*) There's a way of eluding the bastards, though! So they can't identify you on their tapes! (*Laughs*)

(STEPHANIE *has taken out her door key, fumbles while fitting it into the lock, drops it; stoops to pick it up but can't seem to find it in the dark.*)

MURIEL: . . . I *said* everything is fine. Hunky-dory, sweetie. I called 'cause I guess I been a sort of negligent mother . . . these thirty-odd years. (*In a rush of feeling*) I just want you to know I love you, honey. Love my two little girls more than anything on earth or . . . anywhere. Remember that, honey, will you? (*Stricken with feeling*, MURIEL *touches her head, dislodges the turban, which falls to the floor, revealing her thin, short hair and the jagged scar in her scalp.*) Oh, honey, you know that—don't you? You and Stevie?

(STEPHANIE *rings the doorbell.* MURIEL *freezes.*)

MURIEL: . . . It's the doorbell. (*Frightened, excited*) But he's supposed to come tomorrow night, not tonight. It's too soon. I'm not ready. Oh, God! (*Picks up the turban and tries to put it on, but it falls off again*) 'Bye, honey!

STEPHANIE: Mother? Are you there?

(MURIEL *approaches the door cautiously.*)

STEPHANIE: Mother? It's Stephanie. Open the door.

MURIEL: It's . . . *who*?

STEPHANIE (*impatiently*): It's me. Your daughter Stephanie. I lost my key.

MURIEL (*alarmed*): You're in Denver, Colorado. It's two hours earlier there. You can't be in two time zones simultaneously.

STEPHANIE: Mother, don't *joke*. For God's sake, don't *joke*. Just let me in.

MURIEL: Unless you're subatomic particles you can't be in two time zones simultaneously.

STEPHANIE (*half screaming*): Damn it, *let me in!*

MURIEL *pushes the chair away from the door; unbolts and unlocks the door.* STEPHANIE *steps inside, stumbles against the chair and almost falls. She drops her handbag and her suitcase but hangs on to the package.*

STEPHANIE (*a mild drunken slur to her voice*): What's this chair doing here?

MURIEL: It's a barricade.

STEPHANIE: A what? I almost broke my neck. (*Squinting*) Why's it so dark in here?

MURIEL: You aren't supposed to be here. (*Confused, alarmed*) Why are you here? What day is it?

STEPHANIE: Why did you barricade the door? Did someone try to get in?

MURIEL: There was . . . someone named Hugh. One of our neighbors, remember? Causing trouble. (*Presses her fingertips against her eyes*) I refused to let the son of a bitch in.

(STEPHANIE *walks swaying to the circle of light, sits in a chair, legs outstretched. Her face looks flaccid, her eyes unnaturally bright.*
MURIEL *shuts the door, locks and bolts it, and, grunting, pushes the chair back in place.* STEPHANIE *observes her without comment.*)

MURIEL: You . . . aren't supposed to be here. Is it my fault you're here?

(STEPHANIE *makes a gesture as if to indicate it doesn't matter.*)

MURIEL: *Is it my fault . . . ?*

(STEPHANIE *removes a pint bottle of Scotch from the paper bag, unscrews the top, carefully takes a swallow, and wipes her mouth daintily with the back of her hand. She hiccups.*)

MURIEL: Oh! Shame on you! My own daughter . . . reeling drunk.

STEPHANIE (*with dignity*): I am not reeling. I have never in my life . . . *reeled.*

MURIEL (*guiltily, defensively*): You flew to Denver on the six o'clock flight. You know you did.

(STEPHANIE *shrugs.*)

MURIEL: You . . . didn't?

(STEPHANIE *shrugs again, hiccups. She starts to unbutton her coat but fumbles and gives up.* MURIEL *comes to help her, but she too is clumsy and can't force the buttons through the buttonholes.*)

MURIEL: Oh, I won't be blamed! I won't be a . . . scapegoat!

STEPHANIE (*dreamily*): I watched the plane leave without me. No one is to blame.

MURIEL: But . . . why? (*Angrily*) They stopped you, didn't they? The airport police?

STEPHANIE: . . . Sat in a cocktail lounge talking things over. In the inside of my head. (*Raps on her forehead with her knuckles; giggles*) Just sat.

MURIEL (*muttering*): There are TV monitors everywhere in that airport, it's so obvious they don't even try to hide. You get X-rayed just walking minding your own damn business.

STEPHANIE: They can't see the inside of your head, though.

MURIEL: Oh, yes they can.

STEPHANIE: They *can't*. Not if you know how (*giggles shrilly*) to block 'em.

MURIEL (*disgusted*): You're drunk. My own daughter—reeling *drunk*.

(MURIEL *secures the turban on her head, tries to tidy up both* STEPHANIE *and herself.*)

STEPHANIE (*drinking from the bottle*): Oh, Momma, don't be mad at me, everybody's mad at me. I . . . want to *die*. So *ashamed*. I called them and I told them, "How can I leave my mother?" I told them, "Momma isn't well and she needs me," I told them (*voice rising, childlike*), "Nobody loves me like my Momma on this earth." (*A pause*) Now they're mad at me 'cause I told the truth. (*A pause*) Once in my goddamn life I told the truth—now they hate me. So *ashamed*.

MURIEL: Oh, Stevie.

STEPHANIE: I don't care, Momma, I told the truth for once. I can't leave *here*. (*At the word "here"* STEPHANIE *stamps her feet on the floor like a child in a tantrum.*)

(MURIEL *draws away, as if frightened.*)

MURIEL (*to herself*): They made a tape of this—they *know*.

STEPHANIE (*starts to cry, softly*): I said out there, at the airport I was saying, maybe it's 'cause I saw some pilots walking by in their uniforms, y'know, I said, "I want to see my father's picture just once. I have a right," I said.

MURIEL (*alarmed*): Your father? What about him?

STEPHANIE: I was telling them, I have a right to see that man's *face*.

MURIEL (*guiltily*): Dwight James Washburn walked out in 1957. He took his face with him forever.

STEPHANIE: I was his little girl but I can't remember.

MURIEL: Because the man was nothing special.

STEPHANIE: Yes he was, he was. You loved him once, so he *was*. I want to see that for myself, Momma. (*Voice rising, pleading*) Momma, I am thirty-eight years old.

(MURIEL *in a sudden fury of activity slams out of the living room, rummages around in her bedroom, snaps on the crook-necked bedside lamp.* STEPHANIE *watches blinking as she pulls out cartons from beneath her bed and out of a closet, tosses them about, etc. She is murmuring inaudibly to herself, "I won't be blamed, I won't be blamed." We see her actions through her opened door and through the transparent wall of her room.*)

(MURIEL *reappears, triumphant, waving a glossy photograph.*)

MURIEL: *I* will not be blamed.

(STEPHANIE *reaches for the photograph with a quavering hand. Her expression is open, hopeful, childlike.*)

STEPHANIE (*bringing the photograph to the light, squinting; after a pause*): This is . . . my father?

(STEPHANIE *turns over the photograph, examines it closely, suspiciously.*)

STEPHANIE (*in a flat, accusing voice*): This . . . is Errol Flynn.

MURIEL: So? I warned you he was nobody special.

(STEPHANIE *gives a little scream, laughing or half sobbing, and tears the photograph into tiny bits.*
   A pause. Lights begin to fade. MURIEL *gingerly approaches* STEPHANIE *to comfort her. Focus upon the couple:* MURIEL *eases into the chair beside* STEPHANIE, *to embrace her;* STEPHANIE, *weeping softly, presses her head against* MURIEL's *breast.*)

MURIEL (*sings an improvised tune*):

In the green of the year
When there's nothing to fear . . .

(*She hums, stroking* STEPHANIE's *face and hair.*)

In the green of the year
When there's nothing to fear . . .

STEPHANIE: I couldn't leave you, Momma. You know that.

MURIEL: Oh, Stevie. I know, I know.

STEPHANIE: I love you, Momma. I'm right here.

MURIEL: But is isn't fair, honey. (*Strokes* STEPHANIE's *face, hair*) It isn't fair for you, honey. (*A pause*) Stevie! Stevie the bear—remember your teddy bear, honey, how you'd pretend *he* was Stevie when you went to bed? Remember, honey?

STEPHANIE (*quietly*): No, Momma. I don't remember.

Lights out.

Scene 8.

Darkness: sultry tango music.
Lights up: very dim light, as MURIEL (*her identity at first unclear*) *moves about the living room lighting candles. These are unusually tall, elegant candles in silver candlestick holders placed strategically about the set.* MURIEL *moves to the tango beat, with obvious delight and anticipation.*
   As the light comes up, we see that MURIEL *is wearing a new wig, a silvery-blond wig styled rather like the hairstyle made famous by*

Marilyn Monroe. Her dress is long, black, slinky, glamorous. In the soft, mellow light she appears young, transformed, beautiful.

Stage right, in the shadows, are boxes filled with MURIEL's *belongings. There are a number of them, neatly stacked, perhaps shading off into the wings. We do not see the end of them.*

STEPHANIE *has passed out in the chair extreme stage left. She wakes, confused; shaking her head. A liquor bottle, apparently empty, falls to the floor.*

STEPHANIE: . . . Mother? Where are you? (*She tries to stand, sinks back. She has a violent headache.*) . . . Mother? (*Craning her neck, staring at* MURIEL) Is that you?

(*As the tango continues,* MURIEL *performs a dance step, solo, facing the audience and* STEPHANIE, *who seems to be paralyzed in her chair.*)

STEPHANIE: You'll . . . injure yourself. You know you've fallen. Mother—*you know you've fallen.*

(*As* SEÑOR RÍOS *appears, stage right, in the corridor, approaching the front door of the apartment,* MURIEL *primps in a mirror.* STEPHANIE *becomes agitated, though she's incapable of rising from her chair.*)

STEPHANIE: He isn't coming, Mother! You know he isn't! You made it all up! You've invented everything! Your mind . . . isn't right! You know it, and I know it!

(SEÑOR RÍOS, *flowers in hand, rings the bell.* MURIEL *hurries to answer it, trying to disguise her excitement.*)

STEPHANIE: There's nobody there! Your mind isn't right! Don't answer that door, Mother!

(MURIEL *opens the door.* SEÑOR RÍOS *enters. He bows to her graciously, takes her hand and kisses it. He is a tall, even massive man; swarthy-skinned, with a handsome moustache; an old-fashioned courtliness to his bearing and manner. He wears a tuxedo with a red cummerbund and highly polished black shoes.*

We hear near-inaudible murmurings. SEÑOR RÍOS *speaks in Spanish;* MURIEL *seems almost to be singing or humming, interrupting herself frequently with bursts of light, girlish, tinkling laughter.*

The flowers are orange gladioli, which MURIEL *puts at once in a waiting vase.*)

STEPHANIE: Don't touch them! Don't smell them! They're out of the garbage dumpster! Oh, Momma, they're *poison*!

(MURIEL *and* SEÑOR RÍOS *whisper together, then begin to dance. They dance for perhaps a full minute, performing the tango flawlessly. It is an urgent, sensuous, romantic beat.*)

STEPHANIE: Momma, you'll fall—you'll hurt yourself. You know you can't dance . . . (*Agitated*) Come to bed, Momma. Oh, Momma, it's so late.

(SEÑOR RÍOS *escorts* MURIEL *to the door; the two are both affectionate and rather formal in their behavior. At the door,* MURIEL *suddenly remembers something.*)

STEPHANIE: Mother . . . ?

(MURIEL *tiptoes almost stealthily to* STEPHANIE, *as if approaching a sleeping child's crib. She leans over her, kisses her.* STEPHANIE *raises her arms as if to retain her but cannot.*)

STEPHANIE: Mother, where are you going?

(MURIEL *returns to* SEÑOR RÍOS, *links her arm through his, and the couple leave through the front door. Tango music ends.*)

STEPHANIE (*her voice a high, thin wail, trailing off to silence*): Mother . . . !

A *beat or two, then lights out.*

(THE END)

APPENDIX

Notes for STEPHANIE's speech as she rehearses.

. . . Politics is war, let us admit it . . . but there is hope in unity . . . a hope whose name is "feminism" . . . the "women's movement" . . . a hope at all times imperiled . . . at the present time especially so.

. . . Women's political perspective . . . the only vital, vigorous alternative in American politics . . .

. . . Deep skepticism among youth . . . (male) graft in politics, business . . . (male) corruption . . . (male) violations of ethical standards . . . The Senate . . . Speaker of the House . . . former Presidents . . . business leaders . . .

. . . Our enemies fear us . . . the antiabortion forces . . .

. . . After years of struggle, women's income in America is only 75 percent of men's for equal work . . .

. . . must unite: *Feminism* is the *only way of the future.*

How Do You Like Your Meat?

CHARACTERS

WOMAN: early thirties
DRIVER: no specific age (though not elderly)
BIN: early thirties
SANDY: early thirties
DAUGHTER: ten
SON: six
LIMOUSINE DRIVERS: one man, one woman

Darkened stage. Lights come up to illuminate the WOMAN *at stage left. She is in her early thirties; Caucasian; attractive and immaculately groomed but not glamorous or overly "feminine"; a "career" woman, presumably—in a smart tailored navy-blue suit and white blouse, red leather pumps, with a red leather over-the-shoulder purse. The spotlight focuses upon her face and shoulders.*

The WOMAN *addresses the audience with an air of shared confidentiality and barely suppressed excitement. She is slightly breathless but not hysterical. Throughout the play, it is crucial that the* WOMAN, *even when upset, not be depicted as "hysterical."*

WOMAN: You would not *believe* what happened to me . . . ! What *almost* happened to me . . . !
(*Pause*)
I was returning from Omaha, the first time the company sent me out—I mean, on my own, not just as someone else's assistant—

and my flight was forty-five minutes late getting to Newark, and . . .

(*Stage darkens. Lights come up to show the* WOMAN *entering from stage left, hurrying, with an air of mild anxiety. She is carrying her shoulder bag, an attaché case, and a single suitcase. Her accessories are of high quality but not luxurious.*

Onstage are a uniformed MALE LIMO DRIVER *holding a handpainted sign, "R. Curtis," and a heavyset* FEMALE LIMO DRIVER, *also uniformed, holding a sign, "American Limousine." Overhead is a sign, "Limousine & Taxi Pickup."*)

WOMAN (*trying to remain calm*): Excuse me—have you seen a driver from the A-Plus Limousine Service?

MALE LIMO DRIVER (*shaking his head, politely*):   No, ma'am.

(*The* FEMALE LIMO DRIVER *shakes her head also.*

From stage right, the DRIVER *appears. He is a light-skinned black or Hispanic of no special age, of moderate height, wearing a dark gabardine suit, a wine-colored shirt, a matte black leather necktie, and amber-tinted sunglasses; his lacquered black hair is combed stiff and wavy against his head. Perhaps he wears a visored cap, but the cap has no insignia or identification on it.*)

WOMAN (*anxiously, a little shrilly*): Are *you* from the A-Plus Limousine Service?

DRIVER (*speaking with a slight accent, as of the West Indies*): The *who?* Ma'am?

WOMAN (*speaking as if believing him deaf*): The A-Plus Limousine Service.

DRIVER: No, ma'am, don't think so, sorry—you looking for a taxi?

WOMAN (*upset, speaking generally*): A driver was supposed to be here, right *here*, waiting for me—the company arranged it, the company always arranges it—he was supposed to be here by six-fifteen when my flight was due—my flight was late but drivers are supposed to *wait*, they're supposed to *know* when a flight is late—

(*The* MALE *and* FEMALE LIMO DRIVERS *speak variously: "Maybe he was here and left"—"I didn't see nobody from A-Plus"—"Could be he's making a telephone call"—"Nah, nobody here from A-Plus," etc.*)

DRIVER (*courteous but forceful*): Ma'am? You looking for a taxi? I'll take you.

WOMAN: Oh, but my driver—what if he's here—somewhere—

DRIVER (*pointing to sign overhead*): He ain't here, ma'am, he ain't *anywhere*. You maybe better come with me, then.

WOMAN: I can't understand it. The company always uses A-Plus— the driver is *always* waiting right here.

FEMALE LIMO DRIVER: *I'm* looking for a party named Anderson, coming from Pittsburgh. *You* aren't Anderson, are you?

WOMAN (*annoyed*): Of course not!

MAN (*shaking his sign*): R. Curtis—?

WOMAN: I—I'm scheduled to be picked up by A-Plus.

DRIVER (*moving in upon her, jiggling his car keys*): Ma'am? I better take you. You gonna get stranded here. Where you going?

WOMAN: Oh—I live in Dutch Neck. It's about an hour away. But I —I don't quite know what to—if the driver from A-Plus is—

DRIVER: Nah, he ain't here. Happens all the time. My limo company, we don't let customers down. (*He reaches rather peremptorally for the* WOMAN's *suitcase. There is a moment's—but only a moment's—subtle tug of war before the* WOMAN *surrenders it.*) Okay—we better go. That traffic's bad.

WOMAN (*worriedly*): But—what if the other driver *is* here— somewhere?

DRIVER (*smiling, impatient*): Ain't no concern of ours, ma'am, is it? A-Plus just ain't reliable. Let's go.

WOMAN (*looking at her watch*): Oh dear. It *is* late. (*As* DRIVER *is about to move off with her suitcase*) Oh—sir? You *do* know where Dutch Neck is?

DRIVER (*over his shoulder, mumbling*): Yes, ma'am.

WOMAN (*following nervously*): How—how much do you charge?

DRIVER: Ma'am?

WOMAN: How much do you charge? To go so far from Newark?

DRIVER: Ma'am, I'm gonna check the book.

WOMAN: It shouldn't be more than seventy-five dollars . . . should it?

(DRIVER *mumbles "No, ma'am" or "Don' know, ma'am," then exits stage right;* WOMAN *hurries after him awkwardly in her high-heeled shoes.*)

WOMAN (*to herself*): Nothing like this has ever happened before. I suppose I'm doing the right thing. But what if—

(*Lights out.*
Lights up. Simulated drive in the taxicab. If the taxi is represented onstage, it should be a luxury car now past its prime: a rear window finely cracked like a spider's web, subtle rust spots on fender—nothing exaggerated or comic. DRIVER *unlocks doors, unlocks trunk, places suitcase in trunk;* WOMAN *gingerly climbs into the backseat.* DRIVER *takes his place behind the wheel and the drive begins.*)

WOMAN (*chattering nervously*): I'm so lucky you came along. I'm certainly going to complain on Monday, about that other driver. Leaving me stranded—at rush hour! (*She is fussing with the seat belt, which is broken.*) Oh, driver—the seat belt back here is broken.

DRIVER, *intent upon maneuvering his car, seemingly through traffic, does not hear.*)

WOMAN (*raising her voice, politely*): Oh, driver? I'm afraid the seat belt back here isn't in working order.

DRIVER: Ma'am, you don't need 'em back there, you only need 'em up here.

WOMAN: Oh, but I—I always buckle up. It doesn't feel right not to.

(DRIVER *turns on radio: loud pop music, static.*
A brief lull: the WOMAN *searches through her purse and attaché case as if looking for something. She finds it, then looks for something else. An air of distraction, vague worry.*)

WOMAN (*peering out the window*): Driver? Are you headed for the turnpike? (*When he doesn't respond*) You do know where Dutch Neck is, don't you?

DRIVER: What's that?

WOMAN: You do know where Dutch Neck is—don't you?

DRIVER (*emphatically*): Yes, ma'am. Said I did, didn't I? It's right by . . . (*He mumbles something indistinct.*)

WOMAN (*leaning forward*): What? I didn't hear—

(DRIVER *mumbles again: a strongly accented word.*)

WOMAN: Oh—that radio! Did you say "Manalapian"? Dutch Neck isn't anywhere near Manalapian—it's the other way, east of here. It's a suburb of Trenton. You take the Hamilton exit. . . .

DRIVER (*regarding her in the rearview mirror, grinning, perhaps angrily*): Yes, ma'am. I know Dutch Neck.

WOMAN: Oh—but I thought you said "Manalapian."

DRIVER (*brusquely*): You want to go to Manalapian or Dutch Neck?

WOMAN: Dutch Neck.

DRIVER (*excitedly*): What's this "Manalapian"? Said "Dutch Neck" before.

WOMAN: Oh, but I thought *you* said—

DRIVER: Ma'am, *you* said. You're the fare, ain't you? You want to go to Dutch Neck or Manalapian?

WOMAN (*nervously*): D-Dutch Neck, please.

(*She holds the hand grip to steady herself as the* DRIVER *drives rather roughly. He shakes his head, murmurs to himself; turns up the radio: jarring rock music.*)

WOMAN (*flinches, watching traffic*): Oh dear, we came close to that—that truck. (*She is thrown to one side of the backseat; pulls herself upright.*) Driver . . .

(DRIVER *ignores her: radio music intrusive.*
The drive is a little calmer now. WOMAN *checks her reflection in compact mirror, fusses with her hair.*)

WOMAN (*timidly, yet persistently*): Excuse me—driver? We never did quite settle it, about the fare. Does your company charge a flat rate? (*Pause.* DRIVER *does not hear.*) You don't seem to have a meter up there, so I assume it's—a flat rate?

DRIVER (*regarding her in the rearview mirror; truculently*): Ma'am? What's the problem now?

WOMAN: Please, could you turn down that radio?

(DRIVER *reluctantly turns it down, but only minimally.*)

WOMAN (*leaning forward*): The fare? From the airport to Dutch Neck? Does your company have a flat rate?

DRIVER: Ma'am, I told you I'm going to check the book. We get there, I'll check the book.

WOMAN: But—

DRIVER: Sure can't check the book *now*. (*Sounds his horn; he's an aggressive driver.*)

WOMAN: The . . . the limousine service—I mean A-Plus—usually charges seventy-five dollars. I mean—exclusive of gratuity.

DRIVER: Huh? "Nuity"? What's that, lady? A "nuity"?

WOMAN (*speaking as if he were partly deaf*): Gra-tu-ity. *Tip.*

DRIVER: What's that?

(*He throws on the brakes and the* WOMAN *is thrown forward.*)

WOMAN (*a bit flustered*): I don't intend to pay more than seventy-five dollars. I mean, the company won't pay more than seventy-five dollars. That's the flat rate with A-Plus Limousine Service.

DRIVER: A-Plus Limousine ain't *here*—right?

(WOMAN *is momentarily rebuked. The* DRIVER *is evidently tied up in traffic. He talks to himself irritably:* "Shit!" "Damn—lookit that!" "Oh, fuck!" *etc. The* WOMAN *seems not to hear.*
   Suddenly a jetliner passes overhead; the noise is deafening. An enormous shadow passes ominously across the entire stage.)

WOMAN (*hands to her ears*): Oh—those jets! How on earth do people endure their lives around here! (DRIVER *seems to be turning the wheel energetically, maneuvering through traffic.*) Excuse me— aren't you going to get on the turnpike here?

(DRIVER *sounds his horn, gestures out his window, ignores her.*)

WOMAN (*weakly, yet persistently*): The other drivers usually take the entrance here . . . then exit at the Hamilton exit. (*Pause*) I don't intend to pay more than seventy-five dollars. (*Pause*) Exclusive of gratuity, I mean.

(*Lights down.* WOMAN, *spotlighted, addresses the audience in an amplified, breathy voice.*)

WOMAN: I should have known—should have suspected something was wrong. But I was so exhausted from the flight, and the un-expectedness of being alone at Newark Airport, that frantic place —and the man seemed legitimate—at first. (*Pause.*) Oh!—I can scarcely believe it now, but what I did—(*as if confiding in the audience, certain of sympathy*)—I actually tried to relax: told my-self I'd be safe at home in an hour! I laid half the seat belt across my lap (*indicates the action*) as if that would help in an accident! *That's* how my poor frazzled brain was working! I even tried to *work.* (*Opens attaché case, takes out papers*)

(*After a minute or so the* WOMAN *glances up. Now the drive has become jolting.*)

WOMAN: Oh dear—those potholes! (*Puzzled, looking around*) Driver, where are we? Why aren't we on the turnpike? (DRIVER *has not heard: the radio music is loud again*) Excuse me? Oh— sir? Why are we—here? Are we still in Newark? Is this somewhere in Newark? (*Jolted, she seizes the hand grip; papers and attaché case slide to the floor.*) This neighborhood—where are we? *Where is the turnpike?*

DRIVER (*exasperated*): Yes, ma'am? You say something, ma'am?

WOMAN (*trying not to become upset, staring out windows*): This neighborhood—I don't recognize it. Where are you taking me? (*A look of frightened revulsion*) Oh—the air *smells.*

DRIVER (*switching off radio, exasperated*): Ma'am? What's the prob-lem?

WOMAN: Where are we? Why aren't we on the—

DRIVER: You saw that traffic back there—didn't you? Backed up a mile?

WOMAN: But—

DRIVER: I'm taking a short cut. Gonna pick up the turnpike off Route 1.

WOMAN: This isn't the way the other drivers have taken me. I—I don't know where we are.

DRIVER: Lady, I been driving out of Newark eight years! You got a better idea, lady, you tell me!

WOMAN (*suddenly, looking around*): Is this a—taxi? Is this really a taxi? A limousine service? (*Frightened*) Driver, where is your identification? The outside of the car—it isn't marked, is it?

DRIVER: Eight years I been driving out of Newark! Nine years! You don't tell me, lady, how I'm gonna get onto the turnpike fastest! (*Excited*) You know what time it is? Rush hour! It's still rush hour! All them cars—you saw 'em, didn't you, lady? Backed up a mile back there?

WOMAN (*trying not to become panicked*): Excuse me—I think I would like to get out here.

DRIVER: You got a better way to get on the turnpike, lady? *You tell me.*

WOMAN: Excuse me, please: I think I would like to get out here. (*Pause*) Driver—*let me out here.*

DRIVER (*half shouting*): Yes, ma'am? What in hell you askin' now, ma'am?

WOMAN: Stop this car, please. I want to get out.

DRIVER: What? What's it now?

WOMAN (*shrilly*): Just stop the car, let me out. This isn't a—a real taxi, is it? It isn't a limousine, is it? Oh, please just let me out—just let me *out.*

DRIVER (*astonished*): What? What the hell, lady? What you sayin' now? You don't like my driving, lady? Huh?

WOMAN: Just let me out here. (*Turning door handle*) Slow down, let me out. Oh! slow *down!*

DRIVER: This ain't no nowhere, here! Jesus Christ, you sayin' you want to get out *here?*

WOMAN (*screaming*): Let me out! Oh—help!

(*Desperately, yet with enough presence of mind to take her belongings with her, including the sheaf of papers, the* WOMAN *manages to get the door open and stumbles out of the moving car. She falls, scrambles to her feet, continues to run, crying "Oh! Oh!" in a breathless voice, but not screaming.*)

DRIVER: Jee-zuz! (*Sits staring after her in disbelief*) Ma'am! Hey, ma'am! Wait! (*Has braked the car, now leans out the door*) Ma'am? What's all this? *What you got against me?*

(*Lights out.*)

(*Lights up. Rear of a suburban bungalow. Terrace, picnic table and benches, a portable barbecue, lawn chairs, children's toys, tricycle, etc. A family—*BIN *and* SANDY, *and their ten-year-old* DAUGHTER *and six-year-old* SON—*are about to sit down to a picnic supper.*

BIN, *a tall, broad-shouldered man in his early thirties, is cooking hamburgers and shish kebab on the grill. He wears a comical cook's apron, a white T-shirt, and chino trousers; he is fair, perhaps freckled, with a wide, moon-shaped face that shows his emotions explicitly. He is drinking from a can of beer.* SANDY, *his wife, is approximately* BIN's *age, pretty, wearing snug-fitting pink slacks and a pink cotton sweater and sandals. Her fingernails and toenails are painted. She is arranging things on the picnic table—bowls of salad, a large box of potato chips, soda pop in cans, bottles and jars of ketchup, mustard, pickle relish, paper plates and plastic cutlery, and so forth.* DAUGHTER, *a plump, aggressive child, snatches some potato chips and thrusts them into her mouth before* SANDY *can stop her.* SON *is standing close by, sucking his thumb.*

The WOMAN *runs into this scene with as much desperation as if she were being chased. Her hair is disheveled, her eyes shining; the color is up in her face. She clutches her shoulder bag, her attaché case—which is opened—and some papers. The family stare at her incredulously.*)

WOMAN: Oh! Thank God! Someone is home here! Oh—please! I tried three houses and no one would answer the door, and— Oh, just let me hide *here!*

(*A beat or two as the family members continue to stare at her.* BIN *stands with his double-pronged fork over the sizzling grill, and* SANDY *makes an unconscious gesture toward scooping* SON *up in her arms.*)

BIN: Hey, what is this? What's going on here?

WOMAN (*beginning to sob*): Oh, thank God! I—I need help!

DAUGHTER (*excitedly*): I'll call the police, Daddy! Mommy! Let me call the police!

SANDY: Who—who are you? What is this?

WOMAN (*hiding her face*): I've had such a fright. . . .

BIN: What is it? (*He lays down his fork and approaches the* WOMAN; *he's still a bit guarded. He looks in the direction she came from, toward the front of the house.*) Did somebody attack you, lady?

WOMAN (*trying to calm herself*): Oh . . . oh . . . oh . . . thank God you're here!

SANDY (*seeing that the* WOMAN *is nicely dressed*): Why, you poor thing—you're white as a sheet! Sit down here.

DAUGHTER (*dancing about excitedly*): Can I call the police, Daddy? Mommy? I know the number to call!

SANDY: Sit down before you *faint*!

(SANDY *helps the* WOMAN *sit down on the picnic bench; fusses over her, etc.* SON *is hiding behind the barbecue.*)

BIN: Did somebody attack you, lady? What's going on?

WOMAN (*speaking rapidly, not quite coherently*): The taxi driver— he—he wasn't one—I got in the car without—I opened the door and jumped out—oh, my ankle hurts—I turned my—my ankle. . . .Oh, my heart is pounding—I—I'm so . . . My flight was late —at the airport—I missed my limousine—and this man—this— this man—oh . . . (*Begins sobbing again*)

BIN: We'll see about this! (*In a rough gesture,* BIN *yanks off his apron and throws it down. He trots off to check the street.* DAUGHTER *runs after him.*)

DAUGHTER: Daddy, wait for me! Daddy, I'll call the police!

WOMAN (*breathlessly*): He threatened me, this—this false taxi driver. I *think* he was false—he didn't have any identification, and the car wasn't marked, and—and he *looked* at me so—he was going to kidnap me—oh, I've never been so—so frightened—I—

SANDY: My God! Right out there? In our neighborhood? Did he lay his hands on you?

WOMAN: He's a black man or—or Hispanic—he's not a—a white man. But that isn't why—I mean—I mean, that isn't the reason—

SANDY (*calling after* BIN): Honey, come back—it could be dangerous! Bin! (*To the* WOMAN, *her eyes moist*) He never listens to me! He's the most hotheaded man I know!

(SANDY *hugs* SON *against her knees; he is frightened. The* WOMAN *tries to compose herself, dabbing at her face with a tissue and examining her reflection in her compact mirror.* SANDY *murmurs words of comfort to* SON.

DAUGHTER *comes running fatly back.* BIN *strides behind her, his cheeks ruddy, an air of excitement about him.*)

DAUGHTER: Daddy saw him! Daddy saw him!

BIN: Is this character driving a dark maroon car? Buick Le Sabre sedan? Three, four years old?

WOMAN: I—think so. I don't actually know the makes of cars.

BIN: He's up the block stopped in the middle of the street like he's *waiting.* (*Laughs, rubs hands together*) Right in plain daylight.

SANDY: Oh, Bin, he tried to kidnap this poor woman, she says. We'd better call the police—

DAUGHTER: Mommy—I'll call them! (*Dancing around*) I know the number: 747-3100!

WOMAN: Oh—I don't want trouble. He didn't actually—

BIN: In this neighborhood, lady, we don't like strangers scaring white women. Kidnapping white women. (*Flexing fingers*) We don't like strangers driving our streets at *all.*

WOMAN: But—he might sue for false arrest. If—

SANDY: He was *after* you! Tried to *kidnap* you! Poor thing, you're pale as a ghost!

WOMAN (*confused*): He—he didn't actually *do* anything to me. It was just the way he was driving—he wasn't going the usual route, he started shouting at me—oh, I think he was drunk, or high on some drug, his eyes were so—oh, I've never seen eyes like that—like an animal's eyes glowing, so yellow and glowing and—ferocious.

BIN: Well—he isn't going to get you *here*. You can bet you're safe *here*.

SANDY: Oh, look how she's trembling!

WOMAN: It was—just the way he behaved—he—turned into a madman—shouted at me like he wanted to murder me, *looked* at me with his yellow eyes—

SANDY: Looks can kill!

BIN: You want me to call the police?

WOMAN (*hesitantly*): Oh—I don't think so. I—I don't want to press charges. He didn't actually—

BIN (*wide grin*): *I'd* be tempted to—take care of this myself. I have in my possession—

SANDY: Bin—don't you dare! You leave that thing where it *is*.

BIN (*poking her in the breastbone*): I have a permit for it, and I have a right to use it if I or my family or anybody else is in danger. I bought it for emergencies like this.

DAUGHTER (*excitedly, to* SON): Oh—Daddy's gonna get his gun! Daddy's gonna get his gun!

SANDY: Daddy is *not*.

BIN: Look, sweetheart—don't tell me what to do.

WOMAN (*embarrassed*): Oh, I—I seem to have—caused all this. Oh dear, I'm so—sorry. Why don't I call another taxi? May I use your phone?

SANDY (*to* BIN): Do you want to get us all in trouble? What if that man is armed? What if he's *un*armed?

BIN (*laughing, speaking generally*): It's always good for a laugh, isn't it—a woman talking about things over her head!

SANDY: I'm afraid for the children!

(BIN *and* SANDY *step to one side, arguing; not loudly, but earnestly. The* WOMAN *tries not to eavesdrop. She smiles at* SON, *who stares at her, half hiding behind the barbecue.*
DAUGHTER *runs out toward the street; returns excitedly.*)

DAUGHTER: He's gone! The bad man—he drove away!

WOMAN: Oh—that's a relief. (*Pause.* BIN *and* SANDY *are still engaged in their discussion:* BIN *pokes* SANDY *in the breastbone;* SANDY *slaps at his muscular arm.*) My—what a pretty playsuit you're wearing! Did your—uh—mommy make it?

DAUGHTER: *Make* it? How?

WOMAN: Well . . . What is your name?

DAUGHTER: That's for me to know and you to find out!

WOMAN (*to* SON): What is *your* name, little boy?

DAUGHTER: That's for us to know and you to find out!

WOMAN (*wincing*): Well—you're a lively little girl. You look just like your daddy.

DAUGHTER: *He* looks like Mommy. He's autistic. (*She pronounces the word "aw-tist-tic."*)

SANDY (*overhearing*): Brooke, what are you saying? What on earth? Your brother is *not.* Your brother is not autistic, and you know it.

DAUGHTER: He's a moron.

(SANDY *makes a slapping gesture at the* DAUGHTER, *who eludes her around the table, giggling.*)

SANDY: Brooke! Aren't you ashamed! Making your baby brother cry in front of company! You'd better apologize.

DAUGHTER (*to* WOMAN): He isn't a moron—he's too young. You have to be twelve years old to be a moron.

SANDY: Why, Brooke!

WOMAN (*standing nervously*): Oh . . . I've done such a selfish thing, interrupting you in the midst of—your supper. I really should be—

BIN (*flush-faced, but making an effort to be friendly*): Nah, no problem. We got to stick together, people like us.

DAUGHTER: The man's gone! The bad man, the nigger—he's gone!

SANDY: Brooke! I've told you—we don't say words like that.

BIN: Oh, Christ—the meat! I forgot the meat! (*He hurries to the grill.*) I guess it's okay. (*Drinks thirstily from his beer can*)

SANDY: My goodness, I seem to have forgotten my manners! May I get you something to drink, miss—?

WOMAN: Oh—oh no, thank you! I've caused enough trouble.

SANDY (*warmly*): It isn't the slightest bit of trouble. We're glad to have you. It's the least we can do, after the terrible scare you had. There's soda pop—diet pop; there's beer—light and regular; there's what I'm drinking, a Bloody Mary. *Please* sit down.

WOMAN: Oh, I wouldn't hear of it. Interrupting your picnic supper. . . . Why don't I just call another cab, a real cab, and get on home.

SANDY: Where do you live?

WOMAN: Dutch Neck.

SANDY: Dutch Neck—where is that? Bin, do you know where Dutch Neck is?

BIN: Maybe we'd better drive you home ourselves, after supper. (*Laughs*) No telling who else might show up.

WOMAN: Oh, I've inconvenienced you quite—

DAUGHTER (*pouting*): Doesn't anybody want me to call the police? I called them one time—when we had a prowler, and Daddy wasn't home. I know the number: 747-3100.

SANDY: Brooke, be quiet. Help set the table. (*To* WOMAN) Let me make you a Bloody Mary, it's just perfect for calming the nerves. I need to freshen my own.

WOMAN (*hesitating*): Are you sure it wouldn't be—too much trouble?

SANDY: Not at all! You sit down and relax!

(SANDY *exits;* BIN *turns hamburgers on the grill with his splendid fork and turns the shish kebab spit.*)

BIN: Dutch Neck—that's some distance away. Must be an hour?

WOMAN: If traffic is bad on the turnpike, it can be longer.

BIN: Where were you coming from?

WOMAN: I—I don't remember. I mean—the airport. (*Laughs, confused*) Oh, yes—Omaha. Nebraska.

BIN: Then this character, this impostor, tried to kidnap you?

WOMAN: Oh, I'm not sure—what he meant to do with me.

(SANDY *returns with Bloody Marys, one in each hand—bright, festive drinks with a fresh sprig of celery in each glass.*)

WOMAN: Oh, thank you. So much. I—my nerves *are*—a bit strained. (*Drinks*) I will never forget your kindness.

SANDY: Oh, I'm sure you'd do as much for me, if I turned up at— at your house. Do you have a family waiting at home?

WOMAN: I'm—I'm a career woman. (*Giggles self-consciously*) What is called a—professional woman . . . I guess.

SANDY: I hope you'll stay and have supper with us—we have tons of food.

WOMAN: Oh, dear *no,* I—

DAUGHTER (*squatting at* WOMAN'*s feet, squinting up at her*): Did you get his license-plate number?

WOMAN: I'm afraid I didn't.

DAUGHTER: That's the first thing you're supposed to do—write down their license-plate number. They told us that at school.

WOMAN: I just didn't. I'm sorry now. (*To* SANDY) May I use your telephone? I'll just—

SANDY: Oh—I'll call a cab for you myself. No trouble. Or maybe Bin and I should drive you home? You still look upset.

BIN (*guffawing, yet solicitous*): No telling who's gonna show up the next time, driving a cab.

WOMAN: No, please. I'm sure I'll be all right.

(SANDY *exits to make the telephone call.*)

DAUGHTER (*peering up at* WOMAN): Was he crazy? There's lots of them—crazy people. The niggers smoke crack and the spics sniff glue.

BIN (*wagging his finger*): Brooke! We don't talk like that around here.

DAUGHTER (*earnestly*): You see it on TV every night. Not that it's any secret or anything.

BIN (*laying down fork*): I'm gonna check on that guy one more time. (*He trots out toward the driveway,* DAUGHTER *fatly following.*)

WOMAN (*to* SON): Your mommy and daddy and sister are—so nice. (*Drinks; wipes at her eyes*) They've saved my life practically.

(BIN *returns, flexing his fingers.*)

BIN: I *think* he's still around. Up the block in the other direction, cruising through the intersection—

DAUGHTER: It was him! It was him! I betcha!

BIN: Nervy bastard! (*Smiles*) I've got a notion to . . .

WOMAN (*apologetically*): I feel like such a fool, not remembering to write down the license-plate number.

BIN: That's the first thing Sandy always does—when, y'know, it might happen or it might not.

WOMAN (*drinking, eating potato chips—daintily, yet clearly hungrily*): I feel like such a fool.

BIN: *Trusting* is what you were. It could happen to any of us, even a man. Some of these cars for hire, y'know, the limousine services, they don't mark their cars on the outside. Like regular taxis, I mean.

WOMAN: Oh—don't they?

BIN (*drawing up a lawn chair, sitting close by the* WOMAN): What's in Omaha?

WOMAN: What? Omaha?

BIN: What's in Omaha? You were there on a trip?

WOMAN: Oh—was it Omaha? Yes. A—a business trip. I am a . . . (*Pause*) professional woman.

BIN: Y'know, things like this (*gestures vaguely toward the street*) are happening more and more around here. On account of Newark— y'know what that's like. Bad as Harlem or the South Bronx. I belong to a vigilante patrol team—we started last year.

WOMAN: Do you!

BIN: Thursdays and Sundays, evenings, are my shifts. But of course I'm vigilant all the time. (*Ominously*) You got to be.

(*The* DRIVER *reappears, at rear, cautiously sets down suitcase, backs off.*)

WOMAN: Oh, yes.

(SON *suddenly comes to life: tugs a cellophane wrapper down over his head as far as it will go, begins running around in erratic circles, buzzing with his lips like a wasp.* BIN *ignores him.*)

DAUGHTER (*derisively*): Show-off! Show-off! What a silly little baby! (*To the* WOMAN) He is too autistic. You see it on TV.

BIN (*idly cuffing* DAUGHTER): That's enough, Brooke. (*To* WOMAN, *earnestly*) My wife and I, what we want for our children—y'know, your children outlive you, right, but they *are* you, right?—they carry on your—your—what's it called?—your genes. It's heredity—it's the struggle for survival. Just 'cause we're civilized it doesn't mean we're not carrying on the—the struggle. (*Flexes his fingers*) So, what we want for the kids is—a future. A—future. (*Seems puzzled.*) A life just like ours.

(DAUGHTER *wanders off, disappears; now comes running excitedly back.*)

DAUGHTER: Daddy! Oh, Daddy! Guess what! There's a suitcase on the sidewalk out front! I bet it's got a bomb in it!

WOMAN (*clapping hand to forehead*): *My* suitcase!—I forgot all about it.

BIN: You mean he tried to run off with your suitcase too?

WOMAN: I hope it hasn't been tampered with!

(BIN, WOMAN, *and* DAUGHTER *return with the suitcase, which* BIN *is carrying.*)

DAUGHTER: You can't tell by putting your ear against it. If there's a bomb inside. (*Excitedly*) You can't tell by X-raying it if they use plastic bombs.

WOMAN (*examining suitcase carefully*): It doesn't *look* as if it's been tampered with. The lock hasn't been broken.

BIN: That character's nowhere in sight. I'll bet you he's miles away by now.

WOMAN: I feel like such a *fool*—a naive, trusting *fool*.

DAUGHTER: If he stole it, that could be reported to the police.

WOMAN: But he brought it back, didn't he?

DAUGHTER: But he stole it first.

WOMAN: What I should have done was take down his license-plate number. The least I could do was spare this happening to another woman.

BIN (*lifting the suitcase in one hand, like a weight, to exercise his arm muscles*): What *I* should have done was get my trusty little .32-caliber Smith & Wesson.

(SANDY *returns, carrying a bottle of vodka, Bloody Mary mix, and picnic items.*)

SANDY: Those taxi companies! I hope you won't be upset—the taxi won't be here for maybe an hour. I called three of them, and they were all so—so sort of surly—one of them had such an accent I'd swear it was Ethiopian! (*To* WOMAN, *warmly*) Let me freshen your drink. So you'd better have a bite with us after all—you still do look a little pale.

WOMAN (*smiling, hesitant*): I guess I am—a little hungry.

BIN: Her suitcase is back. That bastard'd been driving around with it all this time.

SANDY: Oh—that's nice! I didn't know it was missing! But is he still here?

DAUGHTER: I bet he is! I bet he won't ever go away! I bet he knows right where we live!

BIN: He's gone, I'm sure. He got a good look at me a couple of times. Hell and high water won't get him back *here* again.

SANDY (*to* WOMAN): That's such an attractive suitcase! And it hasn't been damaged?

DAUGHTER: You can't tell just by pressing your ear against it. If something's ticking inside.

WOMAN: It's a little scratched, but—I'm grateful to have it back.

(SANDY *refills* WOMAN's *Bloody Mary glass. Both drink.*)

SANDY (*in a lowered voice*): Hon—you're sure that awful man didn't touch you? (*Makes an ambiguous gesture*) Y'know . . .?

WOMAN: Oh, I'm sure.

SANDY: Sometimes a woman is in such a—a traumatic state, she will forget everything. Won't remember.

WOMAN: Oh—I didn't give him a chance. I escaped.

SANDY: It's called blocking. It's like shell shock, sort of. Like soldiers get after a—a trauma. Like amnesia.

DAUGHTER: I know the number for the Rape Crisis Line!

WOMAN: Oh, I'm sure he didn't touch me—I . . .(*Glances down nervously at her body*) Oh—my stocking is torn.

SANDY (*concerned*): Let's see.

(SANDY *and* DAUGHTER *stoop to examine the* WOMAN's *ankle, which appears bruised.*)

WOMAN: When he chased me—out front—and I ran—I turned my ankle, and—

SANDY (*touching the skin*): Does it hurt?

WOMAN (*wincing*): Oh! Just a trifle!

DAUGHTER: I know the Rape Crisis number! It's 747-4100!

SANDY: You're sure he didn't—do anything more?

WOMAN: Oh, I'm sure.

SANDY (*as if with a special significance, so* BIN *cannot hear*): Sometimes . . . a woman will forget. Won't remember.

(*A pause*)

WOMAN (*fluttery, laughing*): Your neighbors aren't too—friendly! I ran to a house across the way and—and I rang the doorbell—I was screaming, I guess, I was so scared—and I could see someone inside, watching TV I think, and whoever it was, they just hid around a corner. And the house right next door here—almost the same thing happened.

SANDY (*as if incensed*): Well. That did not happen *here*. We're always happy to help people *here*.

BIN (*heartily*): Right. People like us have got to stick together.

(BIN *claps his hands to change the subject and the mood; strides to the grill.*)

BIN: Okay, gang—y'know what time it is? Time to eat.

DAUGHTER: Yayyy!

BIN: Everybody's famished! Too much excitement! Adrenaline!

SANDY: My, yes! It's late—it's almost eight o'clock! (*To* WOMAN) Of course you *are* staying. That cab won't be here probably until nine o'clock.

BIN (*cheerfully*): How do you like your meat, hon? Rare? Medium? Medium rare? Medium well? Well done? (*Winks at* DAUGHTER, *who giggles excessively*) Burnt to a crisp?

WOMAN (*hesitant, but clearly pleased to be invited*): Well, I—I know I shouldn't, but (*laughs*) I guess I *am* famished. I like my meat medium well.

BIN: Shish kebab or hamburger, or both?

WOMAN: Oh—I guess both. (*To* SANDY) I guess it *is* adrenaline. Or something.

(*The two women set the table, in a sisterly manner. The Bloody Marys have had an agreeable effect upon them both.*
    BIN *brings a platter of meat to the table, and everyone sits down.*
DAUGHTER *and* SON *are placed at opposite ends of the table to prevent*

scuffling. The mood is gay, festive, almost celebratory, as if a danger were past.)

WOMAN (*with a girlish giggle, as she tucks her skirt in beneath herself*): I guess I'm not dressed right for a backyard barbecue!

SANDY: Where did you say you flew from?

WOMAN: Oh—I can barely remember!

(*Overhead, a jet plane passes deafeningly; its ominous shadow passes swiftly across the stage, but no one seems to notice.*)

BIN (*chewing*): How's that shish kebab? Okay?

WOMAN (*beginning to eat, inclining her head seriously*): I've never tasted anything so delicious in my *life.*

BIN (*heartily*): There's plenty more where that came from!

Lights out.

(THE END)

The Ballad of Love Canal

A Play in One Act

CHARACTERS

BAMA: in her forties, but girlish; slightly plump; hair hidden by a kerchief (may be in rollers); in housedress

MEDRICK: in his forties; burly, muscular; may have tattoo on forearm; wears thick-lensed glasses; nondescript sports- or work-clothes

DUGAN: eighteen; husky, blemished skin; wears clothes, or a costume, suggesting youthful rebellion/small-town chic (ripped jeans, black leather, heavy metal gear, skinhead haircut)

GIP: mid- or late forties; may resemble MEDRICK; may have a tattoo; wearing a visored cap, inconspicuous but definitely "sporty" inexpensive clothes

Each of the NOONANS *has a mannerism (nervous tic, twitch, gesture, stammer, habit of scratching, etc.) which should be subtly modulated through the play; never allowed to become mechanical, predictable, or obtrusive. After the first several minutes, the speech-difficulties should be* only *suggested, in the way that a stammerer has learned to accommodate his or her stammer.*

The underlying emotion for the men is rage; for BAMA, *terror.*

The setting should be stylized, suggesting the front yard of a modest bungalow-style house. In the foreground, lying face down, is a sign which, when lifted, should be large enough to be read by everyone

in the audience: "THIS PROPERTY IS CONDEMNED—NIAGARA BOARD OF HEALTH." *(A skull and crossbones above the words.)*

Love Canal is a hazardous-toxic waste dump of approximately sixteen acres located in the center of a residential community in Niagara Falls, New York. In the 1950s, residents began to complain of conditions (black sludge, nauseating odors, burnt children, an alarmingly high percentage of respiratory illnesses, neurological problems, miscarriages, heart trouble, cancer, etc.) but were systematically lied to by government officials, including doctors in the hire of the government. Not until spring 1978, and not after much agitation by homeowners, did the New York State Health Department initiate an investigation.

Since then, "Love Canal" had become synonymous with the phenomenon of both hazardous-toxic waste dumps in the United States and the hypocrisy, venality, and indifference of government officials.

Lights up, but flickering. Throughout, until the very end, the stage lighting should suggest a quavering and uncertain mental condition.

BAMA, MEDRICK, *and* DUGAN *are arguing together, in not-quite-audible muttering voices.* *("He said—" "I did not—" "Yes you did—" "Nah, I did not—" "Nah I did not—" etc.) As lights come up, they turn, blinking, to face the audience. There is a tense, defensive air about them as if they are obliged to correct a misunderstanding they don't fully comprehend.*

BAMA *(staring, startled)*: So many of ya!—whazis, a block party I guess—

DUGAN *(muttering, embarrassed)*: Shit-ma, it ain't no block party it's—*them.*

BAMA *(blinking)*: You'all from the—State? Boarda Health?

MEDRICK *(gruff, to her)*: You gonna talk to 'em or you gonna lem*me?*

BAMA *(coming forward, nervous, excited, making an effort to enunciate her words as carefully as possible)*: Uh—we are the NOO-NENS, 826 Syc'more Court, thisis our h-h-h—

DUGAN *(furious, embarrassed)*: *Hauz* Chrissake!

BAMA: —*hauz* right here. (*Points behind her, proudly, if confusedly.*) Thisis our— (*She stares at the ground, trying to think of the word for lawn.*)—uh our, howyacallit our—

MEDRICK (*tapping his foot inappropriately hard on ground*): Yah like, uh— Whadayacallit uh—

BAMA: —grasses, green-like, uh—

MEDRICK (*miming the motions of lawnmowing*): Yah like ya, uh— keepin the godamn grasses *down*—

BAMA (*squatting, plucks at soil as if letting it fall through her fingers*): —s-s-soil, unnerneath g-g-grassss—

MEDRICK: Our prop'ty ona Earth—our shara ["share of"] th' Earth—

DUGAN (*gritting his teeth*): *Lawn.*

BAMA: "Lawn"—! (*laughs apologetically, continues quickly*) Yes we are the NOONINS livin here, MEDRICK (*indicates* MEDRICK) my huzbin, DUGAN (*again indicates* MEDRICK, *then corrects herself and indicates* DUGAN, *who squirms with embarrassment, muttering,* "Shit-ma!"), our boy. An Ima BAMA, like—BAMA. Hiz wife. (*pause*) Guessitz a nunusul ["unusual"] name huh?—ALIBAMI, ALIBAMAY—

DUGAN (*muttering*): Chrissake Ma *they* don't give no goddam 'bout it! (*fierce gesture toward audience*)

BAMA (*stubbornly*): Why, they do too, maybe!—some wimmen, 'speci'ly, they wanna know, an ask me—'Howja get sucha pretty n-name' so I tellem, uh—(*pause, puzzled*) I tellem uh—it's how my momma named me 'cause she—(*pause, laughs*) I don know why she named me ALI–BAMI guezz she just *did.* (*Overlapping begins, as* MEDRICK *cuts her off*) Momma loved me oh yes she *did* now Ima mother m' self an I *know.*

MEDRICK (*means to establish a jocular-macho relationship with audience, at* BAMA's *expense*): My mutherinlaw ol' BESSIE she was nutz from Day One lemme tellya an it hadna nuthin to do with TOZZINS ["toxins"] ina WAWATER you betcha! (*slaps fist into palm, grim and amused satisfaction, as* DUGAN *overlaps*)

DUGAN (*smirking at audience*): Yah you tellem Pa, fuckit. Azzholes!

BAMA (*shocked*): Oh D-Dugan! You watch yur—(*as if faint, presses hand to forehead, heart*) Uh—the whassis—ground—ina *spin*— (*taps foot against ground*)

MEDRICK (*impatient*): Nuthin wrong with t'Erth itz *you*. You taken your yur pills, Ma?—or forgot agin?

BAMA (*hotly*): I taken *all* if em the docter gimme why my brain's ina spin thaz *why*!

MEDRICK (*to audience*): Tryin to say itz TOZZINS inur ["in our"] backyard also FISHLEAD un from N'gra River tryin to scare us so we sellur prop'ty dirt-*cheap*. Okay ya crooks I say MEDICK NOONAN AINT EATEN ANY FUCKIN FISH IN 39 YRZ I toldem. (*incensed*) Azzholes from noozepapir— (DUGAN *overlaps*) with a fuckin c-c-c— (*mimes photographing*) snoopin inur *lives* Chrissake!

DUGAN (*sneering*): Azzholes from NUUU Y'RK TIMZ fancy fuckin noozepapir betta gettheir azz outa *here*! (MEDRICK *overlaps*)

MEDRICK (*raw appeal suddenly*): I sayz t'em, I sayz prac'tly beggin WE AINT FREAKZ YOU COMIN HERE—WRITIN BOUT *US*!

DUGAN (*overlaps, sneering, fists clenched*): Kickem azz! Killem!

BAMA (*deeply embarrassed by the men's belligerence, tries to restore calm by pushing them back*): I was sayin—why we made our d'cision to stay an not sell our hauz cause we been livin here on Syc'more howmany yrs, Dugan went t'school right nearby, there's the el'men'try school—

DUGAN (*overlapping, holding nose*): Been shut down eleven yrs!

BAMA: —goin to church the Meth'dist no moren two milz away oh we been real happy here DON MAKE UZ MOVE we been—

MEDRICK (*overlapping, flailing for words*): —happy as—PIE!

DUGAN (*clownish*): PIZZYA PIE. OH YUMMM. You saidit Ma.

BAMA: We aint 'shamed we're proud livin on LOV KENEL, *we* aint sellin our—

MEDRICK (*angry gesture toward neighbors*): Damn bastids! traytrez! ["Traitors"]

(GIP *strides across the stage behind the* NOONANS, *unobserved by them. He carries a lightweight vinyl-covered kitchen chair over his head, from stage left to right. He seems oblivious of the* NOONANS *too who continue uninterrupted.*)

DUGAN: Yeh KILLUM! (*as if correcting himself*) KILLYUM!

BAMA: Yes, the NOONINS, you can count uz *stayin*—

MEDRICK (*overlapping*): Yah shit LOOVVE C'NALZ our fuckin *home* been here howlong (*counting on fingers*) 19-uh whazzis uh '58 I wuzin th' Army—

BAMA (*tries to help, counting on fingers, too, but* MEDRICK *overlaps*): 19-uh 61 got marr'd— 19-uh 66— (*fumbles count*) Oh I hate math'matics, wasnt ever any good at em.

MEDRICK (*loudly*): 19-uh-72 okay, 19-uh whazzis, take away 2, un, take away 10, uh— (*confused*) Nah it's gotta be—*one*—*two*— (*happily*) TWEL-VE.

DUGAN: Nah, twenny-two!

BAMA: Huh? Yur not twenny-two yur *eighteen*!

MEDRICK (*screwing up face in concentration*): One-EIGHT. He is one-EIGHT. Can't be twenny-two, no way.

DUGAN: Tell em bastids go away (*meaning audience*) so we can *eat* Chrissake. I wana, a— (*describes big circle with arms*) zinnia— zinna—zizza—cheez an pep'roni an all kinda shit—

BAMA (*incensed*): Why Dugan you aint hungry you just *ate*— (*much overlapping here*) Sunday dinner you *did*.

DUGAN: Did not!

MEDRICK: Thatzth' ["that's the"] fuckin med'cation makes the kid starvin like some kinda *jackel* Chrissake!

DUGAN: Say what? Who'sa 'jack'l' you ol' bastid!

BAMA (*prevents* DUGAN *from rushing at* MEDRICK): Oh oh Dugan! You know yur father's not a well man you know!

DUGAN (*aggrieved*): I say I'm fuckin hungry Ma I wanna a, pizzya!

BAMA: Just had our Sunnay dinner like always, big bake-ham you love spreadin muzzard ["mustard"] all over, an mash-potattos—

DUGAN: That was last Sunnay, Ma. Chrisske!

MEDRICK (*sternly*): Nuffa that, boy. No DIS-RE-SPECK to ya Momma in fronta strangers. (*to audience, as if on TV, "winning," almost articulate*) Cert'ly Bama pre'pared Sunnay dinner, sheza wonerful cook she sure *is*. Knows howta please a man! (*rubs stomach, and* BAMA *playfully swipes at him*) Nah only kiddin hon! (*to audience, confidentially*) Roast pork kinda pink-like an blood seepin on the plate thatzwhat *I* like! yah an steaks ona grill ch'coal-broil an the ch'coal in stripes-like an jusawiffa ["just a whiff of"] whatyacallit—k'rosene! (*sniffs the air, ecstatic*) Yah an batt'rfried shrimp an french frize an muzzard-an-relish an— (*ecstatic overlapping from* DUGAN) —and c'shews ["cashews"] —an 'ginia bake ham an pottattos an-onionz fried ina pan in greeze—God!

DUGAN (*rapidly*): —yah an gravy inth' mash-pottattos an muzzard-an-relish an ketzup an cherrypie an icz cream all big fat scoopsa ICZ CREAM JESUS GAWD!

MEDRICK: —lotza greeze an salt an pork sausage an ketzup an fried eggs inth' pan swimmin in bacon greeze! Yah an piez an cakz an whip-cream! My momma wuza damn good cook she wuz, like my daddy usta say, "Toss it on th' plate goddam it," wimmen fussin in th' kitchen and a man gets hungry like you do workin construction FOUR-OH hourz a week plus o'rtime you rile up a real kinda appetite Goddamit. "Toss it on th' plate, Ma," I'm alwayz sayin to this one, Chrisske a man gets hungry.

DUGAN (*overlapping*): Thatz what I been saying Pa—IM HUNGRY! STARVIN!

MEDRICK (*suddenly cuffing him*): Hey shaddup!

GIP *strides behind the* NOONANS, *as before, left to right, with chair.*

DUGAN (*reacting from having been cuffed, as if a mechanism inside his head has been triggered*): Uh—oh—nooo—ANTZ! (*brushing spasmodically at himself, panicked*) ANTZ ALL OVER!

BAMA: Dugin *no*—honey there's no antz, that's just your (*pause*) magination. Like the doctor said—

DUGAN (*frantically shaking his trouser legs, brushing at hair, etc.*): ANTZ ALL OVER OOOH HELP!

MEDRICK (*poking son*): Nuthin wrong with you 'cept your head Chrissake!

BAMA (*trying to embrace* DUGAN): No no honey yur safe with Momma.

MEDRICK: Antz is all in yur head.

DUGAN: Oh thatz worst— (*grips his head as if to remove it*) Oh help HELP oh GOD!

BAMA (*to* MEDRICK): It's the, the Tri-chloro-phenol (*pronounces word carefully*) in my baby's blood— All over the playground—

MEDRICK: Nah—don get him started, ya know better!

BAMA: Now now Dugan, now—there's no antz anywhere not even in yur head.

DUGAN: There ain't?

MEDRICK: You know there ain't! Goddam baby!

BAMA (*to* MEDRICK): Don be cruel to him, he's just a, a—y'know a child. He's a child. (*Tries to embrace* DUGAN *who wrenches away*)

DUGAN (*recovering, glaring at audience*): You—spyin on us huh? Noozepapers, teevee—like we wuz freakz huh? Hey Pa— (*points into audience*) one of em's gotta, a, cammel, Golly dam.

MEDRICK (*aroused immediately*): Say what? Cammel—

DUGAN (*miming taking a photograph*): Cammel-la! (*frustrated*) Shit-pa!

BAMA: *I* don see no camm'ra—these people are our *friens*—

MEDRICK: We got no friens Chrissake!

DUGAN (*sneering*): PEEEPLE MAG'ZINE, TIIIME! Like we wuz freakz contam'ated glowin inth' fuckin dark!

MEDRICK (*cuffing* DUGAN): Nuffa that, we don glow in no fuckin dark, that ain't us glowin in no fuckin dark don *say so*, could be yur on teevee! (*aggrieved*) How we gonna sell the hauz, y'all takin pictures? Ya got no right we're A-, A-. Am-, Am-mer'can citzens too!

BAMA (*trying to hush* MEDRICK): Ohhhh shhhh Meddick, we don wanna *sell*—remember? Weren't that us? The Gov'ment man came visit, an the man from the chem'cal plant, an—

DUGAN (*frightened*): Wherez he?—oh God I ain't takin no liver enzine ["enzyme"] test agin!

MEDRICK (*incensed*): One thing's for sure: we ain't gonna sell this hauz, this hauz I done all kindsa repairs an 'provements, howmany yrz, thatz HOME to us—

BAMA (*wildly*): Twenny-nine yrz! Thirty-nine!

MEDRICK (*pulling slips of paper out of pocket, dropping some but unable to pick them up; peering myopically at figures on slips*): Offerin us, thissis the State C'mmiss'ner's Office, offerin us THREE-SIX-FOUR-OH-OH dollarz, fuckin in-sult, how're we gonna re-locate Godamit can't buy none other decent hauzze for shit-THREE-SIX-FOUR-OH-OH fuckin dollarz! Whatre we gonna do, live ina tent, huh? (*slaps thigh, slips of paper fall, flutter, scatter*) Live inur ["in our"] car, huh? Ona s-, s-, sidew'lk like them HOMELISS peeple poor bastids (*loudly*) IM NOT ONEUV EM I GOTTA HOME CHRISZAKE! IMA U.S. ARMY VET'RAN. Silver Star Godamit. MEDDICK NOOYIN you can check my record, Priv'te First Class MEDDICK NOOYIN was shipped to LEB-YON to BAY-ROOT in 1958. Got th' doc'ments to prove I WAS I WAS.

BAMA (*embarrassed*): Shhhh Meddik—talking so *loud*.

MEDRICK: Tryin to' crurce ["coerce"] us inta sellin sayin ev'body else is sellin, thought I c'ld trust the Gov'ment now I know betta! An the docters lyin sayin the X-rayz an all an blood-tests an all don show up nuthin, fuckin lyin sunzabitches Im gonna SUE I'm gonna SUE f'r a hunnert milyun dollarz I gotta Silver Star Godamit gotta WAR WOUND (*pulls up shirt, a fatty scar on his midriff is revealed*) t' prove it!

BAMA (*smooths hair, tries to begin another time*): WELL. Y'all look frienly to *me*, I'd say thissiz a block party I dint know better. (*smiles*) Like I was sayin, my fam'ly an me, we have been lived in this houz, two-bedroom gung-low ["bungalow"], azphalt sidin like real red brick, attached g'rage an nice trees an shrubs an flowers I'd usta grow before they toldus 'bout the soil, thissiz th's city of N'g'ra Falls thatz so famous thr'out th' world but — (*laughs*) —the Falls don mean muchta us, us born here like we were—Medyick an me. (*confiding*) We wuz high school sweetheartz us too!

DUGAN (*muttering, embarrassed*): Shit-ma!

BAMA (*earnestly*): Yes an we bought this gung-low, howmany yrz back, Dugin was the tiniest sweetest baby only three months old! an nobody warned us about no c-, c-, c'nal—NOBODY TOLD US NUTHIN FOR SURE NOT THE PEOPLE SOLD US THE HAUZ. Oh this c'nal dug in, uh back in, 1892 by someman name W'LL'M T. LOVE therez nuthin there, no water or nuthing, itz covered with dirt an this nasty sludge they callit, the City of N'g'ra Falls used th' c'nal fora dump an the U.S. Army won't confess they were dumpin chem'cal warfare stuff—the M'nhat'an Project thatz radyoactive!—everybody knows thatz radyoactive!—an this Hooker Chem'cal Comp'ny—dumped 20,000 tonz—all kindsa tozzins—so our drinkin water an soil an, like the inside of our basement, an air we gotta breathe c-, c-, con—

MEDRICK: Bama, hush! Dontcha sayit!

BAMA: I—gotta right. Just speakin the *truth*.

MEDRICK: How we gonna sell the g'dam hauz—blab'mouth!

DUGAN (*teasing*): Mamma's trying to say CON TAM YIN ATED. (*ducking* MEDRICK's *clumsily aimed blow*) CON TAM MIN YATED.

MEDRICK: Therez nuthin wrong with *uz*—the docters say so.

BAMA (*sudden tearful outburst*): Oh my little Baby Boo!—my lit'el-lit'el girl!—dint even get *born*—went into layber too soon—poor Baby Boo—come out justa, justa— (*holds hands out, palms upward, as if holding bloody evidence*) —blood an mess-like! (*weeping*)

MEDRICK: Oh Bama don go into *that*—we been all through *that*!

BAMA (*weeping*): Then we tried agin an Baby Boo hada same thing happen—preg'ant six monthz an come out TOO SOON poor in'cent baby-girl—the docters sayin was *my* fault an I ast Why? why? an therez no answer.

MEDRICK (*embarrassed*): Now Bama, hon—

BAMA (*weeping harder*): Then we tried agin Medrik an me an Baby Boo dint even makeit *five* monthz! There I'z ["I was"] in the Ay'nPee ["A&P"] pushin a cart by the frozzin stuff an Baby Boo — (*indicates her belly, as if swollen*) —givez a real hard kick like shez cryin out an Oh my God Ima feelin all this, this—hot-stuff-like, blood-like, comin down my legz—

MEDRICK *and* DUGAN *look a bit sickish.*

MEDRICK: Oh hey Bama c'mon—thatz enough!

BAMA (*bawling*): Itz Baby Boo comin too soon! Right there! All down my legz an ona, ona floor, an— (*sobs*)

MEDRICK (*sternly*): Ya hadna oughta talk like that, Bama, should be, a wimmen'd be *shamed* talkin like that—in pub'ic.

BAMA (*weeping*): Then, then—then WE TRIED AGIN MEDRIK AN ME AN—

MEDRICK (*silencing her*): O.K. Bama, uh-huh, uh-huh.

BAMA (*surprising sarcasm*): 'Therez nuthin wrong with *uz'* the docters say.

DUGAN (*seeking attention, pulling upper eyelids up to expose eyeballs*): POIZONNED Chriszake! DIE-OX-INN. TRI-CHLORO-PHENOL!

MEDRICK: You gonna get yur azz warmed, boy!

BAMA (*recovering, a bit dazed*): Oh dear oh pleaze!—its Sunnay, a nice day no bullzoners up th' street—

DUGAN: Bull-dozzers.

BAMA: —no sewermen an no nasty sludge-smell—

MEDRICK (*disgusted*): Shudyap!—blab'mouth! Just like a, a wimmen—"nasty sludge-smell"—"Baby Boo" an tellin all our secretz—how we gonna sell our prop'ty if yur tellin em—what kinda azzholez gonna buy it I ast ya!

BAMA (*hurt, perplexed*): But—I thought we l-l-loved our hauz an refused to sellit—

(GIP *appears, kitchen chair held above his head, striding briskly from stage left to stage right. This time the* NOONANS *see him and express surprise.*)

MEDRICK: Hey Chrizze! Whoin hell're *you?*—stealin my chair!

GIP *continues to hold the chair over his head as he blinks and grins at* MEDRICK.

GIP: Say what? You kiddin?

MEDRICK (*fists clenched*): I'm askin ya—WHOIN HELL'RE YOU STEALIN MY CHAIR RIGHT IN FRONTA MY EYES!

GIP: You kiddin, Meldyick? Haha very fun-ny!

BAMA (*hand over mouth, aghast*): Oh—honey! (*restraining* MEDRICK) Thissis yur—

DUGAN (*sneering*): Thatz UNCLE GIP Chrissake pops!

GIP (*sets down chair, confronts* MEDRICK): Whatsis—you don 'knowledge ["acknowledge"] yur own brother? huh?

MEDRICK (*squinting*): Uh—Gip?

GIP (*incensed, hurt*): Just what kinda b'havior's this—a man not knowin his own brother that's pract'ly his *twin!*

MEDRICK (*genuinely embarrassed*): Uh—I—sure I knew ya, Gip—

GIP (*hurt*): Nah ya never did!

DUGAN (*laughing, derisive*): A man don know his own brother—thatz *weird.* Thatz the "higher cort'cal functionz" on the fritz you betcha! Shit-pa!

MEDRICK (*half-pleading*): Oh hey Gip—I know ya, I saw who it w-was right away.

GIP: Nah—ya lyin!

BAMA (*touching* GIP's *arm*): Oh Gip, Meddick was only jokin, ya know how he is.

GIP: Yah—Ima here helpin y'all move an wonderin why nobody's liftin the least finger 'cept me—y'all standin yakkin in the front yard like th' teevee camella's rollin. An the goodam U-Haul's right there waitin to be loaded! (*Points stage right*)

MEDRICK, BAMA, *and* DUGAN *stare to the right, amazed.*

MEDRICK: Jeezuz! How longz that been there?

BAMA (*hand to heart*): Oh!

DUGAN (*vague grin*): Whatahell—we *movin?*

GIP: Whatsis? *You* called me an ast me would I helpya move Chrizzake!

MEDRICK: But—*where* we goin? Gip?

(GIP *strides to stage apron, picks up the fallen sign, which he bran-dishes, then fixes in place as if pushing the stake into the ground:* THIS PROPERTY CONDEMNED BY NIAGARA COUNTY BOARD OF HEALTH. *The skull and crossbones is prominent.*)

BAMA: Oh! Hallerwe'en!

MEDRICK (*dazed*): We—movin? Outa our—gung'low?

GIP: Been evicted, ain't you?

MEDRICK: "E-victed"? Uz?

GIP: No bettern anybody else are ya?—what'd ya think, y'allz somethin special?

BAMA (*frightened*): But—I got nuthin packed!

DUGAN (*strikes palm with fist, grinning*): Hot gollydam! 'Bout time! All the guyz in my gang, theyz all moved out, or dead! Now itz MY TURN!

MEDRICK: Oh but, oh but—where we movin *to?*

GIP (*rubbing stomach*): Know what yur big-bro could go for, Spike?—nice cold canna beer.

MEDRICK (*to* BAMA): Uh—the Gov'ment, musta been. FBI come an wired uz inour sleep, elect'odes an paste onth', onth' (*touches tem-ples with fingertips*)—fronta-th'-head. Oh Gawd.

DUGAN (*exiting stage left*): Cel'bration! Hot golly*dog!*

MEDRICK (*to* BAMA): The Gov'ment gottuz to sign them documents, give us in-jections so we sold our hauze against our will! I don remember!—I *do* remember! (*wipes forehead on sleeve*) Oh Bama hon' I tolja I shouldna had them X-rays piercing my brain—I *tolja* it was wrong! (*pause*) Once, I was a soljer, proud of my country an them proudof me an—(*pause*) I was a, a well man, then.

BAMA (*fiercely protective*): Yura a well man *now* Medick! My Medick!

MEDRICK: Uh—wherez my car? They took my car too—?

GIP (*pointing*): Carz inth' driveway, Spike, can'tcha *see*?

MEDRICK (*squinting*): Docters told me downtown, one eyez "leg'lly blind"—but dint say which. Bastids!

BAMA (*pressing herself against* MEDRICK): Oh hon—where they sendin us? I'm so scared!

GIP (*defensively*): Look: me an Lucille're damnhappy where they sent *us*. We gotta pen-shion an th' settlement an a real nice view of Lake Ontaryo. Retired age FOUR-THREE—thatz somethin th' ole man woulda croaked over, huh Spike!

BAMA: Uh—Lucille's dead, ain't she?

GIP: Say what?

BAMA: Why—wenta her funeral last spring, poor woman, dint we, hon?

MEDRICK (*shrugs*): *I* don know for Chrizzake.

GIP (*upset*): Bama, what kinda talks that! Lucillez in excellent health, the cheemo-, cheemo-, un th' thrppy ["therapy"] went real *well*. She wuz sayin, just this mornin, "We gotta have Bama an Meldrick an th' boy over for Sunnay dinner *soon*."

BAMA (*doubtfully*): Oh—she wuz?

GIP (*earnestly*): Her an me, now I'm retired, anytime we want we go fishin on the lake—no worries *nuthin*. Only FOUR-THREE yrz old an I'm free as uh—some guy thatz NINETY.

(*As the men talk,* BAMA *goes to inspect the "CONDEMNED" sign; shakes her head sadly.*)

MEDRICK: Yah—fishin? Whatcha catch?

GIP (*boastfully*): Laketrout an pike an bass an whatsis name: sammon.

MEDRICK (*skeptically*): Sam-mom? In Lake Ontaryo?

GIP (*indicates size of fish, which is large, with his hands*): Sammon I said.

MEDRICK (*worriedly*): Nah thatz gotta be carp'r somethin—some garb'ge fish you betta oughta not eat, Gip. Dosed to th' gills with mer-, mer-, merc— (*frustrated*) —POIZZON.

GIP (*defensively*): The fish me an Lucille catch is *safe* for consumers, it ain't glowin in the dark at least!

MEDRICK: Yah I'd be careful, I was you. Don wanna end up like, uh, me, d'ya?

BAMA (*looking around*): Uh wherez—him? Our son?—wherez he gone?

MEDRICK: Who?

BAMA: Wuzn't somebody here, just now? (*Points to spot on stage where* DUGAN *was standing.*) Just now.

MEDRICK: Say what?

BAMA (*shivering*): Oh itz too much!—this life, now. Th' Erth spinnin so fast, an tozzins e'erywhere, no matter their name. (*as* MEDRICK *comforts her, an arm around her shoulders*) Oh honey Ima just so *scared*. I wuz a li'l girl I b'lieved adultz would pretect me an now an now—IMA 'DULT MYSELF.

GIP (*defensively*): The sammon Lucille and me catch is safe to eat an anyway— (*laughs*) —nobodyz gonna live forever are we?

MEDRICK (*strongly, in an almost lucid voice*): What breakz yur heart is—alluvem ["all of them"] lyin to ya. The Prezident on down. Ya vote for em then they don give a damn ya live or die, ya eaten up with c-, c-, ca-, canzer or ya blood go bad or—Jeezus, ya nameit! (*pause: as if summarizing his experience*) HATREDZ A RAZOR-BLADE CANT BE TOO SHARP, BITTERNESS A POIZZON CANT BE TOO TOZZIC.

BAMA (*shocked*): Oh Medick!—those're hard wordz.

DUGAN *trots back carrying a case of beer and a football. His manner is boyish and transformed; lights brighten.*

DUGAN (*happily*): Dad-dee! Unc Gip! Lookit what I found!

MEDRICK (*squinting*): Huh? Whatzis?

GIP (*big grin*): Hey boy thatz th' boy huh!

MEDRICK: Why—th' ole f-. f-, f'b'll, *we* usta play with, Gip, r'member! You an me an—wuzzit Dad-dee? And then my own boy an me—

GIP: Thingz turnin for the betta, 'bout time!

(GIP *takes a can of beer for himself and hands one to* MEDRICK. GIP, MEDRICK, *and* DUGAN *open cans and drink thirstily.*
Lights brighten. The tone is now that of a television advertisement. A bar or two of "commercial" music.)

GIP (*sighing, wiping mouth on sleeve*): Ah Jeezuz don that hitta spot!

MEDRICK (*blinking, amazed*): My headz feelin better awready!

DUGAN: Yah an *my* headz gettin that nice rumblin buzz—nuthin else c'n crowd in *now*.

GIP (*holding a beer can aloft*): Ina can like this—the 'luminumz ["aluminum's"] gotta good 'tallic ["metallic"] taste, huh! I loveit!

MEDRICK: Beer ina glass—phoo! (*spitting gesture*)

GIP: Oh man—sharin a good cold beer an a, a— (*takes out a pack of cigarettes from his pocket, offers cigarettes to* MEDRICK *and* DUGAN *who each accept, and light up happily*) —a whazis—a smoke—sharin with a broth'r an a, a, a— (*lights cigarette, inhales, coughs wheezily*) —whatdayacallit, sonuva broth'r—oh shit—*him* — (*pats* DUGAN *on head*) —yah thatz th' life ain't it! The old man'd go along with *that*.

MEDRICK (*exhaling smoke luxuriously*): Jeezus my headz real—woken up, an my eyez, my eyez, (*blinking*) dazzlin bright now, liketh' sun. Hot dawg!

BAMA (*fondly chiding*): Hey—ya guys not goin to spoil yur app'tite are ya?—Gyp ya stayin for dinner I hope?

DUGAN (*philosophically*): Firzt time I hadda beer, in fifth grade theze guys is screwin arond in th' lockerroom and I, an I dint know no better, dope as I wuz, skinny li'l bastid, "Chugalug!" they sayz so I tried ta so I'm chokin an coughin beer outa my nose an pract'ly pukin an them laughin at me— (*fond reminiscence*) Yah—an now look! (*finishes the can of beer in one or two enormous swallows*)

MEDRICK: Uh Gip—ya know I recog'nized ya face, huh?—just now?

GIP: Sure, sure, Spike!

MEDRICK (*earnest, maudlin*): I mean—Jeezus yur my only broth', right?

GIP (*puzzled*): Thatso? What happ'n'd ta—

MEDRICK (*not listening*): —blood broth'r likea, a twin Chrissake— know ya face bettern my own! Itz bloodkin that countz, an, an, whassis name: LOVE.

GIP (*coughing*): Oh yah Spikey-kid—I know.

MEDRICK: Ya shouldna doubt me, huh? I rec'nized ya face, Gipper I *did.*

GIP: Nah I dint doubtya!

(MEDRICK *and* GIP *embrace awkwardly, yet with emotion. Tears glint on* MEDRICK'*s cheeks.*)

MEDRICK: Ya shouldna doubt me, huh?

GIP: Nah I dint!

(DUGAN *has withdrawn a few yards, has set down his beer and cigarette and is tossing the football up into the air and catching it. Radiant, boyish grin.*)

DUGAN: Heyyyyy ya two! Lookzharp!

(DUGAN *tosses the football at* MEDRICK, *who manages to catch it. He passes it to* GIP *who runs with it. Immediately,* MEDRICK, GIP, *and* DUGAN *take up an energetic improvised game of touch football; laughing loudly, grunting and swearing, enjoying themselves like children. As* BAMA *takes prominence in the foreground, the men play toward the rear of the stage.*

During BAMA'*s concluding speech, the men continue with their game, exclaiming breathlessly, grunting, swearing, laughing, etc. Their commands to one another are muffled as if coming from a distance: "TOSS!" "PASS!" "PEN'LTY!" "OFF-SIDE!"*

"T-F'RMATION!" "CENTER!" "SPLIT-END!" "STRAIGHT-ARM!"
"LAT'RAL!" "BACKFIELD!" "HAND-OFF" "TOUCHDOWN"
"TOUCHDOWN" "TOUCHDOWN YAH!" (These exclamations can
be used in any sequence and should overlap, echo, and repeat, like
discordant music. Some may even be amplified.)

BAMA *has removed her kerchief, shakes out her hair; if her hair*
has been up in rollers, she now removes the rollers and quickly
brushes out her curls.)

BAMA *(approaches audience wide-eyed, girlish, blushing):* Oh—y'all
so *sweet.* Never saw a Welcom Waggin with so many folks!
OH—! *(someone has handed her a giant pizza which she accepts,*
pleased and grateful: she holds the pizza up proudly so that the
audience can read the inscription, which is in slices of pepperoni
sausage) OH what's this—"WELCOME NEW FRIENDS"—y'all
so *sweet! (dabs at eyes*—BAMA *is now her young self, just moving*
into the house on Sycamore: the change in her should be dramatic
and perceptible, yet not overly obvious) My husband Medrick and
I thank y'all, thank y'all from the bottom of our heart! Oh gee 'scuze
me! *(wiping away tears)* I'm a baby, gee, my age! *(Laughs)* Oh—
there's nothing the HUMAN SOUL so yearns for, being welcome
here on Earth, being liked by folks, and, and *loved* by friends and
neighbors, sure we all believe in God and in Jesus Christ the
Redeemer oh yes but, but it's lonely here on Earth so we must
love one another and trust one another, yes TRUST all of us TRUST
(as in an appeal to the audience), we must be friends, my honey
and me we only been married a short time and this is our first
house we're just so . . . happy . . . so grateful . . . *(weeping)* y'all
making us welcome in your neighborhood, LOVE CANAL oh that's
the perfect name for it it is!—we know we're gonna be happy here
and our li'l baby-boy Dugan three months old— *(mimes holding a*
baby in her arms) —he's gonna be happy growing up here and
going to school right over there! *(points off-stage)* And, when we
get settled in— *(confidentially)* —we're gonna have a li'l baby girl
li'l BABY BOO—oh I can't wait I can't! *(Giggles, finger to lips)*
Medrick don't know yet, don't tell 'im! *(Coming forward)* Yes, this
is our house 83 Sycamore we're crazy about, no matter it's a thirty-
year mortgage, that's okay! all you want is a place on Earth that's
HOME so y'all welcome *in* for refreshments, oh please come in,
all you good people and neighbors oh please? yes? y'all come *in?*

(Arms wide, heartfelt appeal to audience: but who will accept her invitation?)

Lights fade. As men continue their game.
Lights out. The sounds of the men continue for two or three beats, in darkness.

(THE END)

Under/Ground

A Play in One Act

CHARACTERS

NOLA HARVEY: twenty-eight years old
MILES HARVEY: forty to fifty years old
KEITH: thirty to thirty-five years old

Lights up. Extreme stage right, KEITH, NOLA, *and* MILES *are standing preparatory to entering the underground bomb shelter. Most of the stage is dark.* KEITH, NOLA, *and* MILES *may be standing on a raised platform to indicate "ground level"—a sidewalk—outside the shelter. There are double doors leading into the shelter; stairs, a landing, more stairs, corridors, doors to rooms, etc. The shelter need not be represented realistically but should be suggestive in its labyrinthine, gloomy, sinister, surreal complexity. The play itself begins in apparent realism and moves gradually toward surrealism.*

KEITH *is a foreign-service officer of modest rank at the American embassy of this capital city of an unnamed European country: seemingly upbeat, optimistic, ebullient, "patriotic" in the professional manner of foreign-service employees abroad.* NOLA HARVEY *is the young wife of* DR. MILES HARVEY, *an American historian of some reputation. The* HARVEYS *are attractively dressed:* NOLA *in a tasteful, "feminine" dress or suit;* MILES *more conservatively.* KEITH *wears regulation diplomatic attire—a dark blue suit, conservatively cut, a plain necktie. As these three descend into the bomb shelter, their personalities gradually shift—from their "daylight" or "social" personae to deeper, more primitive personalities.*

As the lights come up, KEITH, NOLA, *and* MILES *are laughing com-*

panionably. KEITH *fumbles for his wallet and extracts two small plastic card-keys to unlock the shelter doors. The locks on the doors are prominent.*

NOLA: Oh, I've had too much to drink—that luncheon went on and *on.* Is it always like that at the embassy?

KEITH (*suavely, boyishly*): Only when our visitors are VIPs.

MILES: We weren't treated half so well in Frankfurt after my lecture.

KEITH: That's because it was Frankfurt—a major post. Here—(*lowering his voice, smiling*)—well, things are sort of *minor,* as maybe you've noticed.

NOLA: This is a lovely country. The people are so—warm, and curious, and *interested* in us.

KEITH: Yes, they adore Americans—at least to our faces. (*As he peers at the card-keys and fits one into the lock of the outer door, without success*) They're eager for visas to "study"—to get scholarships to pay their way to the States. (*Smiling*) Wait'll you see this place— as the ambassador was saying, they lost most of the capital city's historic architecture in the war, so they've poured money into government buildings. (*Fussing with key-cards, still pleasant, but getting impatient*) This bomb shelter is quite something, y'know, for a country so—limited in resources as this.

NOLA (*a bit apprehensive*): This—bomb shelter—is it big?

KEITH: Mammoth!

NOLA: I've never been in a bomb shelter before.

MILES: Nor have I, come to think of it. They've lost popularity, back home.

KEITH (*sly smile*): They still exist, back home—but they're reserved for VIPs, you bet!

NOLA (*uneasily*): Well. I guess we don't like to think about that.

KEITH: That's the idea.

NOLA (*to* MILES): I—I'm wondering whether I really want to go in here. It's such a lovely, sunny day.

MILES: Certainly you're coming along. We want to "share every-thing," don't we? (*Gives her a significant look, squeezes her hand*)

KEITH (*as a guide; "booster" voice*): When it was built in 1964, this was as modern as any shelter in the world, even the Kremlin's—even our own leaders'. Now, I guess it's outmoded in certain respects, like for instance a chemical attack—toxic chemicals *sink*, y'know—but in case of a conventional nuclear war, it should be adequate. Ah! (*Succeeds in unlocking the door; turns the knob and pushes the door in, producing a sharp, creaking, jarring noise*)

NOLA (*startled by the noise, laughs nervously*): I—I think I—

MILES (*displeased*): Nola, dear, don't be silly.

NOLA: —I'd rather wait in the car.

KEITH (*like a salesman*): Oh, the shelter is perfectly safe, Mrs. Harvey. (*Joking, with a gesture toward the sky*) Much safer than "reality."

NOLA (*apologetic, but willful*): My head aches, I must have drunk too much champagne.

MILES (*pulling gently but firmly at her arm*): We are not going to leave you in the car, and *I* want to see the shelter. If Ken says it's safe—

KEITH: Keith.

MILES: —if he's taken visitors through before—

KEITH: Dozens of American VIPs! The most distinguished, last year, was Vice-President Quayle! And he loved it.

NOLA: Loved it?

KEITH: Mr. Quayle is *appreciative.*

(NOLA *acquiesces. The three step through the first doorway into a small vestibule.* KEITH *is enjoying his role as guide.*)

KEITH (*playful finger to lips*): The existence of this shelter is a state secret, so we'll close the door—quickly. (*Shuts outer door;* NOLA *makes an involuntary gesture, as of distress at being locked in.*)

MILES (*bemused*): A state secret? This gigantic door, in a wall fronting a street? Behind Parliament?

KEITH: An open secret, for sure. But—it isn't spoken of. (*To* NOLA) Are you all right, Mrs. Harvey?

NOLA: Oh—yes.

MILES (*overlapping with* NOLA): My wife is *fine*.

KEITH (*familiar, solicitous*): Gee, I used to be claustrophobic too, as a kid. Even through college. Had dreams about being buried alive, choking for air, trapped—brrrr! (*Shudders, but reverts easily to cheerful tone as he inserts the second card in the inner door*) They say it's a basic human phobia—fear of being buried alive.

(NOLA *hugs herself, shudders; sniffs as if smelling something unpleasant.*)

MILES (*professorial, pedantic*): No doubt because in the past, people often *were* buried alive—poor souls who were believed to be dead but weren't. Before modern medical technology. Before embalming.

NOLA (*nervous laugh*): That's what it smells like!

MILES: What smells like—?

NOLA: The air in here smells like formaldehyde.

MILES (*disapproving*): *I* don't smell anything.

KEITH (*cheerfully*): Oh, this is nothing, yet.

NOLA (*accommodating*): Of course, it could be my—imagination.

(KEITH *continues to try to fit the card into the lock, turning it upside-down, jamming it in harder or more gently, etc., but without success. To cover his annoyance, he begins to whistle.*)

MILES (*to* KEITH): Do many people have access to this shelter?

KEITH: Naturally not. This is *the* bomb shelter in the country. The prime minister—high-ranking government officials and members of Parliament—a select number of diplomats and visitors. (*Smiles*) Everyone at the U.S. Embassy, for sure. They wouldn't keep *us* out. (*Muttering*) Damn this lock, I *know* it works.

NOLA (*an edge to her voice; schoolgirl sort of manner*): And what about the others?

KEITH: What others?

NOLA: The seventy million others in this country.

KEITH (*vaguely, blandly*): Oh, I'm sure they'd be taken care of. There are lots of bomb shelters, more conventional ones, built during the war. (*Pause*) Anyway, ordinary folks wouldn't expect to be included in *this* shelter.

MILES: I should think not.

NOLA (*stubbornly*): I thought this was a "parliamentary democracy" —an "egalitarian" society.

KEITH: So? That doesn't affect their tradition.

MILES (*to* KEITH): Keith—it *is* Keith, isn't it?—how long have you been posted here?

KEITH (*shrugging, pleasant*): Oh, forever! . . . Naw, only a few years. They rotate us around. Prevent us from getting "attached." Before this I was stationed in Norway. Before that, Canada. (*Yawns*) Places where nothing much happens. Or if it does, you don't notice. (*An old joke*) Like—tree rings growing. (*Pause, more seriously*) Almost, y'know, you wish for some kind of action—"history"—in backwaters like this. Gee, I envy my colleagues in the Mideast—I *do*.

NOLA (*incensed*): You wouldn't want bombings, would you? Missiles? War?

KEITH (*quickly*): Oh, no, of course not. (*Reverts to an earnest, official voice*) The goal of all U.S. diplomacy is global peace.

(KEITH *has managed to unlock the door, with a cracking, creaking sound, as before. As the three step through the inner door,* MILES *takes a small camera out of his pocket.*)

KEITH (*with sudden authority*): Uh, Dr. Harvey—better not.

MILES: Not even for private use?

KEITH: This *is* an official classified zone.

MILES: But who would know?

KEITH: It's just forbidden.

MILES (*smiling*): Yes, but who would know?

NOLA (*embarrassed*): Oh, Miles, put it away. Please.

MILES (*reluctantly*): Well. All right. But I don't see—

KEITH: It's all right that we're here so long as it isn't *known* we're here. Y'know—diplomacy.

MILES: I understand. Sorry. (*Slips camera back into pocket*)

KEITH: Thanks! (*Switches on fluorescent lights, shuts second door, with a little difficulty.*)

NOLA: What if we're locked in here?

KEITH: Impossible, Mrs. Harvey. (*Waving cards*) What got us in will get us out. Also—there are plenty of telephones.

(NOLA *nudges herself against* MILES, *who slips an arm around her.* KEITH *begins to lead them down the stairs, which are steep.*)

KEITH (*ebulliently*): Hmmmm! It *does* smell a bit, doesn't it? But you get used to it quickly. Nothing to be worried about—it's perfectly empty, and it's perfectly safe. In fact, I find it comforting. I feel so *privileged.*

(*Lights out.*)
(*Lights up.*)

(KEITH, NOLA, MILES *are standing on a landing, illuminated brightly while the rest of the stage remains darkened.* NOLA *and* MILES *glance up behind them a bit edgily, as if to indicate that they've descended a considerable distance.*)

(*Here, we see a large, glossy—though faded—poster giving numbered instructions in a foreign language, an invented language suggestive of Finnish and Russian: "Kyväuoppyio"—"Hyvmespheere"— "Janisijäaratiaj"—"Vytirkborg"—"Svenszeri"—"Väajivilya"—"Reostrov"—"Ostrykyr"—etc. There is a life-sized mannequin in full nuclear defense gear: khaki jacket and trousers, gas mask, boots, gloves.*)

NOLA (*girlish reaction, seeing mannequin*): Oh! It's so—lifelike.

KEITH (*tapping mannequin on head*): Yeah, he's my buddy. Hiya, pal! (*To the* HARVEYS) He's wearing your basic issue, for when the bomb falls. I mean—uh, if—*if* the bomb falls. (*Chuckles*) I've had the gear on—actually, it's a lot more comfortable than it looks.

NOLA: A gas mask can suffocate you, if it's defective.

KEITH: Nah, more likely people put them on wrong. The human factor—no matter how they're educated, some people for sure are going to goof up in times of emergency.

(*A deep, subterranean, near-inaudible throbbing and vibrating has begun.*)

MILES (*cupping hand to ear*): What's that?

KEITH: Generator, ventilation system, hydraulic pumps—everything running constantly, of course. Twenty-four hours a day.

NOLA: So—everything is ready. (*Shivers*)

KEITH: Absolutely! There's a maintenance crew, for sure. And the whole thing is in the process of being computerized.

NOLA (*glancing back up behind her, uneasy*): How deep *is* this place?

KEITH: Oh, we've hardly begun. We're down about twenty-five feet is all. The lowermost level is one hundred seventy-five feet. (*Gesturing expansively*) A regular metropolis!

MILES (*has been examining poster*): What a language! I know German, and Russian, and some Swedish, but this hardly seems Indo-European.

KEITH: Yeah, it's like Hungarian—a real linguistic challenge.

(MILES *stumbles through some of the words on the poster, mispronouncing them;* KEITH *rattles them off with surprising fluency.*)

KEITH: It's just directions in time of emergency. Routine stuff—schoolchildren are drilled in it.

(*Fluorescent lights flicker subtly.* NOLA, KEITH, MILES *notice but say nothing. Lights then stabilize.*)

MILES (*an air of profundity*): How—strange! After millions of years of evolution, and the progress of civilization, a man doesn't know —*really* know—what he's made of. Until he's put to the test.

NOLA (*lightly ironic*): And a woman?

MILES: By "man" I include woman. As in "mankind."

KEITH: It's true, Dr. Harvey! And for entire nations, too. Entire nations can be courageous, or cowardly.

MILES: It's a process of evolution, I suppose.

KEITH: Survival of the fittest!

MILES: I'm a historian, not a scientist, but I've always seen the basic pattern—adaptation or death.

NOLA (*shivering*): It *is* cold.

MILES: Would you like my coat, dear? To drape over your shoulders?

NOLA: No, I'll be all right.

(KEITH *leads* NOLA *and* MILES *down another flight of stairs; or the action is simulated. Lights behind them go out; others come on. The throbbing and vibrating sound is more pronounced. We come to an area of several shut doors; a television monitor; an old-fashioned wall telephone, its receiver dangling loose. Signs on the wall "Út Ysskräjivak-Ylla"— "Czijillo Bvtthliomez."*)

KEITH (*chattering*): Above us—four-ton steel reinforced shields. On all sides—steel and concrete. Tons of dirt. (*Pointing*) Down that corridor, the communications center; down here, the infirmary; and this corridor (*pointing*) is a secret passageway connecting the shelter with the prime minister's residence. (*Turns on light switch, but corridor remains dark*)

MILES: Say, can we see that?

KEITH: Well, Doctor, it's, uh, *dark*.

MILES (*peering into corridor*): I believe I hear—dripping?

KEITH: *I* don't hear anything.

NOLA (*wrinkling her nose*): That smell . . .

MILES: How far down are we now?

KEITH: Approximately one hundred feet. (*Cheerfully, glancing up*) You can feel it, sort of, can't you?—eardrums, eyeballs—a sort of—*force*?

NOLA: . . . like stagnant water.

MILES (*primly*): Leakage in here could be dangerous.

KEITH (*stiffly*): The shelter has *never* leaked, Dr. Harvey, in its entire history.

(NOLA *has wandered to the telephone, lifts the receiver to her ear, out of curiosity. She catches* MILES' *eye, mouths the words "It's dead," shakes her head, and returns the receiver to its cradle.*)

(KEITH, *oblivious of* NOLA, *has gone to a door to open it, switch on lights. The room is cell-like, very small. A single cot.*)

KEITH: Here we have a typical room: a bit compact, but not bad, eh? And a single, if you like privacy.

NOLA (*holding her nose*): Oh, dear! The smell!

(MILES *too reacts, but enters the room; bends to peer under the cot; recoils in disgust.*)

MILES: Ugh!

NOLA (*frightened*): What is it?

MILES: Uh—nothing.

NOLA (*dreading*): Something—dead?

KEITH (*quickly*): Oh, I'm sure it's—nothing.

NOLA (*voice rising*): Something dead?

MILES (*professorial irony, dry wit*): Darling, it isn't any danger to us in the condition it's in—let's put it that way.

KEITH (*peering under the cot too, similarly revolted; turns off lights, firmly shuts the door; apologetic, chagrined*): Whew! That's most unusual, I swear.

MILES (*pedantic*): Decomposition would be very slow in here, of course—no flies, very little bacteria. More likely, since the air is so dry, the process would be like—mummification.

(*A pause.*)

NOLA (*frightened*): A rat?

KEITH (*whistling*): *Most* unusual.

(NOLA *looks around, alarmed, listening to the throbbing, vibrating sound.*)

NOLA: My God, isn't this—madness! This! Down here! How long could human beings survive down here, if there *was* a war?

MILES: Now, Nola.

KEITH: Now, Mrs. Harvey.

NOLA (*pulling away from* MILES*'s touch*): Think of the terror, the disorientation, the hopelessness—

KEITH (*ticking off on his fingers, matter-of-fact*): The alert sounds— you report to your station—the shelter is sealed—you wait out the results of the attack: what's so hopeless about that? Anyway, what's the alternative?

NOLA (*angry*): You don't seem to realize, either of you, that we are surrounded by *earth*. This is a tomb, it's for burial—burial alive.

KEITH (*smiling*): Why, no. It's for surviving. Surviving alive.

NOLA: I can feel the earth—the weight of it. The pressure. (*Swaying, hands to eyes*) It's horrible.

MILES (*embracing* NOLA, *addressing* KEITH *over her shoulder*): My poor darling interprets everything so *personally*.

KEITH: My wife was the exactly same way, Dr. Harvey! I guess that's how women are.

MILES: They lack the gift of abstraction. Of detaching yourself from experience.

KEITH: Exactly!

MILES: Nola, dear, it's just your imagination, whatever you're think- ing of. Mmm? (*Whispers in her ear*)

KEITH: Shall we continue?

NOLA (*easing away from* MILES, *with an expression of dread yet resignation*): There's more?

KEITH: The best is yet to come.

(NOLA *stares at him, laughs incredulously*.)

KEITH (*politely*): I gather you are a disarmament person, Mrs. Harvey? An "ecology" person?

NOLA (*pertly*): And you are a war person?

KEITH (*laughing pleasantly*): I don't care to be reduced to a political stance, Mrs. Harvey, any more than you do. I'm a realist. Americans are realists. Of course, the shelter isn't a luxury hotel, but the fact is, it *exists*. And if there's a nuclear war, you're either *in* or you're *out*.

(*A pause.* MILES *nods professorially.* NOLA *glares at* KEITH, *then turns away, to continue down the stairs.*)

NOLA (*grimly*): Let's get this over with.

(KEITH *hurries to accompany* NOLA; *takes her arm on the steep stairs.* MILES *holds back, surreptitiously removes his camera from his pocket, takes two quick photographs of the secret passageway and the room. Neither* KEITH *nor* NOLA *notices.*
Lights out.
Several beats. "Shelter" sounds—rustlings, scuttlings, echoes of footsteps, distorted voices, distant laughter or cries. An eerie sort of music, underlaid by the throbbing, vibrating pulse.
Lights up.
KEITH *and* NOLA *are on the next level. There is a new rapport between them, as if their outburst has linked them emotionally.* MILES *in background.*)

KEITH: All sorts of Americans come through here, and the cultural attaché foists them off on—I mean, entrusts them to—me. But it's a lonely post.

NOLA: Is it? You seem so sociable.

KEITH: You and the professor are leaving tomorrow?

NOLA: Yes. For Stockholm.

KEITH: Were you—a student of his?

NOLA: Does it show?

KEITH: It's the best kind of marriage, I'm sure. Marriage between equals never works. (*As* NOLA *looks at him, startled*) I mean—somebody always wants to be more equal than the other.

NOLA (*stiffly*): I have an advanced degree too—I'm just not using it right now. I'm (*pause*) . . . just not using it right now.

KEITH: No kids, eh?

NOLA: Miles has two sons, already grown. (*Pause*) He doesn't want more.

KEITH: He dumped his old wife for you, eh? I don't blame him.

NOLA (*offended*): What did you say?

KEITH: *I* was married, but it didn't last. Marriages sort of fall apart in the foreign service.

NOLA: That's—too bad.

KEITH: My wife hung on through Ottawa pretty well, just about made it through Oslo; but here (*laughs*) she started speaking their language, suddenly!—like, y'know, the words would—*erupt*—in the midst of other things, in her sleep, or in—uh—intimate moments with me. (KEITH *emits harsh, crowing sounds, his eyes shut.*) "Kuhvavalaji!"— "Pyajuddik-ut!"— "Uzkavajjikyyo!"

NOLA (*staring at him*): How—

KEITH (*when we think he has finished*): "Hyvskyygizkyi!"

NOLA: —awful.

KEITH (*wiping forehead*): It *was* awful. I'd hafta pacify her, like—(*a gesture as of pressing the flat of his hand over someone's mouth; then pause*) Poor li'l Bobbie went back to Tulsa, where she's from, with the kids. Got remarried to some ol' high-school sweetheart. (*Yawns*) That's how it is.

NOLA: You must miss your children.

KEITH (*leaning closer to her*): I get lonely, but not for my children.

NOLA (*uneasy*): You—uh—must go back home occasionally, to the States?

KEITH (*shrugs*): Once you leave, and live in other countries, you sort of forget about home. (*Slight sneer*) That's another secret everybody knows.

NOLA (*stiffly*): *I* wouldn't forget my home. My birthplace. (*Pause, as if a bit vague*) My family . . .

KEITH (*with a sudden, curious ardor, seizing* NOLA's *hand*): In a place like this, (*drawing out word*) underground, you forget your own name. It's easier that way.

(*Pause.* NOLA *and* KEITH *stare at each other.* NOLA *slowly withdraws her hand.*

MILES, *out of breath, joins them.*)

MILES: Wait for me! (*Pulling at necktie*) It's a little—close in here, isn't it?

(KEITH, NOLA, *and* MILES *descend stairs to another, lower level. The sounds of the shelter are more evident here, especially to* MILES, *who glances about with increasing unease.* KEITH *whistles cheerfully, intermittently, in short outbursts.*

NOLA *loses her footing momentarily, grips* KEITH's *arm; he steadies her.* MILES, *grown querulous, seems not to notice.*)

MILES: Is the air fresh, coming in these vents? It smells like mold.

KEITH (*as if a direct, ingenuous reply*): Mold manufactures oxygen, doesn't it, doctor? "The action of friendly bacteria in fungus." (*Chuckles*)

(MILES *stares at him.*)

MILES (*tugging at tie*): I—I'm thirsty.

(*During the following dialogue, while* KEITH *continues his tour,* MILES *wanders off, toward stage right, to get water from a water cooler. He has some difficulty getting the water to come out the spout. His hands tremble as he lifts the paper cup to his mouth. Then, when he drinks, he reacts immediately to the water—spitting it out, gagging, crying, "Ugh!—ugh!" He has spilled water on himself and dabs at it with a handkerchief, muttering.* KEITH *and* NOLA *do not notice.*)

KEITH (*expansive, ebullient*): Yessir! This is one of many nations with a "tragic history." Hitler punished them for their neutrality—Stalin killed hundreds of thousands in slave labor camps—and the Allies, I'm afraid, bombed the hell out of them—couldn't be helped. That's how history is—cruel to losers. (*Chuckles*)

NOLA (*sympathetic*): The soil of Europe is drenched in blood . . . World War II seems so *recent*.

KEITH: Yeah. People hang on to their history, even when it's fucked them up. (*Shakes head, bemused*) It's an old-fashioned concept, like that's how they know who they *are*.

NOLA (*looking around, indicating door*): What's in here?

KEITH: Medical supplies. But the door's locked.

(NOLA *nonetheless tries the door, which opens, startling them.*)

KEITH: Oops! Guess I'm wrong.

(*It is a closet, with shelves of bottles, vials, first-aid equipment, bed-pans, enemas, rolls of gauze, etc. There is a sudden scuttling noise, as of rodents fleeing, and one of the enema bags is knocked to the floor.*)

NOLA: Oh!

KEITH: God*damn*. (*Kicks enema bag*)

NOLA: What was that?

KEITH: What was what?

NOLA: Some—things— creatures—were in there. I could see them running.

KEITH: A roach, maybe. A mouse.

NOLA (*weakly*): There were more than one. They were bigger than mice.

KEITH: Nah, this shelter is vermin-proof.

MILES (*clutching at* KEITH's *arm*): Excuse me, is there maybe—distilled water in there?

KEITH (*shutting door firmly; officiously*): We can't be breaking into the supplies, doctor. We aren't even citizens of this country.

NOLA (*dismayed, to* MILES): Miles, you look so—

MILES (*querulous, self-pitying*): I don't feel well. It's this impure air. (*To* KEITH) What about oxygen—is there, maybe, oxygen in there?

KEITH: Pure oxygen is a depressant—you don't want that, doctor.

MILES: I'm having difficulty—breathing.

KEITH: Nah, you'll get used to it.

NOLA: If you didn't—talk—so much, Miles, dear. I mean—(*as if genuinely solicitous of him, like a concerned wife, even as he stares at her in disbelief*)—if you didn't take up so much *space*.

MILES: So much space? (*Looking down at himself*) This is all I have.

NOLA (*poking fingers in ears, experimentally*): Oh—something feels so strange! Like—champagne bubbles!

KEITH: It's the pressure—on the brain. Makes the brain cells sort of fizzle and pop—feel it? (*Giddy, he too pokes fingers in his ears and wriggles them playfully.*)

NOLA (*giggling*): So straaange—!

MILES: Nola, Ken—I—I don't feel well. I—

NOLA (*to* KEITH): Where are we now? How far underground?

KEITH: What's it matter? We're here.

MILES (*as they ignore him, as if he were invisible*): I—I'd like to go back to the hotel. I don't feel well. (*Reeling backward, to stare up at the stairs they've descended*) But, my God, how can I ever climb . . . ?

NOLA: I've never felt like this before. (*Sniffing*) I think there's something in the air. (*Sly smile*)

KEITH: The best is yet to come.

NOLA (*pointing at door, childlike, mischievous*): Uh-oh, *that* door—what's behind it?

KEITH: Better not open it!

NOLA: Why not?

KEITH: Mmmm—it's forbidden, that's why.

NOLA: Yes, but why?

KEITH: Maybe it's locked. Maybe there's nothing behind it.

(NOLA *tiptoes to the door, daringly.*)

MILES (*pleading*): Nola, Ken—*please*—I need oxygen—

(NOLA *opens the door, and a figure tumbles out. It is dressed in a gas mask, khakis, etc.: but is it a dummy, or a corpse?* NOLA *shrieks and leaps back into* KEITH'*s arms;* MILES *nearly faints.*)

KEITH (*seems seriously alarmed, disapproving, crouches over the figure*): It's a—dummy. Like the other.

NOLA (*frightened*): Oh, *who* is—?

KEITH (*insistent*): A dummy. Like the other. (KEITH *tries to lift the figure to push it back through the doorway; though lifeless, it seems to be resistant.*)

NOLA: I'm so sorry! Let me help you.

MILES (*backing off, swaying, weakly*): Don't touch it, Nola. It's contaminated.

(KEITH *and* NOLA *struggle to lift the bulky figure. With some effort, they push it back through the doorway, and* KEITH *quickly shuts the door.*)

KEITH (*panting, wiping at forehead with handkerchief*): Only a dummy. We all saw.

MILES (*a bit wildly*): *I* saw! I saw what that was!

KEITH (*incensed*): The prime minister will hear about this. Things are getting shamefully lax. (*To* NOLA) Are you all right, Nola? Mrs. Harvey?

NOLA: A little—out of breath.

KEITH (*staring at her*): Your eyes! Dilated like a cat's.

NOLA: I'm so sorry I—interfered.

KEITH: *I'm* sorry. Perhaps we should wash up.

MILES (*accusing, cowering at stage right*): Nola, how could you? You touched it. That thing. I saw.

NOLA: Wash up? Is the guided tour over?

KEITH: Almost.

NOLA: I want to see everything.

MILES (*faintly*): I want to go back to the hotel.

KEITH: Well! Let's see! (*Opens another door, resuming his official manner; switches on lights, which flicker*) Here is one of the jewels of the shelter—the parliamentary assembly room, with a seating capacity of three hundred.

NOLA (*looking in*): Goodness, it's vast. I can't see the walls.

KEITH (*cups hands to mouth, makes a yodellike sound*): Halloo! Halloo in there! Syvkrikkoya omphysikr!

(*Low, rippling, booming echo of* KEITH's *words*)

KEITH (*whistles, yodels*): Pskyooyiala-ptimi! (*To* NOLA) Hear 'em? The P.M. and the M.P. debating what to do, now the Big One got dropped, that everybody said never would, and Northern Europe is zapped. (*As if listening*) Nothing left aboveground, but down here, chatterchatterchatter, gobblygook talk—Jeezuz.

(*We seem to hear low, murmurous, contentious voices.*)

NOLA: Oh, dear. Is it—?

KEITH: Yeah, it's sad. But, y'know—history. (*Shuts door, and the sounds vanish.*)

MILES (*cowering at stage right, almost inaudible*): Help—can't breathe—

(KEITH *kisses* NOLA, *somewhat grossly, on the mouth.* NOLA *stiffens in resistance but does not shove him away.*)

NOLA (*as if incensed*): You're—crude, that's what you are.

KEITH: *You're* nice.

NOLA: Oh!

KEITH: Some meat on your bones, the way I like 'em. (*Pinches her buttocks*)

(NOLA *slaps at him, shocked.*)

NOLA: How dare you! You know I'm married!

KEITH (*gripping her wrist*): Every American cunt who comes through here is married, for sure.

NOLA: I'll report you to the ambassador!

(KEITH *advances upon* NOLA, *who retreats toward stage left. It is as if she were mesmerized by him, backing away, arms extended gropingly behind her.* MILES *watches helplessly, in anguish.*)

MILES: Nola—Nola! Help me! Can't breathe! (*Opens shirt, sinks to knees*)

KEITH (*in his earlier, ebullient tone*): The luxury rooms come equipped with *saunas*. But it's a state secret.

(*Lights out.*

In the darkness, sinister sounds: vibrating, throbbing, echoes as of voices, laughter, erotic/anguished murmurs, cries.

Lights up. MILES *alone, stage right, sitting dazed on the floor. He has taken his camera out of his pocket, raises it with shaking fingers, to take a flash shot of the audience.*)

MILES: The only evidence. All the dead. No one will believe, otherwise. (*He is breathing hoarsely; perspiration gleams on his face.*)

(*Lights out on* MILES; *Lights up on* KEITH *and* NOLA, *entering from stage left. They are wearing dazzling white terrycloth robes and are barefoot; seemingly naked beneath the robes. Their hair is damp:* KEITH's *is slicked back, and* NOLA *is combing hers. They are amorous, playful; oblivious of* MILES, *who, under cover of darkness, crawls to exit stage right.*)

KEITH (*as they enter, arms around each other's waist, nuzzling* NOLA's *neck*): Toldja, eh? What'd I tellya?

NOLA: That hurts!

KEITH: Eh, sweetheart! What'd I tellya?

NOLA (*glancing around nervously*): Not *here*. Goodness, is this a public place!

KEITH: So? Everybody's *fried*, nobody's *left*.

NOLA: You shouldn't have sealed that door. I can't believe you so selfishly *sealed that door*.

KEITH: We can repopulate, you and me. (*Whistles cheerfully*)

NOLA (*pouting*): I don't know if I—if I love you that much. In that way.

KEITH (*grabbing* NOLA's *hips playfully, roughly*): That's what all the cunts say.

NOLA (*trying to slap him, but he restrains her*): I hate that kind of talk, I really do. I *do*.

KEITH (*discovering camera on floor, whistling sharply*): What's this? (*He snatches it up, opens it, takes out the roll of film and pitches it into the darkness*)

NOLA (*closing robe at throat, as if her modesty were being threatened*): Oh, is that a *camera*?

(KEITH *stuffs the camera into his pocket. Offstage, in the darkness stage right, an ominous chewing and crunching sound has begun, nearly inaudible at first, then building.*)

NOLA: What's that?

KEITH: What's what?

(KEITH *goes to fetch a bottle of wine and two glasses.* NOLA *approaches the darkness at stage right but holds back, fearfully.*)

NOLA: I hear something—strange.

KEITH (*pouring wine into glasses*): *I* don't hear anything. Just the generator. (*Pause*) When that goes out, *we* go out. (*Amorous, cheerful, handing* NOLA *her glass*) But not for billions of years!

NOLA (*distracted by sounds offstage*): Oh, dear, it sounds like—something eating? chewing? (*Listens*) Or being chewed. (*Squints into darkness*)

KEITH: Aw, it's all dark there. It's oblivion. "The darkness upon the face of the deep." (*Smirks*) But the Spirit of God isn't coming this time. *Zap.*

NOLA (*listening, blinking*): Hear it? Little jaws, teeth—so many—grinding. Brrr! (*Turning to* KEITH) Oh, protect me!

(KEITH *slides an arm around* NOLA; *she rests her head against his shoulder; after a moment, they raise their glasses, clink them together, drink.*)

KEITH: It's great, eh? From the P.M.'s private cellar. (*Chuckles*) We're *in* the cellar.

NOLA: I'm so ashamed, I seem to have forgotten your name.

KEITH: Nah, it's all right.

NOLA: But it isn't like me at all.

KEITH: Down here, honey, we don't have names.

NOLA: Don't?

KEITH: It's easier that way.

(*Lights flicker and dim, but remain steady.*)

NOLA: And if the generator goes out?

KEITH: It never has, yet.

NOLA (*gazing up at him, urgently*): But—if it does?

KEITH (*firmly, ebulliently*): We still have each other. There's always—love. And—I have this. (*Takes from his pocket a candle, which he lights*)

Lights slowly out. Noises of chewing, etc., in background. Finally only the candle flame remains, illuminating the lovers' radiant faces.

(THE END)

Greensleeves

CHARACTERS

LEON: late twenties
TAMARA: mid- or late twenties

Lights up. LEON *is seated on a park bench in the sun, reading and annotating a paperback book. His is a face with a distinctive "character." He wears very casual, well-worn clothes—shirt or sweater, jeans, running shoes. His hair is slightly long and unkempt. He may not have shaved for a day or two. As he reads, he shakes his head as if in admiration, marking lines with a pen.*

TAMARA *appears stage right; approaches slowly, like a sleepwalker, staring. She is beautiful in a stylized way, like a model, but wears no apparent makeup, including lipstick. Her clothes are striking and mismatched—a designer jacket, for instance, worn with a long, rumpled skirt. Her hair is long and disheveled as if windblown. Her manner is overly intense, but we can sense her more primary character beneath—practical, self-assertive, perhaps shrewd and defensive.*

TAMARA *regards* LEON *for a beat or two with an expression of yearning. Finally* LEON *glances up, surprised to see her.*

LEON: Yes . . . ?

(TAMARA *continues to stare, as if unhearing.*)

LEON (*puzzled, but trying to be friendly*): Uh—is something wrong?

TAMARA (*shakes head slowly, as if waking from a trance*): Oh, I . . . have I been here . . . long? Here (*indicating where she's standing*) . . . ?

157

LEON: I—don't know. I guess not.

TAMARA: I didn't mean . . . I'm sorry . . . (*Looking around, blinking*) What time is it? God, it must be—well—(*squinting at sky*)—it's obviously *day*time, isn't it! (*Checks wrist, slaps at pockets.*) I forgot my watch.

LEON (*bemused, intrigued by her; checks his watch*): It's precisely 11:08 . . . A.M.

TAMARA: Even if I had my watch, I couldn't trust it. (*Laughs*) I guess we . . . don't know each other?

LEON: I . . . guess not.

(TAMARA *begins to speak,* LEON *speaks, the two of them awkward, words overlapping.*)

TAMARA: I mean—looking at me, you, uh—you don't know *me*—do you?

LEON: It might be that—

TAMARA: We've never—

LEON: Should I? Know you?

TAMARA (*oddly, staring at him, then looking away*): "Should"— "should"— "should." (*Laughs apologetically, almost shyly*) No, I guess you *shouldn't.*

LEON (*attracted to her, yet wary*): It's possible we've met, but I—I doubt that I'd have forgotten you—

TAMARA (*quickly, almost harshly*): Oh yes, oh yes—you would—you *should.* I mean, I'm just a face. (*Touches face as if groping*) All the faces in this city—!

LEON: Are you . . . looking for someone?

TAMARA (*quickly*): No. (*Pause, as if trying to sort out her thoughts, understand her motive*) I mean, I'm not *looking* for anyone in the abstract. It might be, I'm looking for . . . (*Long pause*)

LEON: Someone in particular?

TAMARA (*quickly, resolutely*): Oh, no—*no.* (*Yet she keeps looking at him, in a discomforting way*)

LEON: You *are*—all right?

TAMARA: Yes, certainly. (*Pause*) Well—I'm sorry I've interrupted you—I—I guess I'll be . . . going. (*Self-consciously crosses before* LEON, *who watches her with interest*)

LEON (*faint smile, wave of hand*): Okay—g'bye!

(TAMARA *trails off stage left; but after a beat or two we see her standing uncertainly, watching* LEON *again. He has returned to his book but gradually becomes aware of her; he glances up, frowning.*)

TAMARA (*making a "scene" of it—laughing, slapping the palms of her hands against her thighs as if acknowledging, that, yes, this is a bit odd*): Well—!

LEON (*not knowing how to react*): Well.

(TAMARA *returns, her walk more "controlled"—her determination now is to establish control.*)

TAMARA: I guess I should introduce myself. (*Extends hand briskly for handshake*) I'm Tamara Hudson.

LEON (*still baffled but willing to be charmed*): I'm—Leon Collier.

TAMARA (*gazing at him intensely*): Collier—Collier. Leon. (*Pause*)

LEON (*uneasily*): *Is* something wrong?

TAMARA (*indicating bench*): D'you mind if I—

LEON: Of course not.

TAMARA (*sits with a certain elegance, clearly aware of her posture; arranging skirt nervously, girlishly*): This side of the park!—I never knew it was *here*. I never come this way—I had the idea it might be, well, dangerous—a little. Don't things happen here, sometimes?

LEON: What kind of things?

TAMARA (*looking around, squinting, as if sun were too bright for her eyes*): Those rocks—rock faces. Granite? Like clouds, rocks can have faces. You see what you want to, in them. (*Lifts hair in an unconscious seductive gesture*) I'm—did I say?—Tamara Hudson, I guess I told you?—and you believed me?

LEON: I shouldn't have believed you?

TAMARA (*contemptuous laugh*): "Tamara" is such a phony name—obviously.

LEON: It's a . . . striking name.

TAMARA (*carelessly*): Oh, *I'm* striking. It's my trade. (*Laughs*) All phony. But *Leon*, now . . .

LEON: Are you a model?

(TAMARA *shrugs; checks out cover of* LEON's *book.*)

TAMARA: What are you reading? Oh—(*recoiling slightly, makes a gesture as if to push book away*)—Yeats. Him—the poet! (*To herself*) Never mind *that*.

LEON: You don't like Yeats?

TAMARA (*trying to exert control*): It's a—a coincidence, which means, not design, not *design*, just *accident*. (*Pause*) Like this. (*Pause*) Meeting you. (*Pause, slaps at pockets*) D'you have a cigarette?

LEON: No, sorry.

(TAMARA *fishes out of a pocket a small package, which she examines curiously.*)

TAMARA: These "roasted almonds"—you only get them on airlines. (*Reads package*) "Continental Express"—the commuter plane—propellers—it starts vibrating like crazy in the wind, about ready to fall apart. They heap almonds on you—bags and bags of 'em. (*Giggles*) You know you're in trouble, the more almonds. (*Offers package to* LEON) You want these?

LEON: No thanks!

(TAMARA *returns package to pocket; continues searching for cigarettes.*)

TAMARA: D'you have a—oh I guess I asked you, huh—a cigarette?

LEON: No, I don't. Sorry.

TAMARA: Don't be sorry! It's just as well. (LEON *watches her sidelong as she exhibits classic, perhaps a bit comic, symptoms of unease—crossing her arms tightly beneath her breasts, holding her hands tight under her armpits*) JUST . . . AS . . . WELL.

LEON: What did you mean about "design," "accident"?

TAMARA (*grimly resolute, comical flair*): BEST . . . TO . . . KICK . . . ALL . . . ADDICTIONS.

LEON: You're trying to quit smoking? (*When* TAMARA *nods vigorously*) I quit, nineteen months ago. (*Pause*) Nineteen months, five days—(*checks watch*)—six hours, and fourteen minutes.

TAMARA (*laughing, but then almost hostile*): Well—aren't we proud of ourselves! Aren't we superior!

LEON (*startled at her tone, puzzled*): I—don't feel superior.

TAMARA: You feel superior to me. You have the—advantage.

LEON: What?

TAMARA (*as if conceding*): You should, you should.

LEON: Why?

TAMARA: Oh, for Christ's sake, isn't it obvious! I'm not worthy of . . . (*pause, draws hands over eyes; so low a murmur she can barely be heard*) . . . you.

LEON: What?

TAMARA: That book—those poems—it *is* a coincidence? Or—

LEON: What's a coincidence? I don't get it.

TAMARA: Oh, I have—I have some—in my mind, I mean—certain associations with—with . . . poems, poetry . . . Irish poetry. There was this . . . I mean, I knew . . . someone who . . . set some Irish poems, including some of Yeats's, to music. (*Pause*) A composer, a musician. Not wildly successful.

LEON: Who is it?

TAMARA: No. Not wildly successful. (*Smiles*) *That* never discouraged him.

LEON: Well—most composers, like most poets, artists, actors— aren't very successful. In worldly terms.

TAMARA: I s'pose you're in one of those categories yourself, Leon, huh? (*Assessing him, a bit cruelly, yet teasing*): Maybe—actor?

(LEON *laughs, shrugs.*)

TAMARA: Intermittently employed actor?

LEON: That's a magnanimous way of phrasing it.

TAMARA: And what else do you do? I mean, for a living? (*Slightly sneering*) Work in a secondhand bookstore? No—wait tables?

LEON (*a hurt smile*): I've done both. (*Pause*) And more.

TAMARA (*pursuing this*): Something "real"—like factory work? Meat packing? (*As* LEON *sits stiffly*) And you're from—Ohio?

LEON (*not willing to be led*): You're from—suburban Connecticut?

TAMARA (*shrugging, reacting as if, yes, he has guessed correctly, quick to change subject*): So—you're waiting for fate. To single you out. (*Pause*) No, I mean destiny, don't I? "Destiny" is the preferred term.

LEON (*annoyed at her condescension*): Actually, I'm fairly happy as I am—content, I mean. Things aren't perfect in my life, but—so what? Fate, destiny—those are just words.

TAMARA: Aha! You're not in love, then.

LEON (*laughing*): No, I'm not.

TAMARA: Not at the present time, anyway.

LEON: Not at the present time.

TAMARA (*shrewdly*): And last time you were, *you* walked away.

LEON (*hesitating*): I—wouldn't say that.

TAMARA: Sure you would—c'mon, boast a little—why sure, you're one of the blissful unattached.

LEON: And what about you?

TAMARA (*ironically*): Oh, I'm attached. In ways visible and invisible, attached. (*As if tasting the word, which she finds both bitter and pleasurable*) Attached.

LEON: Meaning?

TAMARA: Meaning—attached.

LEON: Married?

(TAMARA *shrugs, negatively. She dislikes being interrogated.*)

LEON: Do you live around here?

TAMARA (*gesturing vaguely*): Oh—probably. (*Pause*) One of the Yeats poems my friend set to music, it was a "Crazy Jane" poem—the refrain was "All things remain in God."

LEON: That'd be great set to music!

TAMARA: Another was—"Crazy Jane and the Bishop"—I think.

LEON (*half singing, has memorized lines*):

A woman can be proud and stiff
When on love intent;
But Love has pitched his mansion in
The place of excrement;
For nothing can be sole or whole
That has not been—

TAMARA (*quickly, to obliterate and appropriate his words*): "Has not been *rent*." (*Pause*) You have a strong voice.

LEON (*shy about being complimented, changes subject quickly*): You can tell it's great poetry when it can't be changed—I mean paraphrased, in words—into anything other than what it *is*.

TAMARA (*nodding, fatalistically*): I knew. I knew you could sing.

LEON: What? That wasn't singing.

TAMARA: But you have a trained voice—I mean, I *knew*. (*Uneasy, shivering, laughing*) I shouldn't have come over to this side, this side of the—Jesus, I didn't know where, where the hell—I mean, I didn't *mean* to . . . I was . . . drawn.

LEON: Drawn? How?

TAMARA (*carelessly*): By you—obviously.

LEON: That's flattering, but . . . not very likely.

TAMARA (*sharply*): I don't mean to be flattering. I don't flatter men. (*Pause*) Or anyone.

LEON (*deciding to be amused by her rudeness*): Hell, I'm sure you don't.

TAMARA: Where—do *you* live? Close by here?

LEON (*mimicking* TAMARA's *airy gesture*): Probably not. Can't afford it.

TAMARA: Yes, but where do you live?

LEON (*coolly*): A building. An apartment. You know—ceiling, walls, floor. Stairs.

TAMARA: Not an elevator. Stairs. (*Slyly*) No doorman?

LEON: Stairs.

TAMARA (*flirtatiously, accusingly*): You *do* exude happiness, I can tell. Self-sufficiency. Because you're not—in love. Or (*laughs*) in *hate*.

LEON (*annoyed*): You think you know me? You can read me, that glibly?

TAMARA (*rebuffed, meaning to be "sincere"*): You look as if . . . you carry your happiness inside you, like—like one of those—oh, what is it? some kind of a mechanism—some exquisite little bones, in the middle ear, for balance. You don't look as if your happiness depends upon other people.

LEON (*shrugs, self-conscious, a bit flattered*): Well—I try not to blame other people for my problems.

TAMARA: For happiness either?

LEON: That's different.

TAMARA: In what way different? Either you're self-sufficient or you're not.

LEON: I don't buy that. We all enhance one another's lives—don't we? Enhance one another's happiness? Without thinking about it? Without theory? (*Leafs through book, locates poem, reads lines*) "Young we loved one another and were ignorant."

TAMARA: "Young we loved one another and were ignorant." (*Pause*) "Young . . . we . . . loved . . . one . . . another . . . and were . . . ignorant." (*Pause*) People who don't know any better assume that actors and models are alike—their temperaments, I mean—and superficially that's true: we inhabit *otherness*. But there's a crucial distinction.

LEON: Yeah?

TAMARA: Actors have to *think*, and they have to be aware of each other—every moment! every second! Models are (*a languorous gesture*) solitary, mute. Bone structures to hang cloth on. They stand, they wait. They wait, they stand. (*Striking her flat belly with a fist, surprisingly hard*) Salt-free diet to avoid liquid bloat. (*Shudders*) Just—*there.*

LEON: So you're a fashion model?

TAMARA: Right now, no.

LEON: But you *are* a model?

TAMARA: Right now I'm—nothing.

LEON: I think of models—female, male—as objects of—desire. But *impersonal* desire. (*Makes a face*) Which must be weird.

TAMARA: Who said that?

LEON: Said what?

TAMARA: I am not a—a—an—object.

LEON: Yeah? You don't think so?

TAMARA (*as if frightened*): You—don't know me. (*Pause*) Do you know me? (*Half pleading*) You said—you didn't.

LEON: Tamara.

TAMARA: How do you know my name?!

LEON: You told me.

TAMARA (*as if trying to remember*): I . . . told you.

LEON: Tamara Hudson. Phony Tamara.

TAMARA (*laughs thinly*): Oh, yes—sure I did. (*Rubs eyes vigorously, as if to wake herself up*) Actually, it *is* Tamara. The pretensions began at birth, but they weren't mine—they were my mother's.

LEON (*just slightly closer to her*): What did you mean, Tamara, you were "drawn" to me?

TAMARA (*quickly*): I didn't say that.

LEON: You didn't?

TAMARA: I didn't. Not out loud. Did I? Oh, Jesus. (*Pause, sudden anger*) You're putting words in my mouth, trying to coerce me. I—

LEON: Look, you said—

TAMARA: —won't be coerced by you, or anyone.

LEON: Hey, I—

TAMARA: *I won't be coerced.* (*Gets to feet, abruptly*) This part of the park—I've been warned it's—it can be—dangerous. If you're alone. If you don't know the—escape routes.

LEON (*laughing*): It's perfectly safe here.

TAMARA: During the day.

LEON: Yes, but it *is* day.

TAMARA (*squinting up at the sun, which hurts her eyes.*): God! *Is* it! I need my sunglasses. (*Vague, irritable*) I thought—the clock said seven o'clock—seemed to have thought it was—uh—evening— *night.* Somehow, things got reversed.

LEON: You *are* all right?

TAMARA (*excited, slapping at pockets*): My sunglasses . . . my purse! (*Peers beneath bench, etc.*) Oh, God, my *purse!*

LEON: You weren't carrying any purse when you—

TAMARA (*almost frantic*): It *can't* be lost! I just had it! Somebody took it! Did I—lay it down?

LEON: You weren't carrying any purse, Tamara, really, when you came here. You were just—walking.

TAMARA (*describes a sizable object with her hands*): It's this big! It weighs twenty pounds! It's alligator hide, it's worth six hundred dollars, but it—it—*looks* phony, like fake fur—I mean, real fur disguised as fake, to throw off the animal-rights people. (*Laughs*) Actually I'm one of those myself. (*Pause*) Actually it was a gift. It wasn't my fault. (*Pause*) *I* didn't kill the alligator!

(LEON *makes a perfunctory show of looking for purse, then:*)

LEON: I didn't see it, Tamara. Really.

TAMARA: My emergency kit's in it—makeup. Emergency makeup. Plus Diet Coke, diet chocolate-date bar, diet chocolate laxatives—

LEON (*with a placating gesture*): I'll help you look for it, okay? Back in the direction you came from—

TAMARA (*suddenly resigned, even bored with the subject*): What good would that do!

LEON: Maybe you laid it down somewhere.

TAMARA: It would only be stolen by now. Serves me right. (*Pause*) Anyway, there wasn't any "direction" I came from—I came from all directions at once. Walked in circles. (*Slapping pockets again, takes out peanut package, gives a little scream*) Fuck this! (*Throws package down, with childish rage*) Ah! Here. I'm okay. (*She has found keys in her pocket.*)

LEON: Keys to your apartment?

TAMARA: I can deal with this. I'm okay. Nothing's lost. (*Suddenly dizzy, she slumps onto the bench, in the spot where* LEON *had been sitting.*)

LEON (*anxious*): What's wrong?

TAMARA (*weakly fending him off*): I'm—okay.

LEON: You look kind of—pale.

TAMARA: I'm fine, I'm fine—just let me be, Lee—Leroy?—*Leon*— DON'T HOVER OVER ME.

LEON: I—

TAMARA (*disconnectedly*): It's blood sugar. The level. When it goes down, you get—strange. Not yourself. Like adrenaline—the adrenaline rush. But in reverse. (*Shivers*)

LEON: Are you faint?

TAMARA (*rapidly, demonstrating "control"*): It's all chemistry. Blood chemistry. Brain chemistry. I mean, it isn't *spiritual*. Or moral. (*Half pleading*) *It isn't our fault we can't be stronger.*

LEON: How can I—help you?

TAMARA: DON'T HOVER OVER ME, PLEASE! Sit down. (*She pulls him down beside her.*)

LEON: I bet you're hungry—light-headed. Is that it?

TAMARA: I said I was all right.

LEON: When did you eat last?

TAMARA: I CAN'T STAND TO BE TOUCHED AND I CAN'T STAND TO BE HOVERED OVER, GOD DAMN IT.

LEON (*moving away*): Nobody's touching you—hovering over you—

TAMARA: What if I scream, what if—what if I scream *scream* SCREAM—what then, yes, what then—*you'd* get out of here fast, wouldn't you!

(*A pause, a beat or two.* LEON *stiffens, waiting for* TAMARA *to scream, but does not flee: each sits at one end of the bench as if poised, balanced.*)

LEON: I'd like to buy you—how's about some orange juice? An apple? Danish pastry?

TAMARA (*shakes head vehemently, like a spoiled child*): No thank you. (*Expression of distaste*)

LEON: Breakfast? Lunch?

TAMARA: *No thank you.*

LEON (*critically*): You're too thin—that's your problem. Twenty pounds underweight, I bet.

TAMARA (*childish lashing-out*): *You're* too thin.

LEON: Look, I'm only trying to help.

TAMARA (*almost inarticulate, upset*): A skeleton, practically. *You!*

LEON: What?

TAMARA: Don't look at *me!*

LEON: Who's a skeleton? (*Looks down at himself, baffled, partly in dread*) Is that what you said?

TAMARA: It's goddamned rude to make—personal comments. Leave my body alone!

LEON (*laughing*): Who's rude? *You* must be about the goddamnedest rudest woman I've met in memory.

TAMARA: You don't know me! Not the first thing about me.

LEON: Yeah, well I know the genre, sweetheart.

TAMARA: The what?

LEON: Genre—type.

TAMARA (*offended*): I know what "genre" *means*—I just didn't *hear* you.

LEON (*half teasing, half cruel; fascinated by her*): The type that, since she's beautiful, doesn't give a damn about other people, because there's an endless supply of them to admire her—or so she thinks.

TAMARA (*flaring up*): I'm not—like that.

LEON: The type that, because she's beautiful, lives her life being *seen*, so loses her ability to *see*. (*Cruelly*) Even with her contact lenses she's blind.

TAMARA (*stung*): No! I see lots of things. Details. Human things. (*Naively half pleading*) Didn't I see—you?

LEON (*persisting*): The type that, since she's beautiful, is an ideal product of a consumer culture—for sale.

TAMARA: Fuck you! I'm not for sale.

LEON (*relenting*): Oh, hell—we're all for sale, more or less. Some of us do better than others, that's all.

TAMARA: You're wrong about me, Leo—Leon—is it Leon? (*As he grins at her ironically*) You have no right saying such things.

LEON (*as if casually*): Why did you say I was a—skeleton? (*As* TAMARA *looks away*) That *is* what you said, isn't it?

TAMARA: No.

LEON: It sure as hell sounded that way.

TAMARA (*changing subject*): When I was twelve, thirteen years old I was homely—I mean *ugly*. That's my deepest self. (*Pause*) It was better then, I s'pose—people left me alone. Their eyes didn't snag on me.

(LEON *laughs as if what she says is preposterous.*)

TAMARA: Why are you—mocking me?

LEON: I'm not mocking you, Tamara. I'm not even doubting you. Being beautiful, you're inevitably an exhibitionist. Right?

TAMARA: Wrong!

LEON: You probably can't even go to the bathroom without imagining an audience.

TAMARA: What a—a disgusting, juvenile thing to—

LEON: Isn't it true?

TAMARA (*hotly*): Imagining an audience and wanting an audience are two different things.

LEON: Since you arrived here, even talking to me, right now, you seem to be—

TAMARA: Yes? What?

LEON: —like you're in two places at once. Talking to me but somehow not to *me*. (*Grinning*) I bet you don't even remember my name.

TAMARA: Leon. From O-hi-o.

LEON: My last name?

TAMARA (*evasively*): I'm no good at names. I—

LEON: C'mon, what's my last name? (*Snaps fingers under her nose*)

TAMARA: You really hate me, don't you? I—I'd thought—I'd thought m-maybe—you—might—

LEON (*a bit guilty*): What?

TAMARA: Be my friend. Help me.

(*Silence. A beat or two.* TAMARA *looks at* LEON *with a strange half-cringing yearning;* LEON *looks at* TAMARA *with intense curiosity, aroused interest. There has been, and continues to be, an increasing urgency in his manner. He is both sexually and emotionally intrigued by her, though yet wary.*)

TAMARA: I guess I should leave. (*Pause, rubs eyes*) Well. It's your right, whatever you want to feel.

LEON: What's my right?

TAMARA: Any kind of—hatred, loathing—you want to feel. For me.

LEON: Oh—c'mon. You're inventing it.

TAMARA: It has happened before.

LEON: What has happened before?

TAMARA: *This.* (*Pause; shakes head*) Not you—*this.*

LEON: "This"? I don't get it.

TAMARA: But not in this park. No, not *here.* (*Looking around, squinting*) Do you come here often? By yourself? To sit, to read? Is this a secret place of yours?

LEON: I come when I'm free. Yeah, it's a, sort of a—yeah, like a kid might have—a secret place.

TAMARA: I have my secret places too.

LEON: Such as?

TAMARA: In a church somewhere, an empty church. Say I'm in some city I don't know, some neighborhood, I'm walking and I see a church and I go inside—just sit there in the dark—it doesn't work if anyone else is around. (*Pause*) Once I was with this guy, we were in Budapest, I did that, I slipped away into this—this incredible gold-gilt baroque church—he didn't know what had happened to me. It was like—(*she giggles*)—I was catatonic.

LEON: Then what?

TAMARA: Then what what?

LEON: This guy—did he find you?

TAMARA (*indifferently*): I don't remember. (*Pause, naively*) I'm wondering whether I'd ever have come here, this "secret place" of yours, if you hadn't been here.

LEON (*uneasy*): Look, maybe I should walk you home? Your eyes look—like you might be feverish.

TAMARA: Whether, you know, I'd have been—drawn.

LEON (*laughing, embarrassed*): You're lucky it *is* me, not somebody else. The kinds of creeps around here— (*Pause, thinks better of this*) I mean, some guys, they might misunderstand. The kind of things you've been saying.

TAMARA (*as if this is self-evident*): But I wouldn't be here except for *you.*

LEON (*runs hand through hair, perplexed, keyed up*): That's all very flattering, Tamara, but—what the hell does it *mean?*

TAMARA: People do exert magnetic pulls on one another, it's a fact. Like the moon's gravitational pull on us—it's faint, but it's there.

LEON (*peering at her*): Your eyes—they're all pupil—dilated. Are you ill? On some drug?

TAMARA: Morning insomnia—that's when you wake at four in the morning and you can't get back to sleep no matter how desperately you try how you pray for sleep no matter if you haven't slept more than four or five hours in two days so you give up and get dressed and start the day and "the day" from the perspective of four A.M. is a sobering sight I mean *sobering* I mean the day is a SOBERING SON OF A BITCH I'm telling you.

LEON: You're exhausted, spaced out—okay, let me take you home.

TAMARA (*shrinking from him, though he has not touched her*): Not *there.* I'm *here* to get away from *there.*

LEON: Is—someone there? You're afraid of someone? (*Pause*) You could come to my place, and sleep. I'm serious.

TAMARA (*naively, yearningly*): You *are* my friend—I knew it. Would you—hold me? I'm so cold! (*Shivering*)

LEON: What?

TAMARA: Just for a minute? Lee—*Leon.*

LEON (*awkward, embarrassed*): Hold you?

TAMARA: I'm so cold!

(LEON *hesitates, clearly not knowing how to respond.*)

TAMARA: Or—then—will you—sing? Sing for me? (*Suddenly urgent*) Please?

LEON (*incredulous*): *Sing?*

TAMARA: You did before, almost. One of these poems . . . (*The book of Yeats's poems has fallen to the ground; she picks it up and hurriedly leafs through it.*)

LEON: Now—you want me to *sing?*

TAMARA (*excitedly, reading from book, trying to get him to look on*): This one—"All things remain in God." Oh, please!

LEON: Hey, come on. You're kidding me. (*He waves her away.*)

TAMARA (*disappointed, urgent*): But you have a good voice, a trained voice, don't you!

LEON (*embarrassed*): Even if I wanted to sing one of these poems, how could I? There's no music, just words.

TAMARA (*as if momentarily confused*): Oh . . . yes. (*Pause*) Will you sing—"Greensleeves," then?

LEON: "Greensleeves"?

TAMARA: You must know it, don't you?

LEON (*appealing to an invisible audience, laughing*): She wants me to sing "Greensleeves"!

TAMARA: Oh, please. For me.

LEON (*stalling*): What makes you think I *can* sing?

TAMARA: *Please.*

LEON: But—why?

TAMARA (*intense, urgent*): You have a voice for singing—you love to sing.

LEON: Uh—how do you know that?

TAMARA: I know.

(LEON *seems reluctant, yet also rather flattered and excited.* TAMARA *is gazing at him, sitting ramrod-straight, waiting.*)

LEON: Oh, Christ—why not. (*He turns abruptly serious and begins singing for her. He is slightly uncertain at first, then more assured, "masculine."*)

Greensleeves was all my joy,
Greensleeves was my delight,
Greensleeves was my heart of gold,
And who but my Lady Greensleeves?

Alas, my love, ye do me wrong
To cast me off discourteously,
And I have loved you so long,
Delighting in your company.
Greensleeves was all my joy,
Greensleeves was my delight,
Greensleeves was my heart of gold,
And who but my Lady Greensleeves?

(*He skips to the final stanza of this lengthy Renaissance love song*)

Greensleeves, now farewell, adieu!
God I pray to prosper thee,
For I am still thy lover true;
come once again and love me—

(TAMARA *begins to cry, helplessly.* LEON *breaks off his song.*)

LEON: What's wrong?

TAMARA: . . . so beautiful. Oh, my God.

(TAMARA *gets to her feet, paces about distractedly, in her private grief.* LEON *is almost forgotten: looking on, wanting to give comfort, but excluded.*)

TAMARA (*passionate, self-loathing*): I wanted to hold him—to be with him—tell him I loved him—I don't know if it was true, but he would have known I wanted it to be true, and maybe if I'd held him—let him hold me—it would have been true. (*Pause*) But I didn't—of course I didn't—we weren't lovers, "just friends," he had so many friends he didn't need me, why would he miss me? that's what I told myself. (*Crying, beating fists softly together*) They said he was asking about me, but I didn't ask about him—he got sicker and sicker and I avoided them all if I could—I stopped thinking about him, about it—I'm good at that. I loved him, but I—I stopped thinking about him—it's like erasing a blackboard, just—blank—nothing—and afterward they said—they weren't vindictive or even ironic, that astonishes me—they said he understood, he "respected my fear," they said, but I—I *did* go to the funeral (*laughs, disgusted*)—I even met his family. The ones who came.

LEON (*guardedly*): You're talking about . . . who?

(TAMARA, *weeping, is too upset to speak.*)

LEON (*as if in dread*): Someone who died of . . . AIDS?

(TAMARA *nods, mutely.*)

LEON: *I* resemble *him*—is that it?

(TAMARA *nods.*)

LEON (*hurt, deflated*): Which is why you . . .

TAMARA (*breathless*): The first time I heard Alan sing, it was that song—"Greensleeves." The first time I met him. At a recital of Renaissance music . . .

LEON (*trying to absorb hurt*): Okay. I get it.

TAMARA: Alan was such a—a genuinely good man. . . . I know it sounds . . . inadequate . . . it can't mean much to a—a stranger . . . but he . . . *was* exceptional . . . he didn't deserve to die so young, so . . . horribly. He had so much to offer. (*Pause*) I failed him. I know it's too late, but . . .

LEON (*enunciating the terms of his own hurt, deflation of ego*): A friend of yours, a gay friend—died. *I* look like *him.* (*Pause*)

TAMARA (*earnest, not noticing* LEON's *emotion*): Actually . . . probably . . . not . . . not that closely, if . . . (*in a rush of words*) if the two of you were side by side.

LEON (*with growing contempt, fury*): You think that's unique—a good man has died, died "horribly"? You think *you're* unique, your emotion, your grief?

TAMARA: When I saw you—

LEON (*outburst*): *You never saw* ME.

(*A pause.* LEON's *hurt should be evident to* TAMARA *by now, but she is blinded by her own emotion.*)

LEON (*low, contemptuous words*): Nobody's unique—don't think it, don't you dare, least of all *you.* Your grief that's too late, your guilt that's on display, your—fucking arrogance . . .

TAMARA (*stricken, apologetic*): When I saw you here, I—I felt my heart—oh, it was real! (*Approaching him, in open appeal*) I know it's—absurd. It's futile. But I thought if, if *he* would hold me, just for a minute—oh, God, let me hold him—

LEON (*drawing away*): You want *me* to hold you, huh! Like you wouldn't do with your friend, huh!—because you were afraid of being *contaminated*. Now it's too late, and now it doesn't matter a shit, here you are! (*Pause*) Well, you don't know me, but I sure know *you*.

TAMARA: Please? I'm willing to beg.

(LEON *steps back, aside. It is within his power to be generous to this young woman or to punish her as perhaps she deserves to be punished.*

TAMARA *remains standing, hands slightly raised, vulnerable, supplicant.*)

LEON (*looking up with a strange, radiant-cruel smile*): Okay, Tamara. C'mere. (*Opens his arms for an embrace*) You want a hug, I'll give you a hug. (*Subtly taunting*) But what if I, too . . . ?

TAMARA (*uncomprehending*): You? Too?

LEON: I, too. Leon. Collier.

TAMARA: You—

LEON: I'm just inquiring, in theory. What if . . . ?

(TAMARA *stares at him; blinks; looks at ground; is clearly shocked, frightened.*)

LEON (*arms open wide*): Just in theory, Tamara. Dear friend. Just theory. (*Smiles*)

(TAMARA *hesitates for a beat or two, then goes to him, slips into his embrace, sits beside him on the bench. A passionate, desperate embrace, into which they freeze. Neither can see the other's face—the side of* TAMARA's *head is pressed against* LEON's *chest—but each face, visible to the audience, shows tension, anguish, grief.*)

Lights dim slowly. They remain unmoving.

Lights out.

(THE END)

The Key

CHARACTERS

MELISSA: late forties
EDWIN: late forties or early fifties
WAITER: West Indian black, mid-twenties

Lights up. Loud, gay taped music: a bright, synthetic, soulless rendition of a popular calypso song.

MELISSA *is seated alone on the terrace, at a table with a bright-striped umbrella; suggestions of tropical flowers in background. She is reading a paperback book* but nodding and tapping her foot in time with the calypso beat. She is an attractive, fastidiously groomed woman past the bloom of her beauty; with streaked hair, artful makeup, polished finger- and toenails. She wears a stylish straw sun hat and a white dress cut low to reveal shoulders and back; summer costume jewelry, including large dangling earrings; casual yet expensive shoes. As she reads her book she sips nervously from a tall lime-green tropical drink. Her manner is restless and self-conscious, but she is determined to be, or to appear to be, fully absorbed in her book.*

A sound of voices offstage—greetings, laughter, raucous if unintelligible words. The WAITER *appears, stage left, tray and white towel over his arm, as if summoned by a party just entering the terrace offstage right; he is going to bypass* MELISSA *without noticing her.*

---

* The book is Pascal's *Pensées*—a college book of Melissa's she is trying to "rediscover."

177

He is dark-skinned, handsome, with a small moustache, sideburns, one gleaming gold tooth, and snug-fitting jacket and trousers; his manner verges on insolence even as it is a model of professional servility. He glides so quietly past MELISSA *that she glances up, startled.*

MELISSA (*beringed hand to throat*): Oh!

WAITER (*though he would prefer to greet the new customers, he is excessively polite; in richly accented English*): Ma'am?

MELISSA: I didn't hear you there . . . (*Fussing with one of her earrings*) Could you—bring me another of these? "Voodoo Bombshell." (*Laughs, mildly embarrassed*) It's quite—delicious.

WAITER (*token bow, seductive smile*): Yes, ma'am!

MELISSA: Thank you. (*As* WAITER *turns, continues on his way*) This view of the water is so— (*seeing* WAITER *has left the table, she finishes weakly*) . . . beautiful. Isn't it.

(WAITER *exits stage right.* MELISSA *looks after him, a pained expression on her face.*
After a beat, MELISSA *speaks, not to the audience so much as to herself.*)

MELISSA (*throaty, bemused voice*): I shouldn't be here—I shouldn't be here—I shouldn't be here. "Caribbean holiday." (*Pause. Fumbles in oversized straw purse for sunglasses, which she puts on: glamorous white-framed glasses with very dark lenses.*) A woman alone, a Caucasian woman alone on the "unspoiled" island of Saint Kitts, I shouldn't be here . . . I *should* be here—this is a necessary interlude in my marriage, my marriage of twenty-six years—I am an adult and my husband is an adult, two consenting adults— (*speaking more rapidly, half angrily*)—and it's bitterly cold back in Minneapolis, I am suffocating of boredom back in Minneapolis, I deserve happiness no less than anyone else!—any of *you*! (*Gestures stage right at the invisible party on the terrace. A pause; removes sunglasses.*) What time is it? Is this the same day I left Minneapolis? Where is he? *Is* there a he? If I'm a *she* there must be a *he*, but where *is* he? What if there is no one—what if no one arrives—*a secret adventure yet what if no one arrives?* If nothing happens . . . ?

(MELISSA *drains her glass, then freezes, sitting very straight, her expression one of sudden grief or terror, seemingly inappropriate to the situation. The vulgar calypso music ends abruptly, in the midst of a phrase. The muffled laughter and voices also fade.*

A pause. EDWIN *appears, stage right. He is a ruddy, honest-faced man, big-bodied, perhaps stocky; in new, designer resort-ware in which he feels a bit uncomfortable; eyes hidden by rakish metallic-rimmed aviator sunglasses. His bare legs are conspicuously pale. He stares at* MELISSA. *His manner will be both excited and shrinking, eager and timid. He is not a naturally graceful man and gives the impression of mistrusting his body.*)

EDWIN (*biting a thumbnail, musing aloud*): There—there she is! She's—young!—beautiful!—she *is!* Seems to be alone—waiting— is she waiting?—for who?—whom?—maybe me? Her name unknown—*my* name unknown—strangers to each other— mysteries—not expected to tell the truth, am I? (*Chuckles nervously*) "Truth"—what's "truth"—melts like ice—tropical sun— Caribbean holiday— (*Staring at* MELISSA, *running fingers rapidly through hair*) What if there is a husband—to whom she is attached? (*Pause*) Ah! A naked *back.*

(MELISSA's *freeze ends.* EDWIN *approaches* MELISSA, *who comes to life; taped music resumes in the midst of a phrase.*)

MELISSA (*reading, or seeming to read, her book; vaguely signaling to* EDWIN *as if he were the waiter*): Thank you—just set it down —and take this away. (*Glancing up at* EDWIN, *eyes wide*) Oh! Sorry! I didn't see you there.

EDWIN (*a bit clumsy, banging into a chair*): Oh—it happens all the time! I mean (*Pause, awkward joking*) . . . uh, shall I—get you another drink?

MELISSA (*embarrassed, agitated*): I mean, I saw you—I felt a presence. But I didn't see *you.* (*Lowers her voice*) I thought it was the—boy.

EDWIN (*smiling broadly*): Oh, they're never around when you want them, I've noticed. "Natives"—the world over! When you *don't* want them, they hover over you like—like—(*a gesture as if waving off flies, not wanting to say this but backed into a corner*)—uh, like flies. (*Pause*) But let me get you another of these—whatsit—

I was just going into the bar myself. (*Lifting her glass, sniffing*) Smells like lime, vodka . . .

MELISSA: It's delicious, I recommend it—a Voodoo Bombshell.

EDWIN: Voodoo Bombshell. Great.

MELISSA (*hand to mouth, aghast*): Did I say "boy" just now? I didn't mean to—I meant to say "man." I didn't mean to say "boy."

EDWIN: Eh?

MELISSA: The waiter—I didn't mean to refer to him as a—

EDWIN (*a bit gruffly, dismissively*): Oh, I'm sure they don't mind what we call them—the natives. As long as, y'know, we pay for the privilege. (*Cupping hand to mouth, leaning toward* MELISSA, *one white tourist to another*) And we sure do pay, don't we?

MELISSA (*intense*): Yes, but I didn't *mean* to say "boy." It just slipped out! It's racist, and condescending, and truly I know better. Why, my daughter would— (*Pauses, thinks better of this*), Why, I *marched* in—all kinds of—of civil rights rallies, demonstrations, back in the—(*again, pause, not wanting to date herself*)—a while back.

EDWIN: Is that so? *I* marched too. Once, in Washington. Maybe we were there at the same time? Back in . . . (*as if counting*) —uh— a while back.

MELISSA: I think it must be the tropical sun, this lovely, lovely sun —it's almost too much, isn't it, coming in the midst of, well, of winter in our natural habitat—the sun is so *close*, it does something to my head—my thinking processes.

EDWIN (*moving off, stage right, glass in hand*): Oh, I wouldn't worry—that's what we're here for!

(EDWIN *exits.* MELISSA *hurriedly checks her appearance in a gold compact mirror; dabs her face with a powder puff; considers her reflection critically.*)

MELISSA: It *might* be worth it—a face-lift. Someday! But then there's the—blood, bruising—and what if it goes wrong? (*Pause*) He's attractive, isn't he! He *is* attractive. And he *is* the right age. (*To mirrored reflection*) Let the evening develop naturally—if it develops at all. *Don't force.*

(MELISSA *puts her sunglasses back on.*

EDWIN *reappears, eager, smiling like a boyish suitor. He carries two Voodoo Bombshells.*)

EDWIN: May I? Are you—?

MELISSA: You *may*, I *am*—alone.

(EDWIN *sits at the table, a bit bumbling, clumsy, yet not excessively so. There is something plaintive in his eagerness to which* MELISSA *responds with, just very subtly, an air of pity, impatience.*)

EDWIN: Well! (*Raising glass*) Here's to—

MELISSA (*raising glass*): Yes! Well—! (*Sudden attack of giggles*)

EDWIN (*grinning at her, begins to laugh too*): Welllll! Here we are
— Saint Kitts!

(*They drink;* EDWIN *coughs;* MELISSA *chokes a little.*)

EDWIN (*removing sunglasses, wiping eyes*): That *is*—potent stuff. Oh
my, yes.

MELISSA: Potent—oh, yes! (*Fit of giggling, coughing*)

EDWIN (*laughing, red-faced, as if almost out of control*): Hey, I
didn't—mean—

(*They laugh helplessly for a beat or two, until the point at which their laughter comes to seem a bit odd.*)

WAITER *appears stage right: seductive walk, well-practiced smile.*)

WAITER: Ma'am? Sir? Anything you wish?

(EDWIN *and* MELISSA *call out simultaneously, but* EDWIN *drowns* MELISSA *out.*)

MELISSA: No, thank you—we're just *fine*!

EDWIN: Nah, we're okay—everything's okay.

(WAITER *exits.*)

EDWIN (*just thinking of it*): Except—uh—maybe some nuts? Those
macadonia nuts—you have them in little bowls—?

MELISSA (*still giggling, weakly*): Macadamia nuts.

EDWIN (*craning his neck after the* WAITER, *who is out of earshot*): Those nuts? In the bowls? (*Giving up*) Deaf when it suits them.

MELISSA (*wiping eyes with napkin*): Macadamia nuts.

EDWIN: Eh?

MELISSA: You said "macadonia."

EDWIN: Maca *what*?

MELISSA: Anyway—we don't need them.

EDWIN: Well—we're sure as hell paying for them.

MELISSA (*raising her glass again*): Here's to—happiness!

EDWIN (*following suit*): "Caribbean holiday"!

MELISSA: No snow, no ice, no wind, no—*that*!

EDWIN: You said it—*that*! (*Leaning toward* MELISSA) I guess I didn't get your—name?

MELISSA (*a just perceptible pause*): Angelina.

EDWIN: Angelina—that's pretty!

MELISSA: Sometimes called Bunny. (*Giggles*)

EDWIN: Bunny! *That's*—(*not knowing what it is*)—uh, that's—well, that's *something*, eh!

MELISSA: And your name?

EDWIN: Oh I'm—(*blinking*)—Edwin.

MELISSA (*as if a bit disappointed*): Oh—Edwin.

EDWIN (*apologetically*): I guess it isn't a—a very imaginative name. I guess it isn't a—*romantic* name.

MELISSA: It's a fine, solid name. Ed-win. *Ed-win*. (*Pause*) A mature name.

EDWIN (*inspired*): Sometimes called Tickle.

MELISSA: What?

EDWIN: Tickle.

MELISSA: Tickle?

EDWIN (*as if to tickle her*): You asked for it!

MELISSA (*lurching away, startled*): Oh—I—I—

EDWIN (*suddenly sober, wiping mouth with napkin*): Jeez, I'm *sorry*. (*Pause, embarrassment on both sides*) Just a—a joke. Guess it was a . . . pretty poor one.

MELISSA (*stiff; glancing around to see if they are being observed*): Oh, I—well.

EDWIN: Game I used to play with my—my daughter, son, when they were—uh—little.

MELISSA: I—see.

(*A pause. Calypso music quite loud. Offstage laughter.*)

EDWIN (*awkwardly*): This is a—a lively place, eh? You—came here alone?

MELISSA: Yes, I came here alone. And you?

EDWIN: Yes, I— Alone.

MELISSA (*sipping drink*): It's lovely here—the view. The turquoise sea.

(*Both gaze out to sea, into the audience, staring, shading their eyes.*)

EDWIN: The Gulf of Mexico . . .

MELISSA: Actually it's the Caribbean.

EDWIN: Oh, I know *that*! But isn't it the Gulf of Mexico too?

MELISSA: Due south of us, where we're sitting, is Venezuela.

EDWIN: Guess I should study the tourist maps—I sure have a lot of them. (*Sips drink*) I guess I asked you, Angelina—have you ever been here before?

MELISSA (*dreamily, as if making the effort*): Here? Oh, no. (*Pause*) Did you ask me?

EDWIN: I—thought I did. (*Glancing at her covertly*) You are a—uh—a very—uh—very attractive woman—uh—to be—in a place like this—alone.

MELISSA (*frowning, self-conscious*): Well—I'm—I try to be—independent.

EDWIN: Oh, you look like an independent woman! You surely do!

MELISSA: I think I may be beginning a phase of my life, a new and distinct phase of my life, like—like a—a crescent moon that's going to become a full moon, a phase where I will be—become—ever more—and more—independent. (*A bit breathless, removes sunglasses and lays them on the table*) Yes, I think I am! (*Looks at him boldly, blinking*)

EDWIN: That's—fascinating. (*Removes his sunglasses, sets them down, knocking them against* MELISSA's *so that both pairs of glasses topple to the floor*) Oh—shit! Sorry! (EDWIN *picks the glasses up, grunting.*) Jeez, that was clumsy of me! Is this cracked? (*Examines* MELISSA's *sunglasses, as she reaches to take them from him*) A hairline crack—

MELISSA: Oh, that's quite all right—

EDWIN: I'll pay for it—pay for new lenses.

MELISSA (*retrieving the glasses and dropping them into her purse; almost inaudible*): Damn clumsy fool.

EDWIN (*startled*): What?

MELISSA (*as if not knowing she'd spoken, making an effort to smile, even to be flirtatious*): Oh, I said, Edwin, it's quite all right—*perfectly* all right. They were old glasses anyway. Last year's.

EDWIN: Let me replace them—will you?

MELISSA: That isn't necessary.

EDWIN: Oh, but it is!

MELISSA: It was just an accident, after all.

EDWIN: It *was*, but, like—(*at a loss how to speak*)—like *mal*-practice—you can get sued for accidents!

MELISSA (*laughing, a trifle impatient*): Well—nobody's going to sue you over a trifle.

EDWIN (*more soberly*): Yes hell, I *have* been sued over a trifle. More than once. (*Sips drink, with feeling*)

(*A pause. Outburst of laughter stage right, toward which* MELISSA *and* EDWIN *glance, as if hopefully.*)

EDWIN: *They* look like they've been bar-hopping all over the island.

MELISSA: I hope they're not guests of this hotel.

EDWIN (*as if casually*): Are you a guest of—this hotel?

MELISSA (*lowering eyes*): I—uh— Actually, I—have one of those little houses—down along there—(*pointing*)—overlooking the beach.

EDWIN (*delighted*): Do you! So do I! So do I! Real nice, aren't they? Cost you an arm and a leg, but, well, that's what we're here for, eh?

MELISSA (*carefully*): I'm here to—enjoy myself.

EDWIN: Great view of the Gulf—!

MELISSA: Especially, I look forward to waking up early tomorrow—hearing the surf. Waking to the surf.

EDWIN: Not *too* early, I hope! (*Laughs awkwardly, coughs*) I mean —it's your—uh—vacation, isn't it?

MELISSA (*stiffly*): I enjoy rising early, when I can.

EDWIN (*hastily*): Oh, I do too, I do too!—when I can.

MELISSA (*dreamily*): To hear the waves of the Caribbean in my sleep, my dreams . . . to sleep with my window open to the tropical moon that's like a—a—luminous, overripe fruit in the sky . . . to see the sun like an eye afire rising on the horizon of the sea . . . (*Passionately*) How I've yearned for that! All my life, without knowing!

EDWIN (*after a seemingly respectful pause, squinting out toward the sea*): Yes—but—uh—which way are we facing? (*As he points seaward*) Sort of south and west, isn't it?

MELISSA: South and *east.*

EDWIN: But, yes—isn't the sun going *down* over there? (*Pointing*)

MELISSA: My windows face east.

EDWIN: Well—I could be wrong.

MELISSA: *My* windows, in the cottage *I* requested, face east.

EDWIN: I s'pose we could be—uh—sort of—turned around, re-versed. (*Pause*) When you cross the Equator, all kinds of weird things happen!

MELISSA (*as if waving away annoying insects, but unconsciously*): We are nowhere near the Equator.

(*The calypso music has increased in volume.*)

EDWIN (*drawing a breath, awkwardly flirtatious*): So—uh—you're Angelina—eh? Or is it—Bunny?

MELISSA: Depends.

EDWIN: Depends on what?

MELISSA: On the context.

EDWIN: Which context?

MELISSA: The human context.

EDWIN: Meaning—?

MELISSA: Who I'm with.

EDWIN: Oh, yes?

MELISSA: And where.

EDWIN: Oh, yes?

MELISSA: And when.

EDWIN: Ohhhhh, uh-huh. (*Distracted by music*) Jeez—that's getting loud.

MELISSA: It *is*—a bit.

EDWIN (*snapping his fingers, tapping a foot, not quite rhythmically*): Tonight, they're s'posed to have a live band, a steel band. For dancing, I wonder?

MELISSA: I don't know. This is my first day.

EDWIN: *My* first day too. (*Smiles*) Actually, I saw you—spotted you —in the airport. Miami.

MELISSA (*embarrassed*): Oh—come on.

EDWIN: I did!

MELISSA: With all those—gorgeous—young women—on every side?

EDWIN: And I hoped—I swear this is true—I hoped you'd be flying on to Saint Kitts. In my heart of hearts, I swear.

MELISSA (*embarrassed, not knowing whether to be flattered or skeptical*): Oh—you'd say that to—anyone!

EDWIN (*almost offended*): Hey—I'm not a liar, I'm a guy who speaks his mind. (*Pause, then rather daringly*) Heart.

(*Music up stridently.* MELISSA *presses hands over ears, winces delicately.*)

MELISSA: Oh!

EDWIN: Maybe I'd better ask them to turn it down.

MELISSA: Yes, please—Edwin—would you?

(EDWIN *remains unmoving, face creased in a frown.*)

MELISSA: Yes—would you?

EDWIN: You think they'd know better! (*Gets to his feet, blustery, irritable*) Excuse me—waiter? Waiter? (*Pause*) Where is everybody? (*No response, as* EDWIN *moves off stage right*) Excuse me —excuse me . . .

(EDWIN *exits.* MELISSA *hurriedly swallows a large mouthful of her drink; fumbles inside her purse again; checks her compact mirror again; shuts the compact with a snap, drops it back into purse; gets restlessly to her feet, paces about, smooths dress over thighs— the dress is a bit wrinkled—and fusses with straps of dress, hair, earrings.*)

MELISSA (*biting at thumbnail*): I shouldn't be here—I shouldn't be here—I *should* be here! (*Derisively*) What're you saving it for, Bunny, back in Twin Cities? Your heirs? (*Retrieves purse, fumbles inside, takes out little gold pill box, shakes out two pills onto palm of hand, swallows them down with another mouthful of her drink*) Ah!—that will help. (*Pause; head back, eyes shut, lifts hair as if feeling the sea breeze*) That *does* help!

(*Music fades abruptly in the midst of a phrase, but does not die out; continuing, almost inaudibly, as a sort of syncopated drone.* EDWIN, *breathing hard, returns. His expression is one of triumph mixed with* rage. *He has brought along a bowl of nuts, which he slams down on the table.*)

EDWIN: That black—! (*As if choking, can't find right words*) Black *faggot! Pimp!* Insolent bastard! As if I can't see! Rolling his eyes! And the prices I'm paying! (*Seeing* MELISSA *on her feet, startled*) Oh—say! You aren't leaving, are you? Angelina?

MELISSA (*humming to herself, swaying, standing as before with her back to* EDWIN, *perhaps a bit drunk*): Leav-ing? Where would Angelina be—leav-ing?

(EDWIN *stares at* MELISSA *with a curious willed lechery, wiping his damp face with a cocktail napkin.*)

EDWIN: Oh, you're a—tall girl—are you! Those high heels—!

MELISSA (*insouciant, coquettish*): Don't care *how* tall I am! Taller than *any of you men* an' don't care! Just feelin' the—delicious— Caribbean—breeze! Just baskin' in the—pagan beauty! (*Snaps fingers clumsily*)

(EDWIN, *staring, snatches up a handful of nuts and chews them rapidly and noisily, without seeming to taste them.*)

MELISSA (*annoyed*): Why's it so—*quiet?* All of a sudden it's like a tomb. (*She tries a few dance steps, shyly, not very coordinated.*)

EDWIN: Uh—you want to dance?

MELISSA (*not having turned to him, facing outward to sea*): Where's the goddam—music!

(EDWIN *comes stealthily up to* MELISSA *from behind, slides his arms around her, hands cupping her breasts. They freeze in this posture for a beat,* MELISSA'S *face taut, eyes shut in ecstasy, or dread.*

WAITER *appears, stage right. Stares at the white couple incredulously, scratches his head, manages to smile—a smile that slides into a smirk.*)

WAITER: Sir? La-dy? C'n I get you an'thing right now?

EDWIN (*turning, annoyed*): You can *get—*

MELISSA (*sharply*): Edwin!

EDWIN (*angry, but dropping his voice*): —the hell out of here!

MELISSA (*voice lifting gaily, but courteously*): Thank you, we're *just fine!*

(WAITER *shrugs, exits.*

EDWIN *and* MELISSA *return to the table,* EDWIN *holding* MELISSA's *hand, as if they've been dancing; but* MELISSA *draws it from him. He helps her with her chair, and sits himself, rather heavily. Checks their drinks.*)

EDWIN: Oh, hell—we're all out! (*Turns in chair, waves hand in a signal*) Uh—waiter! Boy! Uh—hey! A little service here!

MELISSA (*stiffly*): He isn't a—

EDWIN (*cupping his hands to mouth*): WAI-TER! HEY! Out here on the terrace! Two more Voodoo Bombshells! (*Fingers to mouth, whistles shrilly*) Toot sweet!

MELISSA: —a *boy.* He's a—

EDWIN: Insolent black bastard don't tell *me.* (*Panting, devouring another handful of nuts; a beat or two*) Why's it so *quiet?* No music at all now.

MELISSA (*smoothing dress, hair*): Well—we asked to have it turned down, didn't we.

EDWIN: Turned *down,* not *off.* (*Cranes neck around, squinting*) What's that funny sound?

MELISSA: The surf.

EDWIN: Nah—something else. Like buzzing—and kind of a smell—

MELISSA: The *surf.*

EDWIN (*peering around, though without leaving his chair*): Some kind of a—a—whatsit—big hive or something.

MELISSA: I hear the *surf.* (*Drains very last dregs of drink*) To my ears, nothing is more melodic, more haunting, more peaceful than the *surf.* (*Pause*) The heartbeat of the universe, the great womb.

EDWIN (*whistling again*): WAITER! HEY—OUT HERE! Two more—

MELISSA (*reaching for purse*): I'm—

EDWIN (*almost frightened*): What? What? Oh, no—

MELISSA: —going to my—my place, my place of refuge, going to take a *nap* before dinner—

EDWIN: No, *wait*—we just started to talk—don't you want another drink?

MELISSA: No thank you! (*Giggles*)

EDWIN: You just said you did!

MELISSA: *You* just said you did—Tickle!

EDWIN (*gaping at her, as if uncomprehending*): I—I—uh—don't you—want another drink?

MELISSA (*sighing*): Oh—why not. (*Drops purse, which falls from chair to ground*)

(EDWIN *raises his glass, nervously drains his drink as well; ice dribbles down onto his chin and shirt front.*)

EDWIN (*slapping at himself*): Ooops! God *damn!*

(*Without looking at him,* MELISSA *wordlessly passes him a cocktail napkin, which he uses, gratefully.*)

EDWIN (*mumbling*): Thanks.

(*A beat or two. Very quiet except for a vague buzzing sound.*)

MELISSA: I miss the music—I was ready to *dance.* (*Pause*) He isn't going to come with our drinks. I know he isn't.

EDWIN (*cupping hands to mouth*): HEY—SERVICE OUT HERE! ON THE TERRACE! (*Whistles*)

MELISSA (*fatalistically*): If you want service, you'll have to get it.

EDWIN (*laughing, disgusted*): And this place came *recommended!* Three stars!

MELISSA: Two.

(EDWIN *trots off stage right, a good sport.*)

EDWIN: Don't go away, Angelina—I'll be right back!

(MELISSA *takes up her book, as if desperately; tries to read, absent-mindedly waving away insects, which are circling her head.*)

MELISSA (*reading*): "A mere trifle consoles us, for a mere trifle distresses us." (*Shuts book*) Is that too much to ask, then—a *trifle*? (*Slaps at an insect on her cheek*)

(EDWIN *trots back to the table, panting, pleased with himself; sits heavily; takes another handful of nuts.*)

EDWIN: I just had a few carefully chosen words with the maître d' in there—a native too, I guess, but a *light*-skinned fellow, most reasonable, levelheaded. Amazing English accent—like a Brit. (*Nods*) We should be getting some decent service now.

MELISSA (*worriedly*): You weren't—accusing, were you? Of—the waiter?

EDWIN (*grinning*): Oh, no, not at *all*—no, no, not at *all*—why would I be "accusing"?

MELISSA: Because he can't help it, probably—his attitude.

EDWIN (*sarcastically*): Oh, no—certainly not! Oh, no.

MELISSA: These West Indian islands, they're so beautiful to us, to visitors—tourists—but, well, their history has not been a happy one. (*A little vague*) I *think* they were all slaves, at one time.

EDWIN (*snorting*): Sure! So they hate whites!

MELISSA: A captive people, a noble people, of the race of—kings, emperors—now forced to sell their land, and—

EDWIN: Huh! I was reading on the plane how much these resort places are *worth*. Jeez! Wish I'd invested when I might have! (*Scornfully*) The natives never owned the land anyway—it was mainly plantations.

MELISSA (*ignoring him, glancing stage right, as if anticipating the* WAITER's *entrance*): And they're such a—graceful people, so—at ease in their bodies. Not like us, so—*anemic*.

EDWIN: Huh! *I* don't feel anemic! (*Slaps fondly at belly, torso, belches*)

MELISSA (*continuing, touching fingertips to eyes*): Oh, sometimes I feel so—guilty.

EDWIN: Guilty?

MELISSA: For inhabiting my—lily-white skin. My—legacy of—of—whiteness.

EDWIN (*staring*): Yeah, it *is* sure lily-white— (*Forced sort of lechery*) Smooth and white as cream—for the cat's tongue!

MELISSA (*ignoring him*): My race has dispossessed the races of—of color—made slaves of them—and I, *I* have benefited.

EDWIN: It's us or them! It comes down to it.

MELISSA: In all innocence, *I* have benefited.

EDWIN: Angelina—you're so—uh, you're so—damned attractive a woman for your—I mean, I mean you're beautiful—you're gorgeous—I mean—don't frown! (*Words tumbling out*) I think you're wrong—I think you're *silly* to feel, uh, guilt—

MELISSA (*surprising him, responding naively*): You think I'm—silly?

EDWIN (*with authority*): Yes I do. I really, really do.

MELISSA: You really do?

EDWIN: I *really* do.

MELISSA: I—we—white Americans—all of us—shouldn't feel—guilty?

EDWIN (*pinching her upper arm, sly murmur*): Baby, that depends what the guilt's *for*.

MELISSA (*sharp intake of breath, stifled laughter*): Oh—Edwin!

EDWIN (*grinning, rocking semidrunkenly in his chair*): Baby, that depends on what the guilt's FOR.

MELISSA (*warning finger to her lips*): Hush!

(WAITER *reappears, stage right, bringing two more drinks on a tray. He walks gracefully, very proper, formal, head high; spotless uniform, and spotless white towel over arm.*)

WAITER (*setting down drinks with a flourish*): Thank you, la-dy! Thank you, suh! An'thing else? Please? Your wish? (*No explicit sign of insolence*)

EDWIN (*watching him mistrustfully*): Uh—not right now.

MELISSA (*smiling, "kindly"*): Thank *you* very much, but—not right now. Er—do you live close by?

(WAITER *smiles, nods, but ambiguously, easing away.*)

MELISSA: That village, by the cliff? The shuttle bus goes through. (*As* WAITER *makes a little bow, perhaps a mock-bow, easing away*) Such a—a beautiful little—*quaint*—

(WAITER *exits.*)

EDWIN (*staring after him*): D'ja see *that*? Rolling his eyes!

MELISSA (*forefinger on* EDWIN'*s lips*): Hush!

EDWIN: Rolling his big bug eyes! Thinking I can't see!

MELISSA: He did not roll his eyes.

EDWIN: He rolled them as he *turned*. At about eighty degrees of a circle, the black sonofabitch rolled his *eyes*, don't tell me, baby!

MELISSA: He *blinked* his eyes.

EDWIN: He blinked *one* eye—that's a wink! (*Reaching for glass*) As if I don't know his game!

MELISSA: A man has to be allowed to—to—blink—his eyes.

EDWIN (*tapping* MELISSA'*s glass with his in a genial toast*): Well, here's to—"Caribbean holiday"!

MELISSA (*sipping her drink*): Oh—this *is* strong! There's too much vodka in it.

EDWIN (*sipping*): Huh? Not in mine.

MELISSA: Would you like to trade?

EDWIN: Well—okay. (*They trade glasses; sipping*) Yes—this is better. The prices we're paying! (*Brooding*) I s'pose the bartender's in on it—watering my drink. Probably the maître d' too. Bilking the owner, ultimately. You can be sure it's a white owner without a clue what's really going on down here!

MELISSA (*sharply*): Yes, well—we're here to enjoy ourselves, aren't we. You could always move to another hotel.

EDWIN (*laughs, fatalistically*): Next one'd be worse—that's how it is, tourist-trap places like this. They got you by the short hairs, they don't let go. (*As* MELISSA *makes a gesture of impatience, slapping, then scratching, at her throat*) Y'know, Angelina, you're too *soft*-hearted—that's your problem. You let the rest of us, the bad guys, like, y'know, like the guys who run things—uh, like the President on down, the FBI, police commissioners, businessmen—you let *us* exert the muscle. Fire the shots. (*Leaning toward her, more intimate*) Bet you let your kids walk all over you, eh?

MELISSA (*stiffly*): Kids? You mean children? What makes you think I have children?

EDWIN: You said—a daughter? Didn't you say?

MELISSA: Daughter? Me? I did not say.

EDWIN (*dismayed, blinking*): I thought for sure I heard—

MELISSA: You heard wrong.

EDWIN: I'm—sorry. (*Scratching head, neck*)

MELISSA: I don't care to speak of my private life right now.

EDWIN: Oh, no one's asking!

MELISSA: I've had all I can endure of not *having* any private life.

EDWIN: Me too! The same with me!

MELISSA (*scathing contempt*): What! The same with *you*?!

EDWIN (*quickly placating*): Well—maybe not the—the same—maybe not the identical same. But—I understand.

MELISSA: I will not be *interrogated. Pried into.*

EDWIN: Oh, nobody's—prying into you!

MELISSA: I came here to escape—*that.*

EDWIN: And so did I! And so did I!

MELISSA (*coolly yet dreamily, as if in an aside*): To be "awakened" —if possible.

EDWIN: And so did I!

(*Pause. Lights dim just perceptibly. Faint calypso music is heard.*
     WAITER *appears stage right, bringing a lighted candle inside a small red glass bowl to set on their table.*)

MELISSA: How romantic!

EDWIN (*peering at watch*): What time is it? God, almost nine!

WAITER (*with a little bow*): Lady? Suh? Fresh drink? Yes?

(MELISSA *and* EDWIN *reply simultaneously,* EDWIN *drowning* MELISSA *out.*)

MELISSA: Oh dear, oh no, I *couldn't!*

EDWIN: Right! Great idea!

WAITER: Thank you, suh. Comin' right up, suh. (*Moves off stage right*)

EDWIN (*calling belatedly after him*): And more of these macadonia nuts, please.

MELISSA: Macadamia.

EDWIN (*louder, after* WAITER): And hurry it up, will you?

MELISSA: That's rude.

EDWIN: Comes time for the check, they'll be prompt enough, you bet.

MELISSA: There are—some kind of flying insects here—I've been bitten. (*Scratches*)

EDWIN (*slapping at arm*): Mosquitoes.

MELISSA: No, they're—smaller. (*Catches one*) Sort of a—a hard little shell—oh! (*Insect seemingly escapes, flies away.*)

EDWIN (*sniffing at candle*): Aha! This is bug repellent. That's what this is.

MELISSA: Oh, but it smells—perfumy.

EDWIN (*scratching*): Hope it works!

MELISSA (*gazing up at moon*): The main thing is, the crucial thing is—there's a moon tonight! A great, glowing tropical moon never seen in North America!

EDWIN: They better have screens here.

MELISSA (*quickly*): They did—I checked.

EDWIN: These tiny things, like gnats—little bastards could get right through a screen. Damn, they *bite*.

MELISSA: I'm happy here.

EDWIN: Uh—maybe we better think of—the next phase of—the evening—the *night*.

MELISSA (*quickly*): I'm happy here.

EDWIN: Shit!—excuse my French—you hear that—buzzing, sort of? Droning?

MELISSA (*gaily*): That's calypso!

EDWIN: And there's sure a smell . . .

(EDWIN *gets to his feet, prowls about at rear of stage, poking with his foot.*)

EDWIN (*whistling*): Whew!

MELISSA (*humming, singing to herself*):

They say the men is leadin' th' wimmen a-stray
But I say the wimmen today
Is worser'n the men in ebb'ry way
Oh, yes! The wimmen is—

EDWIN: Oh, Christ! I knew it! (*Has discovered something, which he shoves off stage with his foot*)

MELISSA (*craning around, but not about to rise from chair*): Ed-win? What is it?

EDWIN: Nothing, Angelina! (*A beat or two; returns to table, sits heavily*) God damn! (*Snickering mutter*)

MELISSA: What was it? Was it—anything?

EDWIN: Nah—I kicked it over the side. Down onto the beach. (*Drains glass thirstily, then calls*) Waiter—where're our drinks? (*Cupping hands to mouth*) AND BRING SOME DDT, DAMMIT!

MELISSA (*semidrunk*): They don't make DDT any longer—it's outlawed.

EDWIN: Since when?

MELISSA (*singing tunelessly, prettily*):

It's only a—a cardboard moon
Hangin' in a—a—whatsis sky
But it wouldn't be—hmmmmhmmmhmmm
If you hmmmmhmmmm in me!

EDWIN: You have a—a—lovely voice.

MELISSA: I used to sing. I mean—I was trained.

EDWIN (*disbelieving*): Huh? You *were*?

MELISSA: At Juilliard. I took voice. Mezzo-soprano.

EDWIN: Is that a fact!

MELISSA: I was headed for a career in—in music, in serious music —I—I—loved it so—I was—I was—fulfilled—in music—in singing— (*as if with difficulty*) —in the act of—

EDWIN: Is that . . . so.

MELISSA (*coolly, biting off her words*): Yes—it—is—so.

EDWIN (*wriggling, scratching*): What's keeping him, I wonder! (*Making an effort*) In the moonlight, Angelina, you're so—hauntingly —beautiful.

MELISSA (*giggling, hands over eyes*): In the moonlight, Edwin, you're so—hauntingly—handsome.

EDWIN (*more rapidly*): When I first set eyes on you—back in Miami—I—I saw a woman of—mystery! An ice princess!

MELISSA: I didn't see you.

EDWIN: Beautiful women don't *need* to see—anyone else. (*A bit extravagantly*) That's a law of nature! That's the law of—of—coral! seashells! beautiful, beautiful things that can't see themselves— they're *blind*! (*Pause*) You wanna know what I thought, in Miami?

MELISSA: No—I want my Voodoo Bombshell, that's what I want. (*Giggles naughtily*) Oh no, I *do*, of course I *do* want to know what you thought.

EDWIN (*almost growling*): I thought—I can melt that ice! (*Laughs*) I'm the man, I'm the man can melt that ice—mmmmmm!

MELISSA (*lightly slapping him*): Aren't you fresh! Your wife—what's she think of this kind of thing?

EDWIN (*quickly*): She—knows.

MELISSA: Yes? She does? Where you are, Ed-win, right this moment?

EDWIN: She knows and she—she— (*Pause, scratches*) It's complicated.

MELISSA: You're a daddy too!

EDWIN: No I'm not!

MELISSA (*wagging finger*): Yes you are, you *are*! You let it slip!

EDWIN: I did not, I—did not.

MELISSA: You did, you did! (*As if in an aside*) Blabbermouth.

EDWIN: What's that?

MELISSA: Your children call you Tickle—you said.

EDWIN: What's that?

MELISSA: Tickle—they call you—

EDWIN (*lunging to tickle her, a bit roughly*): Aha! Gotcha!

(MELISSA *screams with laughter at first, then shoves at him, jostling the table, knocking one of the glasses to the ground.*)

MELISSA: How dare you, mister! HOW DARE YOU! (*On her feet, nearly spitting*) Your—disgusting sausage-fingers!

EDWIN (*drunken, contrite*): Aw, hey, I'm sorry, honey—just got—carried away.

(WAITER *appears stage right, not bringing drinks, but to intercede. His manner is now not insolent or self-conscious but direct, gallant. We should sense how he is risking his job for the sake of protecting* MELISSA.)

WAITER: Excuse me—ma'am? Suh? Some trouble here?

MELISSA (*to* EDWIN): Pawing—grunting—*drunk*!

EDWIN (*nervously yet belligerently, to* WAITER): Nothing's wrong—the lady's just—

MELISSA: I'm not a—a—body!

WAITER: Ma'am? This gent'man bothering you?

EDWIN (*to* WAITER): Nothing's wrong, I *said*. We're having a private discussion.

MELISSA (*furious, nearly sobbing*): So *crude!* Always—so—*crude!*

WAITER (*doubtful*): Ma'am, you want I should ask this gent'man to leave?

EDWIN (*trying to be genial, clapping* WAITER *on shoulder in a startlingly familiar gesture*): Hey, friend, I *explained* the situation's under control, eh? The lady is just—emotional. (*As if man to man, confidential, sniggering*) Had a bit too much to drink, eh? Kinda —overexcited, y'know? (*Sniggering*) Over*stim*ulated?

(MELISSA *has moved off, stage left, trying to compose herself; takes compact out of purse, checks appearance, murmuring to herself "Oh, why!"—"Oh!"—"Why, why!"; repairs makeup; smooths hair, dress.*
    WAITER *disengages himself, politely but forcibly, from* EDWIN; *approaches* MELISSA *gallantly.*)

WAITER: Ma'am, I need to hear from *you*—this gent'man bothering you?

EDWIN (*belligerently*): *I'm* a guest here too! Don't you turn your back on me!

MELISSA (*making a vague dismissive gesture*): Oh—never mind.

EDWIN: I'll buy this place, I'll buy it out from under you, the lot of you, you think I can't? And you're the first to go, boy! You better believe it!

WAITER: Ma'am?

(EDWIN *grabs the* WAITER *by the shoulder, tries to spin him. The* WAITER *steps aside, seems about to strike out, then restrains himself, his fingers flexing or trembling. A tense moment or two.*)

EDWIN: You'll see! You'll see! (*Wiping face, very excited*) *You* won't even last till morning!

MELISSA (*to* WAITER): Everything is all right, really. You're very thoughtful, but—(*sighing, returning to table*)—just a little slow, you know, with our drinks!

(*The* WAITER *is surprised at* MELISSA*'s abrupt change of mood.* EDWIN *hurriedly helps her with her chair, hovering over her. He seems about to bury his face in her neck, but draws away, as if flaunting the* WAITER.)

EDWIN (*a meaningful glare at the* WAITER): Yes—just a *little* slow.

WAITER (*backing off*): Okay. Bartender's making them.

EDWIN: And more nuts—we're out. (*Calling after* WAITER) And turn up the music—it's too *quiet* out here! (*Calling louder, as* WAITER *retreats*) And d'you know what else we want? Some kind of bug spray—one of those cans—(*makes a shaking, spraying gesture with his hand*)—aerosol spray. We're being eaten up alive, damn it—we're not paying your gyp-prices to be EATEN UP ALIVE, y'understand?

(WAITER *has exited.*

EDWIN *takes* MELISSA*'s hand, kisses it.* MELISSA *giggles.* EDWIN *laughs. Quiet, almost stealthy laughter; an undercurrent of excitement beneath.*)

EDWIN: Did you see his face?!

MELISSA: Oh, you're—*terrible!*

EDWIN: That black bastard—black *stud*—eh?—got the hots for my ice princess, eh? Yum-yum lily-white skin, eh? Smooth like cream for the cat's—rough—tongue! (*Makes a fluttery gesture with his tongue, advancing upon* MELISSA, *who gives a little scream, giggles, shoves him away*)

MELISSA: TER-RI-BLE—YOU'RE—TER-RI-BLE!

EDWIN: *You're* pretty nice. (*Sniffing at her, doglike*) Hey, you're— eh? Worked up, eh? Are you? Eh? That black stud, eh?

(*The calypso music rises. A distinct erotic beat. Lights dim or soften. The sound of other customers arriving, gay, drunken.*)

EDWIN (*lecherous, seductive, incantatory tone*): No last name—Angelica with no last name—I like that, I know what that means, eh? That's what I like and that's what you like, eh? Woman like you, body like yours—(*draws hand across* MELISSA*'s shoulders, down the length of her bare back*)—knowing, eh? Mature—sensuous— *knowing*—

MELISSA (*almost flatly*): Mature?

EDWIN (*continuing, slightly slurred persistence*): —experienced—
widely and—and variedly—knowledgeably—*experienced*—in all
the little tricks of—the trade!

MELISSA: Tricks? Trade? (*She pushes to her feet and begins to dance
to the music, not knowing how to dance to this music but impro-
vising, an awkward, suggestive, yet in a way innocent self-display,
head thrown back, face lifted as if to the moon; humming or singing
without words.*)

(EDWIN *approaches her, from behind; tries to embrace her and she
slips away; does embrace her; turns her; tries to dance with her; the
two of them as if moving to different beats, though neither precisely
to the calypso beat.* EDWIN's *movements are mechanical, "erotic," as
in 1950s rock and roll; but there is little consistency or assurance in
his manner.*)

MELISSA (*giggling*): "Caribbean holiday"! "Unattached"!

EDWIN: You really are—*hot*? Eh? (*Sniggering*) The one thing I
learned, in all my travels I learned, the one thing I absolutely
learned was—was—*is*—a woman's sensuality is far deeper and
more complex and—and astonishing, and—insatiable—than a
man's, eh? Just FANTASTIC, eh?

MELISSA: Are we going to have another drink, or what?

EDWIN (*intense*): You know what I think—I think we should continue
this discussion in absolute privacy, in my room, in privacy, that's
what I think, Angelina—

MELISSA: Bunny.

EDWIN: Bunny—that's right—Bunny. Okay, Honey Bunny . . .

MELISSA (*a bit tonelessly*): Okay, Tickle . . .

EDWIN (*fumbling in pocket*): I have the key right here—we can
adjourn right here, down this path *here* (*indicating stage left,
forward*) to the beach.

MELISSA (*faint complaint*): Drinks?

EDWIN: I'll bring them down. Let's us go down, and I'll come back
and get 'em—I'll get a bottle, that's what, a bottle—(*still fumbling,*

in another pocket)—bring a bottle to our room, okay, Honey Bunny?

MELISSA: Have you lost your key?

EDWIN (*searching pockets*): It's here somewhere—it must be.

MELISSA (*flatly*): You lost your key.

EDWIN: It *must* be here—I remember distinctly—I picked it up from the bureau, I put it in my—

MELISSA (*pushing away from him*): Lost your—key.

EDWIN: Well—*you* have a key, don't you? In your purse?

MELISSA: No, I don't. I don't have a key. *You* have the key. You're the (*infinite contempt*) man.

EDWIN (*embarrassed, apologetic*): Hell. I can pick one up at the front desk, I guess.

MELISSA (*angry, contemptuous*): Can you. Can you really. (*Takes up her purse preparatory to leaving*)

EDWIN: What do you—mean? Why are you—?

MELISSA: Tonight of all nights. Deliberately. And you're drunk, aren't you. You were drinking all day, weren't you. And you saw to it that I'm drunk, didn't you. And that shirt—that shirt doesn't *fit*. You have a dozen good shirts and you wear one that makes you look like a stuffed sausage, oh, deliberately! (*Begins to sob, perhaps without tears; in hurt, frustration, anger*) Tonight of all nights— oh, Edwin, *tonight of all nights!*

(MELISSA *leaves hurriedly, stage left;* EDWIN, *stunned, hands lifted in appeal, stares after her.*)

EDWIN: But, but—I can pick up another key at the front desk, can't I?

(EDWIN *hurries after* MELISSA.
Lights dim. Music subsides. WAITER *enters, stage right, with aerosol insecticide spray. His expression deadpan, though poised on the*

brink of contempt, lips tightly pursed, he proceeds to spray the umbrella table and its immediate vicinity as lights dim further.)

Lights out.

(THE END)

Part

Friday Night

A Play in One Act

CHARACTERS

CHLOE MURCHINSON: twenty-three years old

HILLARD LUDMAN: early or mid-twenties; handsome, "charismatic"

STACEY CONNOR: twenty years old; extremely pretty

POLO SHANKER: early or mid-twenties, of slightly less than average height

LUTHER BRANDT: early or mid-twenties; may be muscular, densely built; some suggestion of Native American features

Lights up. CHLOE *stage right. She is in her bedroom, before a mirror, dressing and making herself up for Friday night. Popular rock music sounds, though not loudly.* CHLOE *is an attractive, not glamorous, perhaps just slightly overweight young woman in her early twenties; her primary emotion seems to be hope tempered by resignation. As she speaks, addressing herself and the audience, she is holding up various articles of clothing, examining her reflection critically in the mirror. She may also be back-combing her hair, applying mascara, lipstick, etc. Her movements are excitable, then consciously "restrained."*

CHLOE (*half singing*): To-night—I have a premonition about to-niiiight. Something's gonna happen—*to-night.* (*She holds up a glamorous sweater, then sniffs one of the armpits, tosses it down*

207

in disgust.) God-*damn*! Meant to get that dry-cleaned. (*Holds up a ruffled blouse*) Nah—got a bad memory attached—coldhearted s.o.b. (*Tosses blouse down*) Good riddance! (CHLOE'*s mother is calling to her from offstage, though we don't hear her;* CHLOE *pauses, then calls back*.) Momma, I don't care who's on "Rich and Famous" tonight—I told you I'm going out! I promised I'd meet somebody! (*Turns her attention back to the mirror and the audience*) Nobody'd think this was a melancholy time for me, hey, would ya? Nobody's sure gonna guess, from looking at *me*. Chloe Murchinson—'way back in grade school—I'm the kind of girl I don't let hurt feelings show—*ever*. (*Mother calls out again, and* CHLOE *responds with increasing impatience*.) Momma, I won't be out late . . . No, Momma, I'm not driving far. . . . God's sake, Momma, I am TWENTY-THREE YEARS OLD. Lived alone for nearabout a year in Traverse City, didn't I? (CHLOE *returns to mirror and audience*) I love Momma and I sure miss Daddy, but —Friday night's FRIDAY NIGHT, for God's sake. On my feet at the A&P six days a week, I deserve some fun. (*Shivering with excitement*) He's gonna be there tonight, I just know it. Maybe— without *her*. Just a premonition! (*Pause*) Heard they were getting engaged—then heard they were *broke up*. 'Course, I'm not jealous, or even, I guess, hopeful . . . exactly. If Hillard Ludman was going to fall in love with me I guess he'd've done it by now. (*Mother calls again;* CHLOE *responds with fond exasperation*.) Momma, I *do* like it real well at home, I *don't* miss Traverse City! Not one tiny bit! But I promised Bonnie, and—uh—(CHLOE *is too honest to be a convincing liar*)—Helen—I'd meet them at Ryan's tonight. So—I'm *going*. (*Pause*) No, don't wait up for me—*please*. (*Returns to mirror and audience; rueful*) The bunch of us—from high school—my girl friends—the ones not married yet or moved away—it's getting *smaller*. Anyway, hell, I don't need them either, Friday nights. I'm not scared of—some kinda *adventure*. (*She is holding a black V-neck sweater against her chest and is suddenly inspired*.) Hey—it's *slacks* that'd go best, I got it!

(*As lights dim and out,* CHLOE *calls to her mother one final time, in the voice of a frustrated child*.)

CHLOE: Momma, sure I love you, but I gotta have my own life, don't I? I'M TWENTY-THREE YEARS OLD—I GOTTA HAVE MY OWN LIFE!

(*Lights up.* CHLOE *approaches entrance to Ryan's—a neighborhood tavern, neither tawdry nor sophisticated; a friendly atmosphere.* CHLOE *enters shyly, expectantly. She is carrying a shoulder bag and is wearing the black V-neck sweater and a pair of black, or black and white polka-dot, slacks; black-tinted stockings; shoes with a medium heel. Her accessories are eye-catching: a belt with a large silver or gold buckle, long earrings, several rings.*

Center stage, in a booth, are HILLARD LUDMAN *and* STACEY CONNOR; *facing them,* POLO SHANKER *and* LUTHER BRANDT. *They are drinking beer, talking, laughing. Sounds of rock music from a jukebox in the background.*)

CHLOE (*to audience*): Friday night—it's okay. Like, if you sort of drop in, alone. Like, on the way home from work or something. (CHLOE *steps inside, waves at someone—very likely the bartender.*) Hiya, Mack! . . . (*As if she has received a compliment on her appearance*) Yeah—thanks! Ryan's is this neighborhood place, nothing fancy, down by the lumberyard where poor Daddy used to work, worked thirty years. He'd hang out in Ryan's a lot—what you'd call a regular. (*Waves to someone else, smiling, buoyant*) Oh, hiya, Mr. Danzig, how's it going? . . . Yeah, me an' Momma we're doing just fine. Tell Mrs. Danzig to drop by sometime, will ya? (*To audience*) Ryan's the kind of place weekends can get kind of rough, but not till late, like midnight. By then I'll be out of here, unless I hook up with a guy. One thing about me: I'm not the kind of girl *hangs out too long.* A small town like this, all you got is your reputation, almost—*that* goes, and *you* go. (*Pause.* CHLOE *has sighted her friends in the booth, presses hand against heart.*) Oh, God—he's *here.* (*Pause*) But Stacey's with him—damn.

(CHLOE *advances bravely, trying to appear at ease, though waiting for her friends to notice her.*)

CHLOE (*to audience*): Coming in alone like this, Friday night, you're taking a chance. Like, you can wind up with the wrong people— (CHLOE *smilingly, but coolly, acknowledges someone who is beckoning to her to come join him*)—or nobody. You can be frozen out by your best friend—(*grimly*)—that has happened. You can leave in fifteen minutes or you can stay till closing—two a.m. It's unpredictable as—as—(*flamboyant metaphor*)—eternity!

(*At last, fortunately,* POLO *has sighted* CHLOE; *he rises from booth and waves.*)

POLO: Hey, Chloe—over here!

(LUTHER, HILLARD, *and* STACEY *beckon* CHLOE *over as well, seemingly friendly enough, but in descending order of interest.* CHLOE, *of course, is delighted—and relieved.*

HILLARD *is the dominant person in the little group, the center of interest and attention even when he isn't talking; then, he appears to be sitting in judgment of whoever is talking, or shows his indifference. His attraction to* STACEY *is evident; but though he is "in love" with her, he may resent the fact, thus resents her, in a subtle way that surfaces from time to time. He has no special feeling for* CHLOE *but may enjoy her obvious adulation of him.* STACEY *is a small-town "popular" girl, a former cheerleader; she is in love with* HILLARD, *and somewhat anxious about him, even as, being very pretty, and accustomed to the attentions of men, she can't resist a generalized sort of flirting, even provoking.* LUTHER *is a high-school acquaintance of* CHLOE's, *with some Native American blood (Chippewa/Ojibway); excitable, and inclined to be sullen; attracted to* STACEY, *but resigned to her and* HILLARD's *relationship. His manner toward* CHLOE *may be patronizing—here is one local girl he doesn't care about impressing.* POLO, *busy with smiles, nods, hand gestures, is clearly attracted to* CHLOE *even as—and this would appear to be an old story—she is not attracted to him, though she is fond of him, as one might be of a younger brother.*

CHLOE, *breathless, comes to the booth, where only* POLO *has risen to greet her.* STACEY *flashes a dazzling cheerleader-type smile that may or may not be sincere—"Hiya, Chloe!—you're looking good!"* HILLARD *nods and mumbles—"H'lo Chloe."* LUTHER *nods, managing a grudging smile, as if his thoughts were elsewhere.* POLO *has gallantly slipped out of the booth to make room for* CHLOE, *beside* LUTHER; *he draws up a chair for himself.*)

POLO: Hiya, Chloe—good to see ya. Where you been keeping yourself?

CHLOE (*flustered*): Oh, I—I've been around. (*Slides in beside* LUTHER) I see you guys got a head start, huh?

POLO (*lifting beer bottle*): You want one of these, Chloe?

CHLOE: Okay—thanks.

STACEY: We just got here, actually—we're not staying long. (*Leans her head against* HILLARD's *shoulder for a moment, to show she means just* HILLARD *and herself*)

CHLOE (*calling after* POLO): Oh, Polo—make that *Lite*—Miller Lite.

STACEY (*with seeming sincerity, though already knowing* CHLOE's *situation*): I thought you were working in Traverse City, Chloe? How come you're back here?

CHLOE: Well, I *was* in Traverse, but, uh, y'know, my mom's alone now, and—it didn't work out too well.

STACEY: Selling real estate, huh? Your mom was telling my mom, back around Christmas.

(HILLARD *lights a cigarette;* STACEY *frowns reprovingly but doesn't say anything.* LUTHER *is already smoking.*)

CHLOE (*embarrassed*): Well, actually—I wasn't an *agent*, a *salesman*—your mom must have misunderstood. You have to take a course, and be licensed, to be a real estate agent in Michigan. Actually, I worked in the office.

STACEY (*persisting*): I'm sure my mom didn't get it wrong—I heard it from somebody else too.

CHLOE (*laughs, shrugs*): Well . . .

STACEY: So, you're back? Doing what, now?

CHLOE: Oh—I'm looking around. Got some applications in. (*Eager to change the subject*) Hillard, I heard you signed up with the National Guard? That so? (CHLOE *is both vivacious and "restrained" with* HILLARD.)

HILLARD (*laughing, marveling, yet flattered*): Christ, word gets around in this town! Can't hardly scratch your butt, a dozen people report on it.

(*General laughter.* LUTHER *guffaws.* STACEY *slaps lightly at* HILLARD's *arm to chide him for his language.*)

CHLOE (*embarrassed*): Well, uh—your cousin Imogene told me. I ran into her at the mall—

HILLARD (*cutting* CHLOE *off, to* LUTHER, *sniggering*): Like that time "Miz" Carlson went ape, or whatever it was—inviting half the team over, and, uh—(*not wanting to be too specific in* STACEY's *presence*)—*you* know. I'm leaving her place at six a.m. and who's coming up the drive but my old man looking for me! How he knew the bunch of us was there, I never found out.

(LUTHER *laughs.* STACEY *and* CHLOE *smile strained smiles.*)

LUTHER: *My* old man, he was too out of it to know.

HILLARD (*shaking head, recollecting*): Christ, that was something, wasn't it? Two nights before graduation!

LUTHER: Bitch got what she deserved.

HILLARD (*grinning, rueful*): I was pretty smashed, Jesus. My old man takes a look at me and just hauls off and wallops me—right there in the driveway. And there's Petko puking in the flowerbed. And Jimmy— (*Laughs*)

STACEY (*a bit primly*): That poor woman, she tried to commit suicide, after. After they fired her.

HILLARD: Well, sure they're gonna fire her—what d'ya think? A teacher, *a math teacher,* got no more sense than to act like that? With her own students?

STACEY: Oh, I don't mean *that,* I just mean—it was, like, a tragedy. She had some kind of mental collapse or something.

HILLARD: It wasn't just *mental,* no way.

(HILLARD *and* LUTHER *laugh.* STACEY *disapproves.*)

LUTHER (*ironic twist of mouth*): That bitch—never invited *me,* I just showed up. Then, then I *was* there—she tried to freeze me out. Just like in class!

HILLARD (*laughing*): Yeah, it was a lot more than *mental.* Talk about "collapse"!

CHLOE: Well, it was sad. She'd been kinda nice. . . .

(POLO *has returned with several bottles of beer and a large bag of potato chips; a glass for* CHLOE.)

CHLOE: Thanks, Polo, you're real sweet.

POLO (*jubilant, beery mood*): Whooo, boy! I guess I *am!*

(POLO *rubs his hands together briskly; he has a habit of "busy" mannerisms, stimulated by his friends'—particularly by* CHLOE's*— presence. Of the five, he is the youngest-behaving.*)

POLO (*grinning*): What're you guys laughing about? Could hear you hee-hawing way over there.

STACEY (*fluttery hands to hair*): Oh, let's change the subject.

HILLARD: Ancient history was what it was.

POLO: Yeah? What?

LUTHER (*sniggering*): "Miz" Carlson. That special graduation party she gave.

POLO (*flatly*): Oh. That.

LUTHER (*laughing*): "Oh. That." 'Cause Polo wasn't invited.

POLO: Yeah, and neither were you, smartass.

LUTHER: I got my foot in the door, though. That's farther than you got, bozo.

HILLARD (*thoughtfully*): Y'know—I kinda wonder what *did* happen to her, after. It's weird—to think that people are still living, I mean if they *are* living, when you don't see them anymore. "Miz" Carlson, nobody at the school now knew her—but they all know *about* her. She's, like, passed into some kinda *legend*.

STACEY (*annoyed, trying to be charming*): Say—why don't we switch the channel, huh, guys? Chloe and me, we're feeling kinda left out.

HILLARD (*relenting*): Yeah, well, it wasn't anything anybody's proud of, like. But it happened.

STACEY (*sharply*): *I* never knew her, anyway. She was before my time.

LUTHER (*to* HILLARD): Camp Grayling, where they're gonna send you for training—my cousin Wayne, he had a helluva time at first. These black guys from Detroit and East Lansing—bad news. You heard about that?

HILLARD (*guardedly*): I heard some things.

LUTHER: Wayne, he's from the Manitou Reservation. Like, he's near-about a full-blooded Ojibway, so they didn't fuck with him too much. But—

STACEY (*to* LUTHER, *flirtatiously*): O-jib-way—that's the real, Indian name? What's "Chippewa," then?

(LUTHER *shrugs.*)

STACEY: Some of us used to wonder—you never looked Indian, much. So we wondered whether you *were*. (*Has been sipping beer, giggles*) I mean—*are*.

POLO (*trying to be funny*): Luther's a redskin, except—he *isn't*.

LUTHER (*flicking hair out of his eyes, defensive, yet pleased by the attention*): Yeah, lemme tell you one thing: I stand outside the white race. (*Everyone laughs*) I say I *do*.

STACEY: It's got to do with blood, huh? What, uh, what's yours?

LUTHER: One-eighth Ojibway. (*Pause. Sly humor*) You wanna know which parts?

STACEY (*persisting*): Do you have relatives on the reservation, actually? Do you ever go to visit?

LUTHER (*coolly*): I got better things to do, honey.

CHLOE (*has also been sipping beer; tries to enter the conversation in imitation of Stacey's vivacity*): My father, one of his best friends at the lumberyard, he was a—a Ojibway. From Peshaw—(*stumbling over the word*)—Peshabay—

LUTHER (*coolly*): Peshawbestown.

CHLOE: He was—I mean is—a real nice guy. *Real* nice. You probably know him—his name's—

HILLARD (*cutting in, to* LUTHER): What d'ya mean, Luther, you "stand outside the white race"? What kinda shit is that?

LUTHER: I don't trust any white men, is what I mean.

STACEY (*giggling*): What about white women?

HILLARD (*almost aggrieved*): Hell, you trust your friends, don't you? Guys you know all your life? Like, who got you in at Allis-Chalmers, it wasn't my old man? And me?

LUTHER (*after a pause*): I trust guys I *know*. But, like, the rest of 'em—fuck it.

HILLARD: On the team, you were just like—anybody else.

LUTHER (*not smiling, but enjoying this*): Naw I wasn't.

HILLARD: Wasn't?

LUTHER: I had to be *better*. A helluva lot *better*.

HILLARD: Says you!

STACEY (*to deflect the tension*): Luther, you don't *look* all that much like any Indian, and your mom either—so, what is it? Why's it matter?

LUTHER: It matters. (*Pause*) Y'know there's the Holocaust, what they call the Holocaust, we studied it, right? In Europe? The Nazis? Killing the Jews? Well, there was a Holocaust here, but nobody knows about it.

CHLOE: Oh—when was that?

LUTHER: It wasn't any special time—it was gradual. Like, there were five million Indians in North America before the white men came; then, by 1900, there were two hundred fifty thousand. (*As if by rote, bitterly satisfied*) That's 'cause you tried to kill us off.

HILLARD: Fuck that! I never did! (*Trying to placate* LUTHER) So, how many Indians are there now?

(LUTHER *pauses; shrugs. Evidently he doesn't know.*)

LUTHER: Depends on how you count them. Us. I mean—full-blood, half-blood, quarter-blood—like that.

STACEY (*shivering*): I saw this documentary on television—the Holocaust. Ugh! You wouldn't *believe*!

POLO: I was watching that too. Jeee-zuz.

CHLOE (*brightly*): We couldn't ever watch anything like that in our house. Momma just wants to watch silly things, and things that make her happy.

HILLARD (*to* LUTHER): Long as you trust your friends, that's the main thing.

POLO: I wouldn't trust no politician either. Like, you vote for some-body, then he doesn't give a shit about you. *I* only voted once—it's a waste of time.

LUTHER: A white man not trusting a white man is, like, what he can choose. Somebody not-white—he can't.

HILLARD (*whistling derisively*): What's that—something out of a for-tune cookie?

STACEY (*brightly, to deflect a possible quarrel*): Is "Holocaust" just that one thing—once? Or is it—a lot of things? Like, it just keeps happening, over and over?

POLO: That was Jews mainly, I guess.

STACEY: No, it wasn't *just* Jews.

HILLARD: It's hard to feel sorry for people, they don't watch out more for themselves. Y'know?

CHLOE: I had a Jewish friend, in Traverse City. Real nice girl. You wouldn't know—I mean, *I* wouldn't know. Anyway, what's the difference?

POLO: I don't know any Jews actually, I mean personally, I guess. They were too smart to settle in Post, Michigan.

CHLOE (*trying for vivacity*): People you meet, and get to like, and they like you—what's it matter what they *are*?

POLO: It matters to them.

LUTHER: These black guys I was telling you about, Hillard, at Camp Grayling—you're gonna have to watch your ass.

HILLARD (*aggressively*): Nobody better fuck with *me*.

CHLOE: When are you going, Hillard?

LUTHER: Wayne, he did okay. He can take care of himself—carries a knife. But some guys, white guys, they have a helluva time. All kinds of weird shit there—drinking in the barracks, smoking dope, snorting coke—you name it. Some of these De-troit dudes, they deal, serious. It's like in a prison, y'know? You can make big bucks, any bunch of guys packed in together.

(CHLOE *and* STACEY *overlap briefly with* HILLARD *and* LUTHER.)

CHLOE: When is he going, Stacey?

STACEY: Last weekend in April, he starts training. Thank God it isn't the real Army.

HILLARD (*incensed, to* LUTHER): Anybody snorts coke, smokes crack—they don't belong in the Michigan National Guard. They don't belong in any U.S. uniform. I'm not any Boy Scout or anything, but—that isn't right.

LUTHER: Beer, that's different, huh?

HILLARD (*drinking*): *That's* different.

STACEY (*checking watch*): Hey—if we're going to Lucille's we better go.

HILLARD: It's early.

STACEY: I told her nine-thirty, it's past that.

HILLARD: Naw, we're fine.

LUTHER (*to* HILLARD): You brought that—uh—my Winchester?

HILLARD: Sure. Out in the car.

LUTHER: Yeah? Everything okay?

HILLARD: Sure.

POLO: What's that?

HILLARD: Twenty-two-caliber Winchester, Luther's gonna buy.

POLO: Which one's that?

HILLARD: You've seen it.

STACEY (*shivering*): I don't like guns—you mean there's a gun in the car, honey?

HILLARD: In the *trunk*. Locked up.

STACEY (*a bit high from beer, giggling*): Long as it doesn't explode or something.

CHLOE: Remember that day, in homeroom, all you guys were absent? And Mrs. Wheeler says, "Is it an epidemic or something?" and we told her, "No, it's first day of deer-hunting season."

HILLARD: It's gonna be weird, at Grayling. Taking orders how to use a rifle, target shooting—that stuff. When I've been using a gun since, God, maybe eight years old!

CHLOE: I feel sorry for the poor deer.

STACEY: I do too! (*Fluttery hands to hair, as if just remembering; histrionic horror*) Oh, God—there was a terrible *accident* with a gun, once. My uncle Roy—him and his buddies went out duck hunting on Traverse Bay—they were drinking, I guess—all night—and in the morning—

HILLARD (*cutting in*): My old man says, "Guns don't have accidents, assholes have accidents."

STACEY (*protesting*): My uncle Roy was just standing there.

CHLOE: Oh, God, did he—die?

HILLARD (*to* STACEY): That's what I mean—assholes have accidents. You got to choose your friends right, too.

STACEY (*incensed, to* HILLARD): Maybe *you* better choose your friends right!

CHLOE: Did he die, or—?

POLO (*boisterous*): Hey—it's a fight! What d'ya callit—lovers'—tussle?

STACEY: You—mind your own business.

POLO (*to* CHLOE *and* LUTHER): These two—they got some news. Some new news.

CHLOE: What's that?

(STACEY *slaps at* POLO *to quiet him;* HILLARD *rabbit-punches him in play.*)

POLO: Tell 'em—go on.

HILLARD (*self-conscious, a bit angry*): Nothing. Not *yet.*

CHLOE (*smiling, bravely*): Is it—? Are you—? (*Looking from* HIL-LARD *to* STACEY *wide-eyed*) Hey, *is* it—?

LUTHER (*grinning*): Hey—no shit?

POLO: Mum's the word! (*Puts hand over mouth*)

CHLOE (*a bit drunk, reaching for* STACEY's *hand*): Oh, lemme see—

STACEY (*withdrawing both hands, blushing*): No, I do *not*. I *am* not. (*Laughing, confused*) I mean, *we* are not. (*Leaning head on* HIL-LARD's *shoulder*) You tell them, honey—go *on*.

HILLARD (*slowly*): There's . . . nothing to tell. (*Annoyed at* POLO) You got a big mouth, y'know it?

POLO: That's 'cause I'm— (*lowers his voice, cups hands to mouth, inaudible murmur*)

LUTHER *and* CHLOE: Huh? What?

POLO (*repeating*): 'Cause I'm— (*again, inaudible murmur*)

STACEY (*to* HILLARD, *giggling*): Stop him.

POLO (*bellowing*): GONNA BE BEST MAN.

CHLOE (*faintly, but with seeming sincerity*): Oh—that's so, so won-derful. . . . When will it be?

(HILLARD *and* STACEY *are whispering together.* HILLARD *has his arm around her shoulders;* STACEY *seems difficult to placate for some reason.*)

LUTHER (*crudely*): No shit?

HILLARD: Look—it's not for public—uh—consumption, yet. (*To* POLO) *What the fuck's wrong with you?* Shithead.

POLO (*minimizing it*): Hey, come on, what's the big deal?

STACEY: My mom and dad are gonna kill me! (*To* POLO) You aren't funny. Also you're jumping to conclusions you got no right to.

CHLOE (*trying to placate her*): Uh, Stacey, actually, I—I'd been hearing—Sharon MacKenzie was saying *she* heard—you and Hil-lard—

STACEY: There is no grounds for—for anything! (*In a flurry, hides face*) Don't look at me, you all! I'm not saying a word.

HILLARD (*disgruntled*): Too many people around here got nothing to do but shoot off their mouths. There's such a thing as privacy, and doing things in their proper time.

POLO (*teasing, pushing it*): Jeez, there's nothing to be embarrassed of, is there? It ain't like you two been exactly a secret item for the past six months.

STACEY: Four months. Four months, eleven days.

HILLARD (*embarrassed*): Oh, Stace—

POLO (*overly boisterous*): Four months, eleven days—what's that the anniversary of, huh? (*As* HILLARD *and* STACEY *wave him away, laughing, annoyed*) WHAT'S THAT THE ANNIVERSARY OF, HUH?

HILLARD (*swift mood change; punches* POLO *on the upper arm*): Shut it, fuckface!

(POLO *winces but does not cry out. A moment's silence.*)

STACEY (*incensed*): Excuse me, please!

HILLARD: Honey, it's okay.

STACEY: Just—excuse me!

HILLARD: Where're you going, hon?

STACEY: To the ladies' room, where do you think! Anywhere away from *here*. (*As* STACEY *slides out of the booth, grabs her purse, strides away, playing a scene*) So *crude*!

(*They watch* STACEY *exit.*)

HILLARD: You jerks shouldn't oughta embarrass Stacey—you know she's sensitive.

POLO: Hell, I wasn't.

LUTHER: *I* wasn't.

HILLARD: She's younger than us, and she's—like, sensitive. (*Pause*) She has allergies too.

POLO: Jeez, I was just talking, Hillard. I didn't mean anything. (*Pause*) When there's good news for once—you kinda want to share it.

HILLARD (*drinking, indifferent to* CHLOE'*s presence*): Like, Stacey's *special*. You don't fuck around her like she's some—ordinary girl.

POLO: Hell no.

HILLARD (*on the verge of drunkenness*): All that goes on in her head, and why—*I* don't know half the time. She can just—start in crying. No reason! (*Runs hands through hair, dramatic gesture*) But—I'm in love with her. First time in my fucking life.

(CHLOE *has been wiping surreptitiously at her eyes, unnoticed.*)

CHLOE (*suddenly*): Excuse me, too. I'll be right back.

HILLARD: Yeah, good—see how she is, willya?

(CHLOE *exits, managing not to cry.* POLO *calls after her.*)

POLO: Another Miller Lite, okay, Chloe? (*To his friends*) She's a nice kid—Chloe. I kinda like her, y'know?

HILLARD (*to* LUTHER): So—you think I should maybe be worried, in the Guard? 'Cause of some Detroit niggers? (*Belligerently*) Yeah? You think so?

(*Lights out.*)

(*Lights up. Ladies' room.* STACEY *is primping before a mirror;* CHLOE *stands beside her.*)

CHLOE (*straining to speak enthusiastically*): Well, I—I think it's just the—the nicest news. (*Pause*) You and Hillard Ludman, you're both so—(*searching for word*)—special. Like—golden, or something!

STACEY (*not overly friendly, but moved by flattery*): Yes. Well. Thanks.

CHLOE: You weren't in our class at school, but—Hillard was—he was—oh, Jeez—you know—real popular, without trying. He was always . . . (*Long pause, as* STACEY *continues to primp, self-absorbed*) . . . the center of things. (*Pause, laughs*) It was me, engaged, *I* wouldn't mind anybody knowing.

STACEY (*relenting a little, almost confidentially*): Oh—it's my father. Daddy thinks Hillard isn't "respectful" enough. To him, or to—me. (*As she applies lipstick*) Like, Hillard vows he's gonna be real careful with Daddy; then, some fresh remark just flies out of his mouth like—a bat or something! (*Giggles*) That kinda thing happen with you, ever? Some guy you're really serious about, and your father can't stand?

CHLOE (*slowly*): Oh—my dad—he got along pretty well, with just about anybody. Any guys I'd bring home—mainly—he liked them.

STACEY (*almost sarcastically*): Lucky you! (*Then, remembering*) Oh, hey, Chloe, I'm sorry—I forgot. (*Pause, embarrassed*) Uh—your mom's okay, is she? Guess it was a pretty bad shock, an accident like that.

CHLOE (*tonelessly*): Oh, she's okay, now. She's got her sisters, and some women friends, and church, and, uh, me. (*Pause*) Mainly, we miss him. (*Pause*)

STACEY (*a commiserating expression, even as she primps*): Well—I never sent any card or anything, I guess, but—I was real sorry to hear. Such a sad thing! (*Pause*) My uncle was saying—the guy that hit him, his insurance company is paying you all? A real big settlement?

CHLOE (*shocked*): What? Who told him that? No, they're fighting it. Damn crooks, fighting it all the way.

STACEY: Mmmm. Must be my uncle heard wrong. (*Pause, indifferent*) Or somebody did.

CHLOE (*the most incensed we have seen her*): The guy who hit him, in the truck, he changed his story, too. Told the police one thing, yes it *was* his fault; then, after he got a lawyer, he retracted it. And the woman Daddy stopped to help—she had this head injury, was lying down in the grass, and didn't see what happened. God, it makes me so mad! And sick! Poor Daddy dying like he did!

(CHLOE *is on the verge of tears;* STACEY *feels compelled to comfort her, though somewhat stiffly.*)

STACEY (*embracing* CHLOE): Oh hey, hon—I know it's hard. I, uh —it sure is *hard*. (*Easing away*) I'll see you out there, Chloe.

CHLOE (*as* STACEY *exits*): Oh, Stacey—I meant to say—I love those earrings— (*But* STACEY *has left.*)

(CHLOE *addresses audience, perhaps by way of the mirror: facing it, looking out. Or there may be no mirror, and she addresses the audience directly.*)

CHLOE (*resigned, wistful smile*): The thing that's embarrassing, in a place like this, I mean a ladies' room, like this, is—you look in the mirror and you catch yourself with hope in your eyes. Like, it's unquenchable—*hope shining in your eyes.* (*Laughs*) Even when you're old enough to know better. (*Serious*) This is a fact: there are insights into life a girl has only in places like this, where there's an odor of drains, and cigarette smoke, and old vomit, all overlaid with air-freshener spray. (*Looks around, quizzical expression*) Somehow I just know—I'm gonna remember these sad, shabby old places, all my life.

(CHLOE *quickly powders her face; back-combs her hair; adjusts her clothing [her sweater may be slightly snug]; examines herself, as best she can, from various angles. Soft rock or country-and-western rock comes up.*)

CHLOE (*reminiscing, wry*): Places like this! Ryan's isn't the worst I've been in, by far. Not knowing what's waiting for you when you go back out. (*Pause*) Once, in Traverse City, in a motel cocktail lounge, I came out of the ladies' room and the people I was with, two guys and a girl, they'd played the cruelest trick on me . . . left money on the table and walked out. Just walked out. I'd been led to believe we were all having a good time so I came back to the table and can't find them and I'm standing there sort of—dizzy—like I'd been kicked in the head—trying not to cry. (*A pause. As* CHLOE *prepares to leave, more briskly, upbeat*) But these guys are my friends, known them all my *life, they'd* never play any cruel tricks on me—!

(*Lights out.*)

(*Lights up. Later. In the booth, as before, are* CHLOE, POLO, HIL-LARD, STACEY, LUTHER. *A semidrunken, giddy, loud-laughing party. The young men are smoking; from time to time,* STACEY *takes a puff of* HILLARD's *cigarette.*)

STACEY (*in the midst of an attention-getting anecdote*): —And here's this big fat Tahitian—or Haitian?—two hundred fifty pounds— black guy looking like murder bleeding from the head but he's got a tire iron in his hands!—and he's swinging it! (STACEY *is girlish in her incredulity*) this is the *real* crazy part—my sister-in-law Irene—*she* gets into it too!—tries to protect Eddy—the black guy knocks her down—and *she gets up again!* The only thing that saved them, the police came by. (*Breathless, basking in attention*) I mean, can you believe it! I asked Irene, "Why didn't you run for the police right away, instead of what you did?" and Irene says, "When I saw Eddy maybe gonna get killed I went wild I guess." Imagine!

LUTHER: So then what happened? They arrest the guy who hit the car, or what?

STACEY: They don't arrest anybody for anything down in Detroit—you'd have to assassinate the President or something.

HILLARD: Well—I met Eddy's wife, once. She's got class. (*Raises beer glass*) A good woman.

STACEY: But—risking her life?

HILLARD (*slightly slurred speech*): It's instinct. It's nature. Like a—a lioness protecting her cubs. (*Sliding an arm around* STACEY's *shoulders, squeezing*) It's love.

STACEY: Anyway, she had a concussion. Now she acts funny, cries a lot—Eddy's on the phone with Mom, complaining.

HILLARD (*pedantic*): Yeah. Nature doesn't give a shit for the individual, it's the whatdyacallit—the species.

POLO: People do all kinds of crazy things—they get strength, like, in an emergency.

LUTHER: Remember how Hillard usta be, anytime he got hold of the ball? Like that game against Port Royal, you were a wild man, Christ! Lucky you didn't get your neck broken.

CHLOE (*excitedly*): Oh, I remember that! Hillard was fantastic! Then, the actual *ambulance* on the field—

HILLARD (*almost embarrassed*): Well. Shit. You got the ball in your hands . . . it's up to *you*. (*Pause*) I'd've been willing to—die, I guess. If needed.

STACEY (*protesting*): Oh, but it's just a *game*! *Foot*ball.

HILLARD: Nah, you'd know if you were out there—the team depending on you—everybody depending on you. It's—life or death.

POLO (*marveling*): Jesus, that was some night. And the Port Royal team, they lost every game after that. Wasn't that them?

LUTHER: This kid I saw on TV, he's a twin, eleven years old, and he gives a kidney or something to his brother—*that's* something. I don't know if I'd do that or not.

HILLARD (*drunken logic*): Hell—it's your own brother, you got any choice?

LUTHER (*drunken logic*): Yeah, but he's a twin—he's, like, *me*.

STACEY: Hey, guys, this isn't, like, nice, is it—considerate—ya'll know how Chloe's poor dad got killed last year.

CHLOE (*quickly*): Oh—that's all right.

HILLARD (*to* CHLOE, *feelingly*): Yeah. Man. *That* was something. What'd he do, stop his car 'cause there was an accident? In the sleet or something? And he's helping this woman and her kids and somebody comes along in a semi and plows right into him? (*Moved*) Jee-sus.

LUTHER (*respectfully*): Yeah, that was real—sad. Then the woman driver just pulled away, and left him, too?

CHLOE: Oh no!—she didn't. Who said that?

POLO (*awkwardly*): Your dad was about the nicest guy in town, Chloe. It was a—a damn shame. . . .

CHLOE (*wiping eyes, too flustered to know what she's saying*): Oh— that's all right!

LUTHER (*aggressively*): You guys should sue 'em for a million bucks! At least!

CHLOE: Oh—mainly—mainly we miss him—

LUTHER (*A gesture at his throat as if with a knife*): Plus taking care of the fucker who—

(*As* LUTHER *speaks,* CHLOE *is already intent upon leaving the booth.*)

CHLOE (*trying not to cry, stoic*): Excuse me—!

(CHLOE *slides out of the booth—there is some awkwardness. Now it is clear that she is upset, the others are repentant; especially* POLO, *who follows after her.* CHLOE *takes a few steps away, her back to the others, pressing a tissue to her eyes.*)

POLO: Aw geez Chloe—you okay? (POLO *is not certain how to relate to her: touches her, but tentatively*) You—want me to take you home?

(CHLOE *shakes her head.*)

POLO: We, uh—didn't mean—

CHLOE: That's okay. (*As if to leave.*)

POLO (*disappointed, concerned*): You going—?

(STACEY *has poked both* HILLARD's *and* LUTHER's *arms.*)

STACEY: C'mon back, Chloe! C'mon!

HILLARD (*loudly, sincerely*): Hey, Chloe—c'mon!

LUTHER (*embarrassed*): Yeah—Jeez.

(CHLOE is sincere in her indecision; but, with POLO so intent upon escorting her back, she gives in. She's embarrassed, blowing her nose. Slides back into the booth.)

STACEY: *I'm* such a coward, I fainted, sophomore year, donating blood at school.

POLO (*grinning*): I sold some blood, once—in Port Huron. They only give you twenty-five dollars for—I guess it's a—pint?

STACEY (*playfully slapping at* POLO): Oh! A pint! You'd be dead! Or am I thinking of a quart? I don't want to *think* about it, I'm gonna faint!

HILLARD (*flexing a muscular arm so that the veins stand out*): Hell, I'd give a gallon of blood for somebody I loved—no questions asked. (*Teasing* STACEY, *erotic undertone*) 'Specially if she'd be the nurse, and draw it out herself with the syringe. Mmmmm. Or, like, suck it out, like here. (*Indicates artery in throat*)

STACEY (*squealing, hiding face*): Oh, you *stop*!

HILLARD (*slurred voice*): Hell, I'd give blood here—here and now —anybody had a syringe.

LUTHER: Here—next-best thing! (*Takes a jackknife from his pocket, drops it on table*)

(*Brief commotion as* HILLARD *manages to snatch up the knife before anyone can stop him. As* STACEY *screams,* HILLARD *jumps from the booth, opens a blade of the knife, pricks his forearm.* POLO *scrambles up, tries to take the knife from him;* HILLARD *shuts it and passes it back to* LUTHER; *much squealing, laughter.*)

POLO: Man, you're crazy tonight!

HILLARD (*taking seat again, waving his arm about to show thin trickle of blood*): Shit, this is nothing.

STACEY: Oh, Hillard, how could you! (*She blots the blood with a napkin*) Ohhh, this makes me dizzy, I'm gonna faint!

HILLARD: You okay, honey?

STACEY: I think we should leave. Now. I'd better call Lucille.

POLO: Let's go to the Blue Moon—we ain't been there in a long time.

STACEY: Hillard and me, we got better things to do.

POLO (*gaily*): Let's drive out to the Lakeside Inn! Celebrate!

HILLARD (*ponderously*): This sergeant who signed me up, he was telling me, like, in war—*he* was in Vietnam—the hero and the coward are both afraid, equally afraid, but the coward's the guy who gives in, and runs to save his ass, and the hero doesn't run, which is why he's a *hero*.

LUTHER (*scornfully*): So the hero gets his ass blown off, and the coward doesn't. That's all. (*Playing with knife menacingly, though the blade is directed more toward himself than toward anyone else*) Like, the white man gets Indians and blacks to be heroes, so *he* can save his ass. Precious white ass.

HILLARD (*flaring up*): Man, what a shithead you're getting to be, always taking the depressing side of things! Go back to the reservation, you don't like it here! Like it's no fucking wonder you're always so hard up for—(*pauses, considering* STACEY's *presence*)— a girl.

LUTHER (*furious, rising from booth*): Yeah? What? What're you saying, Ludman? *You're* the shithead!

(*Clumsily,* HILLARD *and* LUTHER *lunge at each other. The others cry out—*STACEY *and* CHLOE *cry "Oh no, oh no," "Oh, don't!" etc. Bottles* *topple to the floor.* POLO *manages to intervene, and* HILLARD *backs off, wiping his face on his shirt.*)

LUTHER (*panting, on his feet, brandishing the knife—the blade against his own throat*): You think I'm afraid, do ya? Do ya?

HILLARD: Fuck it, man. Just—fuck it.

CHLOE: What's going on?

LUTHER: Think I'm a coward? (*Pressing tip of blade against throat*) Yeah?

STACEY: Hillard, make him stop!

HILLARD (*as if embarrassed*): Come on, Luther, man. Just—fuck it, okay?

(*A pause.* POLO *makes a move to take the knife from* LUTHER, *but* LUTHER *pushes him away with his opened hand.*)

(HILLARD *turns; someone has tapped him on the shoulder. We assume it is the bartender, telling them to leave.*)

HILLARD: Huh? What? . . . Okay, we're going. (*With a sweep of his arm he knocks the remaining bottles to the floor*) WE HAD ENOUGH OF THIS DUMP—WE'RE GOING, COCK-SUCKERS!

(*Lights out.*)

(*Lights up. A suggestion of dimness.*)

(*In the parking lot,* HILLARD *and* LUTHER *are admiring the .22 Winchester rifle as* STACEY, POLO, *and* CHLOE *look on.* STACEY *is teetering in her high heels and leaning on* POLO's *arm.* CHLOE *is staring intensely.*)

STACEY: Hillard, honey, let's go! I'm scared of that damn thing.

HILLARD (*mean, teasing, to* STACEY): Bet you wouldn't trust me to shoot an apple off your head, huh?

STACEY: You crazy? I sure wouldn't.

LUTHER (*drunk, playful-mean*): *That's* the true test of love!

HILLARD: Nah, that's a test of marksmanship. And courage. (*Sights along the barrel, aiming up*) Lookit the moon! Like a big eye.

CHLOE (*suddenly, daringly*): I'd trust you, Hillard.

HILLARD (*to* LUTHER): You should've tried, to join the Guard. I heard, just a juvenile record, the court seals it—they don't hold it against you.

LUTHER (*flicking hair out of his eyes*): Fuck that.

CHLOE: Hillard, I'd trust you. No questions asked! (*Giggles*)

(*A pause. Everyone looks at* CHLOE.)

HILLARD (*grinning*): Say what, honey?

POLO (*quickly*): Wherever we're going, we better *go*—they're maybe gonna call the cops here.

HILLARD: Whatja say, Chloe, honey?

CHLOE: I'd trust you—shooting an apple off my head. Sure I would.

POLO (*taking* CHLOE's *arm protectively*): Uh—I'll take Chloe in my car. Let's meet at the Lakeshore Inn.

HILLARD (*ignoring* POLO, *to* CHLOE, *in a slow voice*): You'd trust me? (*Pause*) You? (*In a more characteristic voice, mocking* STACEY) That's more'n Sugar Tits here'd do!

STACEY (*sharply*): Hillard Ludman, you're plain drunk. I'm not sure I like you much, drunk.

HILLARD (*snappy*): I'm not sure I like you with your clothes on.

(LUTHER *laughs.* STACEY, *embarrassed and hurt, turns away.*)

POLO: Okay? The Lakeshore Inn?

HILLARD (*with drunken ebullience*): Chloe, Chloe Murch-in-son— you know Hillard Ludman is the best shot in Post, Michigan— right?

CHLOE (*recklessly*): Oh, yes!

HILLARD (*rifle barrel upraised, approaching her, staring, as if he has never really seen her before*): You and me—we're gonna be a *legend.*

(*Lights out.*)

(*Lights up.* CHLOE *in circle of light, addressing audience. As she speaks, the others come forward, out of the shadows; lights gradually up. We see* HILLARD *and* LUTHER, *each with a can of beer;* POLO, *worried;* STACEY, *frightened, angry, disapproving, jealous of the loss of attention, hugging herself as if she is cold.*

Overlapping voices in background. STACEY *is murmuring, whining, pleading:* ". . . all you guys crazy? . . . God damn, I'm not drunk . . . I'm gonna tell Chloe's mother . . . too drunk to know what she's doing. . . ." POLO *is anxious, muttering:* "Maybe not a good idea, Hillard . . . what if . . . accident . . . what if . . . Jeez, Hillard!")

LUTHER (*pointing*): Out there, on that flat rock. That's the place.

(HILLARD, *rifle in hand, steadies* CHLOE *as he begins to walk her, in shallow water, to the rock.*)

CHLOE (*swaying, giggling, slurred voice*): Oh—do I gotta get my feet wet? My nice new *shoes*?

HILLARD: Take 'em off, then!

(HILLARD *squats before* CHLOE, *removes her shoes. This is a brief but tender moment.* CHLOE *gazes down at* HILLARD; HILLARD *gazes up at her. All attention is focused on them. Then, rising,* HILLARD *hooks the shoes, by the heels, rather rakishly, on his belt.*)

HILLARD (*businesslike*): Okay—but where's the *apple*?

LUTHER (*who has been poking around on the riverbank*): Here's the next-best thing. (*It's a tall white Styrofoam cup.*)

HILLARD: Man, that's the *best*. Nice and *white*!

(HILLARD *escorts* CHLOE *out to the rock, then returns to shore.* POLO *and* STACEY *continue to watch, and to speak, in the background, more or less unheard.*)

POLO: Hillard, hey? Maybe—maybe you oughtna better? I mean— it's late—it's *dark*—whyn't you just use the target—by itself— huh?

STACEY (*shivering*): . . . gonna tell your mom about this, Chloe, I sure *am*. And Hillard—goddamn—damn stubborn asshole—gonna get arrested—don't take any advice from *any*body—I HATE YOU!

LUTHER (*giggling, but beginning to be nervous; bringing the cup to* CHLOE *and helping balance it on her head*): Okay! Here we go! HERE—WE—GO!

(CHLOE *repositions the cup on her head, upside-down; smiles bravely, if a bit glassily.* HILLARD, *a short distance away, is wriggling his shoulders, stretching his arms and legs, like an athlete preparing for performance; sights through the rifle's scope; checks the chamber, etc. We have a sense of his enormous excitement, in which fear and pride and defiance and masculine bravado are commingled.*)

HILLARD (*calling to* CHLOE): Honey—you ready?

CHLOE: Ready as I'll ever be!

STACEY (*undertone*): Oh—I can't believe this!

POLO (*undertone*): God, don't let—dear God—oh, *God!*

LUTHER (*almost rattled*): You want me to count for you, Hillard? Like—to five?

HILLARD (*calmly, sighting* CHLOE *through the scope*): Son, I do my own counting.

(CHLOE *remains in the spotlight; lights go down slightly.*)

CHLOE (*addressing audience*): So I was . . . there . . . on the rock . . . but floating. Floating calm and trusting and emptied of myself. (*Pause. She stands motionless, head erect, beatific expression on her face.*) And it was like suddenly I wasn't *her* anymore. Chloe Murchinson. Or, anyway, not *just* her. 'Cause I can see myself in Hillard Ludman's rifle scope like through his eyes . . . through his *soul.* The two of us, *one.* I can see myself through all their eyes . . . all *your* eyes . . . you all looking, for the first time in my life, at *me.* (*Pause, almost weeping*) And I'm so happy. I'M SO HAPPY. I'm gonna die here tonight, amid the rocks and trash I'm gonna die my death, I'm gonna be reborn—no, I have faith in that boy's skill, his cold, unwavering eye—Hillard Ludman is an expert marksman, I have faith, I am not afraid to die—I *am* afraid but floating above all fear.

(*Overlapping with the last sentences of* CHLOE's *speech,* HILLARD *has been counting.*)

HILLARD (*slow, calm*): One. Two. Three. Four. (*Just perceptible pause*) Five.

(HILLARD *fires. The crack of the rifle is very loud; someone has screamed.* CHLOE *has involuntarily ducked, hands to head; but the Styrofoam cup has been blasted off.*
Lights out.)

(*Lights up, stage left, on* HILLARD *and* CHLOE. *The rest of the stage remains dark.*)

HILLARD (*as he raises a can of beer to* CHLOE's *mouth; tender, drunken-admiring*): Bravest girl in this shithead town.

CHLOE (*steadying can with both hands, breathless*): Oh. Gosh. Thank you. (*Dribbles beer on front of sweater*) Oh! Oh, damn! (*Wipes at sweater*)

(*Lights out.*)

(*Lights up. Center stage,* HILLARD *and* STACEY. HILLARD *has walked her to her front door; has evidently been apologizing, or explaining himself in some almost-persuasive way.* STACEY *is sullen but malleable.*)

HILLARD (*embracing her, his face in her hair, almost inaudible*): . . . gonna forgive? Huh? Baby? Sure I love you, baby—oh, God— crazy about you—oh, Stacey honey, oh God—

(STACEY *relents, allows him to kiss her; slides her arms slowly around him, to kiss him, at first a bit stiffly, then with more passion.*)

(*Lights out.*)

(*Lights up stage right. A small circle of light as* CHLOE, *back in her bedroom, is preparing for bed. Her face is flushed, hair disheveled.*)

CHLOE: So. I'm a little, uh, shaky now . . . had too much beer . . . (*Giggles*) In the morning I'll be . . . okay. (*As she removes sweater, inspects stains, sniffs underarms, with regret*) Geez. Damn. (*Tosses the sweater down*) In the morning . . . and forever after . . . a legend. (*Pause, bleary-eyed but resolute*) In Post, Michigan, a legend. Which is why you've heard of me. (*Pause. Though inaudible to us,* CHLOE's *mother has called to her;* CHLOE *responds in a voice of surprise, guilt, exasperation.*) Oh—Momma! You're up? What're you doing up this late? (*As if to prevent door from being opened*)

No, don't you come in here, Momma, I'm undressing, damn it, Momma. . . . (*Pause; listens*) Why, sure I am, Momma, why sure, the proof of is I'm *here*, isn't it? . . . (*Pause, listens, laughs ruefully*) Oh, Momma, hell, you know that, know I love you—I'm feeling tonight like I LOVE EVERYBODY, EVERY LIVING SOUL— like tonight's the first night of—ETERNITY.

(CHLOE *smiles.*)

Lights out.

(THE END)

Black

A Play in Two Acts

CHARACTERS

JONATHAN BOYD: white, thirty-five years old
DEBRA O'DONNELL: white, early thirties
LEW CLAYBROOK: black, early thirties

ACT 1

Scene 1.

Darkness. Several bars of a classic blues number, "Cry Me a River."
Then the music fades, to continue in the background through the
telephone conversation.

Lights up extreme stage right. JONATHAN BOYD *is making a tele-*
phone call at a pay phone in a café.

As the phone rings in DEBRA O'DONNELL's *living room, lights up*
there.

The living room/dining room of DEBRA O'DONNELL's *house is the*
main set. If furnished more than minimally, it should contain at-
tractive "modern" furniture: a sofa and chairs in neutral, subdued
colors; bookshelves (containing both books and CDs); a coffee table;
an end table with a stained-glass lamp; a dining-room table and
matching chairs; perhaps a large potted plant in the background. On
the floor, near the door, are several cardboard boxes (containing
BOYD's *things).*

DEBRA *hurriedly enters from stage left and picks up the receiver on the fourth ring.* DEBRA *is a very attractive, though rather guarded, woman in her early thirties, in a cream-colored outfit (a dress, or a skirt and matched sweater), wearing expensive-looking high-heeled shoes.* DEBRA *is nervous, but* BOYD's *more agitated state has the effect of calming her.*

DEBRA: Yes? . . . Hello? (*A pause, as* BOYD *stands unspeaking; café noises in the background*) Hello—?

BOYD (*guiltily, yet eagerly*): Debra? Is that you?

DEBRA: Boyd? Where are you?

BOYD: It's—you?

DEBRA: Where are you? Are you all right?

BOYD: Your voice is—different.

DEBRA: I'm sorry—what? I can't hear you very—

BOYD: This *is* Debra?

DEBRA (*concerned, impatient*): Boyd, we've been waiting for you—we've been worried. Where *are* you?

BOYD: I wasn't sure—when you wanted me. I mean—exactly.

DEBRA: Come as soon as you can. Where *are* you? Still on the turnpike?

BOYD (*as if anxiously*): I *am* late, then? How late?

DEBRA: Have you been drinking?

BOYD: What time *is* it?

DEBRA (*losing patience*): Boyd, please don't do this. Not tonight.

BOYD: When did you say you wanted me there? Was it eight o'clock? Or—

DEBRA: Just come, Boyd, please—we've been waiting.

BOYD: —was it earlier? seven-thirty?

DEBRA (*becoming upset, as café noises increase*): I can't hear you—where *are* you?

BOYD (*raising voice*): I can't hear you—Debra?

DEBRA: Please, just—

BOYD: Your voice sounds—distant.

DEBRA: —just *come*, Boyd—we're waiting.

BOYD: Was it eight o'clock, or seven-thirty?

DEBRA: I thought we said seven o'clock, but—

BOYD: I'm late, aren't I—oh, Christ!

DEBRA: —don't *do* this. Just *come*.

BOYD: I'm in Passaic. At—you know—the Anchor Inn.

DEBRA (*puzzled, alarmed*): You're *there*? But why? Why didn't you come over?

BOYD: I wasn't sure when you—wanted me.

DEBRA: But why are you *there*? Ten minutes away?

(LLEWELLYN CLAYBROOK *enters from stage left. He approaches* DEBRA *deliberately, graceful on his feet; slides his arms around her, from behind. She is startled, then responds with affection, even passion.* CLAYBROOK *is a black man in his thirties, intelligent, well groomed, casually but tastefully dressed, in a sport coat of a conservative color and texture and a good sport shirt or turtleneck sweater; he may wear a beard or a goatee; he should wear rimless glasses. He need not be handsome, but he should carry himself with a certain measure of dignity—which, we sense, is sometimes willed, self-conscious.*)

DEBRA (*more assertive now*): Boyd, just *come*. We'll be expecting you in a few minutes.

BOYD: But—is it all right?

DEBRA: I can't hear you. For God's sake, please just *come*!

(DEBRA *hangs up the phone, with an exclamation of exasperation and amusement. She turns to* CLAYBROOK'S *embrace and embraces him; hides her face in his neck. They freeze as lights go down and out center stage.*)

BOYD (*still on telephone, angry, despairing*): You don't want me there—I'm out, I'm dead—you know it—you and—*him*.

(BOYD *hangs up the phone so hard that the receiver slips from the hook and he has to replace it.*)

Lights out. Blues number ends.

Scene 2.

Lights up. As doorbell rings, DEBRA *and* CLAYBROOK *open the door to* BOYD, *who is carrying a duffel bag (slung over his shoulder) and a long-stemmed red rose and a bottle of wine. Surprisingly, he appears calm, smiling, charming—keyed-up, but seemingly in control. For the briefest moment, he stares at* DEBRA *and* CLAYBROOK; *then takes* DEBRA's *hand, murmuring "Hello" as* DEBRA *in turn murmurs a near-inaudible greeting and, after a moment's hesitation, leans forward and kisses him on the cheek. One should sense that* BOYD *and* DEBRA *have not seen each other for some time; their feelings are powerful but inchoate and undefined.*

BOYD: God, I'm sorry—I guess I'm late?—it's snowing, the turnpike traffic is—slow.

DEBRA (*just slightly edgy, but seemingly warm, sincere*): We're so happy to see you, Boyd—we were worried. (*She turns to* CLAYBROOK) Boyd, this is Llewellyn Claybrook—Lew—my friend. Lew, this is Jonathan Boyd—his friends all call him Boyd.

(BOYD *and* CLAYBROOK *energetically shake hands, each trying to outdo the other in affability, composure, man-to-man equanimity.*)

BOYD: Hey! Great to meet you!

CLAYBROOK: Great to meet *you*!

BOYD: Yes, I'm—(*merest pause; staring at* CLAYBROOK *as if confused*)—so glad to meet you—Lew. Your name is—?

CLAYBROOK: Some friends call me Lew, some call me Clay.

BOYD (*staring, nonplussed*): Uh . . . Lew? *Clay?*

DEBRA (*an arm through* CLAYBROOK's *arm*): Llewellyn's Lew.

BOYD: Well, I—I'm—so relieved to be here, to be off that turnpike. For you, Debra (*hands her the rose*)—and, uh, Lew (*hands him the bottle of wine*).

DEBRA: Thank you, Boyd.

CLAYBROOK: Thanks!

DEBRA: You aren't wearing a coat, Boyd?

(BOYD *shrugs, smiling. As* DEBRA *closes the door,* BOYD *comes forward, in a manner that is both shy and aggressive; his eyes dart quickly about, taking in the scene. He flicks snowflakes off his hair. Behind him,* DEBRA *and* CLAYBROOK *exchange a significant look;* CLAYBROOK *shows* DEBRA *the label on the wine bottle, eyebrows raised to indicate that the wine is expensive.*

BOYD *is an attractive man of thirty-five, but may appear subtly fatigued, ravaged; with a just perceptible growth of beard and disheveled hair a little too long and uneven. We sense that* BOYD *is but precariously in control of himself and that often he does not know his own motives, though, being intelligent and verbal, he can readily invent and assign motives. His smile—an American boy's quick, sunny smile—is sometimes strained and sometimes genuine. He is wearing a once-good sport coat, a dark shirt with a carelessly knotted tie, chino trousers, and well-worn jogging shoes. He is tall and well-built, vain of his physical prowess and presence.*

BOYD *swings his duffel bag down and sets it onto the floor. As* DEBRA *and* CLAYBROOK *approach, in the manner of hosts welcoming a guest,* BOYD, *his back to them, paws through the duffel bag, takes up an object in his hand, and rises, perhaps leaps, to his feet to face them. His behavior is threatening, as no doubt he means it to be, even as, with his boyish smile, he pretends otherwise.*)

BOYD: Freeze! Like that! Great! *Perfect!*

(BOYD *takes a flash photograph of* DEBRA *and* CLAYBROOK, *who, caught off guard, look very startled and confused.*)

With the flash, Lights out.

Scene 3.

Lights up, immediately. No break from previous scene. As DEBRA *and* CLAYBROOK *manage to compose themselves, exchanging looks,*

BOYD *walks about the living room, rubbing his hands together and blowing on them, as if to warm them, smiling as if in a mild daze.*

BOYD: So warm here—so *nice.* I'd forgotten how—*nice. (He touches the sofa, kneels to touch the rug, drawing his fingers sensuously across the fabric.)* No sign of—damage. So *nice.*

DEBRA *(nervous laugh):* Things aren't much changed.

BOYD: No, the room is larger—the space. The walls back there *(pointing outward, toward rear of theater)* are farther away than they used to be. It's definitely—larger.

DEBRA: A few things are new—

CLAYBROOK *(not certain if BOYD was joking):* What kind of damage?

BOYD: Yes, it's changed. It's the same, but definitely changed. *(At bookshelves, examines CDs)* Mmmm—Ellington, Tatum, Coltrane—the best. *(Pause, as he looks through CDs, of which there are perhaps two dozen)*

DEBRA *(hesitantly touching BOYD's arm):* Boyd, would you—

BOYD *(boyishly, addresses CLAYBROOK):* Could we hear one of these? Would you mind?

CLAYBROOK: I surely wouldn't *mind*—what's your preference?

BOYD *(handing him a CD):* This—this is fine. *(As CLAYBROOK inserts CD and music starts)* Last month, can't remember where, had a fever of a hundred and four, I started hearing *this*—kept me calm and pulled me back to life—like you pull a sagging-heavy boat in the water with just a rope.

(The jazz, which should be cool, mellow, subtly erotic—any familiar piece or sequence of pieces—continues through the scene, gradually decreasing in volume.)

BOYD *(staring at stained-glass lamp on table): This*—this is new. *(As he touches it, DEBRA makes an involuntary protective gesture, as if she's afraid he might knock it over.)*

DEBRA: Lew's father made it. He's—

BOYD *(not hearing; smiling; has sighted boxes on floor):* I guess these are my leftover things? Ready to go?

DEBRA: Well—eventually. Right now, would you—like a drink?

BOYD (*squatting on his heels beside boxes, looking through them*): God, *this*! I'd forgotten all about *this*! (*Lifts tennis racquet*) And these shoes! (*Lifts a pair of shoes*) And—what's this—(*a notebook, through which he glances hastily*)—handwriting I don't recognize, but I guess it's mine. (*He takes up a tape recorder, a single glove, a hat, some paperback books, etc., in turn*) It's so kind of you, Debra, to have packed all this. Another woman, in your place, might have (*as he lets one of the items fall*) tossed all this crap out with the trash.

(DEBRA *and* CLAYBROOK *speak simultaneously.*)

DEBRA: Yes, but I *didn't*, Boyd—

CLAYBROOK: Debra isn't "another woman"—

BOYD (*lifting camera*): My old Sunpack—so it wasn't lost after all. (*Examines the camera almost tenderly, lifts it to sight areas of the room in the viewfinder, including* DEBRA, *who tries not to appear tense or apprehensive*)

DEBRA: Boyd, why don't you sit down, relax. You've come a long way, you must be—

BOYD (*continuing to stare at* DEBRA): So it wasn't lost after all. It was here all the time.

DEBRA (*patiently*): I'm sure I told you that, Boyd. You just never took the time to— (*Pause, tries to smile*) Why don't I get you something to drink?

(BOYD *replaces the camera, gets to his feet; he's unsteady, as if he has been drinking already.*)

CLAYBROOK (*hospitably*): There's beer, wine, Scotch—whatever. Good Kentucky bourbon. (*Raises wine bottle*) Not quite this quality, Boyd, but almost.

(BOYD *sits heavily on the sofa; has surprised himself by the way in which his legs give out. He runs a hand swiftly and nervously through his hair—an unconscious mannerism that recurs, yet should not be allowed to become predictable or obtrusive. We sense that* BOYD *does this when he is trying to position himself.*)

CLAYBROOK (*admiring wine*): *This*, we'll have with dinner.

BOYD (*staring up at him, blinking, as if the light is too strong*): I'll have a, a—club soda.

CLAYBROOK (*as if doubtfully*): Club soda? Uh—with lemon? lime?

BOYD (*suddenly grinning, pointing to* CLAYBROOK *as he tugs at his necktie*): Right, man, that's a good sign—no tie. (*Pulls off roughly and stuffs it in his pocket*)

DEBRA (*another involuntary gesture*): Oh, Boyd—that *tie*.

BOYD: Eh?

DEBRA: That's that—expensive tie—isn't it?—silk, Italian?—your mother gave you.

BOYD (*bemused, to* CLAYBROOK): Yes. Well. My mother isn't *here*.

(CLAYBROOK, *moving toward kitchen, offstage left, takes the rose from* DEBRA *in passing.* BOYD, *not noticing, calls after him, awkwardly joking.*)

BOYD: My mother has been dead for six years—that's one of the reasons why—(*clumsy, now embarrassed*)—why she *isn't*.

(CLAYBROOK *has exited.*
Except for the jazz, there is silence. We expect DEBRA *and* BOYD *to speak, but they do not. They appear suddenly stricken and can barely look at each other.*
DEBRA *remains standing beside the sofa, not quite in* BOYD's *line of vision, as if reluctant to sit down.* BOYD, *on the sofa, stretches his arms wide; sighs; makes sounds meant to suggest both fatigue and relief.*)

BOYD (*as if making decision*): Yes. This is it.

(DEBRA *remains motionless, uncertain how to approach* BOYD.)

(BOYD *turns to look at* DEBRA, *squinting as if, again, the light is blinding.*)

BOYD (*softly*): . . . beautiful.

DEBRA (*as if not hearing*): How hard *is* it snowing out?

BOYD (*as before*): You. Like always. Beautiful.

(DEBRA , *after a pause, takes a seat in one of the chairs; smiles faintly; clasps hands on lap. It is clear that she is very agitated, but she shows little.*)

BOYD (*indicating the room*): All like a dream—but not *my* dream.

DEBRA: You were sick, you said? A fever? When?

(*We hear* CLAYBROOK *whistling offstage.*)

BOYD: Is that—him? Sounds so happy. (*Pause*) He isn't what I'd been—led to expect. (*Pause, as* DEBRA *resists the implications of this*) Oh, I caught malaria—in Africa. Second time, actually. I'm fine, now.

DEBRA: You've lost weight.

BOYD (*trying not to stare*): And you—you've gained. (*Pause*) You've come back to life.

DEBRA (*simply*): Yes. I have.

BOYD (*passionately*): God, when I drove up here just now, the look of the, the house—the lighted windows—the light around the blinds—it went through me like a knife blade. I see that you're *here*, and I'm *not*. (*Laughs*) That's it.

DEBRA: You're back in the country, now? Living in D.C.?

BOYD (*evasively*): I'm looking around.

DEBRA (*lightly ironic*): How's the Anchor Bar?

BOYD: Benny's still bartending—he asked after you. He—was wondering why he hadn't seen us. (*Pause*) In so long.

DEBRA: And what did you tell him?

BOYD: The truth. (*Pause*)

DEBRA: And tonight you're staying—?

BOYD: A motel on the turnpike. I'm fine. (*Pause*) You're so kind to do this. (*Pause*) You and—him. Both. (*Pause; then, boyish-sly*) For a moment, he didn't want to shake my hand. (*Laughs*) At the door. (*Runs hand through hair*) Once, I did that piece on Roberto Durán, the boxer, remember?—for *Sports Illustrated*? (*As* DEBRA *doesn't seem to remember*) Well, Durán was being introduced to a boxer he was going to fight, and the other man put out his hand to be shaken, and Durán jumped away, and screamed at him, "Get away! get away! I'm not your friend!" (*Laughs, demonstrating some of this, then more earnestly*) You let me in that door—you must have—forgiven me? (*Pause*) Maybe—you shouldn't have.

DEBRA (*trying to shift to a lighter tone*): Shouldn't have forgiven you? Or let you in the door?

(BOYD *stares at* DEBRA, *not replying. His eyes are hooded; his manner intense, erotic. It is clear that he is very strongly attached to* DEBRA, *or to something she represents.*

CLAYBROOK's *whistling grows louder.* CLAYBROOK *reappears in the doorway to the kitchen.*)

CLAYBROOK (*smiling, genial*): Uh, say, Jonathan—I mean, Boyd— you're *sure* you want just a club soda? I'm having a Heineken.

BOYD (*as if needing to be tempted*): Uh—Heineken dark?

CLAYBROOK (*with pleasure*): Real dark.

BOYD (*hesitantly*): Well—okay—make that two. Thanks!

(CLAYBROOK *signals "okay" with thumb and forefinger; disappears back into kitchen.*

DEBRA *laughs, then presses fingers to lips.*)

BOYD (*wide smile*): Something funny, Debra?

DEBRA (*quickly*): No.

BOYD: You're laughing.

DEBRA: I'm—smiling.

BOYD (*soberly*): I stick to beer, now. This will be my first of the day. (*Pause*) First in *two* days.

DEBRA: It's fine, Boyd. It's all right.

BOYD: It *is* fine, I promise. (*Pause*) I am not the way I—the way you remember—me.

DEBRA (*almost tenderly*): I know that, Boyd.

BOYD (*flaring up*): You don't *know* it—I'm *telling* you.

(DEBRA *stiffens.*

CLAYBROOK *returns, cheerful, hospitable. He is carrying a tray*

containing two bottles of beer, two tall glasses, a glass of wine for
DEBRA, *a bowl of nuts, and the long-stemmed rose in a slender vase.*
He serves DEBRA *and* BOYD, *takes a bottle of beer and a glass for*
himself.)

BOYD (*lifting glass*): *Chilled.* That's real class! Thanks, Lew.

DEBRA (*sipping wine*): Thanks, Lew. How is the veal?

CLAYBROOK: Everything's under control. (*Checks watch*) I'll start the
pasta at nine. (*As* DEBRA *seems about to rise*) No, sit *still*; I'm in
charge.

(BOYD *is drinking thirstily; scooping nuts out of the bowl to devour.*)

BOYD: Driving on the turnpike—after dark—it's mesmerizing. And
the snow falling. And the oncoming headlights. You start to float
free—don't know where the hell you *are.*

CLAYBROOK: It can be dangerous, at night. Driving alone.

BOYD (*with a smile*): Driving alone is always dangerous.

CLAYBROOK: So! (*Slight pause*) Debra was telling me you've been
traveling?

BOYD: I'm back for good now. For now.

DEBRA: *That* isn't very likely.

BOYD: My bones ache. (*As if amused*) I'm thirty-five years old.

DEBRA: You were treated for the malaria, I hope?

BOYD (*laughs*): If I wasn't, I wouldn't be here now. (*Drinks*) I *am*
here—I guess?

CLAYBROOK (*looking through a pile of magazines on a table, but not*
finding the one he wants): Debra showed me—I mean, I read—
the article you did on Northern Ireland.

BOYD (*surprised and touched*): You read it?

CLAYBROOK: Thought it was here, somewhere.

DEBRA: It's around somewhere.

BOYD: In the *New York Times Magazine.* But that was last year.

CLAYBROOK: It was very powerful, I thought—first rate. Man! You were taking chances, eh? Interviewing the IRA?

BOYD: That was a while back.

DEBRA: This time you were in—? Ethiopia?

BOYD (*flattered by the attention*): In Addis Ababa mainly. It didn't work out too well. I got sick, and I came back, to Europe I mean—I was supposed to go to East Germany, for *Newsweek*, and (*vaguely; drinking*) Poland . . . but . . . Traveling, crossing time zones, you can really displace who you *are*. (*Pause*) One of my cameras was stolen in Budapest. In the Hilton, of all places.

CLAYBROOK: I've been there—the Budapest Hilton. Pretty swanky.

BOYD (*surprised*): *You've* been there?

CLAYBROOK (*ignoring* BOYD's *condescension*): Well—not recently. Back before all hell broke loose in East Europe.

DEBRA (*defensively*): Lew travels too, or did. To professional conferences.

CLAYBROOK (*wryly*): Yeah—*did*. When I was, like, more a theorist —a teacher.

DEBRA (*proudly*): At Rutgers–New Brunswick. The School of Social Work. That's where we met—Lew was my professor.

CLAYBROOK: Now, I'm in the real world, trying to practice what I preach. (*Shakes head*) No more *theory*.

BOYD (*as if puzzled*): I guess I've been told some—inaccurate things about you.

CLAYBROOK (*coolly, not responding to this remark*): Well. People *will* talk. (*Smoothly*) Yes, I surely do envy you, Boyd. I'd always wanted to visit the Iron Curtain countries, and never got there, and now it's all changed. The Berlin Wall—I'd've liked to see that.

BOYD (*shuddering*): The Wall—that was a, a hard fact to deal with. If your mind's susceptible to—things.

DEBRA: Well, the Wall's down, now.

BOYD (*smiling*): Debra doesn't want me to talk about the Berlin Wall—there's bad personal memories associated with the Wall—

so, okay, I won't. (*Pause*) Just a week or so we spent there, once —in West Berlin—I was on assignment for *Life.* (*Searching in pockets for cigarettes, without success*)

CLAYBROOK (*as if to change subject*): Well, we're living in boom times. For history, I mean. Lots of surprises, the last few years.

BOYD (*goes to his duffel bag, to rifle through it*): The thing about West Berlin people aren't going to know, and lots of people, Americans especially, didn't know *then*—the Wall *surrounded* the city. (*Gesturing*) So, you could start hallucinating, there. If you were susceptible. (*He locates a pack of cigarettes, rises, lights cigarette.*)

CLAYBROOK: Susceptible?

(DEBRA *has risen to find an ashtray. In the meantime,* BOYD'*s match slips through his fingers to the rug.*)

BOYD (*quickly stepping on match*): Oh, Christ—sorry! (*Picks up match, drops it in the ashtray* DEBRA *offers*) I guess it didn't— burn.

DEBRA (*annoyed*): Lew doesn't smoke, and *I* don't—much.

BOYD: You've quit?

DEBRA: I'm trying to. (*She squeezes* LEW'*s hand.*) He gives me moral support.

BOYD (*sympathetic*): Well, I hope it lasts. (*Smokes, exhales, coughs a bit*) I've given up giving up. For now.

DEBRA: Women get more addicted to nicotine than men. It's a terrible thing.

BOYD: I guess I'd better put this out.

CLAYBROOK: No—that's all right.

BOYD: Or maybe smoke outside. (*Coughs*)

CLAYBROOK (*expansively*): No, no, Boyd—make yourself at home.

(*At this,* BOYD *laughs and coughs again.*)

DEBRA: Sit down, please, Boyd—don't hover.

BOYD (*to* CLAYBROOK): She used to say that all the time—"Boyd, don't *hover.*" (*Flapping arms*) I used to be a bat.

(CLAYBROOK *laughs;* DEBRA *smiles faintly.*)

BOYD (*sitting, as before; brushes against stained-glass lamp in passing, but doesn't knock it over*): You did miss something historic, Lew—I mean Clay—no, *Lew*—by not seeing the Berlin Wall. Nothing like it. Weird fucking symbol but, y'know, *real*.

DEBRA (*laughing impatiently*): Boyd, the Wall's *down*.

BOYD: It's the ones you can't see that kill you. Walls, I mean. (*A significant glance at* DEBRA) You told him about it, eh?—that time?

DEBRA (*incensed*): I did not tell Lew about that—that sorry episode. Or any other.

BOYD (*regarding her quizzically*): Didn't?

DEBRA: The past is *past*.

BOYD (*looking from* CLAYBROOK *to* DEBRA *and back*): Yes, but you have to share the past, don't you? Good times, bad times? Misfortunes? Happy memories? That's love, right?

(As BOYD *utters the word* "love," DEBRA *interrupts.*)

DEBRA: I've told Lew very *little*. (*She has become a bit shrill, as if the wine has gone to her head; takes* CLAYBROOK's *hand and squeezes it.*) We have plenty of other things to talk about.

BOYD (*slightly mocking-suggestive tone*): And to *do*. Uh-huhhhh. (*He has drained his glass of beer and now drinks from the bottle, emptying it in an extravagant gesture.*)

CLAYBROOK (*restless*): You about ready for another, Boyd? I'm on my way.

DEBRA (*not wanting to be alone with* BOYD): Oh no, honey, wait—I'll go.

CLAYBROOK (*warmly, but also accustomed to having his own way*): No no *no*, Debra. You stay with your—guest. (*His hand on her shoulder, gently but decisively*) Boyd—another beer?

BOYD: Well—if you are.

CLAYBROOK: Sure thing!

(CLAYBROOK *removes the empty bottles, exits stage left. In his wake there is a brief silence. Then, startling her,* BOYD *reaches over to squeeze* DEBRA'*s hand.*)

BOYD: He's—nice. I like him, Debra.

DEBRA (*almost shyly*): I thought you might. (*Pause*) I mean, I thought you might like each other.

BOYD: You think he likes—*me?*

DEBRA (*withdrawing her hand*): Oh, Lew likes *everyone.*

BOYD (*a bit deflated*): What's he, a Christian or something?

DEBRA (*pleased to be talking about her lover*): In fact, Lew's father *is* a preacher—in the African Methodist Episcopal Church. In Philadelphia.

BOYD (*running a hand through his hair, bemused*): Well—I was certainly misled about all this.

DEBRA (*coolly*): What's "all this"?

BOYD (*shrugging*): You, here. And him.

DEBRA (*voice rising*): Who's been talking about me? Our mutual friends? Whose business is my life but my own?

BOYD (*portentously*): I bear a certain—responsibility. We were together eleven years.

DEBRA: We were married nine years.

BOYD: We were *together* eleven years—that can't be changed. (*Pause*) Almost a third of my lifetime.

DEBRA: Don't think about it, that's all. I've stopped.

BOYD: You've—stopped?

DEBRA: I've *stopped.*

(BOYD *drops cigarette, clumsily retrieves it; brushes ashes from trousers, rug.*)

BOYD: Sorry! My hands are—sort of—shaky.

DEBRA: How long were you drinking before you came here?

BOYD (*ignoring this*): He's so sharp, isn't he—just now, he left at the right moment, knowing he can trust me with you.

DEBRA (*laughing, incensed*): Of course he can trust you with me.

BOYD: He can trust *you* with *me*.

DEBRA: What is that supposed to mean?

BOYD (*in an undertone*): Is he—moved *in*? Here?

DEBRA (*implacably*): To a degree.

BOYD: I mean—is it serious, permanent?

DEBRA: On my side it is.

BOYD (*shrewdly*): He isn't married, or anything?

DEBRA (*after a moment's hesitation*): Ask him.

BOYD: I wouldn't want you to be hurt, Debra—that's all.

DEBRA (*laughing*): From *you*—that's funny.

BOYD: He *has* been married, right? His age, he must have children.

DEBRA (*irritably*): Llewellyn Claybrook is a very special person, but he's a very private person. He isn't, in some ways, like *us*.

BOYD (*exhaling smoke*): Not like white people, or not like *us*?

DEBRA: With him, I don't think in terms of *white* or *black*. (*As* BOYD *makes a gesture of disbelief*) I'm in love.

(*A long, painful pause.*)

BOYD (*stiffly*): I see.

DEBRA: There's no reason why you can't be friends with Lew—with us. You and he are both men of—integrity.

BOYD: Are we? (*Tugs at his shirt collar, suddenly warm*)

DEBRA: Your idealism just got in the way of, of *you*—for a while. You had some rough times, but they're over.

BOYD (*mirthless joke*): Yeah, like thirty years. (*Pause, glancing toward kitchen*) You think he's hiding in there? From me?

DEBRA: Lew was genuinely impressed with that article of yours on Northern Ireland. He said, "Here's a *brother*."

BOYD (*moved*): He didn't say that—did he?

DEBRA: You see, I told him nothing—demeaning. (*Pause*) Just that we'd had some hard times—we fell out of love—we got divorced. And that was that.

BOYD (*wincing*): That was . . . that. (*Pause*) As long as you're happy, Debra.

DEBRA (*slowly*): I am very happy. Don't try to change that.

BOYD: But I— (*Pause, looking at her with yearning, perhaps some disbelief, outrage*) I would never—

DEBRA: Yes. Yes you would.

BOYD (*after a pause*): The scar isn't visible—is it?

DEBRA (*touching her upper lip, involuntarily, then lowering her hand*): That depends upon how close you are.

(BOYD, *restless, gets to his feet; moves toward kitchen, glancing in that direction, as if worried that* CLAYBROOK *can overhear.*)

BOYD: I'd heard—upsetting things—about him, and you. That's why I—that's one of the reasons why I—I'm here.

DEBRA: Well, you were mistaken. (*Sharply*) Who's been talking about me?

BOYD: Somebody said he was an unemployed jazz musician, living off you, and mixed up in drugs; somebody else said he was an ex-cop, mixed up in drugs, and maybe a pimp. (*Not noticing* DEBRA's *anger, laughing*) Burt Hartmann—I ran into him in Frankfurt, catching a plane—said he'd heard you were living with a breeder of pit bulldogs. (*Laughs*) The one consensus was—the guy was *black*.

(DEBRA *gets to her feet, quickly advances upon* BOYD, *and slaps him full on the face.*
    BOYD *stares at her, his hand to his stung face; then, unexpectedly, he drops to his knees, takes hold of her ankles, embraces her legs, presses his face against her legs.*)

BOYD (*anguished, rapturous*): These are so lovely—your shoes—your lovely shoes—Debra—I'm so sorry—

(*At this moment* CLAYBROOK *enters, with tray and drinks; an apron carelessly knotted around his waist. He stares at* BOYD *and* DEBRA.)

Lights out.

Scene 4.

Lights up. Later. There is evidence of drinking: a half-dozen beer bottles on the coffee table, a nearly depleted bottle of wine. CLAYBROOK, *seated as before, has removed the apron and laid it on the table beside him.* DEBRA, *seated as before, is flush-faced and uneasy, sipping wine, frequently glancing at* CLAYBROOK. BOYD, *who is squatting by his duffel bag, taking out a portfolio, has removed his sport coat and looks disheveled but eager, happy. Cigarette in mouth.*

BOYD . . . Yes, but each place is the worst, *the* very worst, in Africa. In Ethiopia—here—(*he passes photographs, at which* CLAYBROOK *stares grimly, adjusting his glasses, and* DEBRA, *wincing, can barely bring herself to look*)—I was covering the war—the drought—the famine—the starvation—the AIDS epidemic—me, and the other reporters and photographers, most of us white, some from the U.S. and some from West Europe—we all know one another, by now —covering the world's "trouble spots"— (*Laughs, wiping face with forearm, speaking rapidly*) It caught up with me, made me sick in my guts. (*Pause; watching* CLAYBROOK's *and* DEBRA's *faces closely; then, in an altered voice, with a bit of bravado*) But I filed the story anyway. "One of Boyd's best."

CLAYBROOK (*moved*): Lord Jesus have mercy! This is powerful stuff. Makes the heartbreak I deal with what you'd call *negotiable*. (*Shows a photograph to* DEBRA, *who pushes faintly at his hand, not wanting to see*) Look at those eyes!—poor child.

DEBRA (*quietly*): If you can't do anything to help, it seems wrong to look.

BOYD (*squatting on his heels, keeping his balance with difficulty*): Right! Don't I know it! But—

CLAYBROOK: Where's the story coming out, Boyd?

BOYD (*vaguely*): It's—pending. (*Leafing through photos*) I spent Christmas photographing dying people—children especially. Close-ups like these. Faces, eyes. On film. To sell. Why else? To sell. And there's the byline. (*Pause*) Back in New York, editors shuffle through the contact sheets, discard most of them. The rap is my shots are "too graphic"—or "not graphic enough." The closer to extinction the spark of life is in these kids, the more valuable the photo; but if the spark of life is actually *out*, and all you have is a kiddy-corpse—no thanks!

DEBRA (*impatiently*): Oh, Boyd, let yourself *be*. It's all about you, isn't it?

BOYD (*hurt*): About *me*?

DEBRA: You know.

(*They exchange a significant look.* DEBRA *shakes her head, just slightly.*
CLAYBROOK *continues to look through the photos; then, sensitive to* DEBRA's *feelings, collects them and hands them back to* BOYD.)

CLAYBROOK (*with regret*): Now's not the proper time, maybe. For these.

BOYD (*almost defiantly, taking the photos back*): When is the proper time, then?

CLAYBROOK (*seriously*): Well—some sacred time.

BOYD: Some what?

CLAYBROOK (*holding his ground*): Sacred time.

(BOYD *puts the photos back in the portfolio, a bit carelessly; shoves the portfolio back in his duffel bag as if disgusted with it or disappointed with its reception.*)

BOYD (*sitting on sofa, as before, taking up space*): Some of us don't believe in "sacred time."

CLAYBROOK: There's true courage there, Boyd. In that work. And artistry too. Uh-huh, I'd say beauty—cruel beauty. (*Trying to be congenial*) Like hell might be beautiful. If you've got the eye.

BOYD: If you're not in it.

CLAYBROOK (*to* DEBRA): It's true what you say, Debra—seems wrong to *look* if you can't *act*—like *knowing* and *acting* shouldn't be separated. But say you just bear witness—"They also serve who only stand and wait"—that can be a true course of action too.

BOYD (*drinking*): Debra doesn't buy that, Clay. She knows we're in it for the dough. "Media" men.

DEBRA: Don't put words in my mouth, Boyd, come *on*.

BOYD (*slightly boastfully*): My next big project is private—a book of my photos. *The Eye of the Storm* is the title.

CLAYBROOK: Fine title!

DEBRA (*wanly enthusiastic*): Is this Beacon Press? The one you signed the contract with?

BOYD: No, this is something new. (*Pause*) A better deal.

DEBRA: Well. I'm happy for you.

CLAYBROOK: And I am too, Boyd. (*Glancing at watch*) Uh!—it's *eleven*? How'd that happen?

DEBRA (*makes a motion to rise but sinks back as if dizzy, giggling*): Wow. If we don't get dinner on the table, it isn't going to be *got* on the table.

(CLAYBROOK *and* DEBRA *confer, almost inaudibly;* BOYD *regards them as if from a distance.*)

CLAYBROOK (*murmuring intimately to* DEBRA): Sweetheart, you let me deal with the pasta, okay? No need us both fussing.

DEBRA: I'll make it—hey, c'mon, I'm not drunk—

CLAYBROOK: You toss the salad.

DEBRA: It's *tossed.*

CLAYBROOK: Get the water boiling, then, and call me—that angel hair can't be overcooked.

DEBRA (*to* BOYD, *by way of teasing* CLAYBROOK): He doesn't trust me, fears I'm gonna make a mush of his pasta. (*She gets unsteadily to her feet; leans on* CLAYBROOK; *her shapely body inadvertently displayed.*) *His* pasta—made it himself, on his machine.

(DEBRA *takes up some of the empties, moves stage left.*)

BOYD (*voice raised, aggrieved, dramatic—his self-conscious "summing up"*): I thought that—reporting injustice, atrocities, suffering—I could make a real difference in the world. But one day I had to see—I was just *reporting*. Just a cog in the consumer machine.

(*This moment is lost, however:* CLAYBROOK *is watching* DEBRA, *who has picked up the empty bottles, fumbles, and nearly drops them.*)

CLAYBROOK (*warmly*): Say, honey—you need some help there?

DEBRA (*waving him back*): Honey, no.

(DEBRA *exits.* BOYD *is hurt, offended; from this point onward it is all he can do to control his deep rage.*
Now the men are left together, there is a moment of quiet; they listen to jazz.)

BOYD: Man, that's lovely. The greatest.

CLAYBROOK (*nodding, tapping foot, keeping time with the music*): Mmmmm.

BOYD: Uh—Ellington?

CLAYBROOK: Peterson.

BOYD: Who?

CLAYBROOK: Oscar Peterson.

BOYD: Oh yes! (*Listens*) You probably have a much larger collection, eh?—than just those CDs?

CLAYBROOK (*as if bemused at himself*): I have records—must be hundreds; I have tapes; I'm into CDs. Over at the other place.

BOYD: The other place.

CLAYBROOK: Down the pike, in Jersey City. Where I'm, y'know, located. (*Pause*) Till things get worked out.

BOYD: Till things get worked out. (*Pause*)

CLAYBROOK (*politely*): You're living in Washington?

BOYD: I'm living in (*shrugs*) my car.

CLAYBROOK (*not having heard*): Where's *that*?

BOYD (*drinking, voice slurred, careless*): Living in my *bag*. (*A kicking gesture toward duffel bag on floor*)

(CLAYBROOK *laughs, uncertainly.*)

BOYD (*almost hesitantly*): So, uh, Clay—okay to call you Clay?—my wife was your student, huh?

CLAYBROOK (*carefully*): Debra O'Donnell—that's how I know her, "Debra O'Donnell"—was my student, yes.

BOYD (*smiling*): Looks like, now, she's graduated.

CLAYBROOK: She's getting her degree in May. But she's been working with County Services since last fall.

BOYD: That's where you work too?

CLAYBROOK: Debra's here in Passaic; I'm in Jersey City, like I said. I'm county supervisor, Family Services.

BOYD: Debra O'Donnell—not Debra Boyd. That's how she identified herself, huh?

CLAYBROOK: That's her name, friend.

BOYD: She's—changed. A lot.

CLAYBROOK: She's a fine, strong, good-hearted woman. Just needs faith in her own spiritual *self*.

BOYD: I'm happy for her—now.

CLAYBROOK (*following his own line of thought*): A human being, beneath his or her skin, has got to realize the spiritual *self*. "The Kingdom of God is within." That's what that means.

BOYD (*lighting cigarette, shakily*): That tiny scar on her upper lip—sickle-shaped—you ever noticed?

CLAYBROOK (*taken by surprise*): A bicycle accident, she said—when she was a little girl.

BOYD (*evenly, a bit relieved*): Well. Okay. 'Cause that's the truth—it *was* an accident. (*Pause, smiling ruefully*) My wife is a, a somewhat self-destructive person—you know? (*As* CLAYBROOK *listens, noncommittally*) You saw us—before—sort of—fooling around? (*Gestures toward the spot where he and* DEBRA *had been standing when* DEBRA *slapped him.*)

(CLAYBROOK *lifts his hands, or shrugs, in a gesture signaling that, yes, he saw, but he isn't upset or proprietary.*)

BOYD: I was—complimenting her on her shoes. Her beautiful new shoes. (*Pause*) That wizened little black nail on her smallest right toe—you ever noticed?

(CLAYBROOK *hesitates, then shakes his head "no."*)

BOYD (*smiling*): No? Never?

(CLAYBROOK *shakes his head "no."*)

BOYD: Next time, you'll notice. (*Pause*) *That* was no accident, the toenail. How it happened was— (*Leaning forward, confidentially; draws* CLAYBROOK *into leaning forward to hear*) We'd just moved here, and things were a little rough—y'know how marital life can be? (*Tries to cajole* CLAYBROOK *into nodding, but* CLAYBROOK *does not*) My father told me, at my mother's funeral—he was drunk and sick but he knew what he was saying—"Son," he said, "days can be damned long, but life goes fast and you never learn a thing"— (BOYD *breaks off to laugh, then succumbs to a fit of coughing*) So anyway, we'd just moved here, into this house—Debra claims that I was involved in a "secret infidelity" at the time with a woman in New York, but I was *not*, I swear, Clay, I was *not*—(*a moment of anger, anguish*)—it was just, just—the weight of daily, domestic life—how love's like a bright flame flaring up, y'know? (*gestures with cigarette, dropping ash*)—and this other, this weight, it's like a concrete *sky* crushing your chest—so you *love* people but can't, sometimes, bear them?—to be in the same room with them?—to hear them brush their teeth?—flush the toilet?—blow their noses?—walk across the floor?—*breathe?*

(DEBRA *reappears, stage left. She has come to fetch* CLAYBROOK *but pauses, listening.*)

BOYD (*drunken, maudlin, anger beneath*): I'd blow out my brains before I'd hurt that woman, I loved that woman, I never stopped loving her, but it sort of—wore thin—not *out*, but *thin*—she thinks I stopped loving her but I, I swear, I never did—*never*. Around that time, five years ago, my work wasn't steady 'cause of temperamental differences—never mind about *that*—*that's* a whole other story— and Debra had a job at a mall on Route 1, hated her job and hated her life and hated me I guess, and every day, God knows why, she'd wear this pair of fake-crocodile shoes—high-heeled shoes with a strap—(*an almost lewd expressiveness*)—good-looking shoes, sort of sluttish—showing her legs, her calves—the way high heels are designed to do—and it turned out she was in pain wearing them—I mean *pain*—they were cheap, and they fit badly—almost like Debra was wearing them on purpose?—these glamorous-slutty shoes?—and the nail on one of her little toes turned black—blood accumulated under it—till finally she couldn't walk, she was in such pain, so she told me, and I examined it—*(laughs, exasperated, perplexed)*—and I was so—stunned, kind of—couldn't imagine why she'd done it, how she could be so stubborn—and hurtful to herself. I hugged her, I guess—and I could feel the terrible rage in her. *(Pause)* At first, it looked as if the toenail would have to be surgically removed, then— *(Pause)* The podiatrist said he'd never seen anything quite like it.

(Through BOYD's *monologue,* CLAYBROOK *has been listening sympathetically, looking down at his hands.*

DEBRA *has discreetly withdrawn, and now reappears, smiling, flush-faced and perhaps angry, to fetch* CLAYBROOK. *She is carrying a glass of wine.)*

CLAYBROOK *(quickly, looking up):* Uh—you ready for me out there, honey?

DEBRA: All ready. *(As* DEBRA *comes forward, she stumbles against* BOYD's *duffel bag.)* Oh—!

*(*BOYD *is immediately on his feet, hurrying to her; takes her elbow.)*

BOYD: Christ, Debra, I'm sorry—damn thing's in the way.

DEBRA: Oh, it's nothing.

*(*DEBRA *has stubbed her toe but not seriously; she is rather more embarrassed than in pain.)*

BOYD *(stooping to move the bag):* Let me get this out of the—

DEBRA *(stooping to assist him):* I'll help—it's heavy—

BOYD *(not wanting her to touch the bag, wrenching it from her grasp):* No, no, I've got it—it's okay. *(He hauls the bag up, places it on top of one of the boxes containing his possessions, gives the box a dismissive kick; he is panting, breathless, seems to be acting a bit oddly.)*

CLAYBROOK *(knotting apron around his waist, approaching* DEBRA*):* Didn't hurt your foot, honey, did you?

DEBRA (*quickly, impatiently*): No—of course not.

Lights out.

Scene 5.

Lights up, but subdued, in dining room area. Living room is dim. It is later; BOYD, DEBRA, *and* CLAYBROOK *are seated at the table; candles are lit, and have burnt partway down. Plates have been stacked together; there are two or three wine bottles on the table.* CLAYBROOK, *wineglass in hand, has been talking earnestly.*

CLAYBROOK: . . . No, it surely hasn't been easy, our urban tax base eroding, people moving out, nobody moving *in*—and not what you'd call a mood of generosity, these days. (*Pause*) Seems like there's a true hardness of heart manifested in some folks. A politician wants to get votes, he waves a flag, says he's going to cut down on the "welfare chiselers," "welfare mothers"—hell, everybody knows what *that* means.

DEBRA (*incensed*): Such bigotry!

CLAYBROOK: This guy, this president of Boston University, man, you'd think it was the Gestapo!—he's running in the gubernatorial primary up in Massachusetts, says he's going to cut any welfare mother off the rolls, she has a second baby! (*Pause, angry smile*) So what're we supposed to do with these folks, let them *starve*? Out on the *street*?

BOYD (*a bit drunkenly, hoping to share in emotion*): Like they're starving in Ethiopia!

DEBRA: Lew's got a plan, and he's taking it to the state legislature —a week from Monday?—he's got some friends there, and maybe they'll listen.

CLAYBROOK (*carefully*): I'm optimistic—I *am*. My position is, I start with myself, a black man, okay, and I am responsible for myself. Meaning I don't pity myself and I don't—ever—make excuses for myself. If I'm going to help my brothers and sisters, first I help myself, and no excuses. (*Pause*) I got radical friends, though, white *and* black, believe that the only way to reform the welfare system is—blow it all sky high.

BOYD (*voice slurred*): BLOW IT ALL—FUCKING SKY HIGH! (*Hand on* CLAYBROOK's *arm*) With real bombs, maybe. Like back in the 1960s.

CLAYBROOK: Well—not with real *bombs*. Just dismantle the bureaucracy, the way it *is*.

DEBRA (*passionately*): Easier said than done.

CLAYBROOK: I think things are moving that way. I do.

DEBRA: Budgets cut like they are, things can't get much *worse*.

BOYD (*flamboyant*): Things can always get worse. The—fucking *sun* could come unhinged. (*Laughs*) Serve us right.

CLAYBROOK (*to* BOYD, *a bit sharply*): Serve who right?

DEBRA (*part teasing, part critical*): Boyd is always looking to the Apocalypse to set things right.

BOYD (*pleasantly, but as if rebuked*): That's how you'd sum me up, is it?

DEBRA: Of course not. I'm not in the habit of summing people up.

CLAYBROOK: Yeah—looking to the Apocalypse to set things right— that's a temptation. Man, where I come from, is it ever.

BOYD: Where do you come from?

CLAYBROOK: South Philly.

BOYD: With a faint trace of—is it North Carolina? (*Cupping ear, smiling*) Bet your folks came up from North Carolina, say, 1940?

(CLAYBROOK *laughs, reluctantly; acknowledging it's so.*)

BOYD (*pursuing it, smiling*): I bet you got the highest grades in high school—hell, I bet you were valedictorian. (*As* CLAYBROOK *acknowledges, smiling*) I bet the hot-shot Ivy League schools were all over you—the way the Big Ten are all over the black athletes, begging you to accept their scholarship money—eh? (*As* CLAYBROOK, *embarrassed, concurs*) The admissions officers flew you to their campuses, put you up in the nicest dorms, set the nicest most brilliant most "adjusted" minority students to recruit you—eh? And you had a hard time choosing between Harvard, Princeton, Yale, but you chose—

CLAYBOOK (*wanting to cut if off*): Yale.

BOYD (*snapping fingers*): Right! (*Pause*) I didn't get in.

DEBRA (*eager to change subject*): I guess—no one wants more food? (*Poking in salad bowl*) There's some salad—arugula—left. (*To* BOYD) Lew insists on real olive oil—from Italy. The kind we used to use, he poured it in the sink.

BOYD (*pleasantly, a bit drunk, ignoring* DEBRA*'s "we"*): It's okay, Lew—I went to Cornell. My folks could afford it. And I worked.

CLAYBROOK: That's—good.

BOYD: I never resented it—"affirmative action." I saw the justice of it, y'know?—the history behind it.

DEBRA (*sharply*): It isn't "affirmative action," is it, when a student's grades are good?—highest of the high?

CLAYBROOK (*to avoid controversy, genially*): Your talent for photography, Boyd—you never learned *that* in school. Real talent, you either have it or you don't.

BOYD (*gravely*): You either have it, or you don't. (*Pause*)

CLAYBROOK: Trouble is, we all know how photographs can *lie*.

BOYD (*quickly*): The photograph never lies.

CLAYBROOK: Eh?

BOYD: The photograph never lies. As a photograph.

CLAYBROOK: C'mon, man. Some photographs are just trickery.

BOYD: Compared to—what? (*A gesture around him*) "Reality"?

CLAYBROOK (*passionately*): Working with the outsides—surfaces— of living things, people's faces, skin—what's deep, inside, isn't showing. A lot of it, too, is accidents of light, and fleeting; but, on film, it's permanent. And that's a lie.

DEBRA (*shuddering*): Oh God, I've seen some terrible pictures of myself. I'm always saying, "Ugh! Is that *me*!"

BOYD: That's just vanity.

DEBRA: Yes? It is?

BOYD: A photograph isn't *you*; it's a separate thing. (*Contentiously*) It has nothing to do with you at all. (*Pause*) Anyway, there are some great pictures of you—you know that. The one I took in Miami, y'remember?—you're leaning against that balcony, the sky behind you is all—

DEBRA (*cutting him off, to* CLAYBROOK): Boyd's the quintessential photographer—refuses to allow his own picture to be taken. You should see him, he actually gets scared. Sweats.

CLAYBROOK (*amused*): Why's that?

BOYD (*shrugging, evasive*): She's exaggerating.

DEBRA: Oh—yes? (*Rises girlishly from table, goes into living room, gets* BOYD's *camera, which he has set atop one of the boxes; as she does so,* BOYD, *rather anxious, follows after her, trying to make a joke of it*) Let's see! How's this work! (*Holding up camera, which* BOYD, *not wanting to be rude, clearly wants to take from her*)

BOYD: Debra, please. Don't.

CLAYBROOK (*as if doubting this is a good idea*): More pictures—?

(CLAYBROOK *remains at the dining room table, amused, observing; while* DEBRA *tries to cajole* BOYD *into having his picture taken. She is charmingly, even flirtatiously, "high"; one senses that she is a woman who, in unguarded moments, can't resist provocation. A powerful sense too of how* DEBRA *and* BOYD *are still attracted to each other.*)

DEBRA (*giggling*): How's this damn thing work? (*Fussing with camera*)

BOYD (*reluctantly*): Like this. (*Taking camera, demonstrating*) You push down here, you wait for the little red light—

DEBRA: What is it—Japanese?

BOYD (*exasperated*): That's what you always ask! (*Turning to* CLAYBROOK, *as if he is fearful of* DEBRA) Anything the least bit complicated, she asks, "Is it Japanese?"

DEBRA: C'mon, c'mon! Smile for the camera, Boyd!

(BOYD *steps back, tries to smile.*)

DEBRA (*laughing*): Boyd, you look *ghastly*! C'mon, *smile*.

DEBRA: How's it go again—? "How's it get so late so early—" (*a throaty, seductive voice, though untrained*)

CLAYBROOK: The beat it's got behind it, you know it's a slave gospel—

BOYD (*out of nowhere*): I got back in the States last Sunday I guess, last Sunday?— (*looks to* DEBRA, *who doesn't know*) —so it's just three weeks ago—I guess— (*Pause, as if confused, runs hands through hair*) I had this, this weird insight—in the Tokyo airport.

DEBRA: Tokyo? What were you doing in Tokyo?

BOYD (*ignoring question*): —I saw all these people, swarms and swarms of people, I was on a ramp carrying my bags and I could see, I mean I could *feel*, the motion, the heat—human lives, like, they're *heat*. I got scared, I was thinking, *The earth is hungry, it's going to devour us, all we have is internal radiance to keep us from being devoured.* (*Pause*) Since then, every time I'm walking somewhere, and people are walking around me, there's this little voice, *Not yet, not yet! It isn't my turn to be devoured, yet!*

DEBRA (*laughing nervously*): That's what I mean—"Apocalypse Now." Here's the boy!

CLAYBROOK: How'd you come to be in Tokyo?

BOYD (*waving hand, as if the subject is of no interest, or he doesn't remember*): It was on the way home.

DEBRA (*to* BOYD): That picture I took of you—*you* have the film, so I s'pose you'll destroy it.

CLAYBROOK: Never was in Tokyo, myself. Got invited, once, but the plane ticket was too high, and the per diem too low. (*Pause*) Friend of mine said, the Japanese looked at him like he was a zoo creature wandering loose. (*Laughs*) They'd come right up, like children, and ask to touch his hair. (*Laughs*)

DEBRA: Oh, the Japanese must be more sophisticated than that. You see them all over, traveling.

CLAYBROOK (*reprovingly*): These were people in the street—common folks.

BOYD: The Chinese—they think we're ghosts. (*Pause*) White people, anyway. (*Looks at his hands*)

DEBRA (*pouring remainder of wine into glasses*): Everybody thinks *they're* all that counts.

BOYD: I brought another bottle of my wine—let's open it.

DEBRA: Oh, no—

CLAYBROOK: Another bottle of *this*? (*He indicates the bottle* BOYD *brought; the other bottles on the table are his own.*)

BOYD: It's pretty good stuff, isn't it? Nineteen sixty-two Bordeaux.

CLAYBROOK: *Too* good, almost, Boyd. I mean—for this occasion.

DEBRA: It certainly was delicious, Boyd.

BOYD: So, okay, I'll get the other bottle.

CLAYBROOK: Uh, Boyd, maybe not—thanks—

BOYD: Why not? If we don't finish it, you can keep it, you and Debra. No big deal.

CLAYBROOK: It's too expensive. Save it for another time.

BOYD (*as if casually*): Maybe—there's not going to be another time.

DEBRA (*giddily*): Of course there is!

(BOYD *moves unsteadily on his feet, headed for his duffel bag; he collides with the table supporting the stained-glass lamp, and the lamp nearly falls.* CLAYBROOK, *quick on his feet, catches it;* DEBRA *gives a little cry.*)

BOYD: Jesus—sorry. How'd I do that?

CLAYBROOK: Okay, now. You're fine.

BOYD (*gripping* CLAYBROOK *by both arms, suddenly emotional*): I'm not drunk, I'm—*lucid*. You want to know something? A secret?

CLAYBROOK (*guarded*): Well—maybe.

BOYD (*passionately*): I don't blame her a bit. I don't, I don't, I fucking don't, I *don't*. (*Shakes head emphatically*) Speaking man-to-man— y'know? *I don't blame her.*

CLAYBROOK: Blame her for what?

BOYD (*goofy-sincere smile*): Being in love with *you.*

CLAYBROOK (*embarrassed*): Oh hell, man—c'mon.

BOYD: Well, I *don't*. Why not tell the truth, just once. I'm man enough to tell the truth. (*Flamboyantly*) If I was a woman I'd prefer this man (*indicating* CLAYBROOK) to this man (*indicating himself*). I mean, if I was a white woman. (*Pause, laughs*) As for a black woman—who knows?

DEBRA: Boyd, this isn't amusing.

BOYD (*puzzled*): Amusing? Why should it be—amusing?

(CLAYBROOK *guides* BOYD *back to the table; evidently he has forgotten the wine.*)

CLAYBROOK: What we need is a—little nightcap.

DEBRA: Just a *little*. (*Shakes head, laughs*) I'm drunk.

BOYD (*happily*): I'm not drunk, I'm—lucid. (*Turning to* CLAYBROOK, *shaking hands*) Actually, I'm Boyd. I'm void. I mean, I'm *dead*. (*Laughs, sitting heavily in chair*) I'm dead meat.

CLAYBROOK: What kinda talk's that, man?

BOYD: You're dead meat if, like, you don't have a soul—inside. "The Kingdom of God is within." Well—it *ain't*. With some of us poor bastards, (*pronounced "Negro" intonation*) it sho ain't.

DEBRA: Boyd!

CLAYBROOK (*slurred voice, but with dignity*): God is inside you, man, whether you acknowledge Him or not. That's a fact.

BOYD (*pretense at sobriety*): Oh—I know it, Clay. I know, I know it. I *know*.

CLAYBROOK: I'll make us all a little nightcap. (*Heads for kitchen*)

DEBRA (*rising, unsteadily*): I'll help you, honey.

CLAYBROOK: Nah, I'm fine. Stay still.

DEBRA (*gathering dishes, awkwardly*): I'll just take these—

(DEBRA *and* CLAYBROOK *carry some of the dishes, etc., from the table;* BOYD *rises to help them, but drops a glass to the floor.*)

BOYD: Oh, damn it—sorry!

DEBRA (*scolding*): It didn't break. Just *sit*.

(DEBRA *and* CLAYBROOK *exit*.)

BOYD (*calling after them, but unheard*): That used to be *my* kitchen!
(*Pause, then points stage left*) My bathroom where I laid the tile
from Sears! My bedroom I'm banished from! (*Points in another
direction*) My garage! (*Points down*) My basement that leaks!
(*Louder*) My voice echoes here! I'm the *ghost* here!

(BOYD *rises from the table, returns to the living room; appears to be
headed in a collision course with the stained-glass lamp again, but
at the last moment swerves, adroit on his feet as a basketball player.*)

BOYD ("*Negro*" *intonation*): In you face!

(BOYD *goes to his duffel bag. Glancing over his shoulder, to see that
he's unobserved, he removes from the bag an object wrapped in a
towel. It is a revolver. He checks the chamber, squints along the
barrel, spends a risky several seconds examining the gun; then shoves
it into his trouser pocket. Glancing down, he sees that the object is
too bulky; removes it and shoves it in his belt; but this too is con-
spicuous, so, finally, he pulls out his shirt, shoves the gun into his
belt again, and hides it with the shirt.*)

BOYD (*dampening his hands with his tongue and smoothing down his
hair; in a voice of gravity and menace*): The Kingdom of God is
within. The Kingdom of God is within. (*Pause*) THE KINGDOM
OF GOD IS WITH-*IN*.

Lights out.

ACT 2

Scene 6.

*Lights up. The living room area, some minutes later. The candles
have been extinguished on the table, and the dining area is in semi-
darkness.* DEBRA, BOYD, *and* CLAYBROOK *are back in the living room,
though seated differently:* DEBRA *and* CLAYBROOK *are on the sofa,
affectionately close;* BOYD *is in a chair to their right. His shirttails
out,* BOYD *looks disheveled but not dangerous.* DEBRA *has kicked off
her shoes and, as if unconsciously, moves and stretches her legs, even*

smooths the stockings with slow fingers—*if she behaves in a sensuous, provocative way, it should be very subtle.* CLAYBROOK *has removed his sport coat and appears to be quite warm, perspiration glinting on his face. (He may remove his glasses to polish them.) Jazz with a more hectic beat plays in the background. The long-stemmed rose in its vase is still on the coffee table.*

CLAYBROOK *has brought in a tray of ingredients for the nightcap —bottles, glasses, a tall shaker, a container of ice cubes, etc. He is genial, relaxed, expansive, hospitable—one of those people whom alcohol makes warm and childlike, yet volatile emotionally. His "black"/North Carolina accent is distinctly perceptible.*

CLAYBROOK: Friends, this is a Flintlock I'm gonna conjure up, from my days tendin' bar on Seventh Avenue, workin' my way through NYU (*he stresses each letter of* "NYU") for the Ph.D. (*stresses each letter of* "Ph.D.," *making the sounds comic*).

DEBRA: *Bar*tender? You never said.

CLAYBROOK (*hand on her knee*): Lots of things I ain't said, honey. (*Preparing the drinks,* CLAYBROOK *moves his hands in magician style, basking in the attention.*) First—three and three-quarters ounces bourbon: like so (*into shaker*). Next—two and one-quarter ounces applejack brandy: like *so*. Then—li'l bit of white crème de cacao. Li'l bit lemon juice. Li'l bit grenadine. Okay, now *shake*. (*Shakes liquid, eyes shut; both* DEBRA *and* BOYD *watch attentively.*) Okay, friends, now you pour over ice cubes, and here y'are— straight from yo' man's hands.

(BOYD, DEBRA, CLAYBROOK *touch glasses ceremonially and drink.*)

DEBRA (*between a sigh and a cry*): Oh. God.

BOYD (*trying to sound sober*): Man, this is *good*. What's it called?

CLAYBROOK: Flintlock.

BOYD (*enunciating*): Flint-lock.

DEBRA: Some kind of old-fashioned gun? Musket? (*Laughs*)

BOYD: So, Clay, you were a bartender, too.

CLAYBROOK: Among my many dazzlin' gifts.

BOYD (*almost boyishly*): Are there—other things about you, too? I mean—

CLAYBROOK (*a dismissive gesture of his hand*): Nah, what you see is what you get.

BOYD: Well—that was the finest meal I've had in, in—(*wipes at eyes*)—my *life*.

(CLAYBROOK, DEBRA *laugh. They speak simultaneously:*)

DEBRA: Oh, Boyd, c'mon.

CLAYBROOK: Listen to the man jivin' us!

BOYD: No, seriously, it was *good*. The meat, the sauce, the spices, the pasta—

DEBRA (*proudly, but a bit teasingly*): Lew insists on everything *fresh*, and I mean *fresh*—no canned tomatoes, no oregano or marjoram or basil out of jars. He's the real thing!

CLAYBROOK: The veal got overcooked some. But the pasta turned out pretty good.

BOYD (*as if marveling*): You made the pasta yourself—didn't just *buy* it.

CLAYBROOK: Only way you control quality, it's to do as much as you can yourself.

BOYD: In food as in life! (*Pause, not mockingly but a bit ingenuously*) You take it all seriously, don't you? Making a meal, setting the table, coordinating the wine—all that.

CLAYBROOK (*laughing*): Man, I take *everything* seriously. "We don't pass this way but once."

BOYD (*seeming non sequitur*): A condemned man, he'll eat the pro-verbial hearty meal. A friend of mine did an article—interviewed death row prisoners and officials in Texas. Number-one favorite's T-bone steak and French fries. Some ask for lobster—first time in their lives. (*Laughs*)

DEBRA (*shuddering*): *I* couldn't eat, knowing I was to die!

BOYD: Lucky I brought red wine—that was just a hunch.

CLAYBROOK: Man, that wasn't *wine*—that was *vel*-vet.

BOYD: I was—hoping you'd like it. Both of you. (*Pause*)

(DEBRA *and* CLAYBROOK *may exchange a glance, or* DEBRA *may dab moisture off* CLAYBROOK'*s forehead with a napkin—some small intimate gesture.*)

BOYD (*with abrupt ebullience*): So, Clay my man! Dogs!

CLAYBROOK: Eh?

BOYD: Dogs! You breed pit bulls, eh?

CLAYBROOK (*staring at him, unsmiling*): Say what, Boyd?

BOYD (*smiling, but confused—as if genuinely*): Uh—I mean—you *don't* breed pit bulls. (*To himself*) He *doesn't* breed pit bulls.

(DEBRA *pokes* BOYD *in the leg with a foot, annoyed.*)
(*An awkward moment.*)

CLAYBROOK: What's this—*pit* bulls? (*Emphatically*) Hell, no, man, where'd you pick that up? Those are killer dogs, triflin' and dangerous. I'd vote to make the breed extinct.

DEBRA (*alert, like a student*): Extinct? A breed of animal? Can that be done?

CLAYBROOK (*shrugging*): Why not, honey? Pass a law. The U.S. Congress—let 'em pass a law. Civilized folks can do *anything*, passing the right laws. (*Winking*) Look what ole Abe Lincoln did, folks shamed him enough.

DEBRA (*with exaggerated care, to avoid slurring words*): But, Lew, how can a breed of animal be outlawed? Isn't that like *genocide*? In fact, there are laws protecting endangered species.

BOYD (*eager to join in*): I don't think a pit bull is a species—it's a breed.

DEBRA: So all right, what's the difference? The poor dog doesn't choose his nature.

CLAYBROOK (*gently but forcibly, hand on her knee*): Look, Honeygirl, pit bulldogs ain't your specialty, so how 'bout droppin' the subject?

DEBRA: They're some kind of bulldog, obviously. Something to do with— (*vague*) —*pits*.

BOYD: They're part terrier and part bulldog—

CLAYBROOK: *English* bulldog. (*Mugging*) That's the nastiest kind.

BOYD (*as if to impress with his knowledge*): A pit bull is trained to attack all strangers and kill them, provoked or not. Whether the stranger is an elderly woman, or a baby, or—whatever. And they don't *bark*—that's the eerie thing about them. They give no warning, just leap at your throat.

DEBRA: That's how they're *trained*, but I can't believe that's their *nature*.

CLAYBROOK (*impatiently, hoping to drop subject*): The training *is* the nature, and the pit bulldog isn't natural, it's a hybrid.

DEBRA: But the individual dog—the *creature*! How can it be his fault? her fault? All animals are innocent.

CLAYBROOK: And they don't *bark*—don't give no warning till they're at your throat.

DEBRA: That's how they're *trained*. But what's their *nature*?

CLAYBROOK (*clearly disliking the subject*): The training *is* the nature, and the pit bulldog isn't natural, it's a hybrid.

DEBRA: But it isn't the poor dog's fault! All animals are—innocent.

CLAYBROOK (*voice rising*): I go for setters—grew up with 'em. Yeah, and collies. Dogs that, they look at you with their beautiful eyes, you feel life's worth livin'—right? Tell me it's a bourgeois sentiment—okay, it's bourgeois. Tell me it's WASP—don't care. Lenin loved his dog above the Revolution—or was it Trotsky?— hell, could be Hitler! The fact is, there's anybody or anything you can trust your life with, the dog is *it*—the only mammal that's *it*.

DEBRA (*excited*): That's what I'm saying, that's what I'm saying—you don't *listen*.

CLAYBROOK: Who brought this up? Let's drop it. (*A gesture of impatience; drinks*)

DEBRA (*to* BOYD) He's got a grudge against those poor dogs, that's how he *is*—strong opinions.

BOYD (*to* DEBRA): Why'd you tell me he liked them, then? Didn't you tell me?

DEBRA: What?

CLAYBROOK: What kinda shit's this?

DEBRA: I never said a word, Boyd.

BOYD: Must have been somebody else. Sorry.

(*The subject should be dropped, but* DEBRA *unaccountably picks it up and persists. Half-consciously, she is enjoying the emotional attention, the frisson of arousing* CLAYBROOK.)

DEBRA: I just feel—

CLAYBROOK: Shut up! (*Pause; then speaking as we have not heard him speak before, angrily and ironically*) Look, the pit bulldog is a macho breed, *black* macho breed, got it? That what we're talkin' about? Huh? Baaaad macho breed of killer dog so black men get a charge walkin' the streets with 'em on leashes, sexy feelin', get it?—they give the word, the fucker's gonna tear somebody apart. Real baaad.

DEBRA (*hurt, angry*): I don't care, I still—

CLAYBROOK (*coldly furious*): You want the sociology, okay, I'll provide the sociology, fucking-A right, the pit bull helps com-pen-sate for the male nigger in America being a dog himself but not a killer dog, no way, man, just a runty ole mongrel dog not worth shit. You got it, honey? Like havin' a big cock's s'post to com-pen-sate for not havin' nothin'—including, in fact, the cock. (*Contemptuous*) Now you got it, honey?

(DEBRA, *stricken into silence, edges away from* CLAYBROOK. BOYD *is excited, trying to maintain control.*)

BOYD: You don't have to be rude to Debra, Clay—you don't have to be rude.

CLAYBROOK (*on his feet, upset, walking off, speaking loudly*): Wasn't being *rude* to her, man, was just *explaining.*

BOYD (*on his feet too*): It—sounded rude to me.

CLAYBROOK: Well, fuck you, man—whose problem's that?

BOYD: Just a—

CLAYBROOK: Don't you fuck with me, you—

BOYD: —a minute—

CLAYBROOK (*upset, exiting*): Don't none of you fuck with *me*.

(DEBRA *sits stunned on the sofa;* BOYD *is standing, fingers flexing. Oddly, his facial expression suggests extreme regret, almost as if he is about to cry.*)

DEBRA (*hoarsely*): I think you'd better leave, Boyd. Please.

BOYD (*calling*): Clay? Uh, hey—Lew? Hey, c'mon.

DEBRA (*wiping at eyes*): Haven't you done enough!

BOYD: Me? What'd *I* do? You were the one!

DEBRA (*on her feet, swaying*): I've never seen him like that—and you're to blame. (*Approaching stage left, calling in a weak, apologetic voice*) Lew? Honey? Oh, Lew, *please* . . .

(*No answer.* DEBRA *stands at the kitchen door;* BOYD *looks on, then approaches her and takes her arm.*)

BOYD: If that's what the man is like, Debra—

DEBRA (*fiercely, weeping*): That isn't what the man is like! Get away! Haven't you done enough! (*Calling, as before*) Lew? Please?

BOYD: Debra, I—

DEBRA (*wrenching from him*): Get *away*! Damn you! (*She speaks to* CLAYBROOK, *who is in the kitchen, without daring to enter.*) Lew? Darling? We're so sorry, so very sorry, both of us, we spoke out of ignorance— (*A pause, and we hear* CLAYBROOK's *muffled voice, the words unintelligible.*) You know I wouldn't ever do anything to hurt or offend you, honey—you know that, don't you? (DEBRA *speaks desperately, yet articulately; again there is a pause, and the muffled response, to which* BOYD *also tries to listen.*) Oh God yes, I do. I do. Lew? What? (*Another pause, etc.*) Please accept our apologies. Yes, he is, he's right—

BOYD (*behind her, cupping hands to mouth, guiltily and excitedly*): I'm sorry, Lew—*Clay*—sorry as hell. Believe me!

(*Another pause. They listen; then* DEBRA *quietly leads* BOYD *back into the living room. She wipes her face on a napkin; agitated, not quite knowing what she does, she starts to gather up some of the bottles and glasses, but then stands perplexed.*)

DEBRA (*almost in a whisper*): He looked at me—as if he didn't know me.

BOYD: He's got a temper. Christ!

DEBRA: That wasn't him—really.

BOYD: If I'm to blame, I'm certainly sorry.

DEBRA: No, I was the one who pushed him. You can't push a man like that. (*She drinks from one of the glasses, impulsively.*)

BOYD (*also drinking from one of the glasses*): He's a man of—of passion.

DEBRA: He's a man of pride, and we offended his pride. (*Holds out hand*) Look—how I'm trembling.

BOYD (*taking* DEBRA's *hand*): Debra, I'm sorry. I wouldn't hurt you for the world.

DEBRA (*easing away, distracted*): Is that—? (*Listens*) Is that the back door? (*Listens, urgently*)

BOYD: I don't hear anything. (*More insistently*) I wouldn't hurt you for the world, Debra.

DEBRA: He wouldn't just—walk out? He wouldn't just leave me—

(DEBRA *stands, stricken, looking toward kitchen;* BOYD *circles her as if stalking her. Lights focus on them.* BOYD *touches the butt of the revolver through his shirt, assuring himself it's still there.*)

BOYD (*after a pause*): Debra, I came back tonight for a reason. (DEBRA *doesn't hear; he speaks louder.*) I came back for *you*, Debra. Not my worthless possessions.

DEBRA (*vaguely*): What—?

BOYD: You, and me. I came back for you, and me. (*Pause, as he looks at her with longing*)

DEBRA (*distracted*): I might have been a stranger to him—the way he looked at me. I tried to touch him, and he threw my hand off.

BOYD (*more sharply*): I said, I came back for you, and me. Look at me. (*He takes her wrist, and this time* DEBRA *can't easily twist away.*)

DEBRA: What are you saying, Boyd? You promised it was over.

BOYD: Nothing is ever over. Until—(*laughs harshly*)—it's *over*.

DEBRA (*trying to laugh, faintly, a bit angrily, at the absurdity of* BOYD's *words*): You can see—I have a new life now, I'm changed. I'm not your wife.

BOYD: You're still my wife. Oh yes.

DEBRA: I, I have a certain—regard—for you—I respect and honor you and I feel sorry for you, but—

BOYD: I don't want your pity, for Christ's sake. I want—you know —the way it *was*.

DEBRA (*ironically*): The way it was when? The last few years?

BOYD: No, the way it *was*. You know. (*Almost tenderly*) *You* know.

DEBRA (*quickly*): No. That's over, that's gone.

BOYD: It is *not*.

DEBRA: I can't believe this—after you promised.

BOYD: Debra, I'm the one who loves you—not him.

DEBRA: Never mind him! You don't know anything about him.

BOYD: I'm the one who loves you—I'm your *husband*.

DEBRA (*bravely, defiantly*): Your face! It isn't a face of love.

BOYD (*an expression of barely controlled rage*): If this is my face, it *is* the face of love, God damn you!

(*They struggle.* DEBRA *tries to slap* BOYD, *but he grips that hand too.*)

BOYD (*half pleading*): The other women never meant anything—I swear.

DEBRA: Yes, that was part of it.

BOYD: What? What was part of it?

DEBRA: You used them, and you used me. Nothing meant anything.

BOYD: I made mistakes. I acknowledge that.

DEBRA: We both made mistakes, and now it's over.

BOYD: Nothing is over, I said—until it's *over*. (*Pause*) No survivors.

DEBRA: Are you threatening me?

BOYD: I'm just telling you.

DEBRA: We were getting along so well, I thought—this evening—all of us. And now—

BOYD: *He* doesn't love you, that's for goddamn sure.

DEBRA: I refuse to talk about him with you. You don't *know.*

BOYD: I know what I saw.

DEBRA (*half screaming*): *You don't know.*

BOYD: Debra, please. Hey—c'mon.

DEBRA (*more calmly*): I'll always be your friend, Boyd. But—

BOYD (*unconscious of the import of his words*): You're not my friend, you're my *wife!*

(*At this,* DEBRA *laughs, despairingly;* BOYD, *staring at her, finally smiles—a ghastly grin.*)

(*A pause.*)

BOYD: You don't believe me—but I do love you.

DEBRA (*quietly*): No, Boyd. I don't believe you.

BOYD (*with dread*): You don't—love me? At all?

DEBRA: Not in the way you want.

BOYD: That's the only way there *is.*

(DEBRA *shakes her head "no."* BOYD *stares at her; grips her chin in his hand; seems about to kiss her; but when she goes dead, unresponsive, he doesn't force himself upon her.*)

BOYD: Then it really is over, Debra? It's over?

(DEBRA *does not reply, as she and* BOYD *freeze in their posture. Lights intensify.*)

Lights out.

Scene 7.

Lights up. Only a few seconds have elapsed: DEBRA *and* BOYD *are in the same position, but now* BOYD *has released* DEBRA, *and* DEBRA *is rubbing her wrist, smoothing her disheveled hair, adjusting her clothing.*

As she searches out her shoes, and puts them on, CLAYBROOK *appears, stage left, entering from the kitchen. Both* DEBRA *and* BOYD *look at him.*

CLAYBROOK *enters the living room in a manner that might be described as rueful, yet not repentant. He is wiping his face with a white handkerchief or tissue.*

CLAYBROOK (*after a beat or two; in stiff, "white" diction*): I started some coffee—figured it's about time.

DEBRA (*almost shyly*): That's a good idea, Lew. (*As if embarrassed, he doesn't look at her. To* BOYD) Isn't that a good idea!

BOYD (*ironic, with bravado*): To sober me up, for the road?

CLAYBROOK (*grimly*): To sober us all up.

BOYD: You're kicking me out? Okay, I don't blame you. (*Laughs awkwardly*) Clay, I mean Lew—I'm *sorry.* (BOYD *puts out his hand aggressively; but, looking elsewhere,* CLAYBROOK *discreetly ignores it.*)

DEBRA (*approaching* CLAYBROOK, *speaking hopefully, yet with composure*): *I'm* to blame, I guess—I feel like such a fool.

CLAYBROOK (*squeezing* DEBRA's *arm at the elbow, a quick gesture of affection, an appeal for forgiveness, murmuring*): *I'm* the fool. Let's forget it.

(CLAYBROOK *and* DEBRA *exchange a significant look, as* BOYD *stands to the side, excluded.*)

BOYD: I guess—it's late.

DEBRA (*politely*): I hope you don't have a long drive?

BOYD (*quickly, as if with a double meaning*): Oh no. Not a long drive.

(CLAYBROOK *has been tidying up the coffee table, putting bottles, glasses, etc., on the tray; picking up crumpled napkins from the floor.*)

CLAYBROOK (*trying to speak normally, though still in his "white" diction*): When you leave, I'll help you with those boxes. They're heavy.

BOYD (*as if boyishly*): Thanks!

DEBRA (*trying not to show too overtly how vastly relieved she is*): I smell the coffee—is it mocha java?

CLAYBROOK: Yes, but a fresh package, not the old one.

DEBRA: Good. (*She takes the tray from* CLAYBROOK, *and the two appear, in that instant, domestic, companionable.*) Thanks, honey. I'll take care of everything.

(DEBRA *exits, to kitchen.*)

BOYD (*lighting cigarette, seemingly nervous laugh*): Man, *you're* sure not to be messed with.

(CLAYBROOK *shrugs or grunts a reply. His back to* BOYD, *he is straightening cushions on the sofa; adjusts the stained-glass lamp by a fraction of an inch.*)

BOYD: It was those dynamite Flintlocks—that's what it was.

CLAYBROOK (*bemused*): Maybe.

(CLAYBROOK *indicates that* BOYD *should sit. The men face each other, sitting in the chairs. No jazz is playing.*)

BOYD (*smoking, leaning forward*): Well—it certainly was—is—generous of you, and Debra. Charitable. Having me here, tonight. The ex-husband, the ghost.

CLAYBROOK: Okay, man, that's okay.

BOYD: She's a good woman, and she deserves the best. I'm happy for her. (*Pause, smiles*) I'm not *happy*, but I'm *happy* for her.

CLAYBROOK: Okay, man.

BOYD: After the divorce, for a while—things were a little rocky for her. (*As if considering*) For both of us. (*Pause*) It was hard—she'd try to call me, I was out of the country, on assignment, out of contact. (*Pause, when* CLAYBROOK *doesn't respond*) Y'know, Clay, what you said before—"The Kingdom of God is within"—that made a strong impression on me. Thanks.

CLAYBROOK (*cool smile; in a mock "Negro" intonation*): Don't jive me, man, it's what everybody knows. Or *don't* know—'cause maybe it ain't so.

BOYD (*frowning*): What do you mean? Don't you—believe? (*As* CLAYBROOK *shrugs noncommittally*) Your father's a minister, Debra said? African Episcopal Baptist Church? (*In* BOYD'*s too-solemn intonation, this name sounds ludicrous.*)

CLAYBROOK: African Methodist Episcopal Church.

BOYD (*as if to make a casual joke*): There's a difference?

CLAYBROOK (*a snorting sort of laugh*): Don't push it, man.

BOYD (*leaning forward, eagerly, elbows on knees, as if speaking confidentially*): I wasn't—"jiving" you, Clay. About the Kingdom of God. It doesn't require a supernatural base, does it, or anything theological? Just, y'know, *psych*ological? "Psyche" meaning "soul"? I was thinking—(*runs hand through hair, a bit manic suddenly*) —you and I, maybe, you with your position—in the welfare department—

CLAYBROOK (*interrupting*): County Family Services.

BOYD: —the kinds of things you see—and deal with—the two of us could collaborate—a book of photographs with a text— (*Seeing* CLAYBROOK'*s negative expression*) No?

CLAYBROOK: In my profession, as long as you're *in* it, you don't exploit the people.

BOYD (*hurt*): This wouldn't be exploiting.

CLAYBROOK: You don't use the people as material, that's all.

BOYD (*deflated*): I see. (*Pause*)

(DEBRA *appears, bringing coffee things on tray. She seems to have freshened herself up: her hair is no longer disheveled; her look is less harassed. She is wearing, not her glamorous high-heeled shoes, but flat-heeled sandals.*)

CLAYBROOK (*smiling*): That smells *good*.

DEBRA (*seating herself between the men, speaking brightly, to* BOYD): There's a new food store, Boyd, on Third Street—y'know, where the Italian bakery was? It specializes in all sorts of coffee, it's really wonderful.

BOYD: Is it! (*Smiles*)

(DEBRA *pours coffee, etc., for the three of them.* BOYD, *confronted with his cup, merely sits, smiles, a cigarette in his mouth.*)

BOYD (*as if mischievously, like a small boy*): Maybe I'll stick to—the other. I've got that bottle of Bordeaux in my bag.

DEBRA (*chiding*): Boyd, *no.*

BOYD: No?

DEBRA: You're not serious.

BOYD: I'm always serious! (*Pause*) Like Clay. I mean—Lew. (*Pause*) Since you have a Ph.D., Lew, I guess you're *Dr.* Claybrook?

CLAYBROOK (*easy smile, sipping coffee*): Just when I'm filling out a form, like for a loan.

BOYD: You're sure—nobody wants a little wine? Just a nightcap? One for the road?

DEBRA: Boyd, *no.* You have to drive.

BOYD: We could just start it, and I'd leave the rest of it for you. (*Halfhearted gesture as if to rise*)

DEBRA: Try the mocha java, Boyd, it's delicious.

BOYD (*smiling*): You know that sign you see, sometimes—aimed at commuters—"If you lived here, you'd be home now." (*Laughs*)

(*A moment's embarrassed silence.* DEBRA *and* CLAYBROOK *exchange a covert glance, which* BOYD *notes.*
DEBRA, BOYD *speak simultaneously, but* BOYD *prevails.*)

DEBRA (*forced enthusiasm*): So, Boyd, you're doing a book of—

BOYD (*to* CLAYBROOK): I appreciated your response, Clay, to my photographs. That meant a lot to me.

CLAYBROOK: Well, it's good work.

BOYD (*smiling, stubs out cigarette as if in anger*): So why don't you want to collaborate with me?

CLAYBROOK: Eh? I said I couldn't.

BOYD (*to* DEBRA, *as if teasing*): Clay snubbed me, just now. I suggested we collaborate on a major project—I'd do the art, he'd provide the text. An unflinching look at America's underclass.

CLAYBROOK (*trying to be pleasant*): I didn't *snub* you, friend. I said I *couldn't*, for professional reasons.

DEBRA: Boyd, Lew doesn't have time.

BOYD (*smiling*): Oh, I know! I can imagine. (*Pause*) *I* don't have time, either. Really.

CLAYBROOK: I'm not working just with the "underclass"—whatever *that* is. Family Services deals with all kinds of folks—(*smiling*)—white folks too.

BOYD: That's what the book would do—combat stereotypes.

DEBRA: Maybe you could talk about it with Lew some other time.

BOYD (*eagerly*): I'd like that. (*Pause*) You know, *you* can perpetuate stereotypes too. (*Indicating* CLAYBROOK) It isn't just us.

CLAYBROOK (*smile*): Who's *me*?

BOYD: Talk of "whites"—"blacks"—*that's* irresponsible.

DEBRA: Now, Boyd—

BOYD (*pointing at* CLAYBROOK, *smiling*): For instance—*you* aren't black. I mean—not *black*. Even a really dark-skinned man isn't *black*, so why call yourself "black," then?

(CLAYBROOK *stares at* BOYD *for a long moment, his expression impassive. He grips his coffee cup rigidly, however; sits very still.*)

DEBRA: *Boyd!*

BOYD (*speaking quickly, leaning forward*): I mean—why not speak frankly? For once? A man like you, Clay, with your skin tone, it's absurd to call you *black*—you just aren't! I know, I know—there are historical factors—sure—but it's so extreme. Like primary colors—primary ways of thinking—no subtleties. Am I "white"? Is this (*extending hands*) "white"? Hell, no. Somebody from another planet, arriving on earth, would think we were all color *blind*.

CLAYBROOK (*shaking head, trying to remain calm*): Man, you sure are one, aren't you?

BOYD: One what?

CLAYBROOK: One asshole honky su-*preme.*

BOYD (*aggrieved*): You're not addressing the issue! It's a, a—an epistemological issue!—how we *know* what we think we know, when it turns out we don't know it 'cause it's wrong.

CLAYBROOK (*as if to rise*): Say what, man? I'm tunin' out.

BOYD: Don't go! Sit still! Please! Don't (*pleading, yet with a threat beneath*) condescend to me!

DEBRA: Lew honey, Boyd doesn't mean any insult, he just means— (*embarrassed, concerned*)—what he *says.* He—

CLAYBROOK: I don't give a shit what he *says* long as I don't have to hear it.

BOYD: You're afraid! You're afraid! Man, you surprise me—you're *afraid!* To talk man-to-man, friend-to-friend, to speak the truth for once—like "to bear witness."

CLAYBROOK: Friend-to-friend? (*Echoing* BOYD's *earlier remark attributed to Roberto Durán*) Get away, man, you're not my friend!

BOYD: 'Cause you shut me out. That's why.

CLAYBROOK: Oh, shit! Poor whitey! Ma asshole bleeds for poor whitey! (*Genuine laughter, loud*)

BOYD: What's so funny? What the fuck's so funny?

CLAYBROOK: People of color have got to JUMP UP AN' DOWN WITH JOY they get invited at last to the white-folks' house—my, my! Ain't we lucky! They shakin our hands like our hands was white. Sayin, "Skin color don't mean nothing to me, I'm color blind, ain't I hot shit!" (*Laughs*) Sure, I was the scholarship boy—the "good" boy. 'Cause they was nice to me, they didn't need to be nice to my sister, my cousin—all the rest of 'em. (*Sudden savagery, pointing toward* BOYD's *portfolio*) Like that Third World-victim shit you're peddling!

BOYD: Huh? What?

CLAYBROOK: Share your income with your "tragic" victims—pay *them* for your pictures.

BOYD (*excited*): I'm a, a—witness! You said that yourself! A—

CLAYBROOK: Don't hand me that shit, whitey!

BOYD (*excited*): Why'm I white, why'm I white, c'mon, tell me, why'm I *white*, you think I'm *white*, what the fuck's that, you think you're *black*, real big-deal *"black"*—sit still! (BOYD *takes out revolver, points it at* CLAYBROOK, *who, about to get up, freezes.*)

(*A beat or two of absolute silence, astonishment.* DEBRA *gives a muffled cry, hand to mouth.*)

BOYD: I'm not going to use this—I'm not a man of violence, don't make me use this, okay, man, don't make me use this, okay?— (*as if pleading with* CLAYBROOK) —I just want to *tell* you, I want you to *listen*, I want *respect*, I want—to be your friend—

CLAYBROOK (*frightened, trying to be reasonable*): Hey, man, put that down—hey?

(*Voices may overlap here, in the excitement of the exchange.*)

BOYD: You said I'm not your friend—well, I *am*! I am your friend! I'm the best friend you have, God damn it I *am*, and you shut me out!

CLAYBROOK: Is that—loaded?

DEBRA: Oh Boyd, my God—

BOYD (*swinging barrel toward* DEBRA): It *isn't* me, it's you, and him, it's you shutting me out, you know it *isn't* me—I'm backed in a corner like a rat—

CLAYBROOK: Boyd, don't point that at her. Okay, man? Don't point that at her.

BOYD: I'm not, I'm not pointing it at anyone, I don't want to hurt anyone, don't push me! (*pointing barrel at* CLAYBROOK, *waveringly*)

CLAYBROOK: Man, nobody's pushing you—we're just sitting here talking, we're okay, we're cool, nobody's pushing you, okay?

BOYD: Just don't push me, okay?

CLAYBROOK: Nobody's pushing you, you're cool.

BOYD: I'm not a man of violence, Debra will tell you, I'm a, a pacifist, I believe in peace, I believe in— Stay still! (CLAYBROOK *has not seemed to move perceptibly.*)

CLAYBROOK (*freezing, hands lifted*): Hey, man—I'm cool.

BOYD (*to* DEBRA, *gesturing at* CLAYBROOK *with gun*): You see?—his hands!—the inside of his hands!—call that "black," fuck it it isn't "black"—*I'm* that "black," fuck that shit!

CLAYBROOK: Okay, man, that's right. You're right.

BOYD: I *am* right, but you don't listen. I came as a, a brother tonight, drove 150 miles, treated like shit, condescended to in my own house, and you're doing it right now, sure!—because of this! (*waving gun*) —think I don't know?—I'm unaware?—insulted my profession, kicked me in the balls, the two of you exchanging looks all night like you think I must be blind, hey Debra?—think I can't *see?*—shutting me out and this is my fucking home for Christ's sake—, my *home.* (*Weird grin*) Those tiles from Sears—zigzag lines—I see them in my *dreams.*

DEBRA: Nobody is shutting you out, Boyd—

BOYD (*to* CLAYBROOK): Tried to be reasonable with you—man to man—but you wouldn't *listen.* Calling me "whitey" like I'm shit!

CLAYBROOK: Look, Boyd, I'm sorry. I guess I lost control—

BOYD: You're in my house, with *her*—fucking *her*—think I can't *see?* Some other guy, he'd shoot you both—yeah!—plead "insanity"— "self-defense"! (*Grinning*) The Ku Klux Klan's got more members in the State of New Jersey than any southern state—y'know that? Did y'know that, Professor?

CLAYBROOK: Yeah, I know that.

BOYD: All I ask, a "jury of one's PEERS." (*Laughs*)

DEBRA: Oh Boyd, please—this isn't—you.

BOYD: It isn't—I'm a pacifist. YOU DROVE ME TO THIS—the two of you. (*Gesturing at* CLAYBROOK) Calling me "whitey"—!

CLAYBROOK: I was wrong, man. I mean, I *was* wrong.

BOYD: You know what that is?—That's the fucking Nazis that's what that is! (*As* CLAYBROOK *tries to protest*) THAT'S THE FUCKING NAZIS THAT'S WHAT THAT IS.

DEBRA: Boyd? Please? You can stay here tonight, do you want to stay here tonight?

BOYD (*furious*): Sleeping where? Here? (*Indicating sofa*) Here? (*Indicating floor*) In the cellar, maybe? (*Attention now on* DEBRA) Another guy he'd lose it, a situation like this. *You*—with *him*. "White woman, black prick"—I'm not saying I think that way— but some other guy, he *would*.

DEBRA: Boyd—

BOYD (*waving gun*): Tell him! C'mon tell him! How it really was, you and me—all those times! Hundreds! Thousands! You *know* you're not really going to love anybody but me—like it was—right here —*right here in this house*. (*A pause*) Tell him.

DEBRA (*shrinking*): Boyd, no—

BOYD: Get up! Do it! Tell the truth! For once! For once tonight! Tell him how it *was*, and how it never will be again—with any other man.

CLAYBROOK: Don't point that gun at her—

DEBRA: Lew, it's all right! (*Rises, to comply with* BOYD'*s command, comes forward, frightened, and in a dilemma, her back to the men who stare at her*)

BOYD (*almost pleading*): Tell him!

(DEBRA *must convey to the audience the fact that, though what she says is counter to* BOYD'*s command, it is not true. She is willing to risk death, for* CLAYBROOK'*s sake, rather than tell the truth.*)

DEBRA: I, I—I *can* love another man— (*Pause*) I *do* love another man. (*Pause*) I *can*. I *do*. The past is past. I never think about it.

BOYD: That's a lie!

(CLAYBROOK *makes a gesture as if to protect* DEBRA, *and* BOYD *wheels upon him, seems about to shoot him. Everyone freezes.*)

BOYD: She's lying.

DEBRA (*more firmly*): I love another man. As much—*more*—than—
(*pause*) —that. (*Her expression one of grief, as of an irreparable loss*)

BOYD: LIAR! CUNT!

(DEBRA *hides her face.*)

BOYD (*suddenly tired, winding down, in self-disgust, though still holding the gun on* CLAYBROOK): Okay, I fucked it—I'm drunk, I'm an asshole—but you don't *listen.* Look—I'm in awe of—since I was a kid—black men, women—the special ones—ones like you, no not like you 'cause you *are* special but, like, the Africans, the doomed people, some of them, not all of them, but, Jesus, some of them—you see Death in their eyes, but there's strength there too, it scares me such strength, *I* don't have it—man, *I* sure don't have it. (*Trying to regain control, speaking as if reasonably*) So, okay, friends. I bungled it. Right! I'm drunk, and I'm an asshole-honkey, okay, that's what I came to find out. (*Lays revolver on the coffee table, butt toward* CLAYBROOK) So—blow me away. I'm the one.

(*A beat or two of silence.* CLAYBROOK *again lifts his hands, in appeasement.*)

CLAYBROOK: What're you saying, man?

BOYD: Take it, it's yours. (*Shoves gun toward him*) Your turn.

CLAYBROOK: Man, I don't want—

BOYD: Here's "whitey," blow me away, c'mon. (*Shoves gun farther*)

(CLAYBROOK *takes up the gun, as* DEBRA *makes a muffled sound of protest and fear.*
CLAYBROOK *gets to his feet;* BOYD *too stands, swaying, smiling.*)

BOYD (*opening his shirt*): C'mon—!

CLAYBROOK (*aiming gun, but more to ward* BOYD *off*): Man, you just get out of here—that's all!

BOYD (*taunting*): Here's "whitey," hey, "black prick"—here's "whitey," c'mon!

DEBRA: Boyd, please—

CLAYBROOK (*trying to speak calmly*): You just get your things, and you get out of here, and don't come back!

(DEBRA *stands between them, trying to reason with* BOYD.)

DEBRA (*weeping*): Boyd, oh God. Oh, I can't believe this, oh, Boyd honey—

(BOYD *pushes* DEBRA *aside; advances upon* CLAYBROOK, *who backs up.*)

BOYD: C'mon, pull the trigger, it's loaded, c'mon, black boy, nigger, c'mon you ain't scared, you tellin' me you're scared? (*He makes a wild swing at* CLAYBROOK, *who ducks the blow, eases away; then, aggrieved.*) GOD DAMN YOU PULL IT.

(CLAYBROOK *removes the bullets from the revolver's chambers, drops them in his pocket, tosses the gun down.*)

CLAYBROOK: Now get your ass out of here like it never *was* here!

(*A long pause.* BOYD *is panting; crouching; trembling; but the urgency has left him. He flicks his hair out of his eyes, tries to laugh; wipes his face; approaches the gun slowly, seems about to pick it up, then kicks it across the room.*)

BOYD (*lighting cigarette shakily, faint smile*): Mind if I use your bathroom first?

Lights out.

Scene 8.

Lights up, but subdued. Tone has changed. A few minutes later. BOYD *is at the door, saying goodbye; duffel bag over his shoulder, a box in his arms.* CLAYBROOK *is helping him carry the other boxes out to the car.*

DEBRA *murmurs a goodbye to* BOYD *which we don't hear. She leans forward, quickly kisses his cheek; then backs off.*

The men exit, BOYD *and then* CLAYBROOK. *Door remains open.*

DEBRA *comes forward. Fingertips to eyes. Then she drops her hands, stands motionless.*

DEBRA (*defiantly*): I'm happy. I'm happy. I'm not going to cry—I'm happy.

(A pause. As if DEBRA *is looking into the future. But, when* CLAY-BROOK *returns, framed in the doorway, she turns to look at him—as he looks at her—and both stand motionless.)*

Lights slowly out.

(THE END)

Part

I Stand Before You Naked

A Collage-Play

I STAND BEFORE YOU NAKED

I Stand Before You Naked
Little Blood-Button
The Boy
Wife Of . . .
The Orange
Nuclear Holocaust
Darling I'm Telling You
Wealthy Lady
Good Morning! Good Afternoon!
Slow Motion
Pregnant
I Stand Before You Naked

Though I Stand Before You Naked *is a collage-play, it should be performed in this sequence, with a dramatic high point at* Darling I'm Telling You *and a resolution of sorts at* Pregnant. *The first and final pieces are performed by the entire cast.*
Lights up. The cast appears, alternately from stage left and stage right. Each moving into light, and each claiming the audience's attention, they say, one by one:

291

CAST: I stand before you naked.

"Little Blood-Button" is the last to speak, and, as the others retreat, she claims the stage and begins her monologue, with an air of tough flirtatiousness.

Little Blood-Button

Lights up. A GIRL *in early or mid-twenties, sassy, good-looking, flir-tatious, tough. In tight jeans; a sweater, tank top, or shirt, midriff exposed. No visible makeup. Three studs in each ear. Barefoot. Fin-ger- and toenails painted purple. Long, lavish hair in need of combing.*

GIRL *approaches audience boldly, hands on hips.*

GIRL: One of you's to blame—I could name which! (*Indicates a blood blister on her mouth, at the very* V *of her pert upper lip*) Wakin' up this mornin' to this kinda weird thing: little blood-button, like, little pimple or blister—never had anything like it before in my life, scares me to touch it! (*Incensed*) From you kissin' so hard. Bitin'. *Suck*in'. Things you hadn't oughta done last night, but when I said, "Hey hon stop, I'm a workin' girl I need my *sleep*," you don't pay the slightest heed, just keep right on. So it swoll up, in the night. (*Shivers*) Lessin' it was a bedbug or a *spider*, maybe. (*Pause*) Nah it's from you, kissin' so hard like you do. (*As if peering at herself in a mirror, fascinated; poking at the blood blister*) So *hot*!—like it's afire. Just feel! A thing so—unexpected—reveals itself you can't hardly see your*self*, it's so—noticeable. So swollen and throbbin', hard little button of blood. Howcome it's black blood I wouldn't know. (*Pause. More reflective*) God maybe it's a—what d'you call it—"cyst"—*that's* serious. That's—real serious. (*Pause*) S'pose the doctor looks at it, says— (*Hands over ears*) Nah I don't know *what*! (*Pause*) Just got up, washed my face, gargled my mouth good. (*Glances around; mood changes to sassy, provocative*) Take it easy, hon, I'm right *here*. Damn hard tongue of yours—*that's* to blame. All that kissin', bitin'—I'm hot, I'm wired up tight, gonna give my daddy up in Nome, Alaska, a call, gonna tell him the good news his girl's settlin' down, right now gimme a kiss, yeah suck right down to the roots, suck this damn blood-button out clean. I want me *me* again. (*Pause*) Tastes of salt? sugar? hot brown sugar? Don't you worry, hon, Little Blood-Button's fixed herself up just fine, ain't a single germ livin'. That's the God's-honest truth, guar-anteed. Says so on the label.

Lights out.

The Boy

Lights up. Attractive, just slightly ravaged-looking WOMAN *in her thirties, wearing "artistic" jewelry, a suede suit, modish leather boots. She approaches the audience aggressively.*

WOMAN: This boy named Kit—soon as I started subbing for his class he pestered me with love, called out "Hey, good-lookin' " on the street, eyeing me every chance he could, "Hey, TEACH, you're a PEACH," he's got these incredible brown eyes, smooth peachy-down skin like he hardly needed to shave, didn't look fifteen but claimed he was seventeen which might have been true. (*Takes a deep breath, laughs*) So! "All right," I said, "all right, damn you," I drove us to this place outside town, in the woods, a motel s'posed to look like a hunting lodge, fake logs with painted-on knotholes, I brought along three six-packs of Coors we started drinking in the car, the room smelled of damp and old bedclothes, somebody's hair oil or maybe Airwick, you know the smell—*I* know the smell. (*Confidentially, to audience*) It's my strategy to praise them—oh, actually I mean every word I say, just wanted him to feel good, y'know—*good?* So we're fooling around, out of breath and getting excited, quick kisses, y'know, nervous wisecracks you roar your head off laughing at then can't remember five minutes later. (*Makes dancing, erotic movements, lifting arms, snapping fingers lightly*) "Hey, let's dance, kid," I said, "y'know how to dance, huh?" and we're falling on the bed tangling and kicking. I opened his pants and took hold of him there but he was soft, breathing fast and shallow like some scared animal, was he afraid? but why? of *me?* hey, why? (*Pause*) I blew in his ear and got him giggling, I teased and said, "Okay, kid, now's your chance, Mommy ain't anywhere near," kissed and tickled and rubbed against him, God I was hot, my head sort of spinning, going fast like around a turn in the mountains, ooooooooo! hair streaming out behind me (*lifts hair languorously in both hands, shuts eyes*) like it hasn't done in oh, God, fifteen years. (*Pause; opens eyes*) I was crying, no I was laughing, wanted to get him hard, damn it, big and hard and strong like a man, deep inside me like a man, then I'd whisper how great he was, how fantastic, make both of us feel like a million bucks, I deserve some happiness don't I, I'm a human being aren't I, not just some "sub" grateful for shitty part-time jobs—twenty-three miles I have to drive in one direction, thirty the other, and never anything more than a one-year contract, "Sorry, that's how it is, take it or leave it, Miss Snyder," tough luck. (*Grips her face with sudden violence*) And these pouches under my eyes and a twisty look that scares the nice shy kids. And this voice in my head *Is this me? Oh, God—this? me?* (*Pause*) But he never did get hard, it just felt like something that's been skinned, naked and velvety like a baby rabbit, he was tense and trembling like I'd hurt him or was afraid I might hurt him, finally he whispers, "I guess I don't love you, I guess I want to go home." (*Pause*) But I didn't even hear, I was thinking, Oh fuck, the beer's gonna get warm, shut my eyes seeing the road tilt and spin and the sky opening up like we're all being sucked into it—(*Pause*) "Hey, let's dance, kid," I said, giggling, "let's knock the shit out of this room," he was laughing too, maybe he was crying, nose running like a baby's, and I just lay there thinking, All right, kid, all right, you bastards, this is it.

Lights out.

Wife Of . . .

BETTY LOU, *a plain, girlish woman in her early thirties, is changing from a drab uniform of a kind worn by a cafeteria worker to a "good" dress: something cheaply, though not flamboyantly, stylish and colorful. She makes up her face; primps her hair; changes from flat-heeled shoes to high-heeled pumps. The lenses of her glasses are unusually thick and her engagement and wedding rings are prominent.*

She is standing before a floor-length mirror, but we see only the mirror's rectangular frame, around which have been strung winking Christmas tree lights of various colors. Addressing the audience, BETTY LOU *is alternately nervous, excited, apprehensive; gloating; defiant.*

BETTY LOU: "My cup runneth over!" Oh, golly God, I can't *believe* my life now!

My name is Betty Lou Bisher. I mean—Betty Lou *Fisk.*

You may have heard of me. That is happening more and more often now. (*Giggles*)

When I was a little girl it was believed there was something wrong with me. With my head, that is. That is, with my intelligence. I accepted this, I did not question this. I was living with Grandma Bisher most of the time, Grandma had weak eyes too but nobody made the connection and I just supposed the world was all sort of like—underwater. Y'know, that everybody saw it with their eyes the way I did—faded and blurry like a newspaper left out in the rain.

Oh, I'd misjudge stairs and fall. I'd misjudge curbs and fall. Bump into chairs. I had cuts and bruises on my knees all the time, my elbows, chin (*rubs her chin ruefully*) . . . I couldn't see the blackboard at school, so I'd ask the girl next to me what the teacher wrote, or when the teacher called on me I'd suck my thumb or start to cry, saying I didn't know the answer. It was believed I was slow-witted. I looked so scared all the time, and smiled a lot, they weren't nasty to me, mainly.

In that grade school, there were maybe two dozen slow or retarded or strange children. I was always the smartest of these.

Grandma put up these lights for Christmas, for a little tree and for the front window, that blinked on and off, and I loved the lights because I could *see* them so well! Like coming home in the dusk, in winter. I could see them quite a ways. After Christmas was over, Grandma let me have the lights to put in my room around the window, thinking when Daddy came back the first thing he'd see would be these lights. I was willing to wait for a long, long time. (*Pause*)

When I was in sixth grade Momma got well enough to take me home with her, and the teacher at my new school had her take me to the eye doctor. So it was discovered I needed glasses. There was nothing wrong with my head at all!

Monroe Fisk, my husband, has weak eyes too. Wears glasses. Probably you know this from his picture. Used to be, he wore contact lenses. He got them, he says, purely out of vanity: 'cause a good-looking young guy, such as he was, won't wear glasses if he can avoid it. "It's nothing I'm proud of," Monroe says, "that I was eaten up with pride in my youth." Monroe is thirty-nine now, which is not *old* to be making a fresh start.

He is a Christian, no denomination. He knows from his own past how pride is the root of all sin.

I've changed jobs since the trial—used to work in a junior high school cafeteria, now I work in the cafeteria at the big downtown hospital. It's a place where people mostly mind their own business.

Of course there *is* curiosity. People wouldn't be human otherwise.

Like I said—"My cup runneth over!" Been waiting all my life for something nice to happen and finally it happened—like "I am the Way, the Truth, and the Light" at last declared itself to me and seared my heart.

Would you guess I'm thirty-four years old? Most people say I look years younger.

There's pictures of me too now. Newspapers, TV. Funny—you'd think you would remember each time, but they sort of melt into one another.

First thing these reporters ask is, "How did you meet Monroe Fisk?" and I have to say it was love at first sight. His picture in the paper, on TV—in the paper especially. I saw *him*, and it was like *he* saw *me*. Just reached out, golly God, and claimed me.

The things they were saying about him, I didn't even read them, at first. It was just—*him*. His face, his eyes. His smile. His soul shining in his eyes like something wavy in glass. (*Pause*)

I went to the trial, I was one of the first in line, mornings. Waited

two hours sometimes. Later there came to be less interest 'cause
the trial got sort of slow, what they call forensic testimony, so I
didn't have to get there so early. I didn't mind, though. I took all
my sick leave, and then some. It got so I hardly slept, nights.

I've always been shy, I guess. Blushing easy. And these glasses
. . . so I knew I wasn't pretty. I accepted this.

Grandma was a strong Methodist, she taught me forgive your
enemies, love your neighbor as yourself. TRUST JESUS, she taught
me, and I did. Aged ten, even with my bad eyes, her and me'd
embroider towels and pillowcases and such, saying "TRUST JE-
SUS," and always I did, I accepted what I was told.

Almost every day I attended the trial. Monroe says he noticed.
The verdict was a foregone conclusion.

The jurors meant to be fair-minded, I'm sure. But twelve others,
they'd have come up with another verdict, maybe.

Monroe was charged with only three of them—not eleven.

Still less fifteen, or nineteen, as some were claiming!

They came to an understanding, Monroe's lawyer and the prosecutor, he'd tell police where the other bodies were, of the remaining eight I mean, that were missing, in exchange for life
imprisonment and not the death penalty. (It's lethal injection in this
state.) So the cases could be closed, the families of those poor
women, women and girls, given some rest. You can see the neces-
sity. Monroe's sentences run consecutively—three hundred eighty
years! But that isn't so hopeless as it sounds at first. The governor,
for instance, can commute any sentence he has a mind to.

Well, the verdict came in. And Monroe was taken off to the
maximum security prison up at Schuylersville. And I started writing
to him just to tell him what I *felt*. It came out so easy, the only
time in my life I poured out my soul. Pages and pages. I thought,
*That man has suffered for his sins—no matter his sins, that poor
man has suffered.* I thought, *He doesn't judge others.*

He was so lonely and heartsick, he wrote right back. So we
corresponded. I sent snapshots. I sent some of my poems. Em-
broidered handkerchiefs which the prison facility would not accept,
and returned.

Three months later, I dared to propose—me, Betty Lou Bisher!
proposing to a *man*! Like one of these wild women in a movie or
something where anything can happen!

At first, Monroe claimed he wasn't worthy. Then, he changed
his mind.

Monroe has said he'd had a bad attitude in earlier years, an unhealthy attitude. If somebody offended his pride or decency, be it man or woman, he could not sit silent; he flared up. Those women and girls, they pushed him too far, he said. He knows he did wrong, but sometimes you're provoked. For instance, this one woman, the woman who ran the dog kennel, she'd come right up beside him where he was standing at a bar, started in talking about her ex-husband, telling Monroe things that made him ashamed, him being a man and all. But he was drinking, and so it went. "A woman who'd betray a man she was lawfully wedded to, in sickness and in health, she'd betray any man on earth," Monroe said. Lost to all decency. Just a tramp. But he was weak, and when she inquired did he have a place to stay that night, he said no he didn't, and wound up going home with her, and they started in drinking hard liquor, and . . . (*Pause*)

Well! Enough of that! (*Buoyant, smiling*)

These days I take the bus up to Schuylersville, there's bound to be reporters waiting. How they know when I'm coming exactly, I don't know. You'd think they would get tired of so many of the same questions but they never do. We're man and wife now, since May 16, the facility allows a true wedding ceremony, and a few kisses, but actually being together, like overnight, that will have to wait. Our union remains pure and chaste. We accept this.

Oh, I know, I know—it's a miracle him and I are waiting for. But say some new evidence is discovered. One of those girls turns up alive. Say the governor has a dream where God speaks to him, when he wakes up he knows he's got to commute poor Monroe's sentence. For where there's true repentance for sin, there should be forgiveness too.

My husband has made his peace with God, that's the main thing.

That's what I tell the reporters. Also that I love him, and he loves me. He is a gentleman to his fingertips.

Yes, it's a small, small chance he'll be freed—one out of a million maybe. We accept this. But say it does happen and Monroe comes home, *my* home here he has never seen except in snapshots but it's his home too, and here in the window these lights burning, just waiting for him, I can wait a long, long time. These beautiful lights winking and blinking in the night welcoming my husband home.

Lights blaze up blindingly; then quickly out.

The Orange

Lights up. A painfully thin but attractive girl of high school age, in a form-fitting costume, barefoot, stands facing the audience. She holds a large orange cupped in both hands like a talisman. Her manner is both uneasy and arrogant; a manic, even ecstatic certainty underlies her rambling speech.

GIRL (*half shielding her face, raising elbows*): You're looking at me, I wish you wouldn't. Undressing me with your eyes, like on the bus after school. . . . Oh you may think—but say you're a woman my mother's age, or . . . no, some dirty-minded guy . . . (*Confused*) Like you *think* you got me trapped in a net with your eyes a net of eyes but—(*laughs shrilly*)—you *don't*.

(*She paces about, tossing and catching orange; smells the orange, rubs it against her face.*)

(*Dreamy*) This . . . in fifteen minutes time precisely I'm going to peel, and eat, eat some of it, one segment to begin with, just one, I'll eat it slow, slow slow I'll peel it slow been waiting all day waiting for six, eight, ten hours I know how to wait, I am practiced in waiting in solitude *you* can't know seeing me with just your eyes. I will peel it slow smelling that smell I love I love the rich ripe smell it's a fiery smell kind of, it's a smell goes right up your nostrils like burning wires to your brain, oh God my mouth is (*wipes hurriedly at mouth*) *watering*. That's disgusting isn't it, that's disgusting I hate that. Oh my mouth is afire it scares me, like at, sometimes even at night, asleep I'll wake up, I'm hungry I'll wake up saying Momma, Momma!—it's so alive, like it isn't even *me* alive bleating like a ridiculous little baby for Momma's milk but someone I don't know. (*Pause*) Like between my legs sometimes. Like it's afire. It's damp in its own juices that I hate it's aching throbbing afire but I don't think about it, I hate it, I hate *that*, I'm a good girl I'm a straight-A honor student I hate that, don't look at me with your eyes in judgment, you nasty ones. (*Pause, then with the air of one imparting a secret* I don't have cramps I don't bleed down there anymore, that's a sign of good intentions. God sees into the heart sees good intentions. I have mastered that. I have conquered that. But in swim class I was kind of . . . kind of *weak* . . . (GIRL *drops to knees suddenly, as if faint-headed*) . . . Miss Schrieber says,

"Jill, is it your period? You can be excused you know if it's your period" . . . so I lied I said yes, I said yes it was my . . . that. Or she'd send me to the school doctor and . . . (*Pause; then with vehemence*) I hate to lie I hate lies and liars but sometimes I have to lie, saying I ate some food I didn't, saying I didn't lose any more weight, that kind of lie I'm forced to tell to keep prying eyes away, to keep prying thoughts away, wanting to enter my head like buzzing wasps. Oh I know it's you who own the world but inside here . . . (GIRL *draws a circle on the floor with chalk, herself in the center*) . . . here it's me it's *mine*. You can't enter. (*Defiantly, childlike*) I didn't tell Miss Schreiber, I haven't told Momma, I have not had a, oh I hate that, that word I hate, "*period*," I hate that word "*menstruation*." I have not had any, any of that, that kind of . . . blood . . . in eleven months. I'm counting on my calendar marking secret signs Momma can't decipher should she spy on me. *I* can step out of this—(GIRL *steps out of chalk circle*)—but none of you can step *in*.

(*She circles the chalk circle, provocatively, tossing and catching orange.*)

This . . . oh it's almost time. I will peel it I will smell it I will bite into it . . . one segment at a time . . . my teeth aching, my mouth . . . alive afire . . . tears in my eyes . . . am I trembling? (*Regards hands*) Am I *shaking*? I'll hide away in a toilet stall to eat my orange, oh I don't want anybody watching, I hate that, my girl friends even I hate that, there's Cathy she hides away too but we don't talk about it, just looking at each other we know, the Kingdom of God is within is what we know, a torch inside us, God's hunger, burning throbbing aching, the saints knew but they are all dead mostly. Except . . . Mother Teresa. (*Pause*) But we're not Catholic. We're not *anything*. (*Pause*) It used to be, I'd stick my finger down my throat—(*mimes this, gagging*)—now I don't need to, I'm in control. That first time it just came to me like God allowed me to know it was Thanksgiving it was nine of us at the table and Momma and Aunt Tess fussing over the food, and this, this *gravy*, this turkey gravy in the gravy bowl I saw how it was slick with fat I mean oily globules of fat—oh so disgusting so gross—Momma saying, "Take some gravy, take more mashed potatoes take more dressing more butter more turkey more cranberry sauce more gravy" . . . I locked myself in the bathroom I knew what to do . . . (*Mimes the act of*

vomiting; then wipes her face; relieved, refreshed, radiant) I felt
so good after I knew I was saved. (*Pause*)

So I went from 128 pounds to 120 pounds to 115 pounds to 109
. . . Then it got harder, for a while . . . seems like certain kinds
of flab— (*roughly pinches waist, hips; presses her small breasts
flat*)—are stubborn to melt away. Momma started asking what's
going on? was I on a diet or something? was I trying to starve myself
what's going on? One day Momma barged in my room fouling the
air with her cigarette, took hold of this old ratty sweater I was
wearing, my favorite old sweater I wear around the house, Momma
yanked it tight seeing how thin I was she got scared then I saw it
in her eyes, saying "Oh Jill oh hon oh my God what's wrong"—
and I—(*backs away, speaking rapidly*)—I said "Momma don't
touch don't *touch* leave me alone don't *touch!*"

(GIRL *mimes fending off someone; repositions herself inside the chalk
circle, panting and trembling.*)

Now I weigh 93 pounds . . . this morning I did . . . but I had some
Diet Coke, four cans of Diet Coke, so I'm . . . heavier. Yesterday
I had a 7-Grain Datebar . . . divided it into quarters 'cause it weighs
four ounces I spread out eating it over four hours in my room in
the dark after they'd all gone to bed I'm happiest then. At school
I can be happy too in a different way inside *here* (*indicates circle*)
but it's harder. I divide up the Diet Coke, the diet chocolate-
cream, coffee if it doesn't make me too spaced out, what I hate's
running to the restroom a dozen times a day my stomach bloating
I *hate* that you can see it now can't you! can't you! (*Strikes fist
against belly*) Like I'm, you know, like I'm, I'm pregnant, going
to have a, a baby but oh no I'm not oh *no* never. (*Trembling; on
the verge of mania*) I'm so happy you can't know, inside me, there's
God inside me you can't trap me with your eyes, no nor Momma
either with her threats and tears and coercion, no other word but
COERCION but she can't get me can't touch me, they say—the
doctor she made me go to, the therapist—that woman Ph.D. who
came to talk to us at assembly—saying it's a medical problem an
illness trying to scare us "irreversible liver damage" but it isn't, it
isn't physical at all, it's here, it's God inside me, it's mine. Like
you out there—you're all babbling in some foreign language.
(*Pause; then with ecstatic certainty*) My days my nights I love how
they are divided like this orange divided into segments I pick apart
with my fingers, sink my teeth into slow like on the far side of my

hunger those faces, voices—*you*—sure I see you, and I hear you, I talk with you I smile at you but . . . I don't care about you. I don't. Not a one of you. I am always thinking of . . . this. (*Holds orange high above her head*) Always I am thinking of . . . dreaming of . . . oh it's like fire! it hurts! it's wild in a frenzy like fire the inside of my mouth alive with hunger with wanting to bite to chew to eat to EAT EAT EAT like a frenzy alive like scurrying ants!— the hunger and the food COLLIDE . . . (*Wincing*) It's pain but it's a good pain. (*Pause*) Sometimes, I'm not weak or sick or, I know I must conserve my strength, I'll, like, crawl up a stairs . . . (*on hands and knees*) . . . if nobody's around . . . (*Pause; flaring up angrily*) "I don't want to be *touched*" I said, "I don't love you or anybody love hurts my skin hurts don't touch me" I said "STAY CLEAR." (*Pause*) Now it's time, it's time it's that time now I'm safe nobody can see I'm locked in this toilet stall it's the middle of the hour nobody will barge in nobody can trap me with their eyes I'm safe I can't be touched I . . . (*Orange rolls out of* GIRL'*s fingers, out of the chalk circle, out of reach: she strains to get it but cannot.*)

The GIRL *is frozen in posture, trying to reach orange. Slow dimming of lights.*

Lights out.

Nuclear Holocaust

Lights up. A woman mental patient, middle-aged, in soiled institu-
tional smock, sneakers with white anklet socks. Her hair is disheveled
and her manner disturbing—as if an intense rage were battling to
be released from a narcotic haze. She has, too, a strangely "logical"
attitude.

PATIENT (*addressing audience*): Jesus isn't angry 'cause He brings us
love but (*shakes head warningly*) there's plenty angry in His place.
Praise Jesus! (*Pause*) Yeah, your face shows how "serious" you're
listenin' but I know better—it's just your salary. (*Laughs*) I don't
begrudge it. I have got Jesus and Jesus has got me. (*Pause*) Yeah,
I'm the one they took the name from, got no name now. (*Shrugs*)
I'm the one keeps setting her hair afire by accident. Fallin' asleep
where I am and there's a candle lit or a stove burner. Then you
shaved off my hair thinking it wouldn't grow back BUT IT HAS.
(*Touches hair*) If my face wasn't pimply from this bad food I'd be
pretty like before, that's the Devil's temptation. (*Pause*) Sometimes
Jesus is explainin' things to me and I forget who I was when I
started walkin' somewhere and where it was believed I was going
so when I get there (*laughs*) I can't remember and y'all laugh at
me (*laughs*), walkin' right through locked doors, y'all don't laugh
then. I can fall asleep anywhere. In the cafeteria, in the john. On
the toilet. In the shower with the hot water running . . . I got
scalded and they had to fix my skin. They take it from some place
like your ass—put it somewhere else. (*Pause*) It happened in one
instant like dyin', they put the needle in my arm (*mimes injection*).
After you're dead it's easier.

(*The* PATIENT *crouches slightly, as if to appeal to audience on their*
eye level. Her gaze is disconcerting—too "real.")

I know why y'all are here, you think I'm a freak you're free to stare
and laugh at, that's okay, that's how Jesus came into this vale of
tears and He rose again. He forgives his enemies just like me.
(*Pause; smiles*) This morning, I forgot where I was going and when
I got there (*searches through pockets*) I lost my slip tellin' me why.
(*In fact, she pulls a pink slip out of her pocket without noticing:*
it falls to floor.) I noticed my shadow on the wall and had to laugh.
Jesus says a sinner hurries to get somewhere then when they get

there it's the SAME SHADOW in wait. Once I saw a picture of a Japanese man, I mean just the shadow of him baked into a wall when the—the whatsit—(*shakes head to clear it, remember*)—A-TOMIC BOMB was exploded. I studied that a long time. There's talk of a NU-CLEAR HOLO-CAUST these days but I don't keep up. In that picture it was the man *and* his shadow baked into the wall so the man himself *was nowhere to be found.* (*Pause*) There's a satisfaction in this. (*Pause; dreamy-passionate*) Once I died and was floating on a big silver river under the stars. The element of the river was laughter, it wasn't grief. All those souls floating to Jesus. Any of you there? (*Peers at audience*) There was singing too, gentle and not loud. I joined my voice with the rest but it came out too loud and I was ashamed. Jesus says, "You big cow, clumsy thing, makin' Me ashamed," so He sent me back here so when I saw it, I started cryin'. I was back here in sin. (*Pause*) Now I'm always prayin' for things to get right again. Y'all look at me and hear me talkin' but in my heart I am prayin' for the RETURN OF ALL SINNERS TO GOD. (*Pause; louder*) Dear God, I say in my prayer, send the bomb to punish us at last in Your mercy and bless us in the same instant, for ever and ever. Amen.

Lights out.

Darling I'm Telling You

Lights up. An attractive, youngish woman, a go-go dancer, in a very short tight skirt, fishnet stockings, high heels, exaggerated makeup, hairstyle, dangling earrings, etc. She is "topless" but has slipped on a sweater or a blouse, casually unbuttoned.

One of her eyes is blackened and there are bruises, welts, scratches on her face, throat, breasts, forearms, thighs.

THE DANCER *approaches audience. Her manner is oddly shy and girlish initially. Voice may be nasal, "untrained."*

DANCER (*indicating her eyes*): God it's the weirdest thing, you can't see it maybe where y'all sitting, but—there's *blood* in my eyes. I don't mean bloodshot I mean *blood*. A lot of veins and capillaries burst I guess. That's what they call them?—capillaries? (*Pause*) The coroner said it's a sign of strangulation for sure even if there wasn't the actual evidence. (*In a shrinking gesture, she indicates the strangulation marks on her throat.*) Also, here—Jeez I'm ashamed!— where he bit me. (*Indicates teeth marks on breasts, insides of thighs*)

(DANCER *moves forward; shrugs, smiles, sighs, lifts arms in helpless gesture.*)

Yeah I'm what you . . . I guess you'd have to . . . designate . . . as . . . *dead.* (*Quickly*) Don't hold it against me, huh! I mean, I'm . . . shocked too. I'm *disgusted.* (*Appealing to audience, frankly*) You don't know what the hell to say to dead people, or how to act around them. Like you can't say "How's it goin'?" 'cause . . . you *can't.* Or: "Hey you're lookin' good" 'cause they *ain't.* (*Laughs*) A dead person, even if he was a great guy, or girl, you're gonna . . . like you're gonna cross the street to avoid 'em, huh? (*Shivers*) Ugh! It's a downer for sure! For both parties!

(*Disco music, faint at first. Strong beat.*)

(DANCER *half-consciously and automatically begins a simulacrum of her go-go routine, not emphatically enough to distract from her words.*)

Shit, it's . . . like I say *weird*, being dead. I'm only thirty-two! Thought for sure I'd last longer. Also: this blood in my eyes I can't

see right, and they usta call me "Angel Eyes," the other girls came
up with that and I always felt, y'know, kinda good about it. I mean
. . . "Angel Eyes" has got class. Not crude like "Sugar Tits" or
"Pussy De Vine."

(DANCER *snaps fingers, gyrates, tentatively beginning to be taken
over by the beat. Stage lights darken, with a rosy cast. Neon sign in
background:* "***TOPLESS À GO-GO***")

(*As if "coming alive"*) Uh-huh! Uh-huh! Uh-huh! That's it honey!
Mmmmm! Feelin' good, back where Angel Eyes belongs! Seems
I hardly been *away*! (*Catches sight of someone in the audience, in
a middle row*) Hey—you here? *You*? (*Glancing around, smiling*)
And *you*, sweetie? Like old times, huh? (*Winks*) Don't you worry,
honey, any of you, Angel Eyes ain't gonna tell no tales. Here's the
place (*slaps crotch*) where the secrets OR-IG-IN-ATE and where
the secrets *stay*.

(*Harsh, percussive*) GOT TO GET WHERE THERE'S NO
WORDS TO THE SONG AND NO SONG NEITHER JUST THE
BEAT THE BEAT GIMME THE BEAT OH YES. (*Dreamy; mimes
adolescent self-enchantment before a full-length mirror*) Goin' back
when it was just dancin' in front of a mirror the radio turned up
loud as I dared—hot nigger music—DEtroit MOtown—hair down
to my cute little-girl ass—swinging wild—little white cotton
panties—nobody in the house to know. Nah—nobody. Givin' myself a lipstick kiss in the mirror so DREAMY. (*Pause*) "Damn little
slut," Momma starts callin' me, no reason at all. (*Angry*) NO REA-
SON. (*Pause; with satisfaction*) First chance I got, sixteen years
old, this guy came along (*snaps fingers*), I ran off.

(*She dances, briefly; begins to grow breathless.*)

(*Squinting at someone in audience*): Hey there, you—I see *you*.
How's it goin' honey?—how's the family? (*Winking*) Don't worry,
you guys, Angel Eyes ain't gonna tell, I love you guys watchin' me
'cause it's better than any mirror, ME watchin' YOU watchin' ME
like I'm BE-YU-TI-FUL, mmmmm so DREAMY. (*Pause; tone becomes harsh, flat*) It's when the music stops there's trouble, oh
Jesus three A.M. and and one of you's waiting in his car, fancy black
Porsche, leans his head out the window waving a hundred dollar
bill, "Hey Angel Eyes c'mon and get it sweetheart," so what am I
gonna do?—yeah you know what I'm gonna do. Angel Eyes ain't

no nineteen years old anymore, huh. (*Pause; then half-pleading, frank*) Why doesn't love—love*makin'*—make you guys happy? Why's it, sometimes, make you so—wantin' to hurt? Like— (*pause*)—to *kill*? (DANCER *rubs her neck ruefully.*) Wouldn't pound the earth would you, the soil, wouldn't trample down some green growth would you, like your momma's body's the same, you come out of it and she nursed you and all, so, some other woman's body (*runs hands lightly over body as if defining it:* not *suggestive or salacious*) shouldn't make you—want to hurt, I mean should it? (*A pause of two or three beats*) I mean—should it? (*Pause*) Like there's love, lovemakin'—the bright side of the moon you can see—then there's death, death-makin'—the dark side of the moon you can't see. (*Pause*) But you know it's there. (*Pause*) Okay this last time, Angel Eyes' worst mistake in thirty-two years, I mean WORST for sure (*shivers*) I'd've sworn he was a nice guy—yeah! Didn't act like you others, acted like, y'know, a gentleman. . . . Bought me champagne, an expensive supper, real sympathetic so we started dating, didn't come on at me wantin' to sleep with me or anything, said "How beautiful you are," yeah I was *sweet*. (*Dreamy; even now half believing*) "What's your real name," he asks, so I told him: "Maryanne." And he says "Maryanne" lookin' at me like—I don't know what. (*Wipes at eyes*) So, last Sunday, he drives us up to this cottage in the Adirondacks, on Lake Saranac, only it ain't any cottage like I ever saw, Jeez more like a hotel, only private. Musta been his family place but he didn't say.

(*Lights darken, focus upon* DANCER. *Amplified sound of muffled voices, murmurs, giggles, whispers.*)

DANCER: Well. We got drunk I guess and he's still not touching me or nothin' but he's askin' these things kinda funny at first then, y'know, hurtful—like how many guys I fucked in my life—how many abortions—and I'm kinda shocked—thinking he was *nice*, sayin' he wanted to get married maybe. Oh Christ! So he says, "Okay Maryanne let's go, let's GO-GO," got a tape deck turned up freaky loud (*a burst of disco music, then fading, as* DANCER *mimes this episode*) and we're all alone by this frozen lake in the middle of I don't know where and he makes me do my routine with no top (*mimes removing top*) and him all dressed *even a necktie*, just staring at me his eyes showing kinda white in the dark, finally I said "Can't I stop? please?" I'm hurtin', the backs of my heels bleedin' 'cause I don't have my dancing shoes that're broken in proper. He says, "Oh no you don't Maryanne, oh no you keep *on*," and I says it ain't right, just me and him, sort of—vulgar, like. So he goes crazy starts sayin' "Pig that's what you like isn't it, pig, cunt it's what you like isn't it?—men watchin' *you*—"

VOICE (*eerily amplified: whispered words are muffled, overlapping, indistinct as in a waterfall; overlapping with words in preceding speech*): Oh no you don't, Maryanne, oh no you keep *on*, pig, that's what you like isn't it, pig, cunt it's what you like isn't it?— men watchin' *you*—

(DANCER *mimes being attacked.*)

DANCER (*sobbing, terrified*): So I, I started cryin'—that set him off worse—grabbed my hair, started punchin', kickin,' callin' me every filthy name—

VOICE: —bitch!—whore!—cunt!—human garbage!—filth!—filthy thing!—pig!—bitch!—diseased pig!—don't deserve to live, do you deserve to live pig pig PIG don't deserve to live PIG CUNT—

(*Music grows louder, yet has a blurred quality.*
DANCER *sinks to her knees, under attack.*)

DANCER (*disjointedly*): He starts chokin' me, I begged him, "Don't hurt me, oh don't kill me please I don't want to die, have mercy please," and he says—

VOICE: D'you love me? huh? cunt?

DANCER (*desperate, terrified*): I said "Oh I love you, don't hurt me I love you"—

VOICE: Who's your master, pig? huh?

DANCER: You—you're my master—

VOICE: Who? Who is?

DANCER: —you—only you—

VOICE: Filthy pig-cunt, diseased thing don't deserve to DON'T DE-SERVE TO LIVE—

(*Brief struggle.* DANCER *is no match for her assailant. A miming of beating, strangulation, rape.*
Lights out as music builds to climax.)

Lights up, dimly, to show DANCER *lying motionless on floor, hair fanlike, arms outspread.*
Lights out.
After a beat or two, lights up. DANCER *now on her feet, shakily. She has put her sweater or blouse back on and is smoothing hair, trying to straighten clothes, etc. Approaches audience.*)

DANCER (*brash, matter-of-fact*): Well. That's . . . that. That's how Angel Eyes made her worst and her last big mistake, you better believe it. (*Pause. Music rises again, not strident but faint, dreamy.*) ME watchin' YOU watchin' ME . . . what a laugh. (*Nodding at faces in the audience.*) Yeah—there's some secrets between us—*you,* and *you,* and *you*—okay, but don't worry, ain't gonna tell. (*Pause; smiles*) Look: I don't hate you, none of us hate you, nah—I *love* you. Anybody pays the price of admission—*I love you.*

(DANCER *exits, slowly, provocatively, as music comes up.*)

DANCER: I love you . . . I love you . . . Yeah! I love you.

Lights out.

Wealthy Lady

Lights up. An attractive middle-aged woman in a brocaded dressing gown is seated at an antique table. In the act of writing, she glances up at the audience, smiles.

LADY (*graciously*): I am performing the rituals
of the body I woke up in
sweet smiles writing
checks

I am the lady of the house
this house you've gazed at
from the outside Yes
some of you have wondered
what it looks like
on the inside
Well—it *is* nice! (*Pause*)

Yes I am the lady of the house
this is my boudoir
I am doing what I do best
I am writing writing
POWDER BLUE CHECKS
(*Pause, as she writes, tears check out from book, etc.*)

I am "prolific"   I am much admired
I am happy to be so much   admired
as I smile smile
writing writing
checks FLUTTER BLUE
on! in all directions!
(*As if in a sudden breeze, checks flutter to floor*)

I am performing the rituals
oh! they're sac-red!
of the body I woke up in
I know *my* place
on this third-planet-from-the-sun
HEAPING RICHES LIKE GOD'S GRACE
into.an emaciated face in a photograph—
Cambodian refugee   no it's

is it?—Ethiopian?
SAVE THE ORPHANS FUND
SAVE THE SYMPHONY FUND
SAVE THE REDWOODS FUND
I am smiling upon you all   I'm in a good mood this morning
I slept well last night   and I'll sleep well tonight
smiling upon the FRIENDS OF THE MENTALLY HANDI-
  CAPPED
smiling upon the FRIENDS OF THE ENDANGERED YAK
smiling upon the FRIENDS OF THE ENDANGERED FETUS
I have many adventures   with my checkbook
I SMILE UPON ALL RACES COLORS AND CREEDS

(*Sudden change of mood: yawns*) Ah—I'm a bit bored   my
poor hand is *exhausted*
(*Rises from table, moves a bit stealthily*)
Now I'll leaf through the portfolio
he keeps locked away
(LADY *opens safe*)
I'll finger these sacred papers
the quarterly dividend statements   the money manager's reports
investments   property   interest   oh!
I suppose it's all in order, *I* wouldn't know
and—
(LADY *has a small pistol in the palm of her hand*)
and *here!*—
which *he* keeps in the safe   thinks *I* don't know about
I WILL HIDE IT IN MY CLOTHES

(LADY *paces about the room, fantasizing, excited*)
I will cancel the FRIENDS OF THE ART INSTITUTE luncheon
I will attend today's Sotheby's auction
the van Dusen estate   *poor* Hendrik
there is a Goya up for bidding   or is it a Rembrandt
Andrew Wyeth   van Gogh   Jasper James   oh!
one or another!
I will bid gaily and drunkenly and when
I have bought everything   when
the gallery officers approach me
then I will—
(*Brandishes pistol*)

No I will buy what remains of the   Hinklemann estate
and the old Quaker cemetery north of town
I WILL TURN IT INTO A LUSH LOVELY MEADOW
I want sheep grazing   rail fences   inner-city children
I want languorous mists that linger
cowbells and vespers and shepherds with staves
Lombardy poplars for the balmy evening breeze
if the sheep get too filthy
if the children vandalize the monuments
IF ONE OF THEM APPROACHES ME—
(*Brandishes pistol*)

At the country club buffet I will   toss food onto the floor
I will shake the champagne bottles   FIZZLE-SPRAY ALL OVER
I will gaze upon my lifelong friends without recognition
I will mutilate the ladies'   fur coats
When I am approached   when they say *Won't you come with us*
I will smile smile smile   and
(*Brandishes pistol*)

No—I will park the Mercedes by a   warehouse
in my Gucci crocodile pumps I will go stumbling
through dark alleys
when I turn my ankle   when I whimper
when one of *them* approaches
oh! I will run I will be terrified I will pant like a doe!
when one of *them* touches me
I will—
(*Brandishes pistol*)
YOU THOUGHT I WAS A DEFENSELESS WHITE LADY DIDN'T
    YOU . . . !

(*Abrupt change of mood, returns to table and pen, etc.*)
Oh some other   time
my migraine is
I'll cancel the luncheon though
I almost forgot the FRIENDS OF GAELIC   they depend upon me
the FRIENDS OF THE GRAPE PICKERS   the FRIENDS OF
    THE BLIND
oh! already it's afternoon
the day will flutter by   safely
POWDER BLUE SMILES ON ALL SIDES

but—
I am crossing off my list
the COMMITTEE FOR THE PRESERVATION OF ST. TIMO-
   THY'S ABBEY
for it is chaired by a   swine
who chews
celery
noisily

Lights out.

Good Morning! Good Afternoon!

Lights up. A WOMAN *of trim middle-age, in a tasteful but nondescript navy blue suit, hair bouffant-style and shellacked with spray, enters and takes the stage. She smiles self-consciously at the audience. She wears a costume-jewelry brooch and button earrings; "good" shoes with a small heel. Everything about her is stiffly conventional and proper except for the fact that she has virtually no face. (Yet the malformed face should look as realistic as possible. The facelessness may have a surreal, dreamlike distortion, but she should not wear a mask. Ideally, her eyes are "grown over"—reduced to small holes; her skin the color of curdled milk; her mouth tiny and flat. Yet the mouth is outlined in red lipstick.) The* WOMAN's *effect upon the audience should be one of profound discomfort, of which she demonstrates no awareness.*

WOMAN (*as she enters stage, before taking the light clearly*): Good morning! Good afternoon! (*Chirpy, upbeat*) GOOD MORNING! GOOD AFTERNOON! RING-RING!

(*In spotlight, nervous, smiling*) Oh dear—how should I introduce myself!—I'm, uh, Dorothy Medina!—Dottie!—Aunt Dottie to my sister's children! I'm a—happy person! I'm a well-adjusted person. I have a job I'm SO THANKFUL for and I live in a NICE apartment in a NICE neighborhood, I don't complain. (*Laughs*) I'm not one of those, uh, feminists, those man haters, you don't hear *me* complain EVER. (*Pause*)

(*More intimate, confiding manner*) My brother-in-law Frank, last Sunday, oh he's outspoken!—he was looking through the newspaper, on the cover of the supplement there were these "leading American feminists" sort of posing on display, five or six of them, and Frank was laughing and hooting, "Migod look at these bull dykes, you ever seen any women so shit-face *ugly!*" (WOMAN *clamps hand to mouth, as if scandalized at such language.*) Well Frank is vul-gar isn't he! but—but I mean, really! (*Giggling*) One of these FEMINISTS was wearing, I swear they were Nazi storm-trooper boots up to here (*indicates knees*) and some kind of towel—SER-AP-AY?—over her shoulder—another had long messy *gray* hair down to here (*beneath breasts*) and all of them were middle-aged and what you'd call *hefty*. (*Pause, shaking head*) I mean, I'm all for equal-pay-for-equal-work (*recited mechanically, as her mouth grows stiff, sneering*), but you don't have to be so pushy and *ugly* to achieve it!

(*Pause.* WOMAN *takes out a pink tissue, prissily blows her nose; pats her artificial-looking hair with fussy fingers.*)

In my profession, appearances are crucial—but *attitude* even more. I'm smiling all day long, at the office. On the telephone too! Ring-ring! "Good morning!"—or "Good afternoon!"—as the case may be—"This is Rathauser, Peedie, Cook & Hulit, Industrial and Residential Appraisers and Realtors!" (*Smiles, bobbing head in doll-like fashion*) Ring-ring! "Good morning! Good afternoon! This is Rathauser, Peddie, Cook & Hulit, Industrial and Residential Appraisers and Realtors!" (*Pause*) In one of my bad dreams—oh sometimes I have these dreams—not as if they're *my own* exactly, but I have them!—in this dream I'm at the office and the telephone is ringing and I'm trying to locate it to answer it but there's some substance all over everything preventing me—like glue, or—(*fastidious shudder*)—*mucus*—but finally I answer the phone and there's a voice saying, not *my* voice but oh dear it's coming out of my mouth—"Good morning! This is Peddie, Hulit, Rathauser, & Crook!" (*Hand to mouth, scandalized*) Oh God! Can you believe! Me, Dottie Medina! What *if*! (*Pause*) But that's not really *me*, thank God! I wake up and—oh am I happy!—*it's only a dream.*

(*More somber, philosophical*) Oh I've had my share of sorrow! *Almost* got engaged when I was in secretarial school—*almost* was given a ring—(*stares at left hand, which is ringless; snatches hand away and hides it behind her back*)—oh, how *could* he! when I'd been telling my girl friends! (*Pause; dabs at eyes with tissue*) It's been some years I guess since I've had a, what you might call a, a romantic evening with a man, but I belong to the North Ely Christian Citizens Fellowship, we go on charter trips sometimes, to Miami Beach, to Disneyland, to Mexico City but oh dear (*giggles*) did I get sick! We have picnics, and bingo parties, and square dancing oh I love square dancing—(*square dance music comes up brightly:* WOMAN *executes dance steps with surprising vigor and skill*)—"Do-si-do!" (*pronounced* DOUGH-SEE-DOUGH)—"Curtsy to your partner!"—"Curtsy to your corner!"—"Allemand left!"—"Allemand right!"—"Promenade!" (*Skips about in a circle, smiling and breathless*) Oh it's fun and anybody can be your partner, doesn't even have to be a man! (*Pause*) Saturdays, that's their errand day, I drop by Reverend Mossler's, help him and his wife out a little with the kids, maybe do a little housecleaning which I don't mind in the slightest—*my* apartment's so small. (*Frowns*) It's none of my sister's business, what I do.

(*Pause*) The greatest sorrows of course are losing Momma—that was a long time ago—and losing poor Daddy—just last Christmas. (*Dabbing at eyes*) Poor Daddy had this stroke and heart attack together, I kept him at home till it was just too hard then in the nursing home I visited that poor man every day and every hour I could, practically—yes it was a Christian establishment so it shocked me how they neglected those poor elderly people—nurses not caring if they ate or not—so I'd sit with Daddy holding a spoon to his mouth for, oh dear it was hours sometimes—my arm so *heavy*. (*As if her arm were suddenly very heavy*) Poor Daddy he'd look toward me but he wasn't seeing me, I'd beg him "Daddy please eat! it's your daughter Dottie please eat! it's me it's Dottie I love you I'm the one who loves you please eat! for *me*!" but he wouldn't, it got worse and they fed him with a tube through the nose, he'd try to pull the tube out, went kind of crazy at the end then slipped into sleep, he'd sleep twenty hours a day not even waking up while I was there, I'd sit by his bed for hours waiting for him to wake up to see me but— (*Pause; emotional*) That nursing home! The orderlies were the worst! Once I overheard them saying, "The old guy in 12B"—12B was Daddy's room he shared with two others—"he's about ready to be boxed"—I was so shocked—so—shocked—"ready to be *boxed*" they said—"ready to be *boxed*"— did you ever hear such a cold calloused way of talking—! And a few days later, poor Daddy passed away. (*Pause*) He'd look at me all those years never see *me* never all my life!

(*Regaining control, fearing perhaps she has revealed too much*) Oh!—as I said I am a happy woman, and I would judge that I am a normal woman for my age. Exactly what you *see*, this is *me*. (*Pause*) Except I have this dream, this terrible dream, well nightmare I guess—(*lowers voice*)—where I don't have a face!

(*Simulates dream, with growing agitation, anguish*) I'm trying to make my way through a crowded room, the main room of the old railroad depot here in the city, my train is leaving and I'm desperate to get to it but trying to hide my face too—where my face *was*—

now it's all grown over like scar tissue, or melted away, or—I don't know!—people are staring at me and I'm so ashamed being a, a freak—so ashamed! Then at the train I try to climb on but the conductor blocks my way, "No not *you*" he says—passengers already on the train are looking out the windows at me, staring like they see something terrible that scares them—"No not *you*—NO NOT *YOU*"!

(*Wrenches herself awake from the dream. An earring falls to the floor, unnoticed.*)

Then I wake up, thank God! Thank God! I wake up and of course I'm in my bed—alone, and safe—of course—I have my own face back again like it's supposed to be—*mine*! (*Touches face with blind, groping fingers; pauses, frozen, for a beat or two, eyes shut*) I know I'm all right, then. I'm happy, then—oh so happy! *It was only a dream* I tell myself *only that terrible dream again. I'm* all right.

(*Pause. Lights dim.*) That's all I need to know. That's all.

Lights out.

Slow Motion

Lights up. A young WOMAN *addresses the audience, mimes some of the action in slow motion.*

WOMAN: This is what happened. *(Pause)* It was the wrong time for him to be returning home so I watched him from the upstairs bedroom window, just happened to see him turn in the driveway but he drove past the area where we usually park the car by the garage so I knew, I knew, but what was it, then there was another wrong thing, I didn't hear the car door slam, I wasn't actually listening for it but I didn't hear it slam, so I turned slow and wondering from the window I went downstairs and at the rear door where there was still time for me to be hearing his footsteps I didn't hear them so like a sleepwalker I went outside moving slow as if pushing through water and at the end of the walk I saw he was still in the car still behind the wheel though he'd shut off the motor and the next wrong thing of course is that he was leaning forward with his arms around the wheel and his head on his arms, his face hidden, his shoulders were shaking and I saw that he was crying . . . he was crying . . . and in that moment I knew that our life would be split in two though I didn't, as I made my slow way to him, know how, or why.

Lights out.

Pregnant

Lights up. A very pregnant WOMAN *in her thirties approaches the audience, hands cupping her enormous belly. She wears a clean, shapeless smock; her hair hangs in a single thick braid down her back.*

When the BABY *in her womb speaks, she listens with extreme intensity, for the speech is, of course, interior. At times a barely controlled anguish distorts her face.*

Her own voice is sweet, forthright, pleading.

BABY (*eerie amplified voice, coming from all sides*): WHY DID YOU WAIT SO LONG? (*Pause*) WHY ARE YOU SO OLD? (*Pause*) DID YOU THINK HE WOULD LOVE YOU FOREVER?

WOMAN: I . . . love *you.*

(BABY *responds with a kick;* WOMAN *winces, clasps her belly, staggers.*)

BABY: DID HE TELL YOU YOU WERE PRETTY?

WOMAN: There is no him now, there is only you. Us.

BABY: DID HE TELL YOU YOU WERE PRETTY?

WOMAN: Whoever she was, that woman—on the far side of the abyss of *now* (*indicating her belly*)—I am not that woman.

BABY: DID HE TELL YOU YOU WERE PRETTY?

WOMAN: No! Yes! I don't remember.

BABY: DO YOU REMEMBER ALL THE THINGS (*jeering, laughing*) YOU TOLD *HIM?*

WOMAN: I am not that woman, I am—*this* woman (*Pause, proud*) A mother-to-be.

BABY: THEN WHY DID YOU WAIT SO LONG WHY ARE YOU SO OLD GOD DAMN YOU I DESERVE BETTER AND YOU KNOW IT I WANT A YOUNG PRETTY MOMMA I'M GONNA BE EMBARRASSED PUSHED IN A STROLLER BY *YOU* AND LOOK AT YOUR LEGS: VARICOSE VEINS! LOOK AT YOUR LEGS! THIS IS AMERICA, LOOK AT YOUR LEGS YOU'RE

GONNA GO OUT SUMMER DAYS IN THE PARK PUSHING
ME!

WOMAN (*now addresses a woman friend or acquaintance; her tone
changes—becomes warm, chatty, droll, mock-complaining, a bit
eager*): Oh yes it *is*, I guess that's obvious, my first— Oh my God
yes—isn't it. They say you can prophesize what they will be like,
in the crib, only a few days old, well I can tell right *now*. (*Pause*)
Eight months, three days. (*Pause*) Five hours. (*Laughs*) Oh yes
he's a *he*, no doubt about that. I didn't have any X-ray or anything
but—I know. (*Pause*) Yes he's kicking right now—can you see?
Squeezes, tickles, sort of— (*Winces, tries to disguise pain*) Oh he's
a little devil!—makes me run to the bathroom a dozen times a
day—and night. Makes my nipples get hard right through anything
I wear practically. (*Half shields breasts*) Like I'm already nursing.
(*Pause*) And I'm so BIG. I can't look in a full-length mirror I'm so
BIG I scare myself I'm not MYSELF. (*Pause; then more coolly*)
Yes the father *knows*. Yes we're in—contact yes of course. On good
terms, but— (*Defensive*) It was a mutual decision, not to get
married.

BABY (*mocking*): "IT WAS A MUTUAL DECISION, NOT TO GET
MARRIED."

WOMAN (*now alone with* BABY): It *was* a mutual decision.

BABY (*enjoying this*): YAH—YOU KNEELING IN THE BATH-
ROOM PUKING UP YOUR GUTS SCARED HE'LL FIND OUT
ABOUT *ME*. SCARED HE'LL MAKE YOU GET RID OF ME.
LAY YOU DOWN ON THE TABLE, HUH, LEGS SPREAD
LIKE FOR FUCKING BUT THIS SURE AIN'T FUCKING AND
BIG FEET IN THE STIRRUPS AND THERE'S A VACUUM
TUBE, HUH, JAMMED UP INSIDE YOU, GONNA SUCK OUT
ME. YAH—GONNA SUCK OUT *ME* AND FLUSH ME DOWN
THE TOILET LIKE SHIT WELL NOBODY'S EVER GONNA
DO THAT TO *ME*.

WOMAN (*pleading*): The only truth is . . . I love you. I am living to
. . . love you.

BABY (*mocking echo*): "LOVE . . . LOVE . . . LOVE YOU."

WOMAN: I gave him up, for you.

BABY (*doubting, half believing*): NAH YOU NEVER DID.

WOMAN: He did want . . . that. He wanted you . . . gone. Like you had never been. (*Pause*) So I gave him up, for you.

BABY: THAT AIN'T HOW I HEARD IT, SWEETHEART.

WOMAN: Not that he wanted to marry me or even live with me, I guess he didn't. (*Laughs, wipes at eyes*) I don't care, now. I'm over that. Women don't need to get married, now. They want to have their babies, their babies they deserve, they don't need any . . .

BABY: DID YOU SEE HIM SLEEPING, DID YOU STARE AND STARE AT HIM SLEEPING, DID THE TRUTH OF IT HIT YOU, HOW YOU LOVED HIM BUT IT WAS MORE THAN "LOVE" MEANING SOMETHING YOU CAN SPEAK OF IN WORDS IN THE DAYLIGHT IN A COMMON LANGUAGE, DID IT JUST . . . HIT YOU, A WAVE OF DESPAIR . . . ALL YOU WOULD KEEP OF HIM AND THE THINGS YOU DID TOGETHER IN YOUR SEPARATE BODIES WOULD BE . . . ME?

WOMAN (*as if by rote*): I didn't love him, really. You can't love some-one you don't know; someone who doesn't know you. (*Pause*) Where there's no respect. No dignity.

BABY: THAT'S LATER! TALKING THAT WAY, THAT'S LATER! THAT'S HOW WE INVENT THE STORY OF OUR LIVES— LATER!

WOMAN (*shielding her head from invisible blows*): Don't take my dignity from me—my soul. Oh don't!

BABY (*slyly*): THERE'S ONE WAY OUT. YOU KNOW THE WAY OUT.

WOMAN: (*pleading*): No.

BABY: YOU KNOW YOU KNOW YOU KNOW THE WAY OUT.

WOMAN: Not as long as I have . . . you.

(BABY *laughs, kicks* WOMAN, *who winces, grunts.*)

BABY: SO YOU SAY YOU CHOSE ME, HUH. OF THE BILLIONS AND BILLIONS OF SPERM, THE BILLIONS OF "SOULS" THAT MIGHT BE, OF ALL ETERNITY, HUH, YOU SAY YOU CHOSE ME.

WOMAN: I . . . I was powerless. But yes I did choose.

BABY: YOU'RE GONNA SING LULLABIES, HUH. THAT'S WHAT YOU WANT YOU WANT TO SING LULLABIES YOU WANT TO NURSE YOU WANT TO CHANGE DIAPERS YOU WANT THE "EXPERIENCE OF BEING A WOMAN" I'M JUST YOUR PRETEXT WELL LOOK: I'M HUNGRY NOW, I'M STARVING, I WANT FOOD RIGHT NOW.

WOMAN: *I'm* hungry too, I . . . . my hands are shaking with hunger . . . but when I try to eat (*mimes eating*) I . . . (*Nausea*)

BABY: I WANT FOOD AND I WANT IT NOW, I WANT FOOD, I WANT FOOD RICH WITH BLOOD I WANT MEAT I WANT RAW HAMBURGER I WANT TO CHEW ON BONES I WANT IT NOW.

WOMAN (*determined*): I . . . will eat. I *am* hungry. (*Tries to eat, wipes perspiration from face, etc.*)

BABY: EATING! EATING AGAIN! YOU DISGUST ME! ANIMAL APPETITE!

WOMAN: I must nourish us both . . .

BABY: ISN'T THAT A STRAND OF HAIR IN THAT FOOD . . . UGH WHAT IS *THAT* . . . MAGGOTS?

(WOMAN *shoves plate from her, runs to bathroom, mimes vomiting into a toilet.*)

BABY (*echo, fainter*): THERE'S ONE WAY OUT. YOU KNOW THE WAY OUT.

(WOMAN *slips on sweater or shawl, as if walking outside, briskly.*)

WOMAN (*addressing audience, at first bright and chatty, then more sincerely*): Oh it's an—experience! An—adventure! Sure I'm scared but—I'm happy too. (*Smiles*) Yes he's going to be a real— *boy*. A real *handful*. (*Pause*) No, my mother and I, we're not on good terms I guess, she doesn't approve of my life I guess. (*Pause; hurt, angry*) None of them do, back home. (*Pause*) Last time I called, my father hung up the phone, okay I said, okay that's how you want it you won't see your grandson okay that's fine with me. (*Pause*) Early mornings I like to walk, can't sleep so I walk, before work. Evenings. I keep to myself mainly. I would never bother *you*. (*Pause*) People are okay, I know they're talking about me behind my back, I . . . accept that. Some of the neighborhood women, actually the ones you wouldn't expect to be, they're *nice*. Asking how I am, how far along am I, when's my due date, who's my doctor, be sure to eat right, no smoking . . . Like this (*indicates her belly*) is the one true thing; the thing that . . . makes us one body.

BABY (*teasing, seductive*): HEY YOU'RE IN THE PARK HUH, HEADED UPHILL, WHAT'S IT, THE TOWER HILL . . . THAT STEEP ROCK PATH?

WOMAN (*mimes climbing, with effort; smiling*): It's so lovely here, so peaceful. If I can look out . . . alone.

BABY: A RAZOR BLADE IN THE BATH, HUH, THAT'D BE THE EASY WAY BUT . . . YOU'RE AFRAID OF BLOOD. (*Pause*) SUBWAY TRACKS, A TRAIN COMING LATE AT NIGHT AND YOU STEP OUT INTO AIR AND WHO'S TO KNOW MAYBE SOME MADMAN SHOVED YOU, THEY WOULD NEVER KNOW BACK HOME THEY'D CONSOLE THEMSELVES IT WAS THE CITY THAT KILLED YOU. BUT YOU'RE A COWARD.

WOMAN: I'm drawn to this place, sometimes in my sleep I . . . I'm here. On a sunny day, a clear day . . . I don't mind the litter, the beer cans, bottles . . . sleeping derelicts . . . (*Staring, as if at a body close by on the ground*) I always think, seeing a woman, like that, an old woman, my God how did she come to *that*, I think . . . maybe I should help. Maybe I should . . .

BABY (*briskly*): KEEP GOING. UP TO THE TOP. TOP OF TOWER HILL, C'MON HORSEY LET'S GO. (*As* WOMAN *mimes climbing*) GIDDYAP! GIDDYAP! GIDDYAP!

(*At top of hill,* WOMAN *stands on an observation ledge gazing out over the city, shading eyes, breathless.*)

WOMAN: It's always . . . a surprise. Kind of a shock. The human brain needs . . . perspective. (*Pause*) Everything's so *finite*. (*Excitedly*) What if you could see . . . *time* like this too? (*Gazing out*) Where's my apartment building? Over there? Yes there's the river, the bridge . . . the church spire. (*Close to the railing, swaying*) Oh I could . . . just have to lift my . . . leg. Both legs.

BABY: COWARD YOU WON'T DO IT.

WOMAN: I'm alone, no one would know.

BABY: YOU WON'T YOU WON'T EVERY TIME YOU WON'T.

WOMAN (*forcefully*): Is there nothing I can do or say to make things right between us!

(*A pause of some seconds.*)

BABY (*as if relenting, partway*): IT'S NICE HERE, HUH? THAT WIND—ARE WE HIGH UP? (*Pause*) WHAT DOES "HIGH UP" MEAN . . . ?

WOMAN: I could almost tell myself—I *am* pretty, I *am* beautiful. But most of all—I am alive.

BABY (*echo*): ". . . I AM ALIVE . . . ALIVE."

WOMAN: We are alive.

BABY (*doubtfully*): OF THE BILLIONS AND BILLIONS OF "SOULS" THROUGH ALL ETERNITY BILLIONS OF YEARS YOU SAY YOU CHOSE ME, HUH. EXPECT ME TO BELIEVE THAT, HUH.

WOMAN: Yes.

BABY: OH LIAR!

WOMAN: I stand my ground. I know what I know.

(*She has backed off from the railing.*)

BABY (*teasing*): OH LIAR LIAR—WHAT A LIAR! (*Pause*) NOBODY SAYS YOU'RE PRETTY, NAH NOBODY SAYS YOU'RE BEAU-TIFUL THE HELL WITH 'EM, HUH.

WOMAN (*holding belly tenderly*): I must nourish us both. Have faith in me.

BABY: IS THERE A SUN, TODAY? IS THAT WHAT I FEEL, THE SUN? WHAT *IS* THE SUN?

WOMAN: There is always a sun.

Lights out.

I Stand Before You Naked

Lights up.. The CAST *speaks, each woman taking lines that seem appropriate to her role. The movement should be quicksilver from one to the other, so that the audience is always looking from one to the other.*

I stand before you naked   waiting to be loved.
I stand before you naked and shameless   waiting to be loved.
I stand before you who are strangers to me waiting to be loved
for there is a Mt. Helens of love roiling
inside me   all heat and pulse and rich lava mud!

I stand before you naked   in these carefully chosen clothes.
I stand before you naked   in this hair, this flesh,
this makeup, this luminous bone.
I stand before you naked   not loving you
but hungry to love you   or someone in your place.
I stand before you naked not loving you in the slightest
(whom I don't know and cannot in fact see for these blinding
lights in my face) but waiting to be loved by you.
Or by someone in your place.

I stand before you naked waiting to be loved   thus redeemed.
I stand before you naked waiting to be loved   beyond shame.
I stand before you uttering these words   in our common language
which none of us has created   yet all of us possess.

I stand before you naked waiting to be   loved
or to tear out your throats with my teeth.
I stand before you naked waiting to be   loved
or to suck the very marrow   of your bones!

I stand before you naked   waiting to be loved
and claimed.   I stand before you naked   as the small thin voice
of desire.   I stand before you naked as a salt lick
many soft tongues have tasted.
I stand before you naked as a corpse   prepared for cremation,
or a living fetus   as it becomes a living child.
I stand before you naked   as your soul.
I stand before you naked   lacking the syllables of subterfuge,

and shame.　　I stand before you naked
waiting to be loved, thus saved.

Love me.

(*Each in turn, the* CAST *repeats:* "*Love me.*")

Lights out.

(THE END)

The Secret Mirror

A Collage-Play

THE SECRET MIRROR

The Human Fly
Secret
The Call
The Anatomy Lesson
Cuckold
"I Don't Want to Alarm You"
"I Got Something for You"
Bluebeard's Last Wife
The Floating Birches
A Report to an Academy
The Psychic
The Secret Mirror

The Human Fly

Lights up. The HUMAN FLY, *badly crippled, rolls forward in his wheelchair. He is wearing his* HUMAN FLY *regalia—motorcycle helmet, oversized mask with black markings and elaborate eyeholes; black leather jacket, trousers, boots; large, oddly styled silver gloves. His manner is affable, eager.*

HUMAN FLY: Thank you! Thank you for your applause! (*Nods happily into the silence*) Thank you! That makes me feel just—grand!

(*As the* HUMAN FLY *rolls farther forward, he gets his fingers caught in the spokes of one of his wheels; jerks them out; winces; laughs; turns the mishap into a joke.*)

Ow! Think I'd be used to the damn thing by now! (*Pause, glancing eagerly about*) You have all heard of me, I guess—"THE HUMAN FLY, THE ONLY ONE OF HIS KIND"—of Traverse City, Michigan. Maybe some of you were present, in Tiger Stadium, in Detroit, where I made my first major appearance? (*Peers out into audience, but gets no response*) Huh? No? Gee—thought I saw some familiar faces! (*Pause*) Well. It was, uh, like I say, my first, uh, major appearance—my manager believed the HUMAN FLY should start big—right at the top—Tiger Stadium seating thirty-five thousand! We lined us up some local backers, one of them Teddy Zingler the well-known sports car enthusiast, plus the local Harley-Davidson dealer Buck Halliday—got lots of media attention, yeah, man! Telephones ringing like crazy! (*Pause*) That was five years ago—my twenty-fifth birthday—now the HUMAN FLY is working on his comeback, signed up with a new manager, but —that was *then*! (*Rubs hands together in boyish anticipation. Music comes up: rock, with a ceremonial, dramatic quality.*) We had posters all over Michigan and a sound truck in Detroit, driving through all the neighborhoods, newspaper ad in the sports section of the *News*, everybody I mean *everybody* talking about the HUMAN FLY defying DEATH on his Harley-Davidson leaping over TWENTY-FIVE FULL-SIZED SCHOOL BUSES in world-famous Tiger Stadium. Tickets only nine dollars—all seats. (*Pause. Saddened, yet still affable, upbeat*) Well!—we were kinda disappointed, only one hundred eighty-nine paying customers, plus the fifty comp tickets we passed out, so the stadium's sorta—empty.

Here it's a bright July day, a hot day and kinda hazy, gauzy, like
you get in Detroit in the summer but not *sickish*-hot, thank God
—(I'd been praying for GOOD WEATHER, yeah!)—and there's
the school buses parked side by side, all twenty-five of 'em, so
grand, one for each year of my life, and real pretty, that sharp
carrot-color, just the most eye-boggling—PRO-DIG-IOUS—(FLY
*drawls like a carnival barker who believes his own words, making
grandiloquent gestures with his gloved hands*)—sight you could
expect to see this side of Heaven! Yeah! And the hundred-foot
ramp leading up at just the right angle—seventy-five degrees! And
this ole bike pract'ly bucking under me rarin' to go! (*Sound of
motorcycle revving up*) And the fans goin' crazy with AN-TI-CI-
PATION! Yeah! (*Muffled cheers, whistles*)

(*As he describes his flight, the* FLY *hunches over in his wheelchair,
moving it in jerky, erratic surges, now in one direction toward the
audience, now in another, as if the very chair possessed a demonic
energy.*)

Takin'   her   out   on   the   track—nice   an'   easy—
mmmmMMMMMM!—around a horseshoe curve buildin' up
speed—seventy miles an hour, eighty-eight miles an hour,
mmmmm ninety-nine! one hundred eleven! one hundred twenty-
five! one hundred thirty-two miles an hour SO SWEET—Lord
God be with me headin' up that ramp of no return!—yeah!—Jesus
Christ the Savior be with me!—the HUMAN FLY propelled up
into the SKY—(FLY *makes a quick sign of the cross*)—one hundred
forty-three miles an hour off the ramp and—WHOOOOEEE! (*Ear-
splitting shriek*)

(*Silence. A beat or two.*)

(*Abruptly subdued, apologetic*) Uh—how it happened as it did—
nobody could theorize, afterward. A guy taking pictures caught
me, though, in midair: thirty feet up in the act of flying over those
school buses with the stadium stretching out behind—all these
rows of empty seats like stretching into eternity, there *I* am,
damnedest thing!—like a shot bird!—(*shakes head incredulously*)
—hadn't even cleared the fifth bus when my cycle flew out from
under me and, and—(*drops voice*)—I fell. (*Pause*) To the *ground*.

(HUMAN FLY *now falls out of his wheelchair, to demonstrate. His
helmet, loosely buckled, comes loose; his mask slips, falls off, reveals*

a fresh-faced, youthful man. He draws off the mask entirely. On the floor, he repositions himself deftly, like a snake, head and shoulders erect, continuing his earnest, ingenuous account.)

Actually—I hit the roof of the school bus, bus number five, broke my left leg right away I guess, spinning out, and down, cracked my collarbone, my skull, hadna been for my helmet my skull'd been smashed like a melon!—worst of all my back—y'know, the spinal cord's a weird, weird thing?—like a real *cord*, like with wires inside?—real thin tiny nerves?—you don't know you *got* one till something happens—this spinal cord that's real narrow, hooking up the brain to the body, like, say, you decide you're gonna move your legs, like?—up in your head?—and your legs, a long way away, they gotta obey it?—or maybe *don't*?—and all kinds of other things come off the spinal cord too—oh God. (*Pause. Somber. Then continues with account, as before*) Okay—I hit the damn bus, and I hit the ground, and I hit hard, I mean *hard*, and some things broke inside me, I was swallowing blood but refused to pass out, kept my dignity, raising my hands high in VICTORY. (*Raises both hands high over his head, gripping them*) The TV crew—there was just one, from a local station—they interviewed some of the fans after the ambulance took me away, I saw the tape afterward, guys mainly, a few girls but they were with guys, they were asked, "Why did you come to see the Human Fly today?" and some of them said they'd come to see the Human Fly perform a historic feat in Detroit, and some said they'd come to see the Human Fly get killed, and some said they'd just come to see the jump, and some said they didn't know why they'd come—they just came. (*Pause*) But not a one of them expressed disappointment, and, of all the ticket buyers, only three demanded their nine dollars back.

(HUMAN FLY *now hauls himself back up into the wheelchair: a slow, methodical, practiced routine. Refastens his helmet, mask. Sits panting.*)

(*Head high in pride*) That's all you want, and that's everything— the respect and honor of your fellow man.

Lights out.

Secret

WIFE: in her fifties; attractive, but self-effacing;
conservatively dressed
GREAT MAN: some years older; white-haired, "distinguished"; in good suit, perhaps with a vest,
gloves, fedora.
YOUNG ADMIRERS

Lights up. The WIFE *stands stage right, observing, with a sweet,
placid smile, the* GREAT MAN *as he accepts compliments, congratulations, etc., from several admirers. He is given a book to sign; he
agrees graciously to be photographed with one of his admirers.*

WIFE (*to audience*): You all know me—though maybe not my name,
or face. I'm the wife of the Great Man.

(*Another admirer, a beautiful young woman, hurries up to the* GREAT
MAN *to shake his hand vigorously, ask for his autograph, fawn over
him, flirt. The* GREAT MAN *is seen basking in this attention, taking
down a telephone number in his address book.*)

WIFE: Oh, I've been the Great Man's wife for years, I've hovered
here in the background for years. Naturally, I'm not his first wife,
or even his second—*they're* ancient history. (*Pause*) I'm never
jealous, I'm beyond that. You could say I'm happy, just hovering.
And waiting. (*Pause*) I have a secret.

(*The* GREAT MAN's *admirers disappear, glancing over their shoulders
at him, speaking of him. The* GREAT MAN *summons his* WIFE, *who
hurries to his side; his expression is bland, patient, perhaps bored
or querulous. As they stroll together, the* GREAT MAN *talks and gestures in a pompous manner, taking little notice of the* WIFE, *who
nods in ready agreement.*)

WIFE (*to audience, not meanly or gloatingly but matter-of-factly*): He
basks in my loving attention—he always has. That's how I won
him, thirty years ago. I loved him then, for a while. He doesn't
see me but he sees the love shining in my eyes, that's enough for
him. He sees how completely dependent I am upon him, like a
plant needing the sun. He thinks he sees. My secret is—(WIFE
adjusts GREAT MAN's *necktie as he frowns, stares over her head*)

—I loathe him. He doesn't know how I'm hovering waiting for harm—hurt—sorrow—humiliation—oh, any kind of horror!—to befall him. (*Serene, ladylike smile*)

(*The* GREAT MAN *disengages himself from the* WIFE. *He stands a little way off, takes a letter surreptitiously from his pocket, reads through it. The letter gives him a good deal of boyish-lewd pleasure.*)

WIFE: Of course he's unfaithful to me. I know. I've always known, from the first. And I know that—thinking me hopelessly stupid—he doesn't know I know. (*Smiles*) Yes—I'm faithful to him. A sign in his eyes of my lack of imagination; my "feminine" weakness. Really it's because men don't interest me, much. They never did, to tell the truth. My secret is a simple one: I'm the Great Man's wife so that I can outlive him.

(*The* GREAT MAN *crumples up the letter, lets it fall; returns to the* WIFE, *who meekly takes his arm, smiling up anxiously into his face. She touches his forehead with her fingers. He coughs; she exhibits great concern.*)

WIFE: You've noticed—everyone has, and biographers will comment on it—how my face lights up in his presence. My eyes—oh, my eyes shine like a young girl's! (*As the* GREAT MAN *turns irritably away, makes a rude gesture, etc.*) I repay sarcasm with sweetness; rudeness with gentleness; coarseness with delicacy. A few of the Great Man's closest friends have guessed my secret, it's true, but they can't—and they will never—*know*.

(*The* GREAT MAN, *overcome by a dizzy spell, presses his hand to his chest. The* WIFE *helps him to a reclining chair; adjusts pillows behind his head, a blanket over his legs; removes his glasses, shoes; shakes capsules out of a bottle for him to swallow, etc.*

WIFE *sits beside* GREAT MAN *with an air of satisfaction and expectation.*)

WIFE: Ah—already I'm settling into a comfortable perch at his bedside! It's morning in this nameless white place and the old fool is blind maybe, or deaf, or both, the thing that's devouring him has made his "manhood" an old joke, or was it a stroke that hit him? —like the blow of an ax *I* didn't wield—not *I*!

(*The* GREAT MAN *reaches out with a badly palsied hand for the* WIFE, *but she seems not to notice: she is doing needlepoint.*)

WIFE (*humming, tunelessly*): Lalalala . . . it's so peaceful here mornings . . . I've barred the door against intruders . . . annoying well-wishers . . . professional associates, relatives, friends . . . disinherited children. (*The* GREAT MAN'*s palsied hand reaches blindly for her as she shifts just perceptibly out of his reach, ignoring him.*) Ah, what's that—the mailman?

(*The* WIFE *hurries to fetch the mail; returns with a dozen or more letters. She sits again, with pleasure, opening envelopes. The* GREAT MAN *tries to struggle up from his reclining position, without success.*)

WIFE: Best of all I love reading his mail—our mail. He's popular and his popularity will continue after his death. (*Opens a letter, scans it quickly, critically*) Letters from total strangers, letters from old friends—(*drops the letter, opens another*)—old lovers—(*part crumples this letter, with a look of amusement*)—begging letters, homage letters, letters from students, letters from would-be parasites whose ambition—too late!—is to meet the Great Man and to attach their empty lives to his, hoping to kindle a need in him for their adoration, hoping to burrow into his life, hoping even to marry him—outlive him—become his widow. (*Placid smile, as lights dim on all but the* WIFE'*s face*) Too late.

Lights out.

The Call

Lights up. A MAN, *in his thirties, of moderate height, not overly muscular but implicitly aggressive, addresses the audience. He wears casual clothes, is neither stylish nor poorly dressed. He may be unshaven.*

MAN: Shit!—wouldn't you know it!—we're sitting down for supper and the phone rings and my wife goes to answer it and sure enough it's bad news, I wasn't expecting it but when she said, "Oh no, oh God, *when?*" it hit me in the gut and I *knew.*

Like you *know,* like—your life is cut in half, like—and you can't go back to a minute *before*—when you didn't know.

Because he'd gone into the hospital for tests.
Because his heart— His high blood pressure—
Fuck it!—I knew.
I'm on the phone saying "Okay, Ma, okay," I'm saying, "I'm coming over, Ma, don't cry."

(The MAN *paces about, clenching fists, striking the palm of one hand with his fist. He is both aggrieved and angry; restraining his emotions with difficulty.)*

Just gotta get *out*—in the car—
I'm backing up crazy out of the driveway, burning rubber on the street like I'm eighteen years old fucking wild—
I could kill any bastard gets in my way I mean I'm *wired*
and I hadn't had more than a beer or two all day!—driving like crazy along East Ventnor running a red light and some sonsa-bitches honking at me I don't even hear—
Then, like, it's weird, I'm *calm*—going into the tunnel under the railroad tracks then coming out—thinking, Look: you get that age, his age, it's gonna happen sometime, okay? Thinking, C'mon, asshole, last time you and him got together he threw it in your face, goddamn ten-thousandth time—

(mimicking his father's voice) "Your brother Larry this" and "Your brother Larry that"—"blah blah your brother who's hot shit and you're nothing, got it?—you're nothing just *shit*—you got it? eh?"

(*laughs, returns to his own voice, deceptively affable*) "Okay Pop I'm reading between the lines, yeah I get the drift," I just had to laugh going to the refrig for another ale and the old fuck wants one he can haul his ass over and get it himself, he's got this squinched up you-can't-put-anything-over-on-me look I been living with all my life so I just laughed, I said "Okay Pop let's change the subject, huh?"—last time I saw him alive. Fuck it.

(*Pause*)

So I stop at this place on the east side nobody knows me for a beer or two then go on to another and I should call Ma—but I don't—should call home but I don't—she'd just say something about my old man, my mother, "Where *are* you?" she'd ask—sounding scared like I don't want to hear her.

So I'm driving on Dexter I see this hardware store's still open so I might as well stop and get those heavy pliers so I'm in there sweating trying not to think of him, Jesus just last week walking around like there's nothing wrong and giving me the fish eye on my way out, never did thank me for fixing the washer and mopping up his cellar—that's what Bud's there for, right? And Ma thanks me, like always, says "Look hon you know he loves you, he just expects different things from you than from Larry 'cause you're older" so I'M NOT EVEN MAD I'M JUST SAYING TO HER, "Look don't hand me that crap, Ma, you been handing me all my life." And that shuts the old lady up too.

(*He dramatizes the following, his rage gradually transformed into a kind of euphoria.*) So I get in the checkout line and there's this guy butts in front of me kinda pretending I'm not there so I say, "Hey you I was first," he's pretending he hadn't seen me or heard me and the cashier's this old asshole fart nervous of getting involved, not looking at either one of us just moving the stuff along the counter and ringing up sales so I say "Okay" and throw the fucking pliers down hard, I mean hard, there's a woman screams but I'm halfway out "Okay you sons of bitches, that's it." And I'm in my car trying to get the key in the ignition, jamming it in, I'm gonna tear out of this fucking lot when I see this guy going for his car like he's forgotten all about it like nothing happened and there's nothing over here where I am in my car sitting staring right at him just some kind of fucking empty space, huh?

So I call over, "Wait a minute, you!"—already I'm out of my car with this tire iron I keep under the seat I know I'm gonna kill the sucker, break his ass like it's never been broke wipe the smirk off his face 'cause I'm the baby that can do it, you better believe I'm the baby that can do it. "Hey wait a minute, friend," I'm saying, going for him, "I got something for you."

Lights out.

The Anatomy Lesson

Lights up. A young, neatly groomed MOTHER *and her five- or six-year-old daughter are looking at a large book of anatomical drawings. The* CHILD *is restless, antic, but should not be brattish.*

CHILD (*incredulous, pointing at a drawing in the book*): *That's* where I came from? I did not!

MOTHER: Honey, everyone has to come from *some*where.

CHILD (*thumb in mouth, "shrewd"*): This is just a book.

MOTHER: Yes, but it's a drawing of something real.

CHILD: Just a—dumb—old—BOOK.

MOTHER (*calmly*): This is an anatomical drawing, honey, of something real. Like—where *you* came from.

CHILD: I did not! I did not! (*As if to tear it, mischievously*) This is just—paper.

MOTHER (*preventing her*): Honey, no! (*Adjusting the book, tracing the drawing with her forefinger*) A drawing can be on paper, but it can be of something *real*. You know that. See, this is—

CHILD (*poking book*): *This* is real.

MOTHER: Yes, honey. It *is* real. It's heavy, it has volume. But the drawings in it are *of* real things. Like, for instance, where little babies come from.

CHILD: I'm not a little baby!

MOTHER: No, but you were.

CHILD: *You* say so.

MOTHER: Yes, I do say so. Don't be silly, now. See, here, this is—

CHILD: I don't remember any little baby! (*Looking down at herself anxiously*) I'm big.

MOTHER (*teasing*): Sweetie, I have the photos to prove it!

CHILD: *I'm* big! I'm not in any drawing!

MOTHER (*returning to subject*): Now, this is the mother's body, and this is—

CHILD: You're my—mother!

MOTHER: Yes.

CHILD (*giggling*): *You* don't look like *that*.

MOTHER: This is a drawing, it's an approximation. The important thing is—

CHILD: She's nak-ked!

MOTHER: Yes—

CHILD: She hasn't got any *head*!

MOTHER: Because the subject is the pregnancy, and the pregnancy is in the mommy's belly, and—

CHILD: Is that *you*? Under your clothes?

MOTHER: Well, yes. Sort of. Except I'm not pregnant *now*.

CHILD: You're a mommy's belly.

MOTHER: Body.

CHILD: You're a mommy's body.

MOTHER: No, darling—I *have* a mommy's body.

CHILD (*urgently*): Where do you have it?

MOTHER: I—inhabit it. The way you inhabit a little girl's body.

CHILD: I'm not a baby, I'm a little girl.

MOTHER: You're a very pretty little girl, but silly sometimes, aren't you? Now, come look. You wanted to know where babies come from, and—

CHILD (*loudly*): I wanted to know where *I* come from!

MOTHER: I think we'd better put away this book, for now.

CHILD: No, no, *no*! (*Pulls at book, which tumbles to the floor*) Oh! Ow! Damn old book!

MOTHER: Did you hurt yourself?

CHILD: Damn old dumb old BOOK! (*As* MOTHER *lifts book back onto her lap or onto a little table*) You're my mommy—you're *you*. (*Pause*) Where are you?

MOTHER: Where am I? I'm right here, honey.

(CHILD *hugs* MOTHER, *hard*.)

MOTHER (*laughing*): That *hurts*.

CHILD: You're *here*. You're not *there*.

MOTHER: No, dear. I said—

CHILD: That's some other mommy.

MOTHER: Well, yes and no. It's a drawing of me too, in a sense, the way I *was*, before you were born. Here, you see—

CHILD (*looking worriedly around*): Before I was born, I wasn't *here*. There was nobody *here*.

MOTHER: Well, *I* was here. And your father. We were waiting for you.

CHILD: Why wasn't I here? Where was I?

MOTHER: All safe and snug and warm and waiting too, in your mommy's belly.

CHILD: Who's my mommy?

MOTHER: I am, silly.

CHILD: You talked like—you weren't her. Where is she?

MOTHER: I *was* pregnant, and carried you in my belly; now I *am* a real mommy, and you're a little girl.

CHILD: I don't like that I don't like that I don't.

MOTHER: What? Why? You said you wanted to know.

CHILD: I don't want to know I don't want to know I don't! (*An antic little dance*)

MOTHER (*sighing, shutting book*): Fine with me!

CHILD: *Where* did I come from—really?

MOTHER: From—my body.

CHILD: Not from—you?

MOTHER: Yes, from me. From my body, I said.

CHILD: I'm too big.

MOTHER: You are, now. But you weren't always. Once, you were a little little teeny thing.

CHILD: I WAS NOT! I WAS NOT!

MOTHER (*quickly*): You were *you*, but you were—smaller.

CHILD: How small?

(MOTHER *vaguely shapes something the size of a melon with her hands.*)

CHILD: I was not! (*Pause*) I *was?*

MOTHER: Honey, you've seen babies, you know you have. And puppies and kittens. All little babies are *little*, so they can fit in their mommies' bellies.

CHILD (*giggling*): Why should they?

MOTHER: So they can grow, and come *out*.

(CHILD *giggles, and whispers in* MOTHER's *ear.*)

MOTHER (*chagrined*): What a thing to say! Of course not!

CHILD: That's what it looks like in the book! Where it comes out, where it comes *out!*

MOTHER (*calmly*): It isn't like that at all. A baby is—a baby.

CHILD (*pointing to drawing*): Where it comes *out* yes it *is!*

MOTHER: A baby doesn't come out of the—rectum. You're silly. See?—this is the *womb.*

CHILD: What's the WOOOMMB?

MOTHER: Like a, an—emptiness. Like a balloon. And the little baby grows and grows, and the womb stretches, and— (*Nervous, extravagant gesture*) Because the mother drinks lots of milk and eats lots of good nutritional food, because she loves her baby, and—

CHILD (*carefully*): I came out of *you?*

MOTHER: Yes, you did.

CHILD: How'd I get in there?

MOTHER: You just sort of—arrived.

CHILD: Where was I, before?

MOTHER: You were—waiting.

CHILD: Yes, but where?

MOTHER: I'm not sure.

CHILD: Was I—outside somewhere?

MOTHER: No. You were safe and warm and—safe.

CHILD: Did somebody put me in there? In the WOOOMMB?

MOTHER: Actually, your father and I—well, we didn't put you there, exactly, but—

CHILD: Did it hurt?

MOTHER: Oh, no.

CHILD: Why'd you do it? Did you have to?

MOTHER: We didn't have to, we—wanted to. Daddy and Mommy both love you very much, so—

CHILD: When?

MOTHER: When what?

CHILD: When did you and Daddy stick me in there?

MOTHER: Oh—let's see—(*counts on fingers*)—about six years, eleven months, ten days ago.

CHILD: Why'd you do it? (*Giggles*) It's nasty.

MOTHER: Honey, it is *not* nasty.

CHILD: That's the nasty place, it is it *is*.

MOTHER: I told you, there are different places. The place for the little baby is different from the other, but it's all perfectly natural. It's normal.

CHILD: Grandma slapped my hand when I lifted my dress that time.

MOTHER: Grandma was just worried you were—showing your panties.

CHILD: 'Cause it's nasty.

MOTHER: Where did you pick up that word? It's *private*.

CHILD: What's priv-ate?

MOTHER: Some parts of our bodies are private, that's all. Like secrets.

CHILD: Like going poo-poo. (*Giggles*)

MOTHER: Don't be silly, now. You're too big for that.

CHILD: *Why'd* you do it? You and Daddy?

MOTHER: Because—we love you. I've told you.

CHILD: Where did *you* come from?

MOTHER: I came from—the same place you did.

CHILD: The same place?

MOTHER: My mother's body. The same place.

CHILD: That isn't the *same* place—that's different.

MOTHER: It's different, but it's the same. All mommies are—the same, anatomically.

CHILD: Ana-tom—?

MOTHER: "Anatomically." That means—having to do with the *body*.

CHILD: I'm not the same, I'm different! I am I am!

MOTHER: Yes, honey, you are. But—when you were a tiny tiny baby—when *I* was a baby—

CHILD (*anxiously, looking around*): Where was the mommy, then?

MOTHER: The mommy is on the *out*side, I guess you could say. And the baby's in the *in*side.

CHILD (*excited*): It's too *little* in there! It hurts!

MOTHER: It didn't hurt *then*—*you* were little.

CHILD: I was not! I don't remember!

MOTHER: Maybe we'd better stop the lesson, for now. You're getting feverish.

CHILD: I wouldn't fit in there I wouldn't!—would I?

MOTHER: Of course not, honey. Not now.

CHILD: You won't make me go in there will you will you?—you and Daddy will you?

MOTHER: Of course not. Shhh! you're too loud.

CHILD: You won't make me, will you, again? Stick me in there again?

MOTHER: Please, honey. Calm down.

CHILD: How did you know it was me?

MOTHER: What?

CHILD: When I was real real little, Mommy, how did you know it was me?

MOTHER: We—knew.

CHILD: Was my face like it is now?

MOTHER: Well—not exactly.

CHILD: How could you tell, then?

MOTHER: There's a "you" that isn't just your—(*vaguely*) face.

CHILD: Did Daddy tell you, or did you tell Daddy?

MOTHER: We—told each other.

CHILD: But how did you *know*?

MOTHER: Know what?

CHILD: It was *me*.

MOTHER: I told you—we were waiting for you.

CHILD: But how did you know it was me you were waiting for?

MOTHER (*passing hand over eyes*): Honey, enough. Some other time.

CHILD: You don't know, do you? You don't know.

MOTHER: Yes, I do.

CHILD: Then tell me, then!

MOTHER: Some other time, I said.

CHILD: No, no, I want to know *now*!

MOTHER: Shhhh—please!

CHILD: I won't SHHHH I won't SHHHH I want to know *now*!

MOTHER: But—what do you want to know?

CHILD: WHERE I COME FROM THAT'S WHAT I WANT TO KNOW!

MOTHER: I told you, babies come from—

CHILD: WHERE *I* COME FROM I WANT TO KNOW! I WANT TO KNOW!

MOTHER (*startled by* CHILD'*s vehemence*): Why, honey—I—

(*Lights begin to dim.*)

CHILD: I WANT TO KNOW I WANT TO *KNOW*.

(MOTHER *holds out arms to* CHILD, *as if to hug her;* CHILD *dances away.*)

CHILD: *I WANT TO KNOW.*

Lights out.

Cuckold

Lights up. A well-dressed, well-groomed MAN *in his thirties or early forties speaks to the audience, "dramatizing" his account as an ordinary person (i.e., not an actor) might do.*

MAN: This is what happened.

Last Friday I deliberately left the office early—just an hour. But it was enough!

I let myself in the apartment, right away called her name as always but there was no answer.

I called her name but she wasn't in the living room.

I called her name but she wasn't in the kitchen.

I called her name but she wasn't in the bedroom.

I called her name but she wasn't in the study.

I called her name but she wasn't in the bathroom.

Calling her name, beginning now to be worried, unless I was frankly upset, I hurried back to the living room switching on the lights, like a fool or a madman or a desperate husband I looked under the sofa (though I knew she wouldn't be in such a place!), I returned to the kitchen opening cupboard doors though I knew it was futile, "*Where are you?*" I called, "*where are you hiding?*" and in the bathroom calling her name I heard the . . . the strangest echo . . . as of the interior of a seashell . . . and in the bedroom I threw back the covers of the bed, lost control kneeling to peer beneath the bed, I called her name like a prayer translated from a Middle Eastern tongue, I threw open the closet doors, I rummaged in the hanging clothes, I kicked shoes about, I ran into the hall calling her name ran outside to knock on neighbors' doors, my face was beet red, my pride in a puddle at my feet, I hardly knew what I was doing climbing the stairs to the roof but of course she wasn't on the roof, I took the elevator down eleven storeys to the street but she wasn't on the street, I lost control I circled the block in the rain, crossed through the park, my heart beating like crazy like *I had already died and this was hell* then I gave up and went back home, let myself in the apartment and when I stepped inside the living room there she was . . . oh my God, there, restored to me . . . simply sitting there looking at me with her lovely ironic imperturbable eyes in whose tawny pupils I was reflected no more than an infinitesimal fraction of an inch tall, and I whispered "Bitch!

Where have you been all this time!" and knelt to feel her pads: were they damp? were they cold? were they gritty from the street? But I couldn't tell.

Lights out.

"I Don't Want to Alarm You"

Lights up. A young or youngish WOMAN *in black approaches the audience, smiling. At first her smile seems quite normal; then we see it is a little too intense, and her teeth too prominent. She is the nightmare embodiment of the "best friend": she who bears a lethal message beneath seemingly beneficent words.*

She may carry a small, commercially wrapped bouquet or a potted plant wrapped in gaudy tinfoil.

WOMAN: I don't want to alarm you! Oh no. *(Pause)*
I know how hard a time you've had of it lately. *(Pause)*
Soooo brave. *(Nods)*
I know how, your back being broken, it's painful
for you to walk here with me
as if we were *(faintest of pauses)* equals.

(Coming forward, intensely sympathetic)
I *know*—you're trying not to think about it.
And to forgive, where forgetting has failed.
It *is* the wisest strategy, I think, for you—to assume
that air of subtly modulated hurt, a bit of "dignity"
in which no one much believes. Oh yes!—
"saving face" is *courteous.*
And we, your dearest friends, are grateful.

(More intensely smiling, but now as if "confidential," voice lowered)
And if, these days—oh, I know! I know!—it's so *hard!*
(Finger to lips as if she, your friend, can keep your secret)
—If, these days, you are happy in
that sea-green haze between sleep and wakefulness where
the body floats placid . . . paralyzed . . . on the very cusp of . . .
extinction . . . *(now more briskly, smiling)* I think too that is
the wisest strategy for you, for now.

*(*WOMAN *holds out flowers.)*

Lights out.

"I Got Something For You"

Lights up. RICKIE's *bedroom: it is part of an affluent household, but its qualities need not be specified. Stage right, a closed door; stage left, a window, with an attractive curtain and a venetian blind, its slats drawn shut. The window is open about a foot, the blind raised to this height. We see a pair of hands grasp the underside of the window from the outside and tug upward. There is some difficulty— the window sticks.*

Muffled curses from the other side of the window, though we can't see anyone yet: "Damn!" "Shit!" "Fuck it!" "Come on!" etc.

BARRY *finally gets the window raised high enough so that he can climb through, with his clumsy bundle; unfortunately, he gets caught in the venetian blind, flailing and shoving at it impatiently.*

BARRY (*To* RICKIE, *behind him*): Why didn't you pull this fucking blind *up?* Asshole!

RICKIE (*protesting*): Hey, gimme a hand, willya? (*He too has trouble climbing through the window—*BARRY *doesn't help him.*) *Damn* you!

(RICKIE's *bundle slips from his grasp and falls to the floor.*)

BARRY (*furious, but keeping his voice low*): You knew we'd be coming in here, why didn't you get things ready? Do I have to think of every fucking detail *myself?*

RICKIE (*uncertainly, may be lying*): I *did* leave it up. The maid must've let it down.

BARRY (*raising hand as if to cuff him, as in a familiar routine*): Don't hand me that shit, okay?—not tonight. *Not tonight.* (*Disgusted*) *And close the damn thing, will you?* (*As* RICKIE *tugs down window, readjusts venetian blind*) We're not going back out this way—right? So *close* it. (*As if to invisible audience, fuming, "wired"*) Big brother's got to think of every fucking thing *himself*—well, fuck that shit! (*Ominously*) After tonight, we're *equals.*

(RICKIE *manages to shut the window; lowers the venetian blind, adjusts the curtain, neatly. He is breathing hard.*

BARRY *and* RICKIE *come forward, and we see them distinctly.* BARRY

*is in fact peering at his reflection in a mirror—he's in a state of
controlled mania, yet still vain about his appearance.*

BARRY *is twenty years old,* RICKIE *eighteen. They are brothers,
very good-looking, with a distinct family resemblance;* RICKIE *is perceptibly younger than* BARRY, *less mature and less certain of himself.
Both are athletes—tennis players—but not conspicuously muscled or
swaggering. Both wear casual but expensive clothes, in dark colors;
prominent wristwatches; sporty shoes [not running shoes]. Their
haircuts are styled to the latest fashion.*

*They have each carried into the room a large, bulky bundle
wrapped in a plastic garbage bag, and these they have set on the
floor. Each bundle contains: a slick moisture-repellent or rubberized
raincoat, long, oversized; rubberized or plastic headgear; a rubber
mask; rubber overshoes, or fishing boots; long rubber gloves; a dou-
ble-barreled shotgun and a box of shells. These items, of course, are
hidden from the audience initially.)*

RICKIE (*as if struck*): It's—weird!—isn't it?

BARRY (*frowning into mirror, running hands through his
hair*): What's weird?

RICKIE (*with a vague giggle*): Like, uh, unnatural—breaking in our
own house. Climbing over the roof! (*Looking about, grinning, as
if the room has become unfamiliar to him*) My room, where I've
just *been.* (*Picks up a tennis racquet, turns it in his hand as if
wonderingly*)

BARRY: Nobody broke in. Where's any sign of "forced entry"? (*Points
to window*)

RICKIE: How'd they get in, then?—you-know-who.

BARRY: Must have walked in. Been invited, maybe. Who knows? (*A
sneering smile*) Some old business buddies with a score to settle.

RICKIE (*shrill giggle*): Yeah! Dad sure has a lot of those!

BARRY (*raising a forefinger, in correction*): *Had* a lot.

(*As* BARRY *squats to remove items from his bundle,* RICKIE *tiptoes
with exaggerated caution to the door. He opens it a crack, listens for
a moment, shuts it carefully again. Wipes hands on trousers.*)

RICKIE: Don't need to worry about fingerprints—in my own room!
(*Pause*) They're down there, huh? Watching TV?

BARRY (*contemptuously*): What else? They sure aren't playing chess! They sure aren't *fucking*! (*Taking no note of* RICKIE, *who winces; removing items of clothing from bag, seemingly talking to himself*) Last guy who's gonna see them is Lin-Lang-Loo (*mocking approximation of a Chinese name*)—"H'roe! Housa Lee! De-rirv-ery! Thank you!" (*Pause, then with childish resentment*) What burns my ass, he's always got to order that fucking walnuts duck; then he doesn't eat it, he eats what *I* order—Three Treasures in the Nest—'cause it's better. And *she's* got to order tofu, or that crap bean curd with Chinese greens, that *nobody* wants. And you: sesame cold fucking noodles!

RICKIE (*staring at wristwatch*): Eight-twenty-four p.m., Wednesday, that's—what? "Unsolved Mysteries"?

BARRY: Never mind what's on TV, asshole! We're not going to see it.

RICKIE (*sheepish grin*): Oh, yeah. We're at the movie.

BARRY: Which movie?

RICKIE (*nervously, but by rote*): *Jacob's Ladder*. At the Cinemax 7. Parkett Boulevard. Seven-fifteen show. Which we know 'cause we had to get there on time. It's a twenty-minute drive each way, and—

BARRY: What's *Jacob's Ladder* about?

RICKIE (*clumsy laugh*): Uh—that's a good question!—uh—Tim Robbins is this troubled Vietnam vet, who was actually killed—I mean he's dead—or almost?—but he's, uh, like dreaming—I guess. (*Slipping into gear, rote recitation*) This guy and his platoon were experimented on by the U.S. government—chemical warfare—made them into animals—cut loose and shot one another instead of the enemy—*he's* bayoneted—by a buddy—carried by helicopter through the jungle to—

BARRY: What's the final shot?

RICKIE (*has lost thread of recitation*): Uh—he's climbing up to Heaven, like, with his little boy that's dead?—or, no: he's on the operating table, they tried to save him but couldn't, his guts are all—(*makes a motion as if to indicate his own intestines spilling out; pause; as if frightened*) . . . Oh Christ.

(BARRY, *not troubling to glance up at him*—BARRY *is removing items from his bag*—*reaches out toward* RICKIE *and snaps his fingers.*)

RICKIE (*roused from trance*): Oh, yeah! "Sure I do, officer—*here!*" (*Reaches in pocket, takes out a ticket stub*)

BARRY (*frowning up at him*): You wouldn't find it so *fast*—I told you. What the fuck, you're forgetting already?

RICKIE (*staring at stub, replacing it in his pocket*): There's so much to remember.

(BARRY *makes a disparaging gesture at his brother, as if he's both impatient and amused.*)

BARRY (*lifts rubber mask, peeks through eyeholes at* RICKIE): C'mon, get a move on.

(RICKIE *squats and removes items from bag, as* BARRY *has done, in the same order. He whistles, hums, or sings under his breath, a current rock hit; moves his body suggestively.*
  From this point onward, BARRY *and* RICKIE *are costuming themselves. It seems evident that they've taken drugs, perhaps cocaine, to give them energy and courage.* BARRY, *of course, is the more composed;* RICKIE *is clumsy, drops things, but is determined. Glances repeatedly at his brother as they dress, as if in childlike imitation.*)

BARRY (*savage giggle*): Hey, Dad—here's your fortune cookie: "I got something for you!"

RICKIE (*giggling*): "*I* got something for you!"

BARRY (*lifting shotgun from bag*): Walnuts duck! Okay—I'll give you walnuts duck *all over.*

RICKIE: Tofu!—bean curd!—Chinese fucking greens *all over!* (*In a gesture mimicking his brother's, he lifts his shotgun, peers through its sight.*)

BARRY: Remember, Rickie—*you* go first.

RICKIE: I go first.

BARRY: You take the first shot.

RICKIE: I take the first shot. (*Pause*) How come?

BARRY: I *told* you: just *do* it.

RICKIE: Yeah, but—how come, exactly?

BARRY (*as if evasively*): To make sure you do your share.

RICKIE: Yeah, but—how come *first?*

BARRY: So you don't—freak out.

RICKIE: *I'm* not gonna freak out—didya see how I played the net today? I was *hot.*

BARRY: Yeah, you *were.* Your backhand's coming along.

RICKIE: The funeral and stuff—how long will it be? The TriState Tournament's a week from Saturday.

BARRY: You wouldn't be thinking like that, so don't.

RICKIE (*giggling*): Yeah, but I *am* thinking like that, like—wow!— I'm in two time zones at once, y'know?

BARRY: You just wouldn't be thinking about tennis, but, like, when the date comes up, we'll *go.* We're not gonna let Coach down, huh?

RICKIE (*breathing fast*): *I'm* not gonna let Coach down, I'm not gonna let Dad down, "at the price I'm paying for those lessons"— (*Pause*) How come I take the first shot, Barry?

BARRY: It's what we decided.

RICKIE: She's gonna look at me, and she's gonna say—

BARRY: Don't give her time! Just blast away!

RICKIE: What if I miss?

BARRY: You won't miss.

RICKIE: Yeah, but what if I miss?—and she knows who I am—

BARRY: You don't miss with one of these babies. (*Lifts shotgun*)

RICKIE: *You* take her, *I'll* take Dad.

BARRY: *I* got Dad.

RICKIE: Yeah, but—if I miss?

BARRY: It's all worked out, for Christ's sake—we had the fucking *chalk marks* down there, didn't we! Just do it like it's rehearsed. ("*Wired,*" *breathing fast*) Do it, do it, *do it!* (*Jubilant*) "Thirty-love!"

RICKIE: They'll know.

BARRY: What?

RICKIE: They'll know. Who we are.

BARRY: They won't know.

RICKIE: *He'll* know.

BARRY: How the fuck will he know!

RICKIE (*as if resigned*): "Sixth-sense business acumen"—"investment wizard"—he'll know. (*Pause*) *She'll* know.

BARRY: Not if you keep your mouth shut. (*With shotgun, miming*) Just, like, *fire*. We walk in there—we're already aiming—we *fire*. You, then me! Left barrel—right barrel! Reload, and *fire!*—left barrel, right barrel! Reload, and *fiiiire!* (*Pause, calming down a bit*) Too bad, actually, he *won't* know. Fucker might've broken down and said, "Congratulations, Barry, you didn't fuck up for once!"

RICKIE (*has just thought of this, tries to joke*): Big bro, you're not gonna, like, *waste* me, are you? In the back?

BARRY (*staring at him*): What?

RICKIE: When I take the first shot, and, uh—

BARRY (*hurt, incensed*): What the fuck are you saying, Rickie?

RICKIE (*backing down*): I was only joking. I—

BARRY: That is sick, Rickie. That is obscene.

RICKIE (*embarrassed*): Well, I, uh—I was only joking.

(BARRY *clamps a hand on* RICKIE's *shoulder. His manner is utterly sincere, "moving."*)

BARRY: We're brothers, aren't we? All the way?

RICKIE (*wiping at eyes*): Yeah.

BARRY: Nobody's as close as we are, right?

RICKIE: Yeah.

BARRY: Like Mom's always telling people—"Barry and Rickie are *friends*." (*Pause*) We're going to inherit together, aren't we—fifty-fifty—split right down the middle?

RICKIE: I guess.

BARRY: Eleven million each—at *least*! Hell, *I* don't want any more than that, do you?

RICKIE (*eager to please*): That's enough for me.

BARRY (*passionate, earnest*): I only want my fair share, that's all—not a penny more! So—what's the problem?

RICKIE (*vague smile, confused*): What's the problem?

BARRY: Do like we rehearsed, you'll be okay, Rickie. Just don't give them a chance to talk. If she says anything—don't listen.

RICKIE: Don't listen.

BARRY: *He'll* try to stop us—you know him!—but he won't have time. (*With shotgun, mimes pulling the trigger*) Remember: AIM FOR THE HEAD.

RICKIE (*imitates his brother, with exaggerated intensity*): AIM FOR THE HEAD.

BARRY (*giggling*): No mercy!

RICKIE: No mercy!

BARRY (*shotgun brandished*): Remember Scarface—"How d'ya like my baby?"

RICKIE: How d'ya like my baby! (*Raises voice*) MY BABY!

BARRY: Shhh!

(BARRY *puts on overshoes;* RICKIE *does the same, awkwardly.*)

RICKIE: These are—waterproof, for sure?

BARRY: For sure.

RICKIE: Jeez, they're kinda tacky!

BARRY (*conceding the point*): Yeah, well—it's only this once. (*Pause*) Okay, now—let's run through the scenario.

RICKIE (*by rote, quickly*): We do it. We pick up the shells and put them in our pockets. We walk out the back. We drive away. To our destination. We get rid of the stuff. Where nobody's gonna find it. We drive back. It's, uh, nine-thirty. Maybe ten. We come inside—the door's unlocked. (*Pause*) We can tell right away something's wrong. (*Pause*) Something isn't—right.

BARRY (*prodding him*): Where are they?

RICKIE: The rec room.

BARRY: Is the TV on?

RICKIE: The TV's on.

BARRY: All the lights?

RICKIE: The lights are on.

BARRY (*prodding him, impatiently*): So?

RICKIE: We, uh, we come in the door, we—can tell right away something's wrong. (*Pause*) Something isn't—right.

BARRY: Okay!—then—?

RICKIE (*slowly*): We—find—them. Yeah.

BARRY (*impatiently*): Then—?

RICKIE (*enunciating words carefully*): We—find—them.

BARRY: *Then*—?

RICKIE: We, uh, freak out. We—run outside. On the lawn. We're crying—yelling. (*Zombielike recitation*) The neighbors hear us— call the police.

BARRY: Yeah!

(BARRY *and* RICKIE *are completely costumed now except for their masks.* BARRY *has carefully folded up the plastic garbage bags, pushing one into a pocket of his raincoat and one into his brother's pocket.*

He sees that RICKIE *is standing very still, staring into a corner of the room, a peculiar look on his face.)*

BARRY: Hey, kid, don't worry: it's all gonna come *naturally.* Afterward. We *will* miss them, sure!

RICKIE (*wiping at nose*): I'm kinda worried, Barry, if Mom sees me —I mean, y'know—she's gonna feel kinda—bad.

BARRY: She won't see you, asshole, I *explained.* (*Exasperated*) You walk in—you're already aiming—you give it to her in the face. (*As if reasonably*) She's got no face, how's she gonna *see* you?

RICKIE (*dazed*): In the face. In the face. In the face. (*Pause*) Oh God—she's gonna see me, I just know. She's gonna say, "Rickie—" (*Draws out word*) "Riii-ick-ieee—"

(BARRY *has been adjusting his rubber mask, which, with the headgear, completely covers his head and face, except for narrow eyeslits. There is a certain swagger in* BARRY's *manner: he seems to have drawn power from the very fact of disguising himself.* RICKIE *stares at him.*)

BARRY (*voice slightly altered by the mask*): How? How's she gonna know you? With this on? (*Indicating mask*) The two of us are gonna look identical: twins.

(BARRY *helps* RICKIE *with his mask.*)

RICKIE (*now masked, somewhat reassured*): Yeah—I guess.

BARRY: C'mere! (*Pulls him to the mirror, where they stand side by side*) What d'ya mean, "I guess"?—"I *know.*"

(*For two or three beats,* RICKIE *comtemplates their reflections. Then, suddenly convinced, energized, he picks up his shotgun.*)

RICKIE: I *know.* Yeah! Right! Okay! Nobody's gonna know *who* goes first!

(*The brothers move toward the door.* BARRY *prods* RICKIE *into the lead. As lights dim:*)

BARRY (*sly, insinuating, singsong*): "Hey, Daaaddddy: I got something for you!"

RICKIE (*as an echo, overlapping with* BARRY): "—got something for you!"

(RICKIE, BARRY *exit, giggling. The door is left open.*

A beat or two. *One of them returns, pokes his head into the room, glances around. Satisfied that all is in order, he switches the lights off.*)

Lights out.

Bluebeard's Last Wife

Lights up. BLUEBEARD, *distinguished, patrician, and his* WIFE, *a beautiful young woman, walk ceremonially together, her arm linked through his. His gaze is on the horizon, his expression inscrutable, perhaps just faintly contemptuous.*

WIFE: How you all—my sisters!—must envy me. (*Pause*) For I am Count Bluebeard's new bride.

BLUEBEARD (*pointing overhead*): The stars you see, my dear, in the night sky, this great vast winking sky—have vanished thousands of billions of years ago. It is the stars that exist now, which you cannot see, that exert their influence upon you.

WIFE (*to audience, as they resume walk*): He takes me—suddenly! Anywhere! Inside the castle walls, or outside! (*As* BLUEBEARD *roughly embraces her*) If anyone sees us, my husband will have his eyes gouged out. Or hers. (*Pause*) When we lie together in the tall cold grasses, the grasses curl over us to hide us.

(BLUEBEARD *retreats.*)

WIFE: A man's passion is his triumph—some of you, my sisters, have forgotten that fact. And to be the receptacle of a man's passion is a woman's triumph. (*As if confidentially*) I am Bluebeard's youngest bride, of the many he has wed. *And it is my vow to be Bluebeard's last wife.*

(BLUEBEARD *joins his* WIFE, *walks with her, as before.*)

WIFE: It's said my family "sold" me—and what if they did? (*Flouncing hair, self-satisfied*) At least I am of value: at least a great nobleman, who could buy nearly anyone in his kingdom, chose *me*. (*Shivers as if in excitement or anticipation*) And brought me to Bluebeard's Castle—of such legendary renown. (*Pause*) This great house—smelling of time, death, Fate. Stone passageways and rooms with such high ceilings you can barely make out their elaborate gilt ornamentation; immense fireplaces, in which small thin fingers of blue flame burn; ancient tapestries; tall leaded windows looking out onto—nothing.

BLUEBEARD: My bride, have you ever loved another man as you love me? Have you ever gazed upon another man like me? Do you give your life to me?

WIFE (*gaily, girlishly, recklessly*): What is a woman's life if it cannot be thrown away? (*To audience*) Bluebeard told me of the doors in his castle that I may unlock, and the rooms I may enter freely; he told me then of the seventh door, the forbidden door, which I may *not* unlock—

BLUEBEARD: For behind it lies a forbidden room, which you may *not* enter.

WIFE (*to audience*): "Why may I not enter it?" I asked, for I saw that he expected this question of me.

BLUEBEARD (*rather coolly, formally kissing her brow*): Because, my bride, I have forbidden it. (*Pause*) But here is the key to the door, in any case. For I am going away on a long journey.

WIFE (*taking key*): Dear husband, where are you going on your long journey? Cannot I come with you?

(BLUEBEARD *turns away. His* WIFE *stares after him—but there is no reply and no response.*
BLUEBEARD *withdraws indifferently into the shadows.*)

WIFE (*to audience*): Here it is—a golden key, weighing no more than a feather in the palm of my hand. (*Examining it*) What's this?—a stain? A faint rust-colored stain? How the key glistens when I hold it to the light! (*A pause*) Best not to examine it too closely. (*A pause*) I am young, as you can see. And innocent. *Very* much the virgin —until my wedding night. (*She winces, as if involuntarily, with a recollection of pain; then steels herself.*) The happiest night of my life—I swear by my soul. (*Earnestly*) Yes, I know, of course, that my husband's previous brides have died in this castle; that, one by one, they excited his outrage, thus deserved their fates. I know, I know!—everyone in our country knows the legend! (*Hugs herself, shivering; then, with defiant happiness*) I will slip this precious key into my bosom, to wear against my heart, as a token of Bluebeard's trust in *me*.

(*A beat or two.* WIFE *moves about, as if along a passageway.*)

WIFE: Of course I'm tempted too. Like my sisters—my sister brides—who preceded me—and are now dead. (*Approaching door*) Ah—the door! The forbidden door! The lock that must not be opened! (*As if drawn against her will, resisting*) I too feel the tug of a terrible hunger—the human need, not simply to know, but to know that I possess the courage and strength to seek out knowledge; not to shrink from it. (*Strokes, caresses door; touches key to lock; sensuous, erotic manner*) Yes—I too am tempted by this door that must not be opened, this lock that must not be penetrated. (*Pause; then turns abruptly away, as if wrenching herself free.*) But I am a good wife, I am *his* wife. (*On knees, impassioned prayer*) Our Father—oh, lead me not into temptation!

(*A beat or two.* BLUEBEARD *appears: he has been watching from the shadows.*

BLUEBEARD *rejoins* WIFE. *A rough embrace, kisses.* BLUEBEARD *presents* WIFE *with a single blood-red long-stemmed rose.*)

WIFE (*to audience, with pride*): When my noble husband returned from his long journey he was gratified—and, I think, somewhat surprised—to see that the door to the forbidden room remained locked; and when he examined the key, still warm from my bosom (*as* BLUEBEARD *examines the key*), he saw that the stain was untouched. And he declared—

BLUEBEARD: Truly, you are now my wife; not merely in flesh, as the church has decreed, but in spirit as well. And I, in my turn, vow to love you above all other women.

(*Lights dim slightly, then rise, to suggest change of time and mood.* BLUEBEARD *withdraws into shadows.*)

WIFE: Here, in our bedchamber, I see, through the opened windows, the unfathomable night sky—so many stars, so many worlds that know us not! Where does God our Father dwell, in such a honeycomb? (*Pause*) The silence of these infinite spaces terrifies me! (*Pause*) Except: I am *his* wife, the wife of Bluebeard; the last of Bluebeard's wives. (*A beat; then smiles, defensively*) Of course— it has been charged against me that I betrayed my sisters—I abandoned them to a common grave, and cast my lot with their enemy. Some of you resent me, don't you?—ah, I know. But—so be it. (*Pause*) When I sleep in our sumptuous marital bed I sleep deeply, the untroubled sleep of an infant; for, in Bluebeard's Castle, I am without sin. I dream dreams I cannot recall in the morning, of extraordinary beauty, and magic; dreams of sacrifice, and blood, and valor. Sometimes my beloved husband will recall these dreams for me, for their marvels are such they invade even his dreams. "How is it that you, of all people, can dream such dreams," he exclaims, "such works of art!" (*Pause*) And he kisses me, and holds me to his bosom. (*Pause*) Soon, I will be bearing his child—I pray for a son. The first of his many sons. (*Pause, then with grim satisfaction*) Without me, the lineage of Bluebeard would have died out.

Lights out.

The Floating Birches

Lights up. An elderly, disheveled MAN *addresses the audience. He is barefoot; may be wearing pajamas, or badly wrinkled, partly un-zipped trousers and an undershirt. Skin sallow, eyes recessed.*

MAN: You lied to me!—saying it was an ambulance but—UP THE
DRIVEWAY COMES A HEARSE.
(*Struggles, as if being restrained; manages to throw off invisible hands*) I'm not going 'cause I'm not dead God damn it I'M NOT
DEAD YOU CAN'T SAY THAT! (*calmer, though confused, frightened*) How it began I, I was
coughing, coughing so hard a rib cracked!—Jeezuz!
Now I got this brace—(*opens clothing, shows corsetlike brace around his torso*)—gripping me like a hand.
(*deep, threatening voice*) Hey. I got you, old man.
I know all about you.

(*in his own voice, now annoyed, embarrassed*) One night, I had
to piss, I'm reaching under the bed for a, a shoe—
I don't know why, a—*shoe.*
I guess I was asleep, or—something
But the shoe isn't there so I'm over in the corner in the dark
but there's a fence, not a wall,
it's the fence out behind the barn
and beyond the fence there's—
Jeezuz!—all these junked cars—
that hadna ever been there, before.
But I'm already pissing, I can feel it on my toes hot
and I'm starting to cry knowing I did something wrong
like oh God I made a mistake
but how to make it right?

Pa, this voice is saying—Pa? Hey Pa wake up?

(*He mimes writing a letter, speaking in a gruff, "mad," yet purposeful voice, moving to another part of the stage.*)

TO THE U.S. GOVERNMENT WASHINGTON D.C.—THIS
GOOD WOMAN MY WIFE 50 YRS. IS INNOCENT OF ANY &
ALL WRONGDOING OF MINE. SHE KNEW NOTHING OF
TRANSACTIONS OF ANY FINANCIAL KIND NOR OF

MORAL MISDEEDS & CRIMES. ALL I FORGOT, I CONFESS
& SIGN MY NAME. SHE MUST NOT KNOW OF THIS OR
ANY OF THE CHILDREN AS ALL ARE INNOCENT & I ONLY
AM TO BLAME.

(*Two white-clad female figures appear in the shadows at the rear,
stage left and stage right, but do not advance.* MAN *resumes his earlier
tone, frightened but incensed, angry.*)

You lied, you lied to your father it isn't a, a—(*searching for
word, frustrated*)—'b'lence—'b'*lance*—
it's a hearse come to take me away BUT
I AM NOT READY, I AM NOT—
(*hesitates to say word "dead"*)—ready. You can't make me go
this is my home my, my home, where I live where I was born you
can't make me under U.S. law IF I AM NOT—READY.

(*He struggles as female figures advance.*) God damn you
lying to an old man your own father I wasn't always your father
I am somebody else you never knew God damn you you can't clip
my toenails who gave you permission to clip my toenails—
(*Lifting and grasping one foot, as he hobbles about on the other*)
I can clip my own toenails God damn you thick as horn where the
sledgehammer smashed it—
And you, and—who are you!—I don't know—*you*! washing me
     like a,
a baby, a baby in diapers, I am not a baby I am not a
I am not dead I am not
that one in the, the corset like a woman, I am not him, I
don't know him, let go I don't know him I am not a
corpse, I am not a
dead body I am not that one with the,
the belly like lard, the withered testicles, let me go!
I am not the one the angel touched
in the hollow of the thigh

(*Long pause; then speaks to female figures.*)

One by one you came to me, I framed your faces in my
     hands, in
the reek of the bedpan I bless
I bless you, I forgive
you, I love you, I am your

father am I, am I your father, what has
happened to your father where
has he gone?

(*In a new, transfigured tone, slow-dawning joy, comes forward*)

And now the slow drive through the countryside
by moonlight, the white birches floating—
so many! on all sides so many! so
beautiful the white birches!
You were happy here this was your world, these
hillsides, these woods where
the white birches float. . . .

Lights out.

A Report to an Academy
(After Kafka)

Lights up. An adult APE, *male, with a briefcase enters and takes his place at a podium. He is wearing a suit with a vest; glasses. His manner is friendly, self-effacing; only by degrees does the suggestion of a terrible urgency and recalled agony become evident.*

APE (*acknowledging audience's amusement or skepticism*): Yes, certainly! Oh, yes! (*Nodding*) I don't blame you for your reaction! I would react precisely the same way, I'm sure, in your place!

(*The* APE *opens briefcase, removes papers, etc. Pours water into a glass and hastily sips.*)

To begin—! Ah, how to begin—! (*As if ingratiating*) As all *Homo sapiens* know—beginnings are hard!

(*The* APE *steps away from podium, further exposing himself. To extract the last degree of amusement from his audience, he lifts a trouser leg, shows hairy legs.*)

(*Nodding, laughing*) Yes, yes! It's all over! (*Pause*) It is what is meant by . . . ANIMAL.

(*The* APE *begins to "act out" his story.*)

No way out.
A three-sided cage nailed to a locker in the ship's hold.
The ceiling against the nape of my neck,
the narrow sides cutting into my thighs.

Impossible to stand. Or to sit.
Impossible to sleep.
Oh the days, the nights—without sleep!
My captors, who were human beings, had constructed the
perfect cage:
impossible to forget.
So, ladies and gentlemen, I squatted in the corner.

That is what I did, for the eighteen days of the voyage:
I SQUATTED IN THE CORNER.
No way out.

A statement that, perhaps, *you* cannot comprehend.
No way out.

Squatting in the cage.
Sobbing. A memory of—
my loved ones they'd slaughtered.
But: no way out.
Picking at fleas. Sobbing.
A male ape will sob only when alone.
A male ape will mourn only in solitude.
Over and over the knowledge:
I MUST FIND A WAY OUT OR DIE.

Freedom?
But no. Please do not misunderstand.
Esteemed ladies and gentlemen, please do not misunderstand.
FREEDOM was never my option: only a way out.

I think, ladies and gentlemen, you may have failed, you are
good people, but you sometimes fail, let us acknowledge you
have failed, I don't blame you in the slightest, I would fail
too in your place, thus let us try again:
a three-sided cage:
the ceiling against the nape of my neck,
the narrow sides cutting into my thighs,
the bars raising welts on my hide.
Most of all: a memory of—

(APE *hides his face, cannot continue this line of thought.*)

Bound for the zoological garden in Frankfurt where on Sundays
you and your darling children would dawdle, grinning
and pointing, whistling Isn't he ugly, isn't he comical
tossing peanuts into my cage, crusts of moldy bread,
sharp stones, sticks.
Bound for the zoological garden and a larger cage
I perceived that freedom was not an option.
FREEDOM is not a word in an ape's vocabulary.

Consequently— (*spreads his arms*)
I became one of you.

I charmed my captors who were (*laughs, as if fondly*)—only human,
after all! I learned their mannerisms (*scratches under arms, crotch;*

yawns; blows nose in rag), I learned their speech, I grew ingenious in cunning, I NOW WEAR A NECKTIE.

Please do not misunderstand, gracious ladies and gentlemen:
I am not bitter.
Ah, not I!
Can an animal be bitter?
Ah, surely not!
Only: I had to find a way out of your cage, or die.
So I became one of you. As you see.

(*Approaches audience, "friendly"*)

The first thing I learned from my captors was a frank handshake which, you can be sure, I practice every day. Will you give me your hand?

(*Extends hand.*)

Lights fade.

The Psychic

Lights up. A portly gentleman, white-haired, in a well-cut conservative suit, unlit cigar in hand, addresses the audience genially. Fraternal pin or ribbon in lapel; signet ring; highly polished black shoes. The image of conventional worldly success.

PSYCHIC (*beaming*): Yessir! You folks are a bit taken aback, eh, by the sight of *me*? Julius Jay Glass? Most folks think they know what a psychic looks like—some frazzle-haired skinny gal with pop eyes, clothes smelling of *cats*—the kind of weirdo, if it's a man, you wouldn't let step inside your front door. Sure there's lots of 'em like that, but—not me. Julius Jay Glass. (*Chuckles*) I swear— "Glass" is my family name. They'd have liked for me to change it but I never did. (*Pause; peers out into audience, bemused, but frowning*) Hmm! Getting some emanations from several of you— but, say, I'm not here on business tonight, you'll excuse me if I block them? (*Genial, smiling*) Sometimes, yes indeed, an emanation I receive is, uh, *personal*—like from a lonely woman—could be a lonely *married* woman—those kinds, poor things, are the most desperate. 'Specially some years ago when I was—well, a damned good-looking young man, *coal*-black hair! (*Fluffs hair*) Some town I'd be called to, by the local police most often, I'd return to my hotel and a woman would maybe be waiting, sort of hidden, veiled, in the lobby—a few times, right in my room. So—I acquired a certain reputation as a ladies' man—no fault of mine! Hell, a psychic is only human—like everybody else. (*Pause; brusque*) Now—I block out emanations at the source, if I can. (*Shifting mood, more genial; ambles about stage*) Well—if you've heard of Julius Jay Glass I'd guess it's connected with that case last spring—I'm the "world-renowned psychic" the Tucson police brought in to solve the Bonnie Starr mystery—that poor little four-year-old girl that was kidnapped—in all the papers and on TV—twenty-one days from start to finish. But my career as a psychic goes back, I mean *way* back, to when I was five years old, in Ely [*pronounced "Eli"*], Ohio. Where it was discovered that I had what's called "second sight"—meaning sometimes I could see things at a distance, or forward, or back, in time; things I wasn't supposed to know about; things a child my age would *not* know about. (*Shakes head, smiling. A queer bluish light suffuses the stage.*) Our dog Lucky disappeared and I laid down in his bed, some rags he had for a bed, before Momma could stop me, and I "saw" right away where Lucky was—started bawling real hard 'cause Lucky was dead, mangled and dead, in a ditch where some truck had thrown him. (*Pause*) Wasn't just I *saw* him—some way, I *was* him. (*Trembling*) Oh God! (*Pause*) And the worst kind of nightmares, for a long time afterward. (*Pause*)Brrrr! All the corpses, animal *and* human, I've seen, in my time!—some of them, sorry to say, in an advanced state of DE-COM-PO-SI-TION. (*Nervously sucking on unlit cigar*) Got so damned sensitive by age eleven I couldn't see any picture of any-body in our family that had died, or brush up against clothes that had belonged to dead people, or—curtains, or—piano sheet music, even—'cause if I did, I'd *see*. Some sight I hadn't wanted to see. (*Long pause, as if he's reliving the horror and willing it away*)

(*Blue light gradually fades.*)

(*Reverting to earlier tone, affable and expansive*) 'Course I had to leave Ely, Ohio—young. Aged sixteen. My gift scared my folks, who were simple Christian folks—worried I was getting signals from the Devil. Huh! (*Contemptuous chuckle; peers into audience*) Any of you fool enough to believe in the Devil? Like, you want to think evil doesn't emanate from your neighbor?—or from *you*? (*Pause, then continues as before, a bit self-congratulatory*) 'Course I never married—never "fell" in what's called "love"—not just that Julius Jay Glass sees through you ladies, your beauty and mystery et cetera, but once there's intimacy, Julius Jay Glass *is* you. (*Shakes head, marveling*) This one woman—yes, she was beautiful—high-spirited, proud—she threw herself at me, just about—I took pity on her, told her "Don't waste your time on Julius Jay Glass, he *can't* love, he sees too deep into your heart," and she said, "I can love enough for two—don't send me away!" (*Pause*) But I did. (*Pause*) Later.

Maybe I regretted it, (PSYCHIC *peers into audience, frowning, as if interrupted in his monologue.*) Hmmmm! Is that so! (*Nods, wipes forehead with white handkerchief*) Well now look—I *can't* take on that burden—I *won't*. Yes you are a desperate lady but no—I'm blocking any more emanations from you. I can't be every-body's savior—not at my age!

(*Continuing in earlier tone*) Folks think Julius Jay Glass is a millionaire, *multi*millionaire, all the rich clients I've had through my career—truth is, I give 50 percent of my earnings to charity

—always have. Now I'm retired—or trying to be. Keep retiring every other year, then get summoned back—so damned hard to say *no*. (*Sighs*) This case out in Tucson, now! Brrrr! I'm incognito in my home in Palm Beach receiving signals of desperation from two thousand miles away! Tried to block 'em—*did* block 'em— then it happened the Tucson police summoned me, so I went, couldn't say no—that poor young couple not knowing if their little girl was alive or dead; whether they'd ever see her again. (*Shakes head, moved*) God, the suffering human beings inflict upon one another! (*Pause*) Now the Starrs aren't "poor" actually, they're well-to-do, old Southwest aristocracy which is why the kidnappers chose little Bonnie. Kidnapped her right out of nursery school, two armed men, masked—drove right off—and no trace of them afterward. And everybody, I mean *everybody*, was searching for that poor little girl. The news media went wild. Forty-eight hours she's missing, not a word from the kidnappers, then the Starrs received a single ransom note—"FIFTEEN MILLION DOLLARS OR YOU'LL NEVER SEE YOUR DAUGHTER ALIVE AGAIN"— and after that, nothing. No communication. So—the Starrs were desperate. And Julius Jay Glass was called in.

(*Bluish light rises; slowly intensifies.*)

I'm seated in a windowless room—wax plugs in my ears— isolation—police headquarters—studying snapshots of Bonnie Starr, holding toys, clothes. (*From his pocket he removes a child's pink sweater, which he rubs against his face as he speaks, in an increasingly urgent voice.*) And—long minutes passed in oblivion. Minutes—hours. (*Pause*) I tried, oh how I tried!—to pass over *into* her! (*In a trancelike state, head back, eyes shut, face contorted in a grimace*) But—I was blocked. I was—blocked. (*Pause*) Never wanted anything like I wanted that beautiful little girl to be alive!—even as I knew, oh yes I knew, back East already I'd known, she was probably dead.

(*Pause*) In the sixth hour of meditation I broke through the resistance, saw, suddenly, a road—unpaved—leading off a state highway—past an Exxon station, boarded up—back beyond a 7-Eleven store—I'm like a bird in flight—skimming the earth, riding the air—five, six miles—mountains ahead—scrubby wasteland on all sides—no human habitation—road getting narrower—I'm turning off from the road in a desolate place—dumping ground—there's a ravine ahead—I'm flying along the rim—a half-mile from the road— (*Voice urgent, horrified*) Ah!—I see it—her—*it*—a child's bare legs, feet, protruding from under a tarpaulin . . . where they'd dumped her like garbage, and left her. (*Long pause. Sweater slips from fingers; he stoops to pick it up, returns it to his pocket.*)

So!—that was how it ended. In a ravine, ninety miles west of Tucson. They'd killed her right off, the only mercy was they hadn't raped or mutilated her. Like some do. (*Pause.* PSYCHIC *touches eyes with fingertips, but does not cry; reasserts control; reverts to earlier, genial mood. Bluish light quickly fades.*) Naturally, a psychic isn't always popular, even when he does his job 100 percent perfect! (*Pause*) But they paid me, of course. They always do. (*Pause*) And now I'm retired—I *am*. The strain's got too much for my heart. So—(*sudden shift of tone, as if fearful*)—*don't* send your signals to me—please! I am no one's savior—there is nothing *to* save! Please. (*Quietly, backing off, arms uplifted*) Please. Please.

Lights out.

The Secret Mirror

Lights up. A tall, slender, delicate-featured young MAN *stands facing the audience, one hand, knuckles inward, resting on his hip. His manner through the monologue is shy and self-doubting, yet aggressive; defensive and rueful, yet exalted.*

He shares the lighted space with a large, old-fashioned, possibly antique mirror of the kind that swings, and can be adjusted, on a pedestal stand. The mirror must have a weight and character of its own.

MAN (*addressing the audience*): Say you're alone once again in your rented room. Say you're alone once again before your secret mirror. What a terrible hunger has drawn you here! (*Pause. He pushes the mirror with his fingertips, slowly and carefully, in the way of a ritual, his mirror-image shifting and slanting mysteriously.*) Say you have discovered the place of absolute certainty, for you, in all the universe. In a cheap rented room. In secrecy. Here.

(*He gazes critically, frowning, at his reflection. Then, as if waking from a spell, he turns to lift from a table a wig of the same color as his own hair, but longer, curlier, "feminine." The wig, like all the accessories the* MAN *will employ, is in good taste, not at all tacky, vulgar, or comical.*)

(*Fitting wig onto head, excited, blinking*) Ah!—it's always a surprise, isn't it. (*Stroking surface of mirror as if in wonder*) That *you* are there, inside. (*Pause, almost fearful*) Inside the mirror. Waiting.

(*After a beat or two, he turns eagerly and tremulously to take up some other items from the table: silky, satiny undergarments, all white. One falls to the floor and he picks it up quickly.*)

(*Self-chiding, yet fond*) Putting *your* hair on first is a mistake, it makes the rest so clumsy. But *you* insist. (*Pause. Peers stage right*) And *you* tell me to check the door another time, for what if it isn't locked?—though of course it is. (*Goes to door, checks*) It is.

(*Sighing*) *You* determine the steps, I don't quarrel. A cruel master—I mean mistress!—*you* are.

(*With ceremonial movements, the* MAN *removes his clothes, except for a pair of white briefs; he puts on a brassiere, lacy, elegant, with padded but small cups; raises his arms high as he slides a slip down over his head.)*

(*Staring into mirror*) How *white!*—almost blinding. (*Sniffs*) And this scent, this fragrance . . .

(He takes up stockings, which may be an off-white color, with a patterned texture.)

(*Putting on stockings*) These—to disguise the ugly legs *you* are ashamed of. I only wish they could, completely.

(He holds aloft a pair of shoes: white satin high-heeled pumps.)

Beautiful. If only—not quite so *painful.* (*Laughs, as he steps into the shoes, with some difficulty—the shoes are clearly too tight.*)

(He takes up a dress and holds it against him, contemplating his image. The dress is beautiful, of white linen, or another fine fabric, with long sleeves, a long, full or pleated skirt, and, if possible, numerous pearl buttons.)

How tall *you* are—I'd nearly fogotten. (*As he reverently slides dress down over head*) Of course—it *is* your wedding dress. Which, in secrecy, in this room, only *you* will ever wear.

(He slowly buttons the dress, makes adjustments, etc., gazing at his image hungrily. Then there is a dull thud.)

(*Startled*) Someone on the stairs?—what? But the door is locked. (*Pause*) But you know the door is locked, haven't I locked it, yes and chain-bolted it, you know you *know* that door is locked and we are in no danger. (*Pause, then gives in, sighing*) Oh—all right, I will, *you* know best in these circumstances. (*At door, he tries handle, presses his ear against the door; we hear muffled knocking.*) Yes, you see it *is* locked. He's knocking next door, whoever he is. Didn't I tell you there's no danger here!

(He returns to mirror, holding out badly shaking hands.)

(*Disgusted*) Oh, look at you!—*why!* Can't you trust me by now! Please—have faith! (*After a beat or two the trembling subsides, though not totally.*)
And now—*you* will rise up out of the mirror, complete.

(He takes up an elaborate makeup kit. As he applies makeup in a ritual manner, pausing at moments to lean close to the mirror, the

*light may focus upon his gradually transformed face. Genuine beauty,
however painted, emerges.*)

(*Philosophically*): Strange—how *you* require *me*, to be born; yet
you are my master—I mean, my mistress!

(*He begins to apply makeup—moisturizer cream, liquid foundation,
eye shadow, eyeliner, mascara, rouge, lipstick, powder, etc.—in a
ceremonial manner.*)

Ummm—like this? Yes? No? *Yes!* (*Pause*) Guide my hand—*yes!*
(*Pause, putting on lipstick, covers mouth with fingers, then exposes
it*) The mouth—*our* mouth! (*Shudders, deliciously*) If they knew!
(*Has accident with mascara brush, and repairs the damage with
Kleenex and cold cream*) Oh!—that *hurts!* (*Pause, then quickly*) But
you're all right—don't be upset. (*Then, gazing into mirror*) Yes—
it's *you*. Dwelling in secrecy, here. (*Raps glass with knuckles*) I
wonder you are so patient with me—my clumsiness. (*Laughs*)
My—maleness.

(*He backs off from mirror, contemplating his image critically as he
puts on jewelry: pearl earrings, pearl necklace, bracelets. He walks
about examining his image from various angles—stylized, dancerlike
motions.*)

You!—it *is* you!

(*Pause. Lights dim slightly, to signal change of mood.*
*He approaches audience, eyes shut, holding breasts as if
protectively.*)

(*Dreamy, yearning voice*) Oh?—where?—you're *where?* In the
sun?—in greenery?—a park?—a *public park?* (*Increasing urgency, dread, as he dramatizes this episode*) Haven't I told you no,
never, haven't I warned you, begged you, never! (*Pause*) *You* can't
move freely about the world—*you* can't leave this room—how
could *you*, who are so wise, have made such a mistake! (*Pause,
voice quickening, suspenseful*) Yes, quick! Before it's too late! Out
of the park: hurry! Do you know your way back? *Don't* look at any
of them, don't acknowledge their eyes, walk quickly, if you're not
sure of the way don't give a sign, hold your head high, never betray
weakness, the jackals are waiting to LEAP—profane your beauty
with their ugliness—oh, hadn't I warned you! (*Panting, desperate*)
But you *can't* run in those shoes! Your elegant clothes! Your hair,

your jewelry, your beauty, *you!* (*Hides face with clenched fists*)
Midday in the heart of the city—sunshine blazing-blind—crowds
of strangers staring, gaping—our enemies—throwing the coarse
net of their thoughts over *you*. (*Angrily mimicking voices—we are
startled by the harsh, convincing sounds of these voices*) WHO IS
THAT? WHAT IS THAT? IS THERE A NAME FOR IT? IT? IT?
(*Pause, panting*) That policeman staring at you—don't look. Those
children pointing and laughing. Those workers on that scaffold,
blowing kisses, making sucking noises with their mouths—don't
look. *Beauty is not enough to redeem us.* (*Increasing loss of control,
terror*) Oh God, don't let them touch you, hurry! Hurry here! Those
catcalls, jeers—hands grabbing at you—are you in the street? in
traffic? horns sounding on all sides—can't run in these shoes, in
pain, headband so tight! so tight! (*Grips wig as if to pull it off*)
Beauty is not enough to redeem us. Oh—you've fallen—been
pushed! kicked! in the gutter! in filth! (*Falls to knees, tries to shield
face, body*) Don't, please don't—

(*He mimes being beaten, kicked in the pit of the belly so that he
doubles over in pain.
Brief pause. Then lights up as previously.
The* MAN *returns to mirror, caresses it, but with a look of irony.*)

You can never again leave this room. This mirror. (*Leans to kiss
his image*)

(*A beat or two. The* MAN *turns to audience, defiantly, matter-of-factly,
as he removes wig, jewelry, kicks off shoes, wipes at face with tissue,
etc.*)

Even so—I'm happy here. In this rented room, to which none of
you have entry. In this secrecy. Here. Out of all the universe—
here. (*Pause*) I possess the certitude of happiness. Which of you
can make that claim?

Lights out.

(THE END)

American Holiday

A Collage-Play

American Holiday I

Lights up. Several persons of indeterminate sex, but Caucasians, in colorful sports clothes, move about mincingly, semi-marching, waving small American flags and intoning in unison. One or two of them may wear sunglasses.

VOICE: Today is the day   to honor the dead
    the American dead, the fallen youth   So many dead so many
    it's sad it's a shame somebody has a list   of their names
    It *is* sad so many

(One of them yawns. The others draw away horrified.)

VOICES: Oh! what! oh what! oh we don't know *him* never saw *him*
    before, oh it's Memorial Day it's so sad it's Monday Mondays *are*
    sad but at least we get out of work and where's the picnic basket
    where's the cooler, in the car, whose gonna get it where's the
    blanket where's the fireworks display what time is it oh! look at all
    the graves!

(They stare toward audience, blinking and amazed. One of them takes a photograph with a Polaroid camera as the others cluster around.)

VOICES: Oh it's sort of, gee I don't know it's kinda morbid so many
    so many graves so many flags just like these so many Oh gee

(The photographer tears off the Polaroid print, and all stare at it, a bit disgruntled.)

VOICES: Aw it's just like *that*. *(Indicating the audience)*

(In the sky, aircraft are passing. We may hear the sound of jets and see a shadow passing swiftly across the stage.
    The photographer snaps a picture of the sky.)

VOICES *(with more enthusiasm)*: That's it! that's the real thing that's
    the budget that's it! that's pride! that's tearing a hole in the sky
    mmmm look! *(Shading eyes)*

(One of them unobtrusively exits to fetch the picnic lunch.)

VOICES: Bugles brassy with being right!
    Chemical soda sizzling the drains!
    I want white meat, I hate dark meat!

Flares reddening the hills!
Rough Riders! Manifest Destiny!
Rockets' red glare! Coming of the Lord!
Green Berets! CIA-Intercontinental!
No escape, fellow citizens, from history!

(*The* VOICES *assume a more narrative mode, less vociferous.*)

VOICES: After the first of the mega-explosions
the light moved on the surface of the waters
the air darkened with shrieks and
on the coastline great clumps of oil bobbed in the surf
stuck to fur, feather, fin—stiffened to stone—
to Death.

In the cities, our nostrils were impacted
with burning ashes, or is it hairs?
Or asbestos?

(*One of them returns with a picnic basket and an ice cooler, to the delight of the others. A picnic blanket is spread on the ground and they sit down expectantly, fussing with the picnic things.*)

VOICES: Oh quick before the speeches begin oh *c'mon* the ice is melting the beer's goddamn lukewarm chrissake I *told* you goddamn it now look now look Jeezus these ants! where's the Off, who's got the Off, Jeezus Chrise who's got the Off—

(*Suddenly flat, all buoyancy lost, the* VOICES *speak like computer voices, in unstressed syllables.*)

VOICES: Only Monday
a   long   week   ahead

Lights out.

$

Lights up. A large dollar sign hangs above the stage. (Suggested neon-bright.)

A MAN *approaches the audience briskly. He is in his thirties and conservatively dressed; but he speaks with such passionate intensity that we understand he is baring his soul.*

The MAN *positions himself beneath the dollar sign but does not glance up at it.*

MAN: If you have it you don't think about it
    so acquiring it is the means of forgetting it
    because if you don't have it you must think about it
    and you're embittered thinking about it because
    to think about it is to acknowledge your soul
    incomplete without it because you know you are
    superior to that, yes surely you are superior
    to the many who have it thus need never
    think about it the way, after Death,
    you won't think about Death either.

Lights out.

One Flesh I

Lights up. A MAN *and a* WOMAN, *middle-aged, are seated at opposite ends of an old-fashioned sofa, both of them erect, heads high, hands clasped on laps. They address the audience in an evenly modulated single voice.*

MAN *and* WOMAN: Here. On the horsehair sofa. Waiting. For something. To happen.

(*There is a lengthy pause. The audience begins to feel uncomfortable, but the* MAN *and* WOMAN *continue gazing out toward them, unmoved.*

A grandfather clock becomes visible in the background, ticking with increasing volume, then dies down.)

MAN *and* WOMAN: Here. Waiting. For. To happen.

(*Pause, several beats; couple remains unmoving.*)

Lights out.

Procedure

Lights up. In a hospital bed, motionless, lies the body of a man. He is not elderly; perhaps in his sixties. An IV tube is attached to one of his nostrils; another tube snakes beneath the bedclothes, in the region of his groin. There may be a white screen partly enclosing the bed. A bedside table, with a minimum of items on it. From stage right enter two nurse's aides, A. *and* B. A. *is in her late twenties or early thirties; brisk, self-assured, practiced in her movements.* B. *is not only younger but less assured; her movements are occasionally faltering and timid, but not excessively.* B. *is in every sense the apprentice, determined to learn PROCEDURE, and eager to acquit herself well. Both* A. *and* B. *are healthy, even husky young women, and both exhibit near-faultless posture. Between them they are carrying the "Death Pack" equipment—a kit out of which items (see below) will be taken, plus a small laundry hamper, a large paper bag, two white sheets, a stretcher and litter straps.*

The predominant color of the set is white: stark, dazzling white— the nurses' uniforms, stockings, shoes; the dead patient's gown; the bedclothes. A penumbra of darkness surrounds.

A. *and* B. *approach the bed,* B. *just perceptibly hesitant.*

A. (*sharp, clear, mechanical voice*): PROCEDURE. Open the Death Pack. (B. *opens the Death Pack.*) Take out the "DO NOT ENTER" sign. (B. *does so.*) Affix to outside of patient's door.

(B. *takes out the sign, which measures about twelve by eighteen inches, "DO NOT ENTER" in bold black letters; hangs it from the outside doorknob of a door at the rear.*)

B. (*nervous smile, breathless laugh*): I guess—anybody out in the hall, they'd sure know what we were doing.

A. (*freezing* B. *out by continuing, in the same voice*): PROCEDURE. Remove the contents of the Death Pack and set on available surface in patient unit. (B. *follows* A.'s *instructions, fumbling now and then; conspicuously not looking at the dead man.*) One wrapping sheet. Absorbent cotton. Padding. Bandage rolls. Safety pins. Death tags.

B. (*softly, as if dead man might overhear*): This is—my first time. My first— (*Gestures awkwardly, abashedly*)

(A. *gives* B. *a look of reproof. A beat.*)

A. (*continuing*): PROCEDURE. Remove treatment equipment, if any, from patient unit. (B. *detaches IV tube, etc., with* A.*'s assistance; pushes equipment to the side.*) Lower the head rest, leaving a single pillow. (B. *lowers head rest, fumbling a bit; forgets to remove a pillow.*) LEAVING A SINGLE PILLOW.

B. (*quickly*): Oh yes—sorry! (*Places one pillow on the floor; the dead man's head lolls, which alarms her. As* A. *gestures impatiently,* B. *adjusts the head. Her facial expression is taut, but does not betray distaste.*) Poor guy—wonder who he was!

A. (*continuing, perhaps more forcibly; in an incantatory, ritualistic manner*): PROCEDURE. Place the body of the deceased in as natural a position as possible—arms at sides (A. *and* B. *do this,* B. *a bit timidly*); palms turned toward thighs. (B. *does this.*)

B. (*breathlessly*): Wonder *why*—palms toward thighs.

A. (*coolly*): PROCEDURE. (*A beat*) Close eyelids gently.

B. (*nervous laugh*): Gee—whyn't they have us do this *first?*—so, y'know, the—the—*he* isn't looking at us, like! (*Tries to close eyelids, without success*) Oh my God—they won't *close.*

A. (*as before*): Close eyelids gently.

B. (*tries again*): Oh mister, I wish you'd c-cooperate, I'm just kind of, kind of—NERVOUS. (*She succeeds in shutting both eyelids.*) Hey—okay! Thank God.

(B. *holds out her hands, for* A. *to see how they are shaking, but* A. *is indifferent.*)

A. (*continuing*): PROCEDURE. If the deceased has dentures—

B. (*pointing, frightened; as one eyelid opens slowly*): Oh—he's waking up!

(A., *though exasperated with* B., *says nothing. In a quick, fluid, decisive manner she draws her fingertips down over both the dead man's eyelids; this time both eyelids remain shut.*)

B.: Oh! How'd you do that? (*Pause; abashed*) Well—I guess I'll learn.

A. (*continuing*): If the deceased has dentures, these should be cleaned and—

B. (*nervous attempt at humor*): They *all* have dentures, seems like!

A. (*continuing, without inflection*):　—cleaned and replaced in mouth.

B. (*misunderstanding, leans over to peer at dead man's mouth preparatory to timidly poking her fingers into it*): Oh—mister! You're gonna have to ex-cuse me—

A. (*irritated, but maintaining decorum*):　Dentures should be cleaned and REPLACED. (*As if in an aside, now that she is not repeating instructions from the handbook*) You must know—dentures are not *in* the patient's mouth. (*Points to bedside table*)

B.: Oh! Sorry! (*She locates dentures in a glass on the table; picks them up hesitantly; holds to light.*) They look okay to me. I mean—clean. (*Peering; with a shivery laugh*) Must be weird, wearing 'em. False teeth!

A. (*coolly, as if making a pronouncement*):　Nothing is "weird" in this place.

B. (*approaching patient*):　Well, excuse me, mister, gotta put these back *in*. So that your folks, coming to see you in the—the—downstairs—

A.: In the morgue.

B.: —so they'll see you at your best. (*She mimes replacing dentures in mouth. [Specific action may be hidden, or disguised, by portable bed screen.] Has difficulties; murmurs to herself*) Oh—damn—I just don't know *how*. Like, in real life, this guy'd do it *himself*. (*To* A., *pleading*) Y'know—he's still warm. His mouth, I mean. Inside. Wet too—saliva. (*A pause.* B. *backs away, suddenly frightened.*) Oh God—that's a dead man!

A. (*in official voice*): Sometimes, with the dead, dentures cannot be replaced. (*Looking on as* B. *tries gamely again*) DO NOT FORCE. (B. *fumbles dentures, drops them to floor.*)

B. (*aghast*): Oh God! I'm sorry!

A. (*picking up dentures, setting them on table, continuing as before*): PROCEDURE. Replace top bedding with draping sheet. (B. *covers body awkwardly with large sheet, removes other sheet. The next several steps are done under the sheet, with some difficulty, and distaste, by* B.) Remove patient's pajamas. (B. *does so, folding and thrusting them into a laundry hamper as quickly as possible.*) Press bladder gently to expel accumulated urine. (B. *does so.*) Remove catheter. (B. *does so.*) Place cotton pads over rectum and genitalia to absorb feces and urine which will be expelled as sphincters relax.

B. (*as she is doing this*): Oh! Oh dear. I guess we had a little accident.

(A. *tosses* B. *a towel or more absorbent cotton.* B. *wipes, under the sheet.*)

B. (*trying not to appear repelled*): It's just so—oh Jeez what can you *say.* You start out life soiling your diapers and you end—

A. (*continuing*): Clean old adhesive markings from skin, if any.

B. (*peering under sheet*): Poor guy—he's got 'em. (B. *busies herself with this task.*)

A.: Prop sagging jaw with folded pads.

B.: That's how *my* mouth comes open, if I sleep on my back! I hear this wet sort of noise, y'know, in my sleep, it wakes me up sometimes, or, a minute later, I'm *snoring*— (*As she props up dead man's jaw, with some initial difficulty*) I'm gonna be so worried someday, when—if—

A.: Pad ankles with cotton and tie together with bandage.

B. (*as she does this*): —I'm married, or something. (*Pause*) My father, he snores so you can hear it through the whole—

A. (*making out tags, deftly*): PROCEDURE. Tie one signed tag to right great toe (*gives* B. *the tag*)—tie one signed tag to left wrist.

B.: Why *two?* The toe and the wrist aren't gonna get separated, are they?

A.: Roll body gently to side of bed. (A. *helps* B. *do this.*) Place one clean sheet diagonally under body. (*Pause*) DIAGONALLY under body. (*Pause*) Roll body back to center of sheet.

B. (*shivering*): He's still warm—some places. Just his fingers and toes, and his face, are *real* cold. (*Pause*) Looks like kind of a nice guy, don't he?—'course any man, no matter how cruel, he's gonna look nice, peaceful, sort of, in a weird way, like a *woman*, at a time like this. Y'know what I mean—?

A. (*freezing* B. *out*): Fold upper corner of sheet loosely over the head and face—(*they do so*)—the lower corner over the feet (*etc.*).

B. (*almost giddy with strain, waving to patient*): Bye-bye!

A.: Secure the arms at the sides by bringing the right and left corners of the sheet over to complete the wrapping.

B. (*performs this action swiftly, keeping pace with* A.*'s words*): Yeah! Right!

A.: Fasten sheet with safety pins. (*Tosses pins to* B.) Fasten additional signed tag to outside of sheet (*etc.*). If dentures could not be replaced, wrap in gauze, identify, pin dentures next to tag (*etc.*).

B.: He could be anybody now. . . .

A.: Lift wrapped body to stretcher.

B.: Here's the hard part, huh? (A. *and* B. *lift body, lay it on stretcher, which is on the floor; they have less difficulty than might be expected.*) Geez he's *light*, isn't he!

A.: Fasten litter straps at chest—(*they do so*)—and just above the knees (*etc.*). Cover body with additional sheet.

B. (*immense sigh*): Well—that's that.

A. (*continuing as before, with perhaps the slightest suggestion of sharing* B.*'s relief*): PROCEDURE. Transfer body quietly and with dignity to the morgue, avoiding if possible public entrances and lobbies.

B. (*as* A. *and* B. *pick up ends of the stretcher; in a loud, somewhat giggly voice*): "—QUIETLY and with DIGNITY to the morgue— avoiding PUBLIC ENTRANCES AND LOBBIES." Yeah! You bet!

(*Lights down as* A. *and* B. *exit with stretcher.*
Lights up. A. *and* B. *are alone, apparently in a nurses' lounge; both have cans of soda, which they open and drink from;* A. *lights a cigarette and offers one to* B.)

B. (*still shaky*): I—uh, thanks but I—I'm not smoking now. I mean, I'm trying not to. (*Wipes face with tissue*) Well. Sure glad I don't work in the *morgue*.

A. (*imperturbably*): It's quiet in the morgue.

B.: I'll say!

A. (*regarding her quizzically; almost friendly*): It wasn't so bad, was it?

B. (*laughing*): To tell the truth, yes.

A.: Just following procedure.

B.: Procedure—! (*Shudders*)

A.: Not the first time you saw a dead patient, was it?

B.: No, not exactly. But the first time I . . . touched one.

A. (*clinical interest*): And how was it?

B. (*staring at* A., *perplexed*): How was it? (*Pause*) It was—something I won't forget.

A.: You won't?

B.: I sure *won't*.

(A *beat or two.* A. *regards* B. *as if bemused. Both sip from cans.*)

A. (*casually*): That man—dead man I mean—he was my father. (*Picking tobacco off tongue, as* B. *stares at her*) I mean—that man, when living, had been my father.

B. (*staring, blinking*): What?

A.: Him. Just now. My father.

B.: You're—joking!

A.: Why would I joke? (*Half-smile*) It isn't my practice to joke.

B.: But—I don't believe it. Him—(*points vaguely offstage*)—us— *you*—

A. (*matter-of-factly*): I should explain—I hadn't seen him in a while. We weren't close.

B.: Oh! You weren't close.

A.: He left us when I was ten. Didn't remarry or anything, just left. He lived in town—I'd run into him sometimes—we'd talk, sort of. Sometimes he'd give me money. (*Pause, smirks*) Other times, he'd avoid me. (*Pause*) Or I'd avoid him.

B.: Did you know he was here in the hospital?

A.: Sure.

B: Did you know he was—dying?

A.: More or less.

B.: And you didn't tell anyone?

A. (*as if genuinely baffled*): Didn't tell anyone—?

B.: Oh—any of the nurses, or—

A.: Why should I? I'm a professional. I do my job.

B.: And it didn't upset you to, to—

A.: I said, I'm a professional. He wasn't *my* first.

B. (*slight attack of dizziness*): Oh—!

(A. *quickly helps* B., *as* B. *leans forward, touching forehead to knees.* A.'s *response is immediate and kindly.*)

A.: You're all right. C'mon.

B. (*recovering*): I'm—all right. (*Pause*) Gee, c'n I borrow a—?

(A. *passes the pack of cigarettes to* B., *who takes one, lights it, exhales smoke gratefully.*)

B. (*emphatically*): My God, I'm so—embarrassed. Here I was thinking of myself, mainly. My first—(*pause*)—death. (*Pause*) I wish I could go through it again, now. See how you did it. Knowing what you told me . . .

A. (*briskly moving off*): Sorry! That's a scene that can't quite be repeated.

Lights out.

Lethal

Lights up. A young, or youngish, MAN *addresses the audience. His manner is loving, seductive, at first; a slow building "lethal" tone; a suggestion of anger, even rage, near the end—but only a suggestion, not at all obvious, self-parodying. The final line seems to him, thus to the audience, a wholly reasonable question.*

MAN: I just want to touch you a little. That delicate blue vein at your temple, the soft down of your neck. I just want to caress you a little. I just want to kiss you a little—your lips, your throat, your breasts. I just want to embrace you a little. I just want to comfort you a little. I just want to hold you tight!—like this. I just want to measure your skeleton with my arms. These are strong, healthy arms, aren't they. I just want to poke my tongue in your mouth. I just want to poke my tongue in your ear. Don't giggle! Don't squirm! This is serious! This is the real thing! I just want to love you a little. I just want to test it a little. I just want to suck a little. I just want to press into you a little. I just want to penetrate you a little. I just want to ejaculate into you a little. It won't hurt if you don't scream but you'll be hurt if you keep straining away like that, if you exaggerate. Thank you, I just want to squeeze you a little. I just want to lower my weight onto you a little. I just want to feel your bones beneath my weight a little. I just want to use my teeth a little. I just want a taste of it. Your saliva, your blood. Just a taste. A little. You're wet, too. You know you are. You give off that smell. It's unmistakable. It's inevitable. It's fate. You've got plenty to spare. You're being selfish. You're being ridiculous. You're being cruel. You're being a bitch. You're just a cunt and you know it. You're hysterical. You're hyperventilating. You're provoking me. You're laughing at me. You want to humiliate me. You want to make an asshole out of me. You want to eviscerate me like a chicken. You want to castrate me. You want to make me fight for my life, is that it?

You want to make *me* fight for my life, is that it?

Lights out.

Imperial Presidency

Lights up. Excitement! Agitation! We are in the midst of preparations for the PRESIDENT's *arrival. A number of men and women hurry about, sometimes colliding with one another, as the* MAYOR *issues directives. There should be no less than four* AIDES—*office workers, city employees, perhaps a custodian or groundskeeper.. They, and the* MAYOR, *are disheveled in this opening scene. The* MAYOR *wears a suit, its coat unbuttoned; his necktie is crooked; hair unkempt, perhaps a bald spot gleaming. A general air of seediness prevails.*

MAYOR (*excited yet quavering voice*): He's coming! He's coming! The President is coming! Our town is entering history!

AIDES (*reverent, chanting*): Entering history! Entering history!

MAYOR: Never before in history has any President visited us! Never! Never so honored! From Federalist times until now! Though our state is one of the thirteen original colonies, and our town is at the crossroads of the state!—where Interstate 911 and the New Jersey Turnpike intersect!

AIDES: Never! Never so honored!

MAYOR: Nothing must go wrong! Everything must go right! The network TV crews will be here! The Secret Service men! The President himself!

AIDES: The President! The President! The President himself!

MAYOR: NOTHING MUST GO WRONG! EVERYTHING MUST GO RIGHT! (*Snaps fingers, points*) There—that! Quickly! Beautify that!

AIDES: Yes, Mr. Mayor! Yes, Mr. Mayor! NOTHING MUST GO WRONG! EVERYTHING MUST GO RIGHT!

(*The* MAYOR *is bossy, bumptious, self-important, yet sincerely anxious. He points, snaps his fingers, etc.; may help with some tasks himself.*

The first beautification task is to erect a new facade over the front of what appears to be an abandoned slum tenement. The new facade includes a homey, domestic window scene—chintz curtains, a potted geranium plant on the windowsill.)

MAYOR (*applauding*): Well done! Just the right touch!

AIDES: NOTHING MUST GO WRONG! EVERYTHING MUST GO RIGHT!

(*The facade begins to slip, and everyone, including the* MAYOR, *fixes it more securely. Outcries, exclamations.*)

MAYOR: The President's cavalcade will take this route! NOTHING MUST GO WRONG!

AIDES: Yes, Mr. Mayor! Yes, Mr. Mayor!

(*During this activity, a* HOMELESS MAN *has entered unobtrusively, another part of the stage where there is a park bench in poor repair. Empty bottles and debris scattered about. The* HOMELESS MAN *takes no notice of the others, but, mumbling to himself contentedly, curls up on the bench and falls asleep.*)

MAYOR (*sighting the* HOMELESS MAN): There—that! Beautify *that!* Dig into the emergency snow relief funds!

AIDES: Yes, Mr. Mayor!

(*The* AIDES *wake the* HOMELESS MAN, *who struggles with them. There is some seriocomic action, as the* HOMELESS MAN *defends himself, but is finally outnumbered by the* AIDES, *who pummel him and drag him offstage.*)

AIDES (*struggling with* HOMELESS MAN): Entering history! Never so honored! EVERYTHING MUST GO RIGHT!

HOMELESS MAN: Ya sonsabitches!—hey! (*As he is dragged off*) I VOTED FOR HIM, TOO!

(*The broken park bench is replaced by a bench in good condition; or, perhaps, a cardboard bench, a bright spiffy green. The debris is swept away. Young trees, shrubs, pots of artificial flowers are hauled onstage.*)

MAYOR (*applauding*): That's it! That's the right idea! We've waited two hundred years for this!

(*As the* AIDES *bustle about constructing, or hauling onstage, a make-shift wooden platform, the* MAYOR *addresses the audience. The platform has a podium and is decorated with numerous American flags. A large flag is draped across the rear wall.*)

MAYOR (*gravely intoning, excitement bubbling beneath*): What a sur-
prise, the President has chosen our town to visit, on Veterans Day!
Such an honor strikes terror to the heart! One asks: Are we worthy?
Am *I* worthy? To shake the President's hand? TO BE PHOTO-
GRAPHED WITH HIM? (*A pause, then, proudly*) Maybe the
President is coming to reward us—our town has, since its settle-
ment in 1746, sacrificed, per capita, more soldier-youths of all
races, colors, and creeds than ANY OTHER TOWN IN THE U.S.!
Yessir! We're in Ripley's Believe-It-Or-Not! We're in the Guinness
Book of Records! We're proud! We're damn proud! We deserve
some media attention! Since 1746 we've deserved some media
attention! (*A pause, then, loudly, as if issuing a proclamation*)
Every war abroad and at home we've sacrificed our youths! We're
always the first!

AIDES (*chanting*): First to enlist—first to see combat—first to get our
legs blown off—first to die! (*Cheers*)

MAYOR: Veterans Day is a sacred day with us, yessir!

AIDE: Even in the State National Guard we have casualties!

SECOND AIDE: —and *veterans*!

MAYOR (*as if remembering*): Oh—oh yes: not just casualties, but
veterans! It's important to have *veterans*!

AIDES: Important to have veterans! Important to have veterans!

THIRD AIDE: —and *civilians*.

MAYOR: Oh—oh yes: some of us are civilians.

AIDES: All of *us* are civilians!

FOURTH AIDE (*slyly*): That's because we're smart.

MAYOR: That's because we're the Mayor. (*Startled*) What did I just
say?

AIDES (*chanting in background, placing flags around platform*): Entering history! At last! About time! Nothing must go
wrong! EVERYTHING MUST GO RIGHT!

(*The* MAYOR *is handed a telegram, which he opens excitedly.*)

MAYOR: It's from the White House! (*Puts on bifocals, reads in a
quavering voice*) "President's schedule altered—instead of from

11:45 A.M. to 1:30 P.M., with luncheon, Veterans Day, November 11, now from 10:50 A.M. to 11:15 A.M., Veterans Day, November 11." (*Looks up, confused*) Oh, dear! That's brief! No luncheon!

AIDES (*disappointed*): No luncheon? No luncheon?

MAYOR (*skimming message, frowning*): But he *is* coming! "—All security measures to be taken—President's speech—unveiling—veterans' monument—checklist of known area subversives requested—" (MAYOR *looks up, confused, blinking*) "Veterans' monument"—?

AIDES: He *is* coming! He *is* coming! (*The large flag falls from the wall, and they scramble to stop it; much fuss*) NOTHING MUST GO WRONG! EVERYTHING MUST GO RIGHT!

MAYOR (*agitated, rereading*): "Unveiling—veterans' monument—" (*A pause*) Oh my God, there must be a mistake!

AIDES: A mistake? A mistake?

MAYOR: We don't have a new veterans' monument to be "unveiled"—

AIDES: Don't have? Don't have? Mistake? Oh my God!

MAYOR (*quickly*): No—no mistake! We'll use our old one, it's a perfectly fine one!

(*The* MAYOR *snaps his fingers, and* AIDES *drag in a badly weathered old statue of a Civil War general on a rearing horse, sword uplifted. The statue appears to be quite heavy; it is mottled with pigeon droppings and graffiti.*)

MAYOR: The sentiment's the same! Universal sacrifice! Brotherhood, valor, honor, rockets' red glare! Good! Yes! (*As the* AIDES *scrub at the statue with steel wool*) Imperial America! Dig into the Children's Aid budget!

(*Lights dim.*

MAYOR, AIDES *quickly exit. The stage becomes a light show of a kind, with whirling, strobe-light effects; the noise of helicopters approaching. Very noisy. A tape of shouted commands, words inaudible; the cheers of crowds; barking dogs.*

The Civil War statue is "veiled" with a white cloth.

SECURITY OFFICERS *appear. They may carry rifles, billy clubs;*

*they may be masked; or plainsclothes. All eyes are turned toward
stage right, where the* PRESIDENT *will appear.*

MAYOR *enters, from stage left.*

Lights up.

The MAYOR *is no longer disheveled. He may wear a toupee; his suit
is now three-piece (he has added a handsome vest); his necktie is
straight; he has a carnation in his lapel. He bears himself more nobly.
Flashbulbs in his face, lights of TV cameras.)*

MAYOR (*momentarily blinded by lights, tries to be a good sport about
   it, grinning, waving to audience*): At last! The great hour is here!
   The President is coming! THE PRESIDENT IS HERE! (*Joins in
   the applause*) WELCOME, MR. PRESIDENT!

(*The noise of helicopters, sirens, barking dogs, applause reaches a
climax. Then there is silence. Then, after a beat, tinny, mechanical
music—"The Stars and Stripes Forever."*

MAYOR *hurries forward to greet the* PRESIDENT, *who enters from
stage right, leaning on the arm of the* PRESIDENTIAL AIDE.)

MAYOR (*both fawning and "dignified"*):   Mr. President! Sir! Welcome
   to our historic town!

(*The* AIDE *nudges the* PRESIDENT, *who extends a hand to be shaken.
It appears that the* PRESIDENT *is unwell; he walks unsteadily; his head
wobbles; he seems confused about his surroundings and parts of his
body. As the* PRESIDENT, *his* AIDE, *and the* MAYOR *mount the platform, they are greeted by a wave of applause and cheers. The*
PRESIDENT *and his* AIDE *take seats; the* MAYOR *takes the podium.
Beaming, he signals for the applause to subside and it is abruptly
switched off.)*

MAYOR (*peering at the crowd, as if into the distance*): Thank you,
   fellow citizens! Can you hear me? (*Static, booming sounds over the
   loudspeaker*) I hope you can *see* me! Those of you who have bi-
   noculars and telescopes—I'm sure *you* can see me! (*Waves of applause, fainter than before*) Well! Here we—are! This hallowed
   occasion is under the auspices of the United States Secret
   Service—thus the "security measures"!—which is why you are all
   cordoned off, at a minimal distance of 200 yards! After all, we don't
   want another "Dallas," do we!

(*Abrupt silence. The* MAYOR *has spoken tactlessly; his smile fades; he glances at the men behind him. The* PRESIDENT *is having a coughing spell and spits into a paper cup held up for him by his* AIDE.)

MAYOR (*embarrassed, blundering, not knowing how to get out of it*): Uh-huh, uh-huh, WE DON'T WANT ANOTHER *DALLAS* DO WE! (*Chuckles*)

(*Mild cheers, distant applause. Static over the loudspeaker.*)

MAYOR (*recovering his pomposity*): Veterans Day! Momentous occasion! "Unveiling of monument!" Deeply honored! *Deeeeply* honored! Mr. President! At last! Two hundred years! Imperial America! "Bring not peace but a sword!" Courage, passion, valor! Sacrifice! May I present—

(*But the* PRESIDENT, *having misread his cue, is already on his feet. He walks, swaying, to the podium, assisted by his* AIDE. *The* MAYOR *is slightly flustered but quickly stands aside.*)

MAYOR (*with the air of an emcee*): Uh—yes—here—MR. PRESI-DENT!

(*Waves of applause, cheers. Barking dogs. Flashbulbs.*
The PRESIDENT *lifts his arm, rather weakly. Clenched fist. His arm shakes perceptibly.*
The PRESIDENT *is a man of moderate height, somewhat gaunt. He wears a three-piece suit like the* MAYOR's, *but it is of higher quality; the shoulders are boxy, obviously padded. The trousers are a size or two too large and the fly zipper is partway open. The* PRESIDENT *wears a lifelike white rubber mask that fits over his face, throat, and head: the mask suggests a subtly deformed face, not wildly grotesque, nor certainly comical. The pink mouth is slack and bracketed by exaggerated smile lines; it must be loose enough so that the* PRESIDENT *can cough and spit through it. The eyes are small, piggish, close-set; the nose is a pug nose, with dark nostrils; dark brown hair, with a shellac-like sheen, has been painted on the rubber head covering, but there are slits in the material through which strands of real hair have been threaded—thus, the "real" hair is combed atop the painted hair. The forehead is creased as if with serious thought. The ears are pink, small, with shallow whorls. The mask is an eerie amalgam of absurd and naturalistic details, and should suggest no historical President, living or dead.*
The PRESIDENT *holds his prepared speech in both hands, which*

tremble slightly. At first, when his speech begins, we think it is his live voice we are hearing; in fact, he is miming a taped speech, piped in overhead.)

TAPE: . . . Thank you, thank you! . . . so deeply honored! . . . sacred occasion! . . . gathered together in homage . . . Veterans Day! . . . as your President, I . . . humility, gratitude . . . the will of the Almighty . . . national destiny! . . . solemn celebration . . . courage, valor . . . men . . . *and* women! . . . United States Armed Forces! (*The speech is interrupted by applause, cheers*) As your President, I . . . no greater privilege! . . . this momentous occasion! . . . VETERANS WE CELEBRATE YOU!

(*Applause, cheers. One of the* MAYOR's AIDES *draws off the cloth covering the Civil War statue slowly, even a bit seductively; the* PRESIDENT *seems oblivious. The statue has been cleaned up slightly, but is still decidedly battered.*

Flashbulbs. Light display. A few bars of "The Stars and Stripes Forever," from the middle of the piece. The PRESIDENT *takes advantage of the interlude to cough harshly, spitting into the paper cup provided him by his* AIDE.

The PRESIDENT *is still coughing when the tape resumes.*)

TAPE (*loud, buoyant voice*): . . . Proud heritage! . . . fearless tradition! . . . forefathers . . . the will of the Almighty . . . valor, selflessness . . . bearing arms! . . . highest ideals . . . DEMOCRACY! . . . moral commitment of your President . . . grave responsibility . . . time of crisis . . . enemies of democracy . . . enemies of America . . . imperial destiny . . . glorious performance: our most recent war . . . WELCOME HOME TROOPS! (*Cheers, whistles; the* PRESIDENT *succumbs to another coughing attack, getting mucus on his chin, which he flicks onto the floor; again, he is still coughing when the tape resumes*) National pride . . . God's will . . . eternal vigilance against our enemies! . . . enemies abroad, and . . . AT HOME! . . . scheming politicians, here AT HOME! . . . certain members of Congress, here AT HOME! . . . undermining executive powers . . . time of global crisis . . . terrorist plots . . . as Thomas Jefferson once said . . . as your President, I . . . executive powers regarding war . . . UPHELD! PROTECTED! EXPANDED! . . . with thanks to Thee on this day of days . . . Almighty God! (TAPE *ends*)

(*Applause, cheers. Barking dogs.*

By the time the TAPE *ends, the* PRESIDENT *has regained some of his control. He mimes the final phrases with dramatic, if wan, gestures; he accepts the crowd's adulation with an air of happy humility. His clenched right fist is raised over his head, and trembles somewhat. He smiles as best he can with the rubber mouth.*

The MAYOR *has leapt to his feet, clapping vigorously, hands over his head.*

The PRESIDENT, *leaning on his* AIDE's *arm, returns to his seat, taking not the slightest notice of the* MAYOR.)

MAYOR (*genuinely moved, cheeks shining with tears*): Mr. President—TH-THANK YOU! (*To audience, voice quavering*) Isn't this a Veterans Day to remember! It *was* worth waiting for!

(*Lights dim except for spotlight on American flag at the rear. The* PRESIDENT, *his* AIDE, *and the* SECRET SERVICE OFFICERS *depart to a few further bars of "Stars and Stripes Forever."*

Applause rises to a crescendo, then is abruptly switched off. Silence.

Lights out.

Lights up. The MAYOR, *necktie loosened, smiling affably, addresses the audience as if recounting an anecdote to friends. As his* AIDES *bustle about cheerfully dismantling the platform, taking down the flags, removing the tenement facade, the trees, flowers, etc., humming as they work. The park bench, too, is hauled away. But the Civil War statue remains.*)

MAYOR (*relieved, chatty*): So!—whew! That was how it was! The President visited our town! Every TV news program—every wire service—every God-damn newspaper in the country—INCLUDING THE NEW YORK TIMES!—took note of *us*. We're in PEOPLE this week, we're in TIME! We're besieged by Japanese investors! (*A pause*) And nothing went wrong. EVERYTHING WENT RIGHT!

AIDES: NOTHING WENT WRONG! EVERYTHING WENT RIGHT!

MAYOR: At last—we've entered history with the rest of you.

AIDES: ENTERED HISTORY! AT LAST! REST OF YOU!

(*The* MAYOR *and his* AIDES *depart, having cleared the stage of everything but the statue. The* HOMELESS MAN *enters, peering guardedly about; finally, he goes to the statue, to curl up at its base. He lies on his side facing the audience, a filthy knapsack, or wadded rags, beneath his head.*

Lights dim but continue to focus upon his face as, contentedly, even blissfully, he falls asleep.)

Lights out.

"Whispering Glades"

Lights up. A WOMAN *in her late sixties or early seventies, a brace on her right leg, is seated in a lawn chair, fanning herself vigorously. Her gray hair is tightly permed; she wears a shapeless cotton shift and orthopedic shoes with white anklets. She is conspicuously over-weight and suffering from the heat.*

WOMAN (*loud, gay, expansive; addressing the audience in maternal voice*): You kids just make y'selves at home! Yeah, sure glad to see ya! Real glad to see ya! (*Waving, swatting with the fan, suddenly violent*) Oh, these flies! All the sprayin' we done, and here they are—buggers! Lookit! Not houseflies like back home, lookit the size of 'em! (*Swatting*) Watch out—they bite.

(*Regaining composure*) Yeah, sure Dad and I are *fine*, we're getting along here real well, real well. Of course there's roaches —Florida's famous for roaches—they don't tell you till you move here. Yes and the dirty buggers fly too—all shiny-black and bright throwing themselves into your food or hair like, uh— whatyacallem—kamyi-kazi—kamikaze?—(*laughs*)—y'know, them *Jap bombers.* (*Pause*)

Oh sure he's fine, I guess you were a little shocked to see him but he's fine over all, he's pretty well adjusted to his new condition, leastways he *can* walk, and he *can* see out of the one eye okay. That ugly rash on his ankles he's so crazy about scratching, scratches it in his sleep, we think it's from fleas—yeah, there's fleas all around here, I'd watch out if I were you, from our neighbor's damn dog we think. The trailer this side (*brusque nod toward stage left*) but we don't want no trouble with 'em, they're real white trash, could be dangerous. (*Pause*) Well, the girl at the clinic gave him peroxide to put on the rash but what's that going to do, I told him for God's sake if he keeps on scratching till it's all scabby and bleeding but you know him, that old man. (*Pause. Pants, fanning herself*)

Oh yes those're marigolds—all that's left of them. Planted them myself with this bad leg and it's the slugs got *them.* (*Laughs in disgust*) I love marigolds though, I love the smell. (*Draws deep breath*) Like the tomato plants, the leaves of the plants, real nice smell sort of, uh, earthy, rich—makes you think of, of—(*vague as if confused*)—the past. (*Pause; then beginning to be angry*) The tomatoes didn't last long in those damn pots we were told to use, the tomato worms got them—ugh—(*violent shudder*)—big and fat and slimy-green nasty things so big!—(*measuring with thumb and forefinger, about four inches long*)—you got to wonder why God invented 'em, what sense there is in His creation! Huh! (*Earnest, passionate*) Yeah I say any kind of DDT, *any* chemical, "toxin,"— napalm!—nerve gas!—I'd say go right ahead douse 'em, kill 'em, all of 'em, it's worth it to kill them nasty ugly disgusting things make you sick to think of! (*Pause, panting; wipes damp face with tissue*)

(*Trying to be more upbeat, "maternal"*): Oh my! here I am going on again, aren't I! made a vow I wouldn't, it's you kids' vacation and all, y'all come down here to relax and have a good time, that's the idea, you're young enough, it's better that way, you kids not knowing what's to come, huh! (*Smiling: then distracted by something on the ground, stamps awkwardly with her left foot, a cold, subdued fury in her voice*) Oh God *damn*! After all that spraying I did! Lookit 'em in a regular *platoon* marching right along here! Big black ants! Ugh! *Ugh!* (*Awkwardly on her feet now, panting, stamping, leaning heavily on the lawn chair*) Like you can see, hon—*they're all over.*

Lights out.

The Pact

Lights up. MATTHEW, *in his thirties, in attractive though conservative resort wear, is sitting at a table, beneath a striped umbrella, reading a newspaper and sipping a "tropical" drink.* MICHAEL, *also in his thirties, less neatly groomed, wearing a grimy panama hat, approaches.*

MICHAEL: Well! *Is* it—? (*As* MATTHEW *glances up*) Hel-*lo*!

MATTHEW (*politely*): Yes—?

MICHAEL: Hello hel*lo*. It *is* you.

MATTHEW: Are you speaking to me?

MICHAEL (*lightly ironic, though excited*): To whom else would I be speaking, Matthew, if I could speak to *you*? (*Extends hand to shake, which* MATTHEW *ignores*)

MATTHEW (*still civil*): Have we met?

MICHAEL: Don't tell me you don't remember me, Matthew.

MATTHEW: Why, I— Matthew *is* my name—

MICHAEL: Of course Matthew is your name! You wouldn't allow anyone to call you Matt.

MATTHEW (*peering at* MICHAEL, *seems genuinely perplexed*): Is it—? You're—? (*Snaps fingers, unable to retrieve name*)

MICHAEL (*smiling*): Yes it *is*—in the flesh. Resurrected!

MATTHEW (*missing this, perhaps deliberately*): I'm afraid I—

MICHAEL: Oh, don't be afraid—c'mon, try!

MATTHEW: It's been—years?—how long?

MICHAEL: Sixteen.

MATTHEW: You *were* in my high school class, but— (*Vague smile*)

MICHAEL: But failed to graduate.

MATTHEW: Really? Why?

MICHAEL: Don't you remember?

MATTHEW: I . . . don't think I do.

MICHAEL: Is it my face you don't remember, or my name? Or—both?

MATTHEW: Perry! Your name is Perry.

MICHAEL: No, but that's close.

MATTHEW: Graham?

MICHAEL: No, but *that's* close.

MATTHEW: Michael?—I mean, Matthew. (*Confused*)

MICHAEL: *You're* Matthew.

MATTHEW: Then you're Michael.

MICHAEL: Well, one of us has to be! (*Laughs, and the men now shake hands.*) Nice to run into you again, Matthew!—after so long.

MATTHEW (*guardedly*): Yes, well. Nice to run into you, Michael.

MICHAEL: After so long.

MATTHEW: I guess, yeah—it *has* been.

MICHAEL: Sixteen years, three weeks. Give or take a few days.

MATTHEW (*as if groping*): Union City, PA: UCHS class of '76.

MICHAEL: Except I didn't graduate. You're forgetting.

MATTHEW: Uh—are you—vacationing here?

(MICHAEL *laughs.*)

MATTHEW: Is something funny?

MICHAEL: Actually, I live here—I couldn't afford to *vacation* here.

MATTHEW: What sort of—line of—work—are you in? (*He now "recalls"* MICHAEL, *turns fearful, guarded.*)

MICHAEL: Ummm—I don't specialize. (*Pulls out chair*) May I?

MATTHEW (*already on his feet*): Actually, I—I—I'm about to leave. (*Tosses a bill onto the table, folds up newspaper*)

MICHAEL: *Are* you? So quickly? About to leave for where?

MATTHEW: Well, I—I—I'm waiting for someone and—we're about to go—back to the hotel.

MICHAEL: Which hotel? The new Hyatt?

MATTHEW: Actually, I—I'm bad at remembering details—

MICHAEL: No no, I bet it's the Conquistador Inn—all that *glass.*

MATTHEW: One of the big ones. On the water.

MICHAEL: Well, I hope so!—on the water.

MATTHEW: So, I can't, uh—

MICHAEL: The name's Michael.

MATTHEW: —Michael, I can't, uh, take time to chat right now, I—

MICHAEL *(almost eagerly)*: Not now—but maybe later?

MATTHEW: Well, I—uh—yeah—except—we're leaving—in the morning—seven a.m.

MICHAEL: Leaving for where?

MATTHEW: For—home. Y'know—the States. We're just here on a —a—short vacation.

MICHAEL: Who—whom—did you say you're waiting for?

MATTHEW: A, a, a—person. And we're—about to—leave—I guess I said.

(A pause. MICHAEL leans smilingly close to MATTHEW, staring.)

MICHAEL: Wow, man. *Did* you? *(Delighted, disbelieving)* You did, you actually *did?*—did you?

MATTHEW *(guardedly)*: Did what?

MICHAEL: Matthew did, after all! He said he never would and he *did.*

MATTHEW: I'm afraid I really don't understand.

MICHAEL *(approvingly)*: Well—look at you!

MATTHEW: What about me?

(MICHAEL sizes him up: clothes, wristwatch, footwear.)

MICHAEL: Crossed over. Made it. Like, y'know, a swimmer, sets out, he doesn't know his strength, whether the fuck he'll make it or drown, but you, you made it—(*whistles*)—sure *did*.

MATTHEW: I—don't get it.

MICHAEL: What are you, what's your line of work, ummm maybe corporate law?—banking?—medicine?—some "challenging" specialization like—hematology?—gastroenterology?—

MATTHEW (*stiffly*): Nephrology.

MICHAEL: Huh? What's that?

MATTHEW: Kidneys.

MICHAEL (*approvingly*): Well—kidneys are certainly *central*, I mean, yeah, they're right *there*— (*He rubs the small of his back.*) Can't get along without 'em, frisky little devils!

MATTHEW: Well. If you'll excuse me, I—I guess I'll—

MICHAEL: You're leaving half your drink. Whatsis?—vodka and banana split? (*Picks up drink, sniffs, tastes*) Wow.

MATTHEW (*glancing worriedly toward stage right*): —I guess—I—

MICHAEL: Kidneys, do your best. You're *on*. (*As if not knowing how desperate* MATTHEW *is to leave*) It's weird, isn't it, the body—human—mammal—whatever—the *idea* of the body—y'know, how it's the habitation of the *soul*—or whatever. Isn't it?

MATTHEW: I, uh—yes—it's a, a—(*lamely*)—miracle.

MICHAEL: We invite the toxins in, and the poor kidneys have got to filter 'em out. And the liver, right? And when they get fed up with the effort, that's it. (*Finishes drink*) Mmmm, *that's* it. (*Pause*) You didn't recognize me at first, did you, Matthew?—I mean, genuinely. I could see it. Wow. It was, like, metaphysical—the blank empty innocence of your blue eyes.

MATTHEW: Well, I, I—had a lot of friends in high school—I mean I guess we all did—sort of.

MICHAEL: Union City High School Class of '76. Guess we've all changed, some.

MATTHEW: I guess.

MICHAEL: Of course, *I* never got my diploma. I was "incapacitated." (*Pause, then broad smile*) Hey: was college fun?

MATTHEW: College?

MICHAEL: Was college a *blast*?—was college a *turn-on*?—did it maybe *broaden your horizons*? Did poor sappy Mikey miss much?

MATTHEW: Miss much—?

MICHAEL: Did Mikey get left behind?—what year *is* this?

MATTHEW (*hoping to edge away*): You—didn't go to college, huh, that's—too bad. Well. (*Vaguely*) I, uh—I liked it okay, but—

MICHAEL: Y'know, some people move with the years, and some people don't, y'know?—y'know why?

MATTHEW: Actually, I—I don't know. (*Looks at watch*) I'm afraid I —it's late, and I—

MICHAEL (*staring, smiling*): You don't know? You truly truly don't know?—or *do* you?

MATTHEW (*keeping a chair between them*): I don't—know. What you're getting at.

MICHAEL: *Should* you know? (*He removes his panama hat: his hair is gunmetal-gray, and thin.*)

MATTHEW: I have to leave—uh, Michael. I'm expected back at the hotel, actually I'm *late*.

MICHAEL: You can wait for this person here, can't you?—right here? Weren't you waiting for this person, when I came along, right *here*?

MATTHEW: No, I was—I was about to—go back. I'm expected back.

MICHAEL: Are you're leaving for home—tonight?

MATTHEW: Well, almost. It's tomorrow morning but we, we, we— have to pack. (*Stares at watch again, as if unseeing*)

MICHAEL: This person, who is this person you're waiting for, this person who's coming to meet you? Who?

MATTHEW: Look, uh—Michael—it *is* Michael, isn't it?—I really have to run, I mean I really have to—run.

MICHAEL: I've seen you hundreds of times, Matthew—hundreds and thousands of times I've seen you, these past sixteen years, but—until now—it was never *you*. I'd look, and I'd blink, and I'd come closer, and—until now it was never *you*. (*Smiles*) America is so—spacious!

MATTHEW: It's nice to meet you, and, uh—

MICHAEL: Keep in touch, huh? Let's keep in touch—huh?

MATTHEW: Yes! Right!

(MATTHEW *is about to walk off, but* MICHAEL *blocks his way; taps his chest with a forefinger.*)

(*A pause.*)

MICHAEL: Who *are* you waiting for?

MATTHEW: I told you I'm not—

MICHAEL: Is it a she?

(MATTHEW *is silent.*)

MICHAEL (*wagging finger*): Oh you did, then, Matthew did, then, he did he *did*!—wanted to die he was so scared he was so ashamed said he never would he never could and he *did*! (*As* MATTHEW *stands silent*) Con-grat-u-la-tions. To the bride, and to the groom. And to the best man, wherever he is.

MATTHEW: Look, Michael—

MICHAEL: Mikey.

MATTHEW: Look, Michael, I—I don't owe you anything, I—I was just a kid.

MICHAEL: *We* were just a kid.

MATTHEW: My head was filled with so much shit, back then—

MICHAEL: Nah! Not you! *You* were the brains of the deal! *You* composed the "farewell note."

MATTHEW: What farewell note?

MICHAEL: *You* heard the "subliminal messages" in the music.

MATTHEW: What music?

MICHAEL: What music, you're asking what music, oh Christ this is fucking fantastic, this is the genuine article, this is—walking on water is what this *is*. I mean, a liv-ing miracle, is what it *is*.

MATTHEW: Excuse me, please—

MICHAEL: What music, he's asking what music, oh fucking fantastic, there's a kind of beauty here. Sheer precipices of oblivion. Oh wow, man.

MATTHEW: You're not—anyone I know. You're a sick person. I can see it in your eyes, and I can hear it in your voice, and I can—

MICHAEL: —smell it on my breath: wetted ashes.

(MICHAEL *pulls up his long sleeves to reveal white scars on both his arms, the interior of the forearm above the wrist.* MATTHEW *flinches, shields his eyes.*
A pause.)

MICHAEL: We made a pact, and you betrayed it. You betrayed us both, dear Matthew.

MATTHEW (*hoarsely*): I don't know what in hell you're talking about.

MICHAEL: We made a pact, Mikey and Matthew, and it was a sacred pact, and you betrayed it, and all your life since then has been a betrayal, you know that, you know that, Matthew, that's the one thing you know, that's the one thing you've never told *her*. Isn't it?

MATTHEW: I—we—we were seventeen years old! Our heads were filled with shit!

(MATTHEW *tugs at* MICHAEL's *sleeves, urging him to cover his terrible scars.* MICHAEL, *laughing, lazily complies.*)

MATTHEW: I—didn't—betray. I—saved us—both.

MICHAEL (*derisively, yet fondly*): "Both"—! You were too frightened to even pick up the razor, after me.

MATTHEW: I saved us—both.

MICHAEL: Is that how you remember it, when you remember it?— "saved us both." (*Laughs, replaces panama hat*)

MATTHEW (*as if rooted to the spot*): Michael—let me leave.

MICHAEL: Is that *her*?—coming from that boutique? (*Pointing stage right*)

MATTHEW (*continuing to look at* MICHAEL): Let me leave, will you let me leave?

(MICHAEL *is intently watching the* WOMAN *approach.*

WOMAN *appears, in her thirties, very stylishly dressed in white resort wear, very beautiful, in sunglasses. She scarcely more than glances at* MICHAEL *and* MATTHEW *and continues off stage left.*)

MICHAEL: Mmmmm! But that wasn't *her*, I guess?

(MATTHEW *stands as before, motionless.*)

MICHAEL: *That* wasn't *her*—I guess? *That* one—?

(*Lights fade as men stand motionless.*)

Lights out.

I'm Waiting

Lights up. An attractive but sullen WOMAN *in her thirties sits facing the audience in a posture that is just slightly odd—her long legs spread, right foot curved so that the ankle rests flat on the floor, suggesting vulnerability. She wears a longish skirt with deep pockets, dark-textured tights, an unbuttoned, loose-fitting jacket (perhaps suede or leather) with a snugly fitting low-cut sweater or blouse beneath; high-heeled shoes that are in no way "feminine." During the course of her monologue, she frequently brushes her long hair back from her face, in an impatient yet provocative gesture.*

The WOMAN *regards the audience for several seconds, nodding just perceptibly to herself; she frowns; she smiles; as if coming to some conclusion.*

WOMAN: Okay. I'm waiting. (*Unobtrusively touching an object hidden in her pocket*) Anybody makes a move on me, I'm waiting. (*Pause*) The first time—I'm not going to talk about it. He was my mother's brother, I never say his name. Nor think it either. I was five years old I guess. I don't remember too clear. That long ago, you mostly don't remember. Or if you do they tell you you're making things up. (*Shrugs*) So, I don't talk about it. Anyway he's dead—so there's no need. (*Pause*) The first time I can really remember, yeah it's like yesterday, I was twelve years old in seventh grade and we lived on Water Street and I was crossing through the park coming home from school, a cold dark day, a spring day but gloomy like the sky was pressing down low and I couldn't hardly tell if it was raining or not, the air was so wet. I was alone, I was *always* alone. (*Mysteriously*) That's how you get selected, but I didn't know it then. (*Pause*) I was crossing through the park and I saw them up ahead but I pretended I didn't see them, I mean I was pretending to myself too. That's what you do when you're scared to death. Like, maybe, you're thinking maybe what's going to happen won't happen. (*Pause*) They weren't even black guys, they were *white*, and I knew them sort of, I knew their faces, from around the neighborhood, guys sixteen, seventeen years old hanging around the bandstand smoking reefer and there I came along, I saw they'd seen me but still I was hoping they hadn't seen me then it was too late. (*Pause*) No they didn't *rape* me or anything, not that, just chased after me hooting and yelling and grabbing hold—(*she grips her breasts roughly*)—they knocked me down into the wet grass, I was sobbing, so scared, paralyzed-scared, and wetting my pants so they laughed at *that*. (*Pause*) Another time, a few years later, it *was* black guys and they pulled me into their car with them and . . . did things to me . . . for three hours . . . made me do things to them. (*Gagging gesture; expression of revulsion; wiping at mouth with the back of her hand*) Three hours. Behind the warehouse, on the river, they terrorized me they told me they'd kill me for sure and dump my body in the river if I told, they said they'd torch our building, where Momma and I lived, just the two of us. So—(*shrugs*)—I never told. Who'd I tell? Momma? She'd have died of shame, I'm not exaggerating. Our priest?—old pot-belly McGuire? (*Contemptuous laugh*) Anyway, the cops in our precinct wouldn't have given a damn, there was nothing I could *prove* even if I'd gone to a doctor or the hospital which I didn't 'cause I . . . didn't. (*Pause*)

(*She gets to her feet, walks springily, sensuously, about; lifting long hair and letting it fall; stretching.*)

I was twenty years old when I fell in love for the first time—*only* time. Oh God!—"fell" is right!—like in quicksand! Working days at Mayflower Moving, all kinds of shit office work, evenings I took courses at Monroe County Community College, where I met Ray Allis, my accounting prof, oh I was crazy for him just looking at him in class shy like I was, I *am* shy, well one evening after class he asked would I have coffee with him at the student union and that was the . . . beginning. (*Laughs breathlessly, caresses hair*) Sure, I knew Ray was married. He never lied about *that*. But he kept saying he and his wife were "irrevocably split," getting a divorce, so I believed him—I'm the kind of girl *always believes*. (*Mysteriously, nodding*) That's how you get selected, but I didn't know it then. (*Pause. Dreamy-urgent voice*) I loved Ray Allis so, I'd lie in the bath till the water got cold till my skin was all puckered like chicken skin! and white! and Momma would knock worried at the door and I'd hardly hear her. Half wanting to die right there, slash my arms with a razor, I was so . . . tensed up . . . hopeful . . . thinking oh he's gonna marry me, he loves me he says, loves loves loves *me* . . . or, like, what if he doesn't smile at me tomorrow night, what if he doesn't call me over the weekend? (*Pause*) Like my heart was all clenched, tight—(*clenches her right fist, raises it high*)—with hope and worry, all *nerves*, I couldn't bear it. (*Pause.*

Sighs, bitter) Well. He didn't leave his wife. And kid. I got a B plus in the course. Which he said was a "gift." *(Pause)* I'd call him, sometimes. Hang up if his wife answered. Till he changed his number. *(Vague)* Used to drive by his house late at night . . . park out there . . . somebody called the police, once . . . I don't know if it was him. *(Pause. She draws pistol out of skirt pocket, sights along the barrel; strokes thoughtfully against the side of her face.)* I didn't have this in my possession, then. *This*, just holding it, the weight of it, restores your pride. *(Smiles)*

(She returns to chair; sits provocatively; studies the pistol in rapt silence for a beat or two.)

(Dreamy-angry, smiling) I'm not twenty years old no more, hell no. Lots of water over the dam since then. Momma died, I grew up, you better believe it. *Try me. (Pause; then, the pistol prominent, she launches into a rhapsodic aria, dreamy, near-ecstatic, yet never quite out of control)* You, mister—there's gonna be a time—an hour—oh yessss you're gonna press up against me all innocent-seeming, like in a bar, some wild Friday night, in a parking garage elevator, or—anywhere: grocery store, 7-Eleven. Mmmmm there's gonna be that time—no way to avoid it—say I'm coming out of a women's restroom at some old dump of a gas station off a country highway, me in shorts, tight T-shirt, sunglasses, and you're going into the men's room, and the two of us collide, right?—you bumping into me accidentally-on-purpose, right? Or: say it's dusk, melancholy brown, been raining off and on all day and you're curious why this woman, a not-bad-looking woman, is sitting by herself at a picnic table in the park, by the kiddie swings, the park deserted and she's sitting there—*(she arranges herself in her initial position, long legs spread, the outside of her right ankle flat against the floor; slips, sensuously, the pistol back into her skirt pocket)*—looking lonely, low, like there's bruises under her eyes from not sleeping or maybe some guy's been beating up on her? —which excites you, right? Mister? Turns you on? *(Laughs almost girlishly)* Sure. Try me. It's a date. I'm waiting.

Lights out.

Social Life; or, The Cannibals

Lights up. As many as a dozen people, but not fewer than five, are
crowded together in a constricted space. (An invisible circle on the
stage might contain them.) They are in near-constant motion, jostling
one another (though not rudely or overemphatically); their words
overlap and interrupt one another; they give little impression of lis-
tening to one another. Mannequins might also be employed, leading
back into the shadows offstage.

VOICES (*divided as the director chooses*): Hello! May I serve you?
This is delicious. Please sit anywhere. Please take off your coats.
You are very generous. You are very *kindly.* Is it still snowing out?
Have you all been introduced? Shall I take your coats? Just slip
your gloves in this pocket. Thank you very much. Please pass it
on. What is the temperature? Please come back soon. This *is* delicious. Is the walk icy? Can you find your way? Let's close the
door—quickly!

(Very brief pause: silence; all freeze in place.)

Will you have another serving? Why won't you have another serving? When was the funeral? Thank you very much. Please sit anywhere. We are in the habit of sitting anywhere. Thank you very
much. May I have the recipe? Is it still snowing outside? The style
is rococo revival, 1845–1870. Can you find your way? Are these
your gloves? Death collects in fatty deposits. You are very *sweet.*
What did the CAT scans say? Two days' uninterrupted preparation
went into this meal. Oh the door, who left open the door? Let's
close the door—quickly!

(Very brief pause: as before)

Parents and siblings devour every second child—in order, it's said,
to gain "mystical strength." Yes thank you. When is the reunion?
Among the Pitjentara tribe of Australia. Who was it? A junior
partner. *You* are so handsome. Which tribe? PITJENTARA. Wasn't
that last Tuesday? Yes she passed away last Monday. Anthropol-
ogists think they devour their own infants for nutrition too but I
find that hard to believe don't you. An infant only a few days old
is a meager feast indeed. Yes we've always lived here. We moved
here last June. Except if it has a name—they can't eat it. What

quaint customs. If they have given it a name. No I don't think baptism, they wouldn't be that advanced. Would savages be that advanced? Well if it has a *name* it can't be eaten, that's TABOO. What curious customs! Some people are so gullible they'll believe anything they are told!

(*Brief pause: as before*)

Thank you, they are artificial flowers. Would you like to sit here? Have you all been introduced? Would you like a second helping? Oh—so freezing outside! So many months! It's warmer by our fire. Please sit here by our fire. Let's adjourn to the other room. Coffee? brandy? cigars for the gentlemen? No the Holocaust did not come within eight thousand miles of our house. Where are our coats? Whose gloves are these? She died suddenly, last Friday I believe. The skull was opened, the brain probed. You can't call them "savages," you'll offend some sect right here at home. How are we responsible for aboriginal behavior in Australia, or here at home—!

(*Brief pause: as before*)

May I serve you? May I take your coat? Must you leave so early? Yes but we must leave. You have just arrived. Thank you *very* much, we are extremely grateful. Our condolences. You can't trust most caterers. You can't trust most lawyers. One of the physicians joked about "morbid obesity." Have you all been introduced? It was a merciful death as deaths go: slow, and then fast. Please take another serving, you've hardly touched a morsel of food! Three days' preparation have gone into this meal. She was secretly disappointed. That is often the case. The sweeter the smile, the deeper the hurt. That is often the case. This is such an honor—where will you sit? *This* is the pièce de résistance! Why are you shivering? Have you all been introduced? It is ten-thirty p.m. It is so frequently ten-thirty p.m. Death rose from the cracks in the sidewalks. Yes death was in the faucets. It is always ten-thirty p.m. in this room. Will you have a canape? Will you have a brandy? Why must you leave so early? Yes but we have just arrived. Please come back soon!

(*Brief pause: as before*)

This is exquisite: may I have the recipe? Does it have a name? Actually they are plastic flowers. You are so sweet to ask. You are

so kind to invite us. She has been dead now, how long? Oh at least
eight months, a year, it happened just past Easter and then the
trip to Hawaii and Roger and Brenda and the children. No I
wouldn't call them "savages" I would call them "cannibals." I
wouldn't call them at all. Fifteen months at least. Yes it is a decent
likeness, you never know. Yes some genetic strains are misleading.
No I don't subscribe to genocide. No there is no geological fault
in our town. The roses *are* exquisite but they are without scent.
Please have another serving. Please pass the bowl on. Is the bowl
too hot? Where are the tongs? Must you leave so early? Have you
all been introduced? But you have just arrived. But we are *very*
grateful. Yes these are my gloves. Let's close the door—quickly!

Lights out.

Love Triangle

Lights up. A WOMAN *and a* MAN, *very attractive, in their twenties or thirties, stand facing the audience.*

MAN (*indicating himself, as if clinically detached*): As he falls in love with her he extracts from her the secrets of her former life.

WOMAN (*with less detachment, yet not emotionally*): As he extracts from her the secrets of her former life he falls in love with her. (*Pause*) "Tell me," he says, "please—"

MAN (*words overlapping with* WOMAN's): "Please tell me," he says. "Don't be frightened. Don't be ashamed. It's only human," he says. (*Pause*) "And don't lie."

WOMAN: He's devoted, he's insatiable. A tawny light comes up in his eyes when he sees her—there's no mistaking that. (*Pause*) No one has ever looked at her like that before.

MAN: He loves her so violently, he resents her. No he loves her so violently he *is* her. (*Pause; a confused smile, as if to shrug off responsibility*) No he loves her so violently he must erase her past lovers. He'd kill them with his bare hands if he could! (*Laughs*)

WOMAN: She has forgotten the texture of life, the very quality of the light, before him. Before his shadow falling upon her own.

MAN: He isn't jealous, he is never jealous, he—

WOMAN (*defensively*): —he isn't that kind of man!

MAN: If he has hurt her sometimes—(*with the suddenness that should shock the audience, the* MAN *seizes the* WOMAN, *twists her arm up behind her, causes her to react in surprise and pain*)—he has never meant it because he loves her oh God he loves loves loves her—

WOMAN (*barely able to speak*): —more than he loves his own life.

MAN (*confronting* WOMAN *directly*): You believe me don't you?

WOMAN (*speaking directly to him*): I believe you.

MAN: You know I love you.

WOMAN: I know.

MAN: And you love me.

WOMAN (*as if blindly*): And I love you.

(MAN *and* WOMAN *assume previous positions, some feet apart; addressing audience.*)

MAN: "Tell me," he says, "your life before me." (*Pause*) "Who were they? who are they? your lovers?—and don't lie."

WOMAN: He is the most passionate of lovers, he is the shining wing of a great plane, a blade slicing the air, all hunger, oblivion. Before him there was . . . so little. (*Pause*) Only her life, her world, *her* being, complete and whole and intact—inviolate.

MAN: She tries to deceive him, holding back certain facts, as women do. Or try to. (*Approaching the* WOMAN *again, as if threateningly*) But she can't deceive him. It's risking death, to deceive him.

WOMAN (*not resisting his advances, as if giving herself up to whatever he wants to do to her*): Sometimes, she thinks it might be best— if he did kill her. Then, in place of pain, there would be—nothing at all. (*Laughs suddenly*)

MAN (*embracing* WOMAN, *not brutally but tenderly*): Oh—tonight he's dying for *her*. He's crazy about *her*. "Bitch," he says, "you sweet bitch," he says, "don't make me beg," he says, "—and don't lie."

WOMAN (*simply*): Eventually, they'll marry. Eventually, they'll reproduce their kind. One, two, three—maybe three children. It's the story of the race. (*Pause*) And then he'll leave, maybe. Her last secret having been exposed.

MAN: Tonight, though, he's crazy with love. "You know it's you," he says. "You always knew it was you," he says.

WOMAN: She knew.

Lights out.

The Suicide

Lights up. A tall, thin young man, x, *in black, with a pale, taut face, is illuminated. Behind him in a semicircle stand* MOTHER, FATHER, GRANDMOTHER, OLDER SISTER, YOUNGER BROTHER. *As these people speak, in rising and falling voices, chanting, overlapping, alternately soft and harsh, cajoling and accusing,* x *sometimes seems to hear, with mild, even amused interest; at other times he hears nothing. As the scene progresses he becomes ever more impervious to them.*

VOICES: Is he—? Did he—? Why—? Where—? Did he thank—? Did he know—? Did he *see*?

(x *preens a bit, yawning. Mimes entering a room, locking the door behind him.*)

VOICES: (Did he talk to *you*? confide in *you*? why not *me*? Oh how could he!)

(*Christmas lights glitter, as on an evergreen tree, a luminescent Star of Bethlehem at the top.*)

VOICES: The gifts we gave him! the gifts! gifts we gave
him! The love! yes it was love! love! we gave him! it *was*!
Did he thank?
Did he care?
Went where?

Didn't sleep in his bed slept where?
Didn't eat at home with us ate where?

(Did he talk to *you*? confide in *you*? then *who*?)

Always elsewhere!

(x *pulls a gym bag out from under a [suggested] bed; removes T-shirt, socks, jogging shoes, and an object wrapped in a towel. He unwraps it slowly, as if reverently, and we see that it is a sharp-glinting long-bladed knife.*)

VOICES (*now more urgent: angry, hurt, frightened, sobbing, plead-ing*): And why! why now! how could he, now! Five SHOPPING DAYS BEFORE CHRISTMAS why now! oh, how! could he! how! could he, now! All the gifts we gave him and this year this year

this Christmas new skis! new skis he said he wanted! said he wanted!
new boots! oh, how could he! a laser printer said he wanted said
he needed! WENT WHERE?

(X *mimes running the knife blade across his throat. Shivery, ecstatic.
Yet startled to see, on his outspread fingers, a faint smear of blood.*)

VOICES (*more gently, pleadingly*): Look at the gifts! for him! under
the tree! the tree! the family loves the tree! Oh we love the tree
—doesn't *he*? New skis new boots new laser printer new clothes
new VCR new car his own car we gave him we gave him at sixteen
at sixteen all the guys have cars he'd said at sixteen skiing
    lessons   tennis lessons   clarinet lessons
      tutorials for SAT   perfect teeth
summers at Blue Mountain   at the old family lodge
      tennis at the club   lessons with the pro
did he marvel
did he thank
did he care
did he *see*
Oh, how could

(X *holds the knife upraised, fascinated by it. Light focuses upon the
blade.* X, *in dancelike movements, low-keyed, subtle, turns about the
still point of the blade. We see that* X *is mesmerized.*

    VOICES *now speak urgently and accusingly, and* FATHER's *voice
breaks through the chorus, agonizing, yet suggesting anger.*)

VOICES: Was he grateful? did he know?
was he human? was he *there*?

Always elsewhere!

FATHER: Was there a reason, was there no reason, I need to know
was there a reason was there no reason is there sometimes NO
REASON is there sometimes NO HELP is there sometimes NO
BLAME is there always a reason is it my fault is it her fault is it
their fault is it ECOLOGY is it LOSS OF FAITH IN AUTHOR-
ITY is it PEER PRESSURE is it EXPERIMENTATION WITH
DRUGS WITH SEX is it FEAR OF AIDS is it FEAR OF LEAV-
ING HOME is it FEAR OF STAYING HOME is it NOT
ENOUGH PARENTAL LOVE AND GUIDANCE is it EXCES-
SIVE PARENTAL LOVE AND GUIDANCE is it REJECTION
BY THE COLLEGE OF YOUR CHOICE (*Voice changes:*

reproachful) Scraped the side of his car the Volvo we gave him goddamn careless when I was that age I'd have been grateful for

VOICES: Always elsewhere, his mind's elsewhere, I touched him and where? where is he? always elsewhere!

Though it was raining elsewhere
though it wasn't "nice" elsewhere
though they didn't love him elsewhere
Didn't thank   didn't kiss
(Did he talk to *you*? confide in *you*? why not *me*? *who*?)

(X, *knife upraised, backs away, slowly. His family steps back to let him pass, reluctantly.*)

VOICES: Was he grateful? was he grateful? was he grateful? why wasn't he grateful? why wasn't he grateful? didn't marvel
didn't thank
didn't kiss

MOTHER (*her voice overlapping*): It began with soiled laundry, it begins with soiled socks, I mean terribly dirty dirty socks terribly smelly socks not changed for days for days not changed Oh how could he! not showering! not brushing his teeth! not using deodorant that's how that's how that's how you can tell, Oh I warn you, oh I know, oh my heart my heart my heart is broken it began with soiled laundry rolled up in balls in anger under his bed he wouldn't let me see he wouldn't let the maid vacuum that's how it began that's how it begins, you'll see, don't pity *me*, *you'll* see, dirty socks dirty shorts dirty shirts boys *are* dirty and their thoughts! their thoughts! their dirty dirty thoughts! their

(*As* X *backs away, mid-stage, into darkness; the* VOICES *are finally the voices of grief, no longer accusing.*)

VOICES: Never said good-bye never   kissed good-bye
never a warning never a note a farewell note
did he know? did he *see*?
was he *human*? was he *there*?

Went where?

Lights out.

Ladies and Gentlemen:

Lights up. The CAPTAIN *of the cruise ship S.S.* Ariel *addresses the audience, as if they are his passengers. He is a ruddy-faced, seemingly genial, smiling man of youngish middle-age; alternately sympathetic (or mock-sympathetic) with the plight of his passengers and coolly, perhaps even sadistically, manipulative. He is a stern, punishing deity in the form of a friendly presence.*

The horror of the situation should be leavened by humor, but not too broad or distracting a humor.

CAPTAIN (*through small megaphone*): Ladies and gentlemen: good morning! And it *is* a good morning, isn't it?—on this lovely sun-warmed January day! I bet the folks back home—in North America—are pretty cold right now, eh? (*Grinning at audience, nodding*) Yes, I bet your friends and neighbors are envious of *you* right now! (*Peers at note*) Ah! listen to this!—it was minus twenty-five degrees Fahrenheit in Butte, Montana, this morning! Blizzards in the Midwest! In Miami Beach, forty-two degrees! Brrrr! Aren't you all glad you're here, on the cruise ship S.S. *Ariel*, not back there!

(*Slight change of tone*) Well!—I wish we of the *Ariel* could claim we'd arranged for this balmy weather, as compensation of sorts for the, shall we say, rocky weather of the past few days!—but it's a welcome omen, isn't it, especially this morning, when, ladies and gentlemen, you'll be enjoying an excursion on the island you see us rapidly approaching off starboard—(*he points*)—small, but *so* beautiful—called by natives of these waters "Screet 'bryk' zzimch'la Ooma'lai'zee"—the Island of Tranquility, or, as some translators prefer, the Island of Great Repose. For those of you who've become real sailors, you'll want to log our longitude at 155 degrees east and our latitude at 5 degrees north—approximately one thousand two hundred miles northeast of New Guinea. Yes, that's right—we've come far! (*Nodding vigorously, humoring his audience a bit*) So far! (*Pause*) And as this is a, uh, rather crucial morning, and today's excursion an important event in your lives, ladies and gentlemen, I hope you'll quiet just a bit—just a bit!—and give me, your captain, your undivided attention. (*He remains genial, as if suppressing annoyance with audience.*) Good, good!—just for a few minutes, now—I promise. Then—you disembark.

(*Another tone, apologetic, confiding*) As to the problems some of you have experienced: let me take this opportunity, as your captain, to apologize, or at least explain. True, many of your state-rooms are not *precisely* as the advertising brochures depicted them: the portholes not quite so large—in some cases, not in evidence. And, well, things *are* smaller, aren't they?—as often, in real life. This is not the fault of any of us on the *Ariel* staff—absolutely not! *We* have nothing to do with the brochures, or the travel agents' promises! So, let me offer my sympathy, ladies and gentlemen: though I'm a bit your junior in age, I can well understand the special disappointment, hurt, outrage, yes and dismay some of you have been feeling—the sense of having been cheated on what, for you, probably, is perceived as being the last time you'll be taking so ambitious and exotic a trip! Thus, my profoundest sympathy! (*More perfunctory, rapidly speaking*) As to the malfunctioning toilets—the loud throbbing or "trembling" of the ship's engines that has kept some of you awake—the over- or undercooked food—the negligent and occasionally rude service—the high tariffs on mineral water, alcoholic beverages, and cigarettes—the re-ported sightings of rodents, cockroaches, and other vermin on board the *Ariel*: I should explain, ladies and gentlemen, that this is the final voyage of the S.S. *Ariel*; and it was the owners' decision therefore to cut back on repairs, services, expenses, and the like. You see, ladies and gentlemen, the *Ariel* is an old, venerable ship, bound for dry dock in Manila, and the fate of many a seagoing vessel that has outlived her time. God bless her! (*Seems genuinely moved*) We'll not see her likes again, ladies and gentlemen!

(*Apparently there is some disgruntlement, buzzing, among the passengers.*)

Ladies and gentlemen, may I have some quiet! *Please!* Just a minute more, before the stewards help you prepare for your dis-embarkment? Thank you!

(*As if in reply to questions*) Yes, the *Ariel* is bound for Manila. But have no fear: You won't be aboard.

(*More buzzing, consternation*)

Ladies and gentlemen, *please.* This murmuring and muttering begins to annoy.

(*Genial smile*) Yet, as your captain, I'd like to note that, amid the usual whiners and complainers, and the bad-tempered old farts, it's gratifying to see some warm—friendly—*hopeful* faces; and to know that there are men and women determined to enjoy life, not complain constantly, and harbor suspicions. Thank *you*!

(*Briskly*) Now, to our business at hand. Ladies and gentlemen: do you know what you have in common? (*Gazing out at audience*) You can't guess?

You *can* guess?

No? Yes?

No?

(*As if this were a game, responding to individuals in audience*): Well, yes, sir, it's true you are all aboard the S.S. *Ariel*, eleven days out of the port of New York; and yes, ma'am, it's certainly true you are all of "retirement" age—which varies considerably, doesn't it? The youngest among you are in your late fifties, the result, I'd guess, of generous early-retirement programs; the eldest among you are—how old? (*Peering into audience, smiling*) Ninety-two? Oh—here's ninety-*four*! And, over here—what, ma'am?—your husband is?—how old?—ah, ninety-*seven*! Congratulations! (*Polite perfunctory clapping of his hands*)

Yes, it's true, sir, you are all Americans. Oh my, yes.

You have expensive cameras, including video equipment, for recording this South Seas adventure; you have all sorts of tropical-cruise paraphernalia, much of it from the Banana Republic—very pretty straw hat, ma'am! All sorts of sunglasses, and sun-screen lotions, and, what a pharmacological stock—thousands of dollars' worth of brand-name pills and medications, my yes! And a supply of paperbacks, magazines, cards, games, crossword puzzles.

Yet there is one primary—elemental—obvious thing you have in common, ladies and gentlemen, which has determined your presence here this morning, at longitude 155 degrees east and latitude 5 degrees north: your fate, as it were. Can't you guess?

(*Dramatic pause*) Ladies and gentlemen: *your children.*

(*As if met with surprise*) Why, yes, you all have in common the fact that this cruise was your children's idea originally, not yours —don't you recall? (*Chuckles*) Though you probably paid for your own passages, which weren't cheap.

Your children made the necessary arrangements, expedited things, saw that your passports and inoculations came through—

yes? *They* presented *you* with our glossy full-color brochures—yes?

Well, ladies and gentlemen, your children—"children" only technically, for of course they are fully grown, a good number of them parents themselves, with near-grown children—your children are, if I may speak frankly, very fond of you; but, oh my!—very weary of waiting for their inheritances.

(Pause, and then quickly, as if to contain audience's astonishment)

Oh yes, oh yes—they *do* love you. Certainly, they *do*. But—they've grown impatient, some of them a bit short-tempered, waiting to come into control of what they believe is their due.

(Evidently there is consternation, disbelief.) Ladies and gentlemen, please! I am requesting quiet, and I am requesting respect.

As captain of the *Ariel*, I am not accustomed to being interrupted. *(Pause. A sense of his power is communicated.)*

Sir?—yes, I believe you did hear me correctly. And you, sir—yes. And *you*, ma'am. And *you*. *(As if lightly chiding)* Most of you aren't nearly so deaf as you pretend!

To continue: Your children, as I've said, love you—of course. But they are impatient with the prospect of waiting for your "natural" deaths. Ten years—fifteen—twenty?—who knows? With today's medical technology, *you* might outlive *them*. And what a loss of money, poured down the rathole of preserving purposeless life!

What's that, sir?—ah!—"Who does that fool think he is, making such bad jokes!"—and you, ladies, giggling like teenage girls, *so* shocked.

(Concern, though fleeting) Steward, will you see to that elderly gentleman over there?—he seems to be having some difficulty. *(Peering into audience)* Is he all right?—mmmm? Perhaps his wife can go to their stateroom and get his medicine—? Thank you!

(Continuing, as if genuinely solicitous, informative) Ladies and gentlemen: your children have come of age in a very difficult, very competitive corporate America. There is a recession—for some, there is *always* a recession. On the face of it, your children are well-to-do; affluent; yet they want, in some cases desperately need, *your* estates—not in a dozen years, but *now*.

That's to say—as soon as your wills can be probated, following our "Act of God" in these tropical seas.

For, however your sons and daughters appear in the eyes of their neighbors, friends, and business colleagues, even in the eyes of their own offspring, you can be sure one fact unites them: *they have not enough money.*

(*As if confidentially*) Just between us—there are several men, beloved sons of couples in your midst, ladies and gentlemen, who are on the brink of bankruptcy; men of integrity and "success" whose worlds are, nonetheless, about to come tumbling about their heads—unless they get money, fast; or find themselves in the happy position of being able to borrow money against their parents' estates, *fast.* Investment bankers—lawyers—a prominent publisher—even a doctor or two—even a university professor!—seriously in debt. Thus, they decided to take severe measures—can you blame them?

Ladies and gentlemen, it's pointless to protest. As captain of the *Ariel, I* merely expedite orders.

Ah, yes, sir!—it *is* "an obscene joke"—as other ladies and gentlemen have protested, on past *Ariel* voyages to the South Seas.

Stewards, come forward, please!

(*Change of tone: brisker, as if the audience is being herded into rows; he may be directing traffic.*)

Yes, it's best to cooperate. Yes, in an orderly fashion. The stewards would rather not use force.

Ah, what a lovely January morning!—and these *are* pure azure waters, just as the brochures promised. But shark-infested—so take care.

No, no picnic baskets today. Nor mineral water, Perrier water, champagne. For why delay what's inevitable?

Ah, it's such a simple, self-evident thing, but, somehow, *you* did not perceive it: You are the kind of civilized men and women who brought babies into the world not by crude, primitive *chance* but by deliberate *choice.* You planned your parenthoods—your futures—your fates. You showered love upon your sons and daughters, at least as "love" is perceived. The very best private schools—even nursery schools. Expensive toys and gifts of all kinds. Closets of clothing, riding lessons, snorkeling holidays, yes and their teeth are perfect, or were made to be; yes, and they had cosmetic surgery when required; yes, and you gladly paid for their abortions or their tuition for law school—medical school—business school; yes, their weddings, their mortgages, their divorces, their children's orthodontist bills. Nothing too good for them!

Yet, always, the more you gave your sons and daughters, the more you seemed to be holding back; the more generous you displayed yourself, the more generous you were hinting you might be, in the future.

And what, what horror!—if you squander their money on your own medical bills?—nursing home bills? What if, worse yet, addle-brained from Alzheimer's disease (how popular *that* seems to have become lately!), you turn against them?—disinherit them?—marry someone younger, healthier, even more cunning than they? Re-write your wills, as elderly fools are always doing?

No, no—impossible. Thus, ladies and gentlemen, step along.

(An undersea light comes up, marine blue, aqua; faint sounds of tropical birds, surf.)

Ladies and gentlemen: the Island of Tranquility, or Repose, upon which you now stand shivering in ninety-five degree heat is six kilometers in circumference, ovoid in shape, with a picturesque archipelago of metamorphic rock trailing off to the north, and, ah, how hypnotic!—that pounding hallucinatory surf! We have here soil of volcanic ash, sand, rock, and peat; the jungle interior (isn't it exotic!) is pocked with treacherous bogs of quicksand.

The fabled Screet'bryk'zzimch'la Ooma'lai'zee—just as the brochures picture it!

Ladies and gentlemen, you *are* troupers, good sports—cooperative—for which we thank you. *Our* task isn't easy, either!

Ladies and gentlemen, you'll quickly become habituated to this island. Fever-dreams await, that will cancel out your already distant *American* lives.

Just look: those dragonflies with eighteen-inch iridescent wings: nothing like them back in Cleveland, Ohio, eh? That red-beaked carnivorous macaw—quite a fella, eh? Bullfrogs the size of North American jackrabbits—two hundred-pound tortoises with thought-ful, pouched eyes—spider monkeys playful as children—the small quicksilver baja snake with the most lethal venom in the world! Most colorful of all—there's one: see it?—up the beach?—the comical cassowary birds with their bony heads, bright feathers, stunted wings—ungainly birds whom millions of years of evolution, on an island lacking mammal predators, have rendered flightless.

(Pause)

By night (and the hardiest among you will survive numerous
nights, if past history prevails) you'll contemplate the tropical moon,
so different from our pallid North American moon, heavy and luminous in the sky like an overripe fruit. You will wonder, "Am I
still on the same Earth?"

Some of you will cling together, yes as you are now—terrified
herd animals. That's fine. That's a way to cope. Some of you will
wander off alone, refusing to be touched, or comforted—ah, even
by a spouse of fifty years.

(CAPTAIN *retreats; or the light begins to change*)

Ladies and gentlemen: I, your captain, speak for the crew of the
S.S. *Ariel*, bidding you farewell. It *was* a spectacular eleven days,
wasn't it?

Ladies and gentlemen: your children have asked me to say farewell in their stead. They *do*—they *do*—love you. But circumstances have intervened.

Ladies and gentlemen: I bid farewell as young children do, who
wave good-bye not once, but many times—Good-bye, good-bye,
good-bye!

Lights out.

Sex

Lights up. A neon sign, in pulsing fleshy-red letters, flashes "SEX"
above the stage. A languorous rock beat is heard, unobtrusively.
   A young WOMAN *approaches the audience. She is dressed as for a*
disco, but her manner is cultivated, not "cheap."
   WOMAN *positions herself beneath the "SEX" sign but does not*
glance up at it.

WOMAN (*speaking rhythmically, suggestively, with some dancelike*
   movement): If you have it you don't think
   about it so acquiring it is the means of forgetting it
   because if you don't have it you must think about it
   and you're embittered thinking about it because
   to think about it is to acknowledge your soul
   incomplete without it because you know you are superior
   to that, you know you know you are superior to the many
   who have it thus need never think about it the way, after
   Death, you won't think about Death either.

Lights out.

One Flesh II

Lights up. The MAN *and the* WOMAN *of* One Flesh I *are again seated at opposite ends of the old-fashioned sofa, erect, heads high, hands clasped on laps. They have, however, changed positions.*

As before, they address the audience in an evenly modulated single voice.

MAN *and* WOMAN: Here. On the horsehair sofa. Waiting. For something. To happen.

(There is a pause of several beats. The MAN *and the* WOMAN *continue gazing out at the audience.*

A grandfather clock becomes visible in the background, ticking with increasing volume. This time, however, it strikes the hour of midnight. Then the ticking stops and silence resumes.)

MAN *and* WOMAN: Here. Waiting. For. To happen.

Pause, several beats; couple remains immobile.

Lights out.

American Holiday II

Lights up. Five figures of indeterminate sex, bloated-looking, in fluorescent-bright summer sports clothes/swimwear, wearing outsized sunglasses, move disconsolately about the stage. One may wear jogging shoes, another sandals; one may be barefoot. One carries a fancy camera, perhaps even a video camera. All are heavily made up so that their faces resemble masks and show little awareness of one another as they intone in near-unison, as in Gregorian chant.

VOICES: How long—?
—until dinner?
What evil has been
perpetrated upon us?
Who took my souvenir lobster trap!

(*A large, garish, synthetic seashell is discovered.*)

This isn't—
It *is*!
I say it isn't—
I say it *is*!
What is a   "cockleshell"
Hello! anybody home! (*Peering into seashell*)
Oh, ugh! it's *dead*—
—been dead for millennia!
Somebody ate it!

(*Dramatic pause*)

Our bodies are filled with HELIUM (*Dreamily*)
we are floating high! high! above Cape Cod!
above Bar Harbor! NO this is Southampton—
It isn't—
I say it *is*—
Weren't we children once—
what evil has been   perpetrated
Our fingers are BREAKFAST SAUSAGE
Oh he's always carsick,
he does it on purpose!
(*As one, turned aside, mimes noisily vomiting into a Kentucky Fried Chicken bucket*)

How long—?
—until dinner?
Not until six. (*Grim pause*)

Why has this happened, why
created in *His* image
WHO IS RESPONSIBLE   ORIGINAL SIN
(*Gigantic yawns*)
pistachio buttercrunch   Rocky Road   cherry marshmallow
It is only 5:13 my digital watch has   stopped
It is only 4:08!   my quartz watch will run   forever
raspberry coffee mocha chocolate banana ripple walnut
What evil has been perpetrated   perpetuated
upon human flesh
Who took my souvenir lobster trap!

(*A stuffed baby seal is discovered.*)

This isn't—
It *is*—
What is a   "crustacean"
(*Examining stuffed seal*) OHHH it's GENUINE SEAL FUR
TORN FROM LIVING BABY SEALS
pineapple passionfruit vanilla persimmon strawberry rum
surf 'n' turf   home fries   grits   lots of ketchup
more beer more butter three stacks of blueberry pancakes to go
pepperoni-mushroom-olives-anchovies-mozzarella pizza to go
Why has this happened
how is it our fault
is it only 3:25?

(*Brandishing small American flags, with varying degrees of spirit*)
   We proclaim the AMERICAN INDEPENDENCE
All the nations of the world wish to emulate *us*
(*Gloating*) Now the Commies wish to emulate *us*
Why is it so difficult to remain   human?
I don't want that video, we saw that video
I want that video, I never saw that video
yes you did   no you didn't   *I* did
Why is it so difficult to remain   human?
Please pass the waffle syrup
no, that's the gravy boat
My thighs! have turned into loaves! of WONDER BREAD!

I *loathe* oysters they're so squiggly-ugh!
I *love* oysters they're so squiggly-ugh!
Oh there he goes again!
(*Another mimed spasm of vomiting into the bucket*)

Who took my souvenir lobster trap!

(*A plastic swordfish is discovered*)

That's PeePee! I want to hold PeePee!
I want to hold PeePee!
You sat on Twinkle, you squashed Twinkle
I did not he sat on Twinkle he squashed Twinkle
Caucasians are biologically superior it's been PROVED
How long—?
—until dinner?
—bedtime?
—teevee time?
—breakfast?
The day has been long, the season
long
(*Gigantic, convulsive yawns*)

(*Now excitement*)
Oh it's time it's time
it's time
      it's six p.m. it's time
that table by the window's ours   by the harbor
Oh look at the sailboats!   Oh—the sunset!
Oh—clouds!   Sky!   Oh!   Where?
JoJo say grace   "Grace"!
JoJo say grace *nice*   "Grace *nice*"! (*Naughty giggle*)
(*Now solemnly intoning, in unison*)
"Let all matter be ground down fine
by our enormous jaws, by the heat of our tongues
Let all matter be transformed into human heat, human flesh,
human waste AMEN"
AMEN   AMEN   AMEN

Lights out.

(THE END)

AFTERWORD

Writing for the stage when one has written primarily for publication, to be read, is an extremely challenging task, though it's difficult to say why. The written word and the spoken word are both *words*—aren't they?

Yet, as the fiction writer begins the task of writing drama, he or she discovers that the techniques of prose fiction simply do not apply to the stage. Still more, the task of "adapting" fiction for the stage is problematic, for one quickly discovers that it is not "adapting" so much as "transposing" that must be done. How much easier, how much more expedient, simply to set aside the fiction and begin anew, from a new angle of vision!

The essential difference between prose fiction and drama is that in prose fiction, it is the narrative voice, the writerly voice, that tells the story; in drama, of course, characters' voices are usually unmediated, direct. In a memory play, the central character may speak to the audience as a narrator, but only to introduce the action in which, then, he or she will participate. The prose writer's sheltering cocoon of language dissolves in the theater, and what is exposed is the bare skeleton of dialogue—action—subterranean/subtextual movement. Suddenly, everything must be dramatized for the eye and the ear; nothing can be summarized. Description simply *is*. Does that sound easy?

Many a gifted prose writer has failed at writing plays for lack of, not talent exactly, but an elusive quality that might just be humility. In itself, humility won't make a fiction writer or a poet into a playwright, but it is a helpful starting place.

Drama, unlike prose fiction, is not an interior esthetic phenomenon. It is communal; its meeting ground is the juncture at which the sheerly imaginary (the playwright's creation) is brought into being by the incontestably real (the living stage). Unlike prose fiction, with its many strategies of advance and retreat, flashbacks, flashforwards, digressions, analyses, interruptions, drama depends upon immediately establishing and sustaining visceral tension; in powerful plays, force fields of emotion are virtually visible on stage. When tension is resolved, it must be in purely emotional terms.

Drama remains our highest communal celebration of the mystery of being, and of our being together, in relationships we struggle to define, and which define us. It makes the point, ceaselessly, that our lives are *now*; there is no history that is not *now*.

When I write poetry and prose fiction, every punctuation mark is debated over in my head; my poetry is a formalist's obsession, in which even margins and blank spaces function as part of the poem. (Not that anyone else would notice, or that I would expect anyone else to notice. Poets quickly learn, and come to be content in, the loneliness of their obsessions.) When I write for the stage, however, I write for others; especially in the hope of striking an imaginative chord in a director whose sensibility is as quirky as my own. Which is not to imply that I am without a deep, abiding, and frequently stubborn sense of what a play of mine is, or an interior vision with which it is inextricably bound. It's simply that, to me, a text is a text—inviolable, yet without life. A play is something else entirely, and so is a film. It is this mysterious "something else"—the something that is others' imaginations in collaboration with my own—that arouses my interest.

Well-intentioned, print-oriented people are forever asking, "Doesn't it upset you to see your characters taken over by other people, out of your control?" My reply is generally a mild one: "But isn't that the point of writing for the theater?"

As soon ask of a novelist, "Doesn't it upset you if strangers read your books, and impose their own interpretations on them?"

In 1985 I attended the West Coast premiere of my play *The Triumph of the Spider Monkey* at the Los Angeles Theatre Center. As directed by Al Rossi and featuring the popular young actor Shaun Cassidy, my grimly satirical posthumous-confessional play about a youthful mass murderer who becomes a fleeting media celebrity in Southern California had been transformed into a fluid succession of brief scenes, with a rock music score and arresting stage devices—a sort of showcase for Cassidy, whose energetic presence in this un-known work by a little-known playwright assured sellout perfor-mances for the play's limited run, and some enthusiastic reviews by critics who might otherwise have been skeptical about the credentials of a prose writer turned playwright. My collaboration with Mr. Rossi had been by way of telephone and through the mail, and my pleasure in the production was enormous, both because it was very well done and because it was in the nature of a surprise. *The Triumph of the Spider Monkey*, reimagined by another, was no longer my play; "my" play, published in book form (in *Three Plays*, Ontario Review Press, 1980), consists of words, a text. This was something else. And it may have been that my fascination with it was in direct proportion to the degree to which I was surprised by it.

Of course, over the years, since I first began writing plays (in 1967, at the invitation of Frank Corsaro, who directed my first play, *The Sweet Enemy*, for the Actors Studio), I have had a few stunning surprises too. Yet, in fact, very few—and even these have been instructive.

In the spring of 1990 I learned with much gratitude what can work—and what can't—on the stage. At the invitation of Jon Jory and Michael Dixon, I accepted a commission to write two linked one-act plays for the Humana Festival of New Plays at the Actors' Theatre of Louisville, *Tone Clusters* and *The Eclipse*. The first began as a purely conceptual piece, devoid of story: an idea, a mood, a sequence of jarring and discordant sounds. "Tone clusters" refers to the eerie, haunting, dissonant music, primarily for piano, composed by Charles Ives and Henry Cowell in the early twentieth century. The music is unsettling and abrades the nerves, suggesting as it does a radical disjuncture of perception; a sense that the universe is not after all harmonious or logical. In conjunction with these tone clusters of sound I envisioned philosophical inquiries of the kind humankind has posed since the pre-Socratic philosophers, but rarely answered—"Is the universe predetermined in every particular, or is mankind 'free'?"; "Where does identity reside?"—being put to an ordinary American couple of middle age, as in a hallucinatory television interview. The horror of the piece arises from its revelation that we reside in ignorance, not only of most of the information available to us, but of our own lives, our own motives: *Death wrapped in plastic garbage bags! in the basement! and we never knew, never had a premonition!* Only later, by degrees, in the writing of the play, did the nightmare interview become linked with a crime, thus with the specific, the time-bound and finite. It is subsequently ironic to me that *Tone Clusters*, which exists in my imagination as a purely experimental work about the fracturing of reality in an electronic era, is always, for others, "about" a crime.

When rehearsals were begun in Louisville, however, under the direction of Steve Albreezi, and I saw actors inhabiting the roles (Adale O'Brien and Peter Michael Goetz), I soon realized the impracticability of my original vision. Why, I thought, there the Gulicks are, and they're *real*.

In my original idealism, or naiveté, I had even wanted the play's dialogue to be random, with no lines assigned to either speaker; a kind of aleatory music. What madness!

Equally impractical was my notion, for the second play, *The Eclipse*, that an actual eclipse—a "blade of darkness"—move from left to right across the stage, in mimicry of an older woman's relentless gravitation toward death. As soon as the gifted actresses Beth Dixon and Madeleine Sherwood inhabited their roles, this purely symbolic device became unnecessary. (I have left the direction in the play, however. My impractical idealism remains—maybe, somehow, it might be made to work?)

In my writing for the theater I always have in mind, as an undercurrent shaping and guiding the surface action, the ancient structure of drama as sacrificial rite. Stories are being told not by us but by way of us—"drama" is our formal acknowledgment of this paradox, which underscores our common humanity. Obviously, this phenomenon involves not only performers on a stage but an audience as well, for there is no ritual without community, and, perhaps, no community without ritual. To experience the play, the playwright must become a part of the audience, and this can occur only when there is an actual stage, living actors, voices other than one's own.

The question of how a writer knows when a work is fully realized is rather more of a riddle than a question. In terms of prose fiction and poetry, one writes, and rewrites, until there seems quite literally nothing more to say, or to feel; the mysterious inner integrity of the work has been expressed, and that phase of the writer's life is over. (Which is why writers so frequently occupy melancholy zones—always, we are being expelled from phases of our lives that, for sheer intensity and drama, can rarely be replicated in the real world.) Theater is the same, yet different: for the living work is communal, and there can be no final, fully realized performance.

I sense that my work is done when I feel, as I sit in the audience, that I am, not the playwright, nor even a quivering network of nerves invisibly linked to what is happening on the stage, but a member of the audience. In the theater, such distance, and such expulsion, is the point.

February 1991

ACKNOWLEDGMENTS

Tone Clusters and *The Eclipse*, under the title *In Darkest America*, were first performed at the 1990 Humana Festival of New Plays at The Actors' Theatre of Louisville. *Tone Clusters*, co-winner of the 1990 Heideman Award for One-Act Plays, was published in *Antaeus*, 1991.

I Stand Before You Naked was first performed at the American Place Theatre, New York, 1990, and published in *Exile*, 1991.

The prose version of *How Do You Like Your Meat?* was published in *Michigan Quarterly Review*, Spring 1990.

Greensleeves was first performed by the Actors Studio, May 1991.

The Key was first performed by L.A. Theatre Works, January 1991.

The prose version of *Friday Night* was published in *Antaeus*, Spring–Autumn 1990.

Procedure was published in *25 More Ten-Minute Plays from the Actors' Theatre of Louisville*, Samuel French, Inc., 1991.

The prose version of *Black* appeared in *Witness*, 1989.

How Do You Like Your Meat? The Anatomy Lesson, Friday Night, and *Darling I'm Telling You* were first performed at the Long Wharf Theatre in New Haven, Connecticut, in April–May 1991, under the title *How Do You Like Your Meat?*

American Holiday was first performed at the Los Angeles Theatre Academy, November 1990, in an early version; in the version published here, at the Ensemble Studio Theatre, 1991.

"The Anatomy Lesson," "I Got Something For You," "The Secret Mirror," and "The Call," were first published in *The Kenyon Review*, 1991

"Lethal," "The Human Fly," and "Secret" were first published in *The Ontario Review*, 1991.

Several of the monologues in the collage-plays are adaptations of works from *The Assignation, The Time Traveler*, and *Heat*.

"The Secret Mirror" was first performed, in a different version, by the Manhattan Theatre Club, 1991.

In Darkest America and *I Stand Before You Naked* are available in performing editions from Samuel French, Inc.

The "Afterword" appeared, in a slightly different form, in *The New York Times*, 1990.